The Politicization of Society

"The state has increasingly replaced the church in determining how we should behave," writes Oxford professor R. M. Hartwell in his introduction to this volume. "Politics is now religion."

The distinguished contributors to *The Politicization of Society* all deal with the central problem of modern society—the growth of the state—and its significance for the individual. Their papers were not produced according to any editorial design; they were written independently, at different times, by different scholars, in different societies, but they share a common concern: "the politicization of society." Among them, they answer three large questions. First, what were the origins of the state and why did it grow? Second, why has modern society become politicized? Third, what have been the consequences of this growth of the state and of politicization for the individual?

The contributors are Robert L. Carneiro, Felix Morley, Murray N. Rothbard, William Marina, Robert A. Nisbet, Jacques Ellul, Giovanni Sartori, Michael Oakeshott, Donald M. Dozer, Herbert Butterfield, John A. Lukacs, Jonathan R. T. Hughes, Butler D. Shaffer, and F. A. Hayek. R. M. Hartwell contributed the introduction, and Kenneth S. Templeton, Jr., served as editor of the volume.

The Politicization of Society

Essays by Herbert Butterfield, Robert L. Carneiro, Donald M. Dozer, Jacques Ellul, F. A. Hayek, Jonathan R. T. Hughes, John A. Lukacs, William Marina, Felix Morley, Robert A. Nisbet, Michael Oakeshott, Murray N. Rothbard, Giovanni Sartori, and Butler D. Shaffer

Introduction by R. M. Hartwell

Edited by Kenneth S. Templeton, Jr.

LibertyPress

Indianapolis

Liberty*Press* is a publishing imprint of Liberty Fund, Inc., a foundation established to encourage study of the ideal of a society of free and responsible individuals.

The cuneiform inscription that serves as the design motif for our end-papers is the earliest known written appearance of the word "freedom" (*ama-gi*), or liberty. It is taken from a clay document written about 2300 B.C. in the Sumerian city-state of Lagash.

The essays in this volume constituted the agenda of a symposium that took place at the Lincoln Center campus of Fordham University on November 17–19, 1977, under the sponsorship of the Institute for Humane Studies, Inc., of Menlo Park, California.

Library of Congress Cataloging in Publication Data
Main entry under title:

The Politicization of society.

Includes bibliographical references and index.
CONTENTS: Carneiro, R. L. A theory of the origin of the state.—Morley, F. State and society.—Rothbard, M. N. Freedom, inequality, primitivism and the division of labor. [etc.]
1. State, The—Addresses, essays, lectures.
JC325.P59   320.1   78-17491
ISBN 0–913966–48–7 (hardcover edition)
ISBN 0–913966–49–5 (paperback edition)

Contents

Introduction
R. M. Hartwell

I

It was liberalism that released remarkable economic initiative and energy during the industrial revolution, and that produced "the magnificent episode of the nineteenth century."[1] Liberalism is here used in the classical sense, not in the modern American sense. The fundamental tenet of classical liberalism was the sufficiency of individual self-determination in belief and conduct as the proper basis of economic and political policy. The main principles of liberalism were: first, in the sociopolitical field, individual freedom and, where it was mutually beneficial, collaboration on a voluntary basis; second, in the juridical field, individual property rights, freedom of contract, and the rule of law; and, third, in the economic field, freedom of enterprise, in the form of the self-regulating market, unrestrained by political intervention. In sum, minimum government and laissez-faire.[2] Liberalism in this nineteenth-century sense

---

[1] This is how J. M. Keynes described the nineteenth century in his introduction to *Population* by H. Wright (London: Cambridge University Press, 1923), p. viii.

[2] In the words of J. S. Mill: "Laissez-faire, in short, should be the general practice; every departure from it, unless required by some great good, is

was novel in history, and, sadly, its brief but massively productive life was cut short by World War I. The twentieth century, in marked contrast to the nineteenth, has seen a continuous retreat from liberalism, in a manner which has confirmed the fears of Herbert Spencer and A. V. Dicey, both of whom were alarmed by the growth of the state, even in the age of laissez-faire.[3]

The great discontinuity in the history of liberalism, undoubtedly, was World War I. No one saw this more clearly than J. M. Keynes, whose liberal instincts were so alarmed by the peacemakers.[4] The Versailles Conference made Keynes acutely aware of the fine edge on which the pre-1914 civilization had perched, and of the combination of forces that had made the civilization possible. "Civilization," he wrote, "was a thin and precarious crust erected by the personality and the will of a very few, and only maintained by rules and conventions skillfully put across and guilefully preserved."[5] He, of course, was one of the few who fully appreciated the uniqueness of the liberal consensus only in retrospect. The crust of civilization, as he understood it, was damaged by the war, further fragmented

---

certain evil" (*Principles of Political Economy, with Some of Their Applications to Social Philosophy,* Ashley edition [London: Longmans, Green, 1915], p. 950).

[3] Spencer, in *The Man Versus the State* (1884), and Dicey, in *Lectures on the Relation Between Law and Public Opinion in England During the Nineteenth Century* (1905), both detailed the growth of the state and the nature of what Dicey called "collectivism." Both gave essentially pessimistic diagnoses of contemporary trends in government. Both were obviously correct in these diagnoses.

[4] These fears Keynes expressed forcefully in a famous polemic, *The Economic Consequences of the Peace* (London: Macmillan, 1919).

[5] J. M. Keynes, *Two Memoirs* (London: Rupert Hart-Davis, 1949), p. 99.

by the peace, and irreparably broken during the interwar years. The liberal world of the nineteenth century, like so much else in European civilization, perished in the trenches of Flanders.[6]

But if the war was so damaging to the world of the few, which included the politicians responsible for the war, why was it waged at all? Certainly it was not the inevitable result of competing imperialisms.[7] The war was made in the chancelleries of Europe, not in its countinghouses. It was blundered into by obtuse and ambitious politicians who were ignorant on three important counts: they had no idea of the capacity of industrialized economies to wage large-scale wars over a long period of time; they had no idea of the political and economic consequences of total war for the growth of the centralized state;[8] and, particularly, they had no idea of the ability of governments, with the aid of the intellectuals, to manufacture appropriate ideologies and to foment hatreds, whether directed at particular individuals or classes, or at other nations.[9]

---

[6] The role of World War I in changing the institutional structure of the political and economic life of Europe has never been adequately recognized. But see, for instance, A. T. Peacock and J. Wiseman, *The Growth of Public Expenditure in the United Kingdom* (New York: National Bureau of Economic Research, 1961), for a displacement thesis about the effects of the war on public expenditure.

[7] The literature on imperialism is vast, but see R. Nurkse, *Patterns of Trade and Development* (Oxford: Basil Blackwell, 1962), on the growth of the international economy, for an objective account of the relationship between "metropolitan" and "colonial" economies in the nineteenth century.

[8] This was particularly true of Germany; see W. F. Bruck, *Social and Economic History of Germany from William II to Hitler, 1888–1938* (Oxford: Oxford University Press, 1938), chap. 2(B).

[9] See, in particular, Julien Benda, *La Trahison des Clercs* (published in

As a result the nineteenth-century liberal consensus was weakened and, in the long run, destroyed. This was most noticeable, in the short run, in economic policy: the institutional framework of the nineteenth-century international economy—based on laissez-faire, free trade, the gold standard, and factor mobility—was ruined by the war and not resurrected by the peace. The international economy never again worked so well. It was the same in politics. The liberal view of politics was based on the principle of individual responsibility, on the freedom and self-interest of the individual constrained by obligations and sympathy;[10] it was strengthened by accepting the mutuality and interdependence of interests in most human situations, and was encouraged by the success of voluntary organizations for social purposes.[11] This harmonious theory of politics, however, gave way to theories of politics and society based on conflict, theories which led to the identification and nurturing of class and national interests, and to the propagation of ideologies of hatred, violence, and revolution. The con-

---

English as *The Treason of the Intellectuals,* trans. Richard Adlington [New York: Norton Library, 1969]). This remarkable book, published in 1927, was one of the first to recognize the trend toward politicization, and to analyze the consequences.

[10] The most famous book on sympathy is that of Adam Smith, *The Theory of Moral Sentiments* (Indianapolis: Liberty*Classics,* 1976; first published in 1759), which was, in the words of T. Sowell, "a cool psychological and social analysis of the origins and mechanics of morality," in *Adam Smith and The Wealth of Nations: 1776–1976 Bicentennial Essays,* ed. F. R. Glahe (Boulder: University of Colorado Press, 1978), p. 168.

[11] As G. Unwin had argued: "The grand achievement of the Englishman in the last century had been the creation of a wealth of free associations . . . as elements of a new social order." See R. H. Tawney, "Introductory Memoir," *Studies in Economic History: The Collected Papers of George Unwin* (London: Macmillan, 1927), p. lxix.

sequences were in the nature of self-fulfilling prophecy:
within a generation Europe was again at war.

Most damaging for economy and politics was the decline
of rationality, and most significant for the individual was
the narrowing of motivation in the determination of choices
and policies. Keynes again was a perceptive observer. He
had grown up in a world in which "the rules of the game"—
whether in intellectual discussion or in personal behavior,
in the conduct of business or in industrial relations, in international diplomacy or in finance, in the rhetoric or in the
actuality of politics—were widely known and largely accepted. Keynes himself had progressed from school to university to civil service, finding himself always able to
conduct, and usually to win, debate by rational discussion.
His world was both pleasant and predictable, and, as everybody believed, was still improving in the manner it had
done since the beginnings of the industrial revolution.

"What an extraordinary episode in the economic progress
of man," Keynes wrote in 1919,

> that age was which came to an end in August 1914! The greater
> part of the population, it is true, worked hard and lived at a low
> standard of comfort, yet were, to all appearances, reasonably
> contented with this lot. But escape was possible, for any man of
> capacity or character at all exceeding the average, into the mid-
> dle and upper classes, for whom life offered, at a low cost and
> with the least trouble, convenience, comforts, and amenities be-
> yond the compass of the richest and most powerful monarchs
> of other ages. The inhabitant of London could order by tele-
> phone, sipping his morning tea in bed, the various products of
> the whole earth, in such quantity as he might see fit, and rea-
> sonably expect their early delivery upon his doorstep; he could
> at the same moment and by the same means adventure his wealth
> in the natural resources and new enterprises of any quarter of

the world, and share, without exertion or even trouble, in their prospective fruits and advantages; or he could decide to couple the security of his fortunes with the good faith of the towns-people of any substantial municipality in any continent that fancy or information might recommend. He could secure forth-with, if he wished it, cheap and comfortable means of transit to any country or climate without passport or other formality, could dispatch his servant to the neighbouring office of a bank for such supply of the precious metals as might seem con-venient, and could then proceed abroad to foreign quarters, without knowledge of their religion, language, or customs, bear-ing coined wealth upon his person, and would consider himself greatly aggrieved and much surprised at the least interference. But, most important of all, he regarded this state of affairs as normal, certain, and permanent, except in the direction of fur-ther improvement, and any deviation from it as aberrant, scandalous, and avoidable. The projects and politics of mili-tarism and imperialism, of racial and cultural rivalries, of monopolies, restrictions, and exclusion, which were to play the serpent to this paradise, were little more than the amusements of his daily newspaper, and appeared to exercise almost no in-fluence at all on the ordinary course of social and economic life, the internationalization of which was nearly complete in practice.[12]

At the peace conference, however, Keynes found himself, for the first time in his life, in a situation in which rational argument was useless and in which internationally impor-tant decisions were being made on the basis of political hatred. Keynes was facing the new passions of the modern age, passions not amenable to logic or facts, passions he found difficult to understand and impossible to control; and so he could not cope with people like Clemenceau or Lloyd George. His reaction was to withdraw from public to the

---

[12] Keynes, *Economic Consequences*, pp. 6–7.

commons rooms of Cambridge where the old rules of argument still prevailed and where the old civilization still survived, and to write that devastating polemic, *The Economic Consequences of the Peace.* Much later Keynes admitted, after the experience of the interwar years, that he had always attributed "an unreal rationality to the other people's feelings and behavior (and doubtless to my own, too)," and that "the attribution of rationality to human nature . . . ignored certain powerful and valuable springs of feeling."[13] The war had tapped these springs, and had unleashed emotions most of which were inimical to civilization, destroying rather than contributing to it.

"Evil, wickedness, and folly" ensued as nonrational criteria determined more and more decision-making, and as more and more decisions were made by politicians whose power had been increased during the war and had not been reduced during the peace. Politicians, in making important decisions about individuals and society, used frankly political criteria: in economic policy, for example, criteria of political expediency rather than of market rationality. Thus an increasing amount of decisions about resource allocation were made outside of the market, for political purposes: for national purposes that were embodied in ideologies and policies of autarky and aggression; or for party purposes that were embodied in class legislation, reflecting ideologies of envy and conflict. The twentieth century, in consequence, has become an era of ideological and physical conflict, both within and between states, of a universality and intensity, and pursued with a barbarism, that have not been seen in Europe for centuries.

---

[13] Keynes, *Two Memoirs,* pp. 100–101.

II

The process I have been describing is now known as politicization. If individualism was the motivating spirit of the Renaissance, rationalism the guiding principle of the Enlightenment, and laissez-faire that of the industrial revolution, politicization is the prevailing characteristic of our age. *Politicization,* however, is a relatively new word in the vocabulary of politics,[14] although the phenomenon it describes goes back to World War I. Politicization can be defined as that now pervasive tendency for making all questions political questions, all issues political issues, all values political values, and all decisions political decisions. As Julien Benda observed as early as 1927: "The present age is essentially the age of politics."[15] Half a century later almost all social phenomena have become politicized, and almost all social problems are assumed to have only political solutions. Politicization can now be seen in the relationship between all people in society: between parents and children, between teachers and pupils, between professors and students, between employers and employees, between producers and consumers, between races, between sportsmen, indeed between men and women. Where once individuals saw their problems as private and sought private solutions for them, now they seek political solutions. Where once private initiative dominated, for example, in areas like cultural entertainment, now political initiatives dominate.

---

[14] See T. Halper and R. Hartwig, "Politics and Politicization: An Exercise in Definitional Bridge-Building," *Political Studies* 23 (1975):71.

[15] Benda, *Treason,* p. 29; also p. 9: "Nowadays it is politics everywhere, politics always, and nothing but politics."

Where once the private investigation of social problems was important, public inquiry now dominates, and with public inquiry there is almost inevitably public solution (remedial legislation and the establishment of a bureaucracy of enforcement and control).

Politicization thus takes the manifest form of increasing the power of the state, of increasing political power as against all other forms of power in society, of increasing the power of the politicians and the bureaucrats as against the power of individuals, private institutions, and voluntary associations. For the individual this has meant increasing political dependence and awareness, along with increasing political ineffectiveness and frustration. "Until August 1914," A. J. P. Taylor has reminded us of England, "a sensible law-abiding Englishman could pass through life and hardly notice the existence of the state, beyond the post office and the policeman."[16] Today the individual Englishman is constantly aware of the state, over which he can exercise little or no control even though it makes more and more decisions about his life. Individual political activity, in consequence, now combines a general sense of powerlessness with a desperate sense of party allegiance, for parties represent power, and party allegiance is compounded of self-interest and artificially generated conviction. Passion becomes a substitute for power.

Powerlessness, and the sense of frustration that accompanies it, has been intensified, moreover, by renewed visions of the millennium, of that better world which the intellectuals dream up, and which the politicians promise but never

---

[16] A. J. P. Taylor, *English History, 1914–1945* (Oxford: Clarendon Press, 1965), p. 1.

deliver.[17] With the failure of promises has come the identification of obstacles to progress, those individuals and institutions which prevent change. Unfulfilled hopes and ideologically stimulated passion in the face of the enemies of progress are the effective ingredients of violence, a specific endemic disease of all modern societies. As Benda also observed, not only was the world becoming more political, it was becoming more passionately political, with an intensity not previously experienced in history. "Today," he wrote, "political passions show a degree of universality of coherence, of homogeneousness, of precision, of continuity, of preponderance, in relation to other passions, unknown until our times. . . . All are furnished with an apparatus of ideology whereby, in the name of science, they proclaim the supreme value of their action and its historical necessity. On the surface and in the depths, in spatial values and in inner strength, political passions have today reached a point of perfection never before known in history."[18]

In this generation of passion, Benda quite rightly gave particular responsibility to the intellectuals who, he declared, "have positively shown genius in their efforts to serve the passions of the layman."[19] The intellectuals have abandoned their traditional attachment to "the purely disinterested activity of the mind," and have espoused political causes; they have replaced dispassionate inquiry with preaching and proselytizing, and objective analysis with dogma. Since they dominate the classroom, the lecture hall,

---

[17] See J. Passmore, *The Perfectibility of Man* (London: Duckworth, 1970), chap. 15.

[18] Benda, *Treason,* pp. 28–29.

[19] *Ibid.,* p. 98.

the library, and the mass media, they have an influential pulpit from which to display their intellectual and moral superiority. It is largely their responsibility that students now live "within a cacophony of slogans, catch-phrases, buzz-words, and other forms of cant," and are "filled with adversary passion."[20] The intellectuals, indeed, have been mainly responsible for "the ideologizing temper" of our times. They have provided the social theory and the political ideology which the politicians have been able to exploit so effectively.[21] In particular, the intellectuals have rejected liberalism, cultivated dreams of an unattainable millennium, and made respectable theories of social conflict, envy, hatred, and violence. This is their treason ("la trahison des clercs," to use Benda's memorable phrase) whereby they replaced the ideal of disinterestedness with "the game of political passions." "Our age," wrote Benda, "is the age of the intellectual organization of political hatreds. It will be one of its chief claims to notice in the moral history of humanity."[22]

But why have the intellectuals become politicized?[23] Why

---

[20] J. Adelson, "Psychology, Ideology, and the Search for Faith," *Public Interest* 46 (Winter 1977):121.

[21] See, for example, Ludwig von Mises, *The Anti-Capitalist Mentality* (South Holland, Ill.: Libertarian Press, 1972), p. 18 ("The Anti-Capitalistic Bias of American Intellectuals"); Ernest van den Haag, "Economics Is Not Enough—Notes on the Anticapitalist Spirit," *Public Interest* 45 (Fall 1976):109.

[22] Benda, *Treason,* p. 27.

[23] This is a neglected problem, but see F. A. Hayek, "The Intellectuals and Socialism," in *Studies in Philosophy, Politics and Economics* (London: Routledge & Kegan Paul, 1967); J. A. Schumpeter, "These Crumbling Walls," in *Capitalism, Socialism and Democracy* (London: Allen & Unwin, 1943); and R. M. Hartwell, "Capitalism and the Historians," in *Essays on Hayek,* ed. F. Machlup (Hillsdale, Mich.: Hillsdale College

have the intellectuals rejected liberalism? Was Benda correct when he wrote: "This denunciation of liberalism, notably by the vast majority of contemporary men of letters, will be one of the things in this age most astonishing to history"?[24] Is it so astonishing? Are not the actions and beliefs of the intellectuals self-interested in a very obvious way? Intellectuals dislike economic liberalism because market economy does not reward them according to their own estimation of their obvious social worth. Intellectuals, therefore, prefer economic systems which give them a place in the sun, in which their cash rewards are almost certainly higher, and in which power rewards are undoubtedly higher. Intellectuals play leading roles in the bureaucracies of the state, as advisers, experts, and administrators, and increasing the power of the state means increasing the power of the intellectuals. Their "cult of the powerful state," therefore, is not disinterested, even though their self-interest is well rationalized.

This rationalization derives from a moral absolute, a false analogy, an historical myth, and an imagined social law. The moral absolute is the assumption that the prime aim of government policy should be not justice, but equality; the false analogy is that of social engineering or social architecture, the belief that because mechanical engineering is possible, then societies also can be socially engineered to fit some predetermined plan; the historical myth is that capitalism (modern industrialization and economic growth) has harmed the living standards and way of life of the work-

---

Press, 1976). See also Benda, *Treason,* pt. II, and K. R. Popper, *The Open Society and Its Enemies* (London: Routledge, 1945).

[24] Benda, *Treason,* p. 104.

ing classes and, therefore, should be replaced by socialism; and the imagined social law is that of historical inevitability, the law of inevitable socialism derived from the study of history.[25] When ambition is added to this formidable intellectual package favoring the powerful state and the politicization of society and economy, then the actions of the intellectuals are understandable, even though they do not become less dishonest and less dishonorable.

III

The following papers are all concerned with politicization, with the central problem of modern society—the growth of the state—and its significance for the individual. The papers were not produced according to any editorial design; they were written independently, at different times, by different scholars, in different societies; but they share a common concern: "the politicization of society." Among them, they answer three large questions. First, what were the origins of the state and why did it grow? Second, why has modern society become politicized? Third, what have been the consequences of the growth of the state and of politicization for the individual? Three quotations will give some idea of the reactions of the various contributors to these important questions. Morley, on the growth of the

---

[25] On justice and equality, see F. A. Hayek, *Law, Legislation and Liberty,* vol. 2 (London: Routledge & Kegan Paul, 1976), chaps. 8, 9; on social engineering, see Hayek, *Studies in Philosophy, Politics and Economics* (Chicago: University of Chicago Press, 1967), p. 187; on the historical myth, see R. M. Hartwell, "History and Ideology," *Studies in History and Philosophy,* no. 3 (Institute for Humane Studies, 1974); and on historical inevitability, see K. R. Popper, *The Poverty of Historicism* (London: Routledge & Kegan Paul, 1957).

state, writes: "The rapid extension of the authority of the state, and its increasing competence to control, discipline, and subordinate not only the individual but also all unofficial forms of social organization, was the painfully outstanding political development of the first half of the twentieth century." Ellul, on politicization, writes: "A society has no reality for us except in its political institutions, and those institutions take precedence over all others. . . . This aspiration, this unconscious assigning of the supreme role to the state leads us immediately to the consideration that everything is now its business." Oakeshott, on individualism, writes: "Morality consists in the recognition of individual personality wherever it appears. Moreover, personality is so far sacrosanct that no man has either a right or a duty to promote the moral perfection of another: we may promote the 'happiness' of others, but we cannot promote their 'good' without destroying their 'freedom,' which is the condition of moral goodness."

Any attempt to summarize these papers would do violence to their breadth of interest, variety of analysis, and richness of documentation. Nevertheless, they do group themselves into the three great problem areas defined above. Carneiro, Morley, Oakeshott, and Hayek are concerned, in varying ways, with the origins, growth, and nature of the state; Sartori on law, Hughes on economy, Dozer and Butterfield on history, and Rothbard, Marina, and Nisbet on dogma and ideology, are concerned with different aspects of politicization; Lukacs, Shaffer, and Ellul are concerned with the consequences of politicization for the individual. Within those broad areas, individual authors emphasized particular themes.

1. *On the origins and growth of the state*
    a. Carneiro rejects the voluntaristic theory of the origins of the state in favor of a theory of coercion. He argues that, although other factors were and are also at work, "only a coercive theory can account for the rise of the state."
    b. Morley argues, similarly, that "state power, no matter how much disguised by seductive words, is in the last analysis always coercive physical power," and makes the important generalization that "the greater the material resources over which it can exercise absolute control, the greater the potential power of the state."
    c. Oakeshott outlines the rise and fall of individualism since the Renaissance: while arguing that "the event of supreme and seminal importance in modern European history remains the emergence of the human individual in his modern idiom," he shows how "antiindividualism" in the form of governments with unlimited authority to make choices on behalf of individuals now threatens "the moral prestige of individuality."
    d. Hayek distinguishes between "organization"—the kind of order produced by "a preconceived plan"—and "organism," the kind of order that results from the actions of individuals without intending to create such an order. He argues that "much of what we call culture is just such a spontaneously grown order," and that "a free system" essentially depends on such spontaneous order.
2. *On politicization*
    a. On the politicization of law, Sartori relates how con-

stitutionalism has changed from a system based on the rule of law to a system based on the rule of the legislators. Far from legislating as little as possible—the liberal ideal—lawmakers are spawning "a fearful inflation of laws," and are weakening the juridical protection of the individual.

b. On the politicization of economy, Hughes describes the growth of government intervention in the U.S. economy: a floodtide of nonmarket regulation, the independent rule of burgeoning regulatory agencies, and the remorseless increase in government spending.

c. On the politicization of history, Dozer and Butterfield show how history has become a tool of politics, a weapon in ideological conflict, and a danger to a free society. Both authors warn against official history. "If the present," writes Dozer, "is made to rest upon only an officially approved past, or an ideally conceived past, its foundations are shifting sand."

d. On the politicization of values, Rothbard, Marina, and Nisbet concentrate on the great modern dogma of equality—the main ideology of politicization. Rothbard demonstrates its incompatibility with "freedom, individuality, the division of labor, and economic prosperity and survival"; Marina associates egalitarianism with empire as part of "a historical syndrome within which civilizations have tended to evolve" and disintegrate; Nisbet points to the conflict between equality and liberty, and argues that centralization and equality are the dominant tendencies of modern Western societies.

3. *On the consequences of politicization for the individual*

a. Lukacs argues that "the modern state and its centralized form of government have become so enormous that large numbers of people fear, distrust, dislike and disrespect it." Historically, the rule of aristocracy, he concludes, was succeeded "not by the rule of democracy but by the rule of bureaucracy."

b. Shaffer seeks to explain violence in modern society partly as a response to excessive government; "political efforts to impose order by coercion or the threat of coercion" frustrate individual expectations and increase the tendency toward aggression and violence.

c. Ellul is concerned with defining politicization, explaining it, and examining its consequences. Politicization, he concludes, is characterized by two factors—ideological debate, and the treatment of all social problems "according to the patterns and procedures found in the political world"; "the moving force" of politicization is "the growth of the state"; the main consequences of politicization are to make the state the "creator and protector of values" and to allow the individual to escape personal responsibilities because they have been transferred to the state.

IV

"Up till our own times," Benda wrote, "men had only received two sorts of teaching in what concerns the relations between politics and morality. One was Plato's, and it said: 'Morality decides politics'; the other was Machiavelli's, and it said: 'Politics have nothing to do with morality.' Today they receive a third. M. Maurras teaches: 'Politics decide morality.' "[26]

In working, living, and believing the state is now arbiter.

---

[26] Benda, *Treason*, p. 110.

It decides about the work place, about the family, and about values. Since the market is no longer allowed to function freely, the state must decide what to produce and how to distribute that production; since the family as a social unit has declined because of the erosion of parental responsibilities largely as a result of state action, the state must decide about education, health, behavior, and all other aspects of growing up and earning a living; and, finally, since the state decides what values should prevail in society, and ensures that such values are embodied in legislation and enforced by bureaucracies, the state has increasingly replaced the church in determining how we should behave. Politics is now religion.

R. M. Hartwell, distinguished economic historian from Australia and Great Britain, is an authority on the Industrial Revolution. In addition to having published several general works in that field, he recently coauthored a major study, British Economy and Society, 1870–1970. *He also served as editor of the* Economic History Review *from 1957 to 1972.*

Before coming to Oxford in 1956, Dr. Hartwell was Professor of Economic History and Dean of the Faculty of Humanities and Social Sciences at the University of New South Wales. He has also been Visiting Professor at the University of Ibadan in Nigeria, the Australian National University, and the University of Virginia. He is currently a fellow of Nuffield College, Oxford.

The Politicization
of Society

Essay One

A Theory of the Origin of the State

Robert L. Carneiro

Born in New York City in 1927, Robert L. Carneiro earned his doctoral degree in anthropology from the University of Michigan in 1957. He has taught at the University of Wisconsin, Hunter College, Columbia University, the University of California at Los Angeles, and Pennsylvania State University. Since 1969 he has been curator of South American ethnology in the Department of Anthropology at the American Museum of Natural History, New York City.

In addition to publishing a number of articles, principally in the fields of cultural evolution and Amazonian ethnology, Dr. Carneiro is the coeditor of Essays in the Science of Culture in Honor of Leslie A. White *(1960), and editor of* The Evolution of Society: Selections from Herbert Spencer's Principles of Sociology *(1967).*

For the first two million years of his existence, man lived in bands or villages which, as far as we can tell, were completely autonomous. Not until perhaps 5000 B.C. did villages begin to aggregate into larger political units. But, once this process of aggregation began, it continued at a progressively faster pace and led, around 4000 B.C., to the formation of the first state in history. (When I speak of a state I mean an autonomous political unit, encompassing many communities within its territory and having a centralized government with the power to collect taxes, draft men for work or war, and decree and enforce laws.)

Although it was by all odds the most far-reaching political development in human history, the origin of the state is still very imperfectly understood. Indeed, not one of the current theories of the rise of the state is entirely satisfactory. At one point or another, all of them fail. There is one theory, though, which I believe does provide a convincing explanation of how states began. It is a theory which I proposed once before,[1] and which I present here more fully. Before

[1] Robert L. Carneiro, in *The Evolution of Horticultural Systems in Native South America: Causes and Consequences; A Symposium,* J. Wilbert, ed.,

doing so, however, it seems desirable to discuss, if only briefly, a few of the traditional theories.

Explicit theories of the origin of the state are relatively modern. Classical writers like Aristotle, unfamiliar with other forms of political organization, tended to think of the state as "natural," and therefore as not requiring an explanation. However, the age of exploration, by making Europeans aware that many peoples throughout the world lived, not in states, but in independent villages or tribes, made the state seem less natural, and thus more in need of explanation.

Of the many modern theories of state origins that have been proposed, we can consider only a few. Those with a racial basis, for example, are now so thoroughly discredited that they need not be dealt with here. We can also reject the belief that the state is an expression of the "genius" of a people,[2] or that it arose through a "historical accident." Such notions make the state appear to be something metaphysical or adventitious, and thus place it beyond scientific understanding. In my opinion, the origin of the state was neither mysterious nor fortuitous. It was not the product of "genius" or the result of chance, but the outcome of a regular and determinate cultural process. Moreover, it was not a unique event but a recurring phenomenon: states arose independently in different places and at different times. Where the appropriate conditions existed, the state emerged.

Antropologica (*Venezuela*), Suppl. 2 (1961), pp. 47–67, see especially pp. 59–64.

[2] For example, the early American sociologist Lester F. Ward saw the state as "the result of an extraordinary exercise of the rational . . . faculty" which seemed to him so exceptional that "it must have been the emanation of a single brain or a few concerting minds." [*Dynamic Sociology* (New York: Appleton, 1883), v. 2, p. 224.]

Voluntaristic Theories

Serious theories of state origins are of two general types: *voluntaristic* and *coercive*. Voluntaristic theories hold that, at some point in their history, certain peoples spontaneously, rationally, and voluntarily gave up their individual sovereignties and united with other communities to form a larger political unit deserving to be called a state. Of such theories the best known is the old social contract theory, which was associated especially with the name of Rousseau. We now know that no such compact was ever subscribed to by human groups, and the social contract theory is today nothing more than a historical curiosity.

The most widely accepted of modern voluntaristic theories is the one I call the "automatic" theory. According to this theory, the invention of agriculture automatically brought into being a surplus of food, enabling some individuals to divorce themselves from food production and to become potters, weavers, smiths, masons, and so on, thus creating an extensive division of labor. Out of this occupational specialization there developed a political integration which united a number of previously independent communities into a state. This argument was set forth most frequently by the late British archeologist V. Gordon Childe.[3]

The principal difficulty with this theory is that agriculture does *not* automatically create a food surplus. We know this because many agricultural peoples of the world produce no such surplus. Virtually all Amazonian Indians, for example, were agricultural, but in aboriginal times they did not pro-

---

[3] See, for example, V. G. Childe, *Man Makes Himself* (London: Watts, 1936), pp. 82–83; *Town Planning Rev.* 21, 3 (1950), p. 6.

duce a food surplus. That it was *technically feasible* for them to produce such a surplus is shown by the fact that, under the stimulus of European settlers' desire for food, a number of tribes did raise manioc in amounts well above their own needs, for the purpose of trading.[4] Thus the technical means for generating a food surplus were there; it was the social mechanisms needed to actualize it that were lacking.

Another current voluntaristic theory of state origins is Karl Wittfogel's "hydraulic hypothesis." As I understand him, Wittfogel sees the state arising in the following way. In certain arid and semiarid areas of the world, where village farmers had to struggle to support themselves by means of small-scale irrigation, a time arrived when they saw that it would be to the advantage of all concerned to set aside their individual autonomies and merge their villages into a single large political unit capable of carrying out irrigation on a broad scale. The body of officials they created to devise and administer such extensive irrigation works brought the state into being.[5]

This theory has recently run into difficulties. Archeologi-

---

[4] I have in my files recorded instances of surplus food production by such Amazonian tribes as the Tupinambà, Jevero, Mundurucú, Tucano, Desana, Cubeo, and Canela. An exhaustive search of the ethnographic literature for this region would undoubtedly reveal many more examples.

[5] Wittfogel states: "These patterns [of organization and social control—that is, the state] come into being when an experimenting community of farmers or protofarmers finds large sources of moisture in a dry but potentially fertile area. . . . a number of farmers eager to conquer [agriculturally, not militarily] arid lowlands and plains are forced to invoke the organizational devices which—on the basis of premachine technology—offer the one chance of success: they must work in cooperation with their fellows and subordinate themselves to a directing authority." [*Oriental Despotism* (New Haven, Ct.: Yale University Press, 1957), p. 18.]

cal evidence now makes it appear that in at least three of the areas that Wittfogel cites as exemplifying his "hydraulic hypothesis"—Mesopotamia, China, and Mexico—full-fledged states developed well before large-scale irrigation.[6] Thus, irrigation did not play the causal role in the rise of the state that Wittfogel appears to attribute to it.[7]

This and all other voluntaristic theories of the rise of the state founder on the same rock: the demonstrated inability of autonomous political units to relinquish their sovereignty in the absence of overriding external constraints. We see this inability manifested again and again by political units ranging from tiny villages to great empires. Indeed, one can scan

---

[6] For Mesopotamia, Robert M. Adams has concluded: "In short, there is nothing to suggest that the rise of dynastic authority in southern Mesopotamia was linked to the administrative requirements of a major canal system." [*City Invincible,* C. H. Kraeling and R. M. Adams, eds. (Chicago: University of Chicago Press, 1960), p. 281.] For China, the prototypical area for Wittfogel's hydraulic theories, the French Sinologist Jacques Gernet has recently written: "Although the establishment of a system of regulation of water courses and irrigation, and the control of this system, may have affected the political constitution of the military states and imperial China, the fact remains that, historically, it was the preexisting state structures and the large, well-trained labor force provided by the armies that made the great irrigation projects possible." [*Ancient China, from the Beginnings to the Empire,* R. Rudorff, tr. (London: Faber and Faber, 1968), p. 92.] For Mexico, large-scale irrigation systems do not appear to antedate the Classic period, whereas it is clear that the first state arose in the preceding Formative or Pre-Classic period.

[7] This is not to say, of course, that large-scale irrigation, where it occurred, did not contribute significantly to increasing the power and the scope of the state. It unquestionably did. To the extent that Wittfogel limits himself to this contention, I have no quarrel with him whatever. However, the point at issue is not how the state increased its power but how it arose in the first place. And to this issue the hydraulic hypothesis does not appear to hold the key.

the pages of history without finding a single genuine exception to this rule. Thus, in order to account for the origin of the state we must set aside voluntaristic theories and look elsewhere.

Coercive Theories

A close examination of history indicates that only a coercive theory can account for the rise of the state. Force, and not enlightened self-interest, is the mechanism by which political evolution has led, step by step, from autonomous villages to the state.

The view that war lies at the root of the state is by no means new. Twenty-five hundred years ago Heraclitus wrote that "war is the father of all things." The first careful study of the role of warfare in the rise of the state, however, was made less than a hundred years ago, by Herbert Spencer in his *Principles of Sociology*.[8] Perhaps better known than Spencer's writings on war and the state are the conquest theories of Continental writers such as Ludwig Gumplowicz,[9] Gustav Ratzenhofer,[10] and Franz Oppenheimer.[11]

Oppenheimer, for example, argued that the state emerged when the productive capacity of settled agriculturists was

---

[8] See *The Evolution of Society: Selections from Herbert Spencer's Principles of Sociology*, Robert L. Carneiro, ed. (Chicago: University of Chicago Press, 1967), pp. 32–47, 63–96, 153–165.

[9] Ludwig Gumplowicz, *Der Rassenkampf* (Innsbruck: Wagner, 1883).

[10] Gustav Ratzenhofer, *Wesen und Zweck der Politik* (Leipzig: Brockhaus, 1893).

[11] Franz Oppenheimer, *The State*, J. M. Gitterman, tr. (New York: Vanguard, 1926).

combined with the energy of pastoral nomads through the conquest of the former by the latter.[12] This theory, however, has two serious defects. First, it fails to account for the rise of states in aboriginal America, where pastoral nomadism was unknown. Second, it is now well established that pastoral nomadism did not arise in the Old World until after the earliest states had emerged.

Regardless of deficiencies in particular coercive theories, however, there is little question that, in one way or another, war played a decisive role in the rise of the state. Historical or archeological evidence of war is found in the early stages of state formation in Mesopotamia, Egypt, India, China, Japan, Greece, Rome, northern Europe, central Africa, Polynesia, Middle America, Peru, and Colombia, to name only the most prominent examples.

Thus, with the Germanic kingdoms of northern Europe especially in mind, Edward Jenks observed that, "historically speaking, there is not the slightest difficulty in proving that all political communities of the modern type [that is, states] owe their existence to successful warfare."[13] And in reading Jan Vansina's *Kingdoms of the Savanna*,[14] a book with no theoretical ax to grind, one finds that state after state in central Africa rose in the same manner.

But is it really true that there is no exception to this rule? Might there not be, somewhere in the world, an example of a state which arose without the agency of war?

---

[12] *Ibid.,* pp. 51–55.

[13] Edward Jenks, *A History of Politics* (New York: Macmillan, 1900), p. 73.

[14] Jan Vansina, *Kingdoms of the Savanna* (Madison: University of Wisconsin Press, 1966).

Until a few years ago, anthropologists generally believed that the Classic Maya provided such an instance. The archeological evidence then available gave no hint of warfare among the early Maya and led scholars to regard them as a peace-loving theocratic state which had arisen entirely without war.[15] However, this view is no longer tenable. Recent archeological discoveries have placed the Classic Maya in a very different light. First came the discovery of the Bonampak murals, showing the early Maya at war and reveling in the torture of war captives. Then, excavations around Tikal revealed large earthworks partly surrounding that Classic Maya city, pointing clearly to a military rivalry with the neighboring city of Uaxactun.[16] Summarizing present thinking on the subject, Michael D. Coe has observed that "the ancient Maya were just as warlike as the . . . bloodthirsty states of the Post-Classic."[17]

Yet, though warfare is surely a prime mover in the origin of the state, it cannot be the only factor. After all, wars have been fought in many parts of the world where the state never emerged. Thus, while warfare may be a necessary condition for the rise of the state, it is not a sufficient one. Or, to put it another way, while we can identify war as the *mechanism* of state formation, we need also to specify the *conditions* under which it gave rise to the state.

---

[15] For example, Julian H. Steward wrote: "It is possible, therefore, that the Maya were able to develop a high civilization only because they enjoyed an unusually long period of peace; for their settlement pattern would seem to have been too vulnerable to warfare." [*Amer. Anthropol.* 51, 1 (1949), see p. 17.]

[16] D. E. Puleston and D. W. Callender, *Expedition* 9 No. 3, 40 (1967), see pp. 45, 47.

[17] Michael D. Coe, *The Maya* (New York: Praeger, 1966), p. 147.

Environmental Circumscription

How are we to determine these conditions? One promising approach is to look for those factors common to areas
of the world in which states arose indigenously—areas such
as the Nile, Tigris-Euphrates, and Indus valleys in the Old
World and the Valley of Mexico and the mountain and
coastal valleys of Peru in the New. These areas differ from
one another in many ways—in altitude, temperature, rainfall, soil type, drainage pattern, and many other features.
They do, however, have one thing in common: *they are all
areas of circumscribed agricultural land.* Each of them is
set off by mountains, seas, or deserts, and these environmental features sharply delimit the area that simple farming
peoples could occupy and cultivate. In this respect these
areas are very different from, say, the Amazon basin or the
eastern woodlands of North America, where extensive and
unbroken forests provided almost unlimited agricultural
land.

But what is the significance of circumscribed agricultural
land for the origin of the state? Its significance can best be
understood by comparing political development in two regions of the world having contrasting ecologies—one a
region with circumscribed agricultural land and the other a
region where there was extensive and unlimited land. The
two areas I have chosen to use in making this comparison
are the coastal valleys of Peru and the Amazon basin.

Our examination begins at the stage where agricultural
communities were already present but where each was still
completely autonomous. Looking first at the Amazon basin,
we see that agricultural villages there were numerous, but

widely dispersed. Even in areas with relatively dense cluster-ing, like the Upper Xingu basin, villages were at least ten or fifteen miles apart. Thus, the typical Amazonian commu-nity, even though it practiced a simple form of shifting cul-tivation which required extensive amounts of land, still had around it all the forest land needed for its gardens.[18] For Amazonia as a whole, then, population density was low and subsistence pressure on the land was slight.

Warfare was certainly frequent in Amazonia, but it was waged for reasons of revenge, the taking of women, the gaining of personal prestige, and motives of a similar sort. There being no shortage of land, there was, by and large, no warfare over land.

The consequences of the type of warfare that did occur in Amazonia were as follows. A defeated group was not, as a rule, driven from its land. Nor did the victor make any real effort to subject the vanquished, or to exact tribute from him. This would have been difficult to accomplish in any case, since there was no effective way to prevent the losers from fleeing to a distant part of the forest. Indeed, defeated villages often chose to do just this, not so much to avoid subjugation as to avoid further attack. With settlement so sparse in Amazonia, a new area of forest could be found and occupied with relative ease, and without trespassing on the territory of another village. Moreover, since virtually any area of forest is suitable for cultivation, subsistence agricul-ture could be carried on in the new habitat just about as well as in the old.

It was apparently by this process of fight and flight that

---

[18] See Robert L. Carneiro, in *Men and Cultures, Selected Papers of the Fifth International Congress of Anthropological and Ethnological Sciences,* A. F. C. Wallace, ed. (Philadelphia: University of Pennsylvania Press, 1960), pp. 229–34.

horticultural tribes gradually spread out until they came to cover, thinly but extensively, almost the entire Amazon basin. Thus, under the conditions of unlimited agricultural land and low population density that prevailed in Amazonia, the effect of warfare was to disperse villages over a wide area, and to keep them autonomous. With only a very few exceptions, noted below, there was no tendency in Amazonia for villages to be held in place and to combine into larger political units.

In marked contrast to the situation in Amazonia were the events that transpired in the narrow valleys of the Peruvian coast. The reconstruction of these events that I present is admittedly inferential, but I think it is consistent with the archeological evidence.

Here too our account begins at the stage of small, dispersed, and autonomous farming communities. However, instead of being scattered over a vast expanse of rain forest as they were in Amazonia, villages here were confined to some seventy-eight short and narrow valleys.[19] Each of these valleys, moreover, was backed by the mountains, fronted by the sea, and flanked on either side by desert as dry as any in the world. Nowhere else, perhaps, can one find agricultural valleys more sharply circumscribed than these.

As with neolithic communities generally, villages of the

---

[19] In early agricultural times (Preceramic Period VI, beginning about 2500 B.C.) human settlement seems to have been denser along the coast than in the river valleys, and subsistence appears to have been based more on fishing than on farming. Furthermore, some significant first steps in political evolution beyond autonomous villages may have been taken at this stage. However, once subsistence began to be based predominantly on agriculture, the settlement pattern changed, and communities were thenceforth concentrated more in the river valleys, where the only land of any size suitable for cultivation was located. See E. P. Lanning, *Peru Before the Incas* (Englewood Cliffs, N.J.: Prentice-Hall, 1967), pp. 57–59.

Peruvian coastal valleys tended to grow in size. Since autonomous villages are likely to fission as they grow, as long as land is available for the settlement of splinter communities, these villages undoubtedly split from time to time.[20] Thus, villages tended to increase in number faster than they grew in size. This increase in the number of villages occupying a valley probably continued, without giving rise to significant changes in subsistence practices, until all the readily arable land in the valley was being farmed.

At this point two changes in agricultural techniques began to occur: the tilling of land already under cultivation was intensified, and new, previously unusable land was brought under cultivation by means of terracing and irrigation.[21]

Yet the rate at which new arable land was created failed to keep pace with the increasing demand for it. Even before the land shortage became so acute that irrigation began to be practiced systematically, villages were undoubtedly already fighting one another over land. Prior to this time, when agricultural villages were still few in number and well supplied with land, the warfare waged in the coastal valleys of Peru had probably been of much the same type as that

---

[20] In my files I find reported instances of village splitting among the following Amazonian tribes: Kuikuru, Amarakaeri, Cubeo, Urubú, Tuparí,Yanomamö, Tucano, Tenetehara, Canela, and Northern Cayapó. Under the conditions of easy resettlement found in Amazonia, splitting often takes place at a village population level of less than 100, and village size seldom exceeds 200. In coastal Peru, however, where land was severely restricted, villages could not fission so readily, and thus grew to population levels which, according to Lanning [*Peru Before the Incas* (Englewood Cliffs, N.J.: Prentice-Hall, 1967), p. 64], may have averaged over 300.

[21] See Robert L. Carneiro, *Ethnograph.-archäol. Forschungen* 4, 22 (1958).

described above for Amazonia. With increasing pressure of human population on the land, however, the major incentive for war changed from a desire for revenge to a need to acquire land. And, as the causes of war became predominantly economic, the frequency, intensity, and importance of war increased.

Once this stage was reached, a Peruvian village that lost a war faced consequences very different from those faced by a defeated village in Amazonia. There, as we have seen, the vanquished could flee to a new locale, subsisting there about as well as they had subsisted before, and retaining their independence. In Peru, however, this alternative was no longer open to the inhabitants of defeated villages. The mountains, the desert, and the sea—to say nothing of neighboring villages—blocked escape in every direction. A village defeated in war thus faced only grim prospects. If it was allowed to remain on its own land, instead of being exterminated or expelled, this concession came only at a price. And the price was political subordination to the victor. This subordination generally entailed at least the payment of a tribute or tax in kind, which the defeated village could provide only by producing more food than it had produced before. But subordination sometimes involved a further loss of autonomy on the part of the defeated village—namely, incorporation into the political unit dominated by the victor.

Through the recurrence of warfare of this type, we see arising in coastal Peru integrated territorial units transcending the village in size and in degree of organization. Political evolution was attaining the level of the chiefdom.

As land shortage continued and became even more acute, so did warfare. Now, however, the competing units were no longer small villages but, often, large chiefdoms. From this point on, through the conquest of chiefdom by chiefdom, the size of political units increased at a progressively faster rate. Naturally, as autonomous political units increased in size, they decreased in number, with the result that an entire valley was eventually unified under the banner of its strongest chiefdom. The political unit thus formed was undoubtedly sufficiently centralized and complex to warrant being called a state.

The political evolution I have described for one valley of Peru was also taking place in other valleys, in the highlands as well as on the coast.[22] Once valley-wide kingdoms emerged, the next step was the formation of multivalley kingdoms through the conquest of weaker valleys by stronger ones. The culmination of this process was the conquest[23] of all of Peru by its most powerful state, and the formation of a single great empire. Although this step may have occurred once or twice before in Andean history, it was achieved most notably, and for the last time, by the Incas.[24]

---

[22] Naturally, this evolution took place in the various Peruvian valleys at different rates and to different degrees. In fact it is possible that at the same time that some valleys were already unified politically, others still had not evolved beyond the stage of autonomous villages.

[23] Not every step in empire building was necessarily taken through actual physical conquest, however. The threat of force sometimes had the same effect as its exercise. In this way many smaller chiefdoms and states were probably coerced into giving up their sovereignty without having to be defeated on the field of battle. Indeed, it was an explicit policy of the Incas, in expanding their empire, to try persuasion before resorting to force of arms. See Garcilaso de la Vega, *Royal Commentaries of the Incas and General History of Peru*, Part 1, H. V. Livermore, tr. (Austin: University of Texas Press, 1966), pp. 108, 111, 140, 143, 146, 264.

[24] The evolution of empire in Peru was thus by no means rectilinear or irreversible. Advance alternated with decline. Integration was sometimes followed by disintegration, with states fragmenting back to chiefdoms, and

Political Evolution

While the aggregation of villages into chiefdoms, and of chiefdoms into kingdoms, was occurring by external acquisition, the structure of these increasingly larger political units was being elaborated by internal evolution. These inner changes were, of course, closely related to outer events. The expansion of successful states brought within their borders conquered peoples and territory which had to be administered. And it was the individuals who had distinguished themselves in war who were generally appointed to political office and assigned the task of carrying out this administration. Besides maintaining law and order and collecting taxes, the functions of this burgeoning class of administrators included mobilizing labor for building irrigation works, roads, fortresses, palaces, and temples. Thus, their functions helped to weld an assorted collection of petty states into a single integrated and centralized political unit.

These same individuals, who owed their improved social position to their exploits in war, became, along with the ruler and his kinsmen, the nucleus of an upper class. A lower class in turn emerged from the prisoners taken in war and employed as servants and slaves by their captors. In this manner did war contribute to the rise of social classes.

I noted earlier that peoples attempt to acquire their neighbors' land before they have made the fullest possible use of

---

perhaps even to autonomous villages. But the forces underlying political development were strong and, in the end, prevailed. Thus, despite fluctuations and reversions, the course of evolution in Peru was unmistakable: it began with many small, simple, scattered, and autonomous communities and ended with a single, vast, complex, and centralized empire.

their own. This implies that every autonomous village has an untapped margin of food productivity, and that this margin is squeezed out only when the village is subjugated and compelled to pay taxes in kind. The surplus food extracted from conquered villages through taxation, which in the aggregate attained very significant proportions, went largely to support the ruler, his warriors and retainers, officials, priests, and other members of the rising upper class, who thus became completely divorced from food production.

Finally, those made landless by war but not enslaved tended to gravitate to settlements which, because of their specialized administrative, commercial, or religious functions, were growing into towns and cities. Here they were able to make a living as workers and artisans, exchanging their labor or their wares for part of the economic surplus exacted from village farmers by the ruling class and spent by members of that class to raise their standard of living.

The process of political evolution which I have outlined for the coastal valleys of Peru was, in its essential features, by no means unique to this region. Areas of circumscribed agricultural land elsewhere in the world, such as the Valley of Mexico, Mesopotamia, the Nile Valley, and the Indus Valley, saw the process occur in much the same way and for essentially the same reasons. In these areas, too, autonomous neolithic villages were succeeded by chiefdoms, chiefdoms by kingdoms, and kingdoms by empires. The last stage of this development was, of course, the most impressive. The scale and magnificence attained by the early empires overshadowed everything that had gone before. But, in a sense, empires were merely the logical culmination of the process. The really fundamental step, the one that had triggered the entire train of events that led to empires, was the change from village autonomy to supravillage integration. This step was a change in kind; everything that followed was, in a way, only a change in degree.

In addition to being pivotal, the step to supracommunity aggregation was difficult, for it took two million years to achieve. But, once it was achieved, once village autonomy was transcended, only two or three millennia were required for the rise of great empires and the flourishing of complex civilizations.

Resource Concentration

Theories are first formulated on the basis of a limited number of facts. Eventually, though, a theory must confront all of the facts. And often new facts are stubborn and do not conform to the theory, or do not conform very well. What distinguishes a successful theory from an unsuccessful one is that it can be modified or elaborated to accommodate the entire range of facts. Let us see how well the "circumscription theory" holds up when it is brought face-to-face with certain facts that appear to be exceptions.

For the first test let us return to Amazonia. Early voyagers down the Amazon left written testimony of a culture along that river higher than the culture I have described for Amazonia generally. In the 1500s, the native population living on the banks of the Amazon was relatively dense, villages were fairly large and close together, and some degree of social stratification existed. Moreover, here and there a paramount chief held sway over many communities.

The question immediately arises: with unbroken stretches of arable land extending back from the Amazon for hundreds of miles, why were there chiefdoms here?

To answer the question we must look closely at the environmental conditions afforded by the Amazon. Along the margins of the river itself, and on islands within it, there is a type of land called *várzea*. The river floods this land every year, covering it with a layer of fertile silt. Because of this annual replenishment, *várzea* is agricultural land of first quality which can be cultivated year after year without ever having to lie fallow. Thus, among native farmers it was highly priced and greatly coveted. The waters of the Amazon were also extraordinarily bountiful, providing fish, manatees, turtles and turtle eggs, caimans, and other riverine foods in inexhaustible amounts. By virtue of this concentration of resources, the Amazon, as a habitat, was distinctly superior to its hinterlands.

Concentration of resources along the Amazon amounted almost to a kind of circumscription. While there was no sharp cleavage between productive and unproductive land, as there was in Peru, there was at least a steep ecological gradient. So much more rewarding was the Amazon River than adjacent areas, and so desirable did it become as a habitat, that people were drawn to it from surrounding regions. Eventually crowding occurred along many portions of the river, leading to warfare over sections of river front. And the losers in war, in order to retain access to the river, often had no choice but to submit to the victors. By this subordination of villages to a paramount chief there arose along the Amazon chiefdoms representing a higher step in political evolution than had occurred elsewhere in the basin.[25]

---

[25] Actually, a similar political development did take place in another part of Amazonia—the basin of the Mamoré River in the Mojos plain of Bolivia. Here, too, resource concentration appears to have played a key role. See W. Denevan, "The Aboriginal Cultural Geography of the Llanos de Mojos of Bolivia," *Ibero-americana No. 48* (1966), pp. 43–50, 104–5,

The notion of resource concentration also helps to explain the surprising degree of political development apparently attained by peoples of the Peruvian coast while they were still depending primarily on fishing for subsistence, and only secondarily on agriculture.[26] Of this seeming anomaly Lanning has written: "To the best of my knowledge, this is the only case in which so many of the characteristics of civilization have been found without a basically agricultural economic foundation."[27]

Armed with the concept of resource concentration, however, we can show that this development was not so anomalous after all. The explanation, it seems to me, runs as follows. Along the coast of Peru wild food sources occurred in considerable number and variety. However, they were restricted to a very narrow margin of land.[28] Accordingly, while the *abundance* of food in this zone led to a sharp rise in population, the *restrictedness* of this food soon resulted in the almost complete occupation of exploitable areas. And when pressure on the available resources reached a critical level, competition over land ensued. The result of this competition was to set in motion the sequence of events of political evolution that I have described.

Thus, it seems that we can safely add resource concentra-

108–10. In native North America north of Mexico the highest cultural development attained, Middle-Mississippi, also occurred along a major river (the Mississippi) which, by providing especially fertile soil and riverine food resources, comprised a zone of resource concentration. See J. B. Griffin, *Science* 156, 175 (1967), p. 189.

[26] E. P. Lanning, *Peru Before the Incas* (Englewood Cliffs, N.J.: Prentice-Hall, 1967).

[27] *Ibid.*, p. 59.

[28] Resource concentration, then, was here combined with environmental circumscription. And, indeed, the same thing can be said of the great desert river valleys, such as the Nile, Tigris-Euphrates, and Indus.

tion to environmental circumscription as a factor leading to warfare over land, and thus to political integration beyond the village level.

Social Circumscription

But there is still another factor to be considered in accounting for the rise of the state.

In dealing with the theory of environmental circumscription while discussing the Yanomamo Indians of Venezuela, Napoleon A. Chagnon[29] has introduced the concept of "social circumscription." By this he means that a high density of population in an area can produce effects on peoples living near the center of the area that are similar to effects produced by environmental circumscription. This notion seems to me to be an important addition to our theory. Let us see how, according to Chagnon, social circumscription has operated among the Yanomamo.

The Yanomamo, who number some 10,000, live in an extensive region of noncircumscribed rain forest, away from any large river. One might expect that Yanomamo villages would thus be more or less evenly spaced. However, Chagnon notes that, at the center of Yanomamo territory, villages are closer together than they are at the periphery. Because of this, they tend to impinge on one another more, with the result that warfare is more frequent and intense in the center than in peripheral areas. Moreover, it is more difficult for villages in the nuclear area to escape attack by

---

[29] Napoleon A. Chagnon, *Proceedings, VIIIth International Congress of Anthropological and Ethnological Sciences* (Tokyo and Kyoto, 1968), v. 3 (*Ethnology and Archaeology*), p. 249 (especially p. 251). See also N. Fock, *Folk* 6, 47 (1964), p. 52.

moving away, since, unlike villages on the periphery, their ability to move is somewhat restricted.

The net result is that villages in the central area of Yanomamo territory are larger than villages in the other areas, since large village size is an advantage for both attack and defense. A further effect of more intense warfare in the nuclear area is that village headmen are stronger in that area. Yanomamo headmen are also the war leaders, and their influence increases in proportion to their village's participation in war. In addition, offensive and defensive alliances between villages are more common in the center of Yanomamo territory than in outlying areas. Thus, while still at the autonomous village level of political organization, those Yanomamo subject to social circumscription have clearly moved a step or two in the direction of higher political development.

Although the Yanomamo manifest social circumscription only to a modest degree, this amount of it has been enough to make a difference in their level of political organization. What the effects of social circumscription would be in areas where it was more fully expressed should, therefore, be clear. First would come a reduction in the size of the territory of each village. Then, as population pressure became more severe, warfare over land would ensue. But because adjacent land for miles around was already the property of other villages, a defeated village would have nowhere to flee. From this point on, the consequences of warfare for that village, and for political evolution in general, would be essentially as I have described them for the situation of environmental circumscription.

To return to Amazonia, it is clear that, if social circumscription is operative among the Yanomamo today, it was certainly operative among the tribes of the Amazon River 400 years ago. And its effect would undoubtedly have been to give a further spur to political evolution in that region.

We see then that, even in the absence of sharp environmental circumscription, the factors of resource concentration and social circumscription may, by intensifying war and redirecting it toward the taking of land, give a strong impetus to political development.

With these auxiliary hypotheses incorporated into it, the circumscription theory is now better able to confront the entire range of test cases that can be brought before it. For example, it can now account for the rise of the state in the Hwang Valley of northern China, and even in the Petén region of the Maya lowlands, areas not characterized by strictly circumscribed agricultural land. In the case of the Hwang Valley, there is no question that resource concentration and social circumscription were present and active forces. In the lowland Maya area, resource concentration seems not to have been a major factor, but social circumscription may well have been.

Some archeologists may object that population density in the Petén during Formative times was too low to give rise to social circumscription. But, in assessing what constitutes a population dense enough to produce this effect, we must consider not so much the total land area occupied as the amount of land needed to support the existing population. And the size of this supporting area depends not only on the size of the population but also on the mode of subsistence. The shifting cultivation presumably practiced by the ancient Maya[30] required considerably more land, per capita, than

---

[30] S. G. Morley and G. W. Brainerd, *The Ancient Maya* (Stanford, Calif.: Stanford University Press, ed. 3, 1956), pp. 128–29.

did the permanent field cultivation of, say, the valley of Mexico or the coast of Peru.[31] Consequently, insofar as its effects are concerned, a relatively low population density in the Petén may have been equivalent to a much higher one in Mexico or Peru.

We have already learned from the Yanomamo example that social circumscription may begin to operate while population is still relatively sparse. And we can be sure that the Petén was far more densely peopled in Formative times than Yanomamo territory is today. Thus, population density among the lowland Maya, while giving a superficial appearance of sparseness, may actually have been high enough to provoke fighting over land, and thus provide the initial impetus for the formation of a state.

Conclusion

In summary, then, the circumscription theory in its elaborated form goes far toward accounting for the origin of the state. It explains why states arose where they did, and why they failed to arise elsewhere. It shows the state to be a predictable response to certain specific cultural, demographic, and ecological conditions. Thus, it helps to elucidate what was undoubtedly the most important single step ever taken in the political evolution of mankind.

---

[31] One can assume, I think, that any substantial increase in population density among the Maya was accompanied by a certain intensification of agriculture. As the population increased fields were probably weeded more thoroughly, and they may well have been cultivated a year or two longer and fallowed a few years less. Yet, given the nature of soils in the humid tropics, the absence of any evidence of fertilization, and the moderate population densities, it seems likely that Maya farming remained extensive rather than becoming intensive.

Essay Two

State and Society

Felix Morley

Felix Morley, educator and journalist, is a former president of Haverford College and former editor of the Washington Post. *Among his honors and awards are a Rhodes Scholarship, a Guggenheim Fellowship, and a Pulitzer Prize. As a keen analyst of public affairs and an authority on U.S. diplomatic and constitutional history, he has lectured widely at American colleges and universities.*

Besides his many writings in newspapers and magazines, Dr. Morley has contributed to symposiums and has authored several books, including Our Far Eastern Assignment *(1926).* The Society of Nations *(1932),* The Foreign Policy of the United States *(1951), and* Freedom and Federalism *(1959).*

This essay, reprinted with permission, is taken from chapter five of The Power in the People *(1949). The Institute for Humane Studies sponsored a new edition of the book in 1972.*

I

" **M**an is by nature a political animal," asserts Aristotle in Book I of *The Politics*. And, a few lines later: "A social instinct is implanted in all men by nature."[1]

These axioms of political science are upheld by all human experience. The prolonged dependency of children, disproportionately long in relation to the offspring of other species, itself attests the validity of the two assumptions. So does the human gift of speech, which Aristotle cites as evidence that man is more political than the bees or other gregarious creatures. There can be no such easy agreement, however, with his simultaneous conclusion that "the state is a creation of nature."

In the fourth century B.C., Aristotle could speak of state and society as though they were the same. Throughout *The Politics* he uses the one word *polis* to represent that for which we have the two nouns. But we must remember that Aristotle was thinking in terms of the Greek city-state, of very limited area and population. "To the size of states," he says, "there is a limit," and even some cities, like Baby-

---

[1] Jowett translation (Oxford: Oxford University Press, 1920), pp. 28–29.

lon, are of "such vast circuit" that they must be regarded as "a nation rather than a state" (Book III). As to population, "a great city is not to be confounded with a populous one." The ideal state should contain enough people to be self-sufficient, but not so many that citizens cannot personally know each other.

Moreover, by listing desirable conditions of statehood, Aristotle makes himself vulnerable to the charge that he has not discriminated between the political instinct and that which is its natural result. A natural result is not the same thing as a creation of nature. In the words of a thoughtful critic: "If the city comes of nature, it does not come of the deliberate will of citizens who get together for the purpose of achieving a certain advantage! There is an inconsistency between the principle first posited and the conclusion reached."[2]

Nevertheless, Americans should be particularly receptive to Aristotle's pioneering thought because to us, as to him, the word "state" still conveys the idea of an autochthonous political entity, with what is well described as "home rule" preserving a jealous independence or at least autonomy in the conduct of local affairs. In political science, however, this word has come to be the technical designation of the sovereign nation-state, and in this national sense the state will be considered in this essay.

The abiding influence of Aristotle in the field of political theory is doubtless largely responsible for the tendency to regard the state as a particular form of society. From our differentiation between liberty and freedom, however, we have learned the importance of verbal precision in political

---

[2] Vilfredo Pareto, *The Mind and Society*, v. I, sect. 272.

thinking. Here again are two distinct words, representing two abstract ideas that are obviously related, but certainly not identical. In the book from which this essay is drawn, I refer to state and society as the separate forms of human organization that they are. Here we must carefully distinguish between them, remembering Pascal's excellent advice: "I never quarrel over names, provided I am told what meanings they are given."[3]

We shall be the more on guard against confusing society and state because American political thinking has in general drawn the clear distinction that is appropriate. The nature of that distinction conforms with the etymology of the words.

II

The noun "society" comes to us from the Latin *socius,* meaning a companion. And, like the related noun "association," society still carries the flavor of voluntary companionship. It would be forcing language to refer to a company of conscripts, or to the prisoners in a tier of cells, as a society. Companionship in both these cases is externally enforced (by the state, as it happens). In a society, companionship between individuals of different tastes and standards is not compulsory. On the other hand, "society . . . tends to suggest a more restricted aim, a closer union of members, and their more active participation" than does the looser term "association."[4] A common interest, a common objective, to some extent a common faith, are elements necessary to a society.

---

[3] *Lettres à une provinciale,* 1, p. 6.
[4] Webster's *Dictionary of Synonyms.*

The idea of association is also involved in the noun "state," though here the association tends to be involuntary, on the basis not of free contract but of *status,* from which, of course, the word "state" derives. The place of birth determines state membership much more definitely than it does social position. In nonpolitical usage, this element of status or condition is always uppermost, as in "a state of good health" or "a state of mental depression." The same sense of subjection to circumstance applies in consideration of the political state. In Great Britain, for instance, individuals as nationals are honestly defined as "subjects," whereas the same individuals are members, not subjects, of a society like the Anglican church.

The state, in short, subjects people, whereas society associates them voluntarily. In a universe of rhythm and pulsation, within "the systole and diastole of time itself," some such differentiation in human groupings is precisely what one might expect. State and society, we shall see, are naturally and continuously in opposition. For that reason, human welfare demands the nicest balance between the appropriate functions of each.

While engaged in the important preliminary of definition, we should note that the word—and the idea of—"constitution" is connected with "state." The "constitution" is inherent in, or literally "stands with," the physical structure. The state "stands with" its constitution, and the character of that organic law, written or unwritten, determines *how* the state shall stand.

Like "state," the word "constitution" has a physical as well as a political meaning, encouraging such picturesque expressions as "the body politic." The political constitution provides the physical linkage between the state and its sub-

jects, with physical connection emphasized by description of
a constitution as "organic" law. Indeed, every political state
must have a constitution—though this may be as arbitrary
as the personal decrees of a dictator—because the very existence of a state implies some accepted relationship, doubtless originating in custom but invariably acquiring the force
of law, between government and governed. This accepted
relationship between sovereign and subject is provided by
the constitution, and a change in the constitution, by executive edict, legislative amendment, or judicial interpretation,
is momentous to all because it signifies a change in that
basic relationship.

The great difference between the British and American
systems of government is that the former has come to vest
complete sovereignty in its representative Parliament, which
by contraction of the power of the House of Lords has become, in effect, the House of Commons alone. In our republic, legal sovereignty is by intent permanently divided, so
that it cannot be located in any single person or organ. "The
basis of law," according to Professor Vinogradoff's searching analysis, is in the United States "provided not by one-
sided command, but by agreement."

Because that unique basis can so easily be undermined,
every constitutional change is of greater importance in the
American federal union than in less delicate governmental
systems. A seemingly innocuous move to alter the method
of appointment to the Supreme Court, for instance, could
easily result in making the judiciary an arm of executive
power. And since the judiciary has authority to check the
legislature, this could in turn mean the development of
executive tyranny. The vital importance of balance in the
American governmental system and the ease with which it

can be upset were well suggested by Justice Harlan F. Stone in his dissent in the AAA case: "While unconstitutional exercise of power by the executive and legislative branches is subject to judicial restraint, the only check on our exercise of power is our own sense of self-restraint."

Thus a great twentieth century jurist rephrased, for members of the Supreme Court, Madison's imperative reminder that we "rest all our political experiments on the capacity of mankind for self-government."

III

The state, to be a state, must have a constitution. The interlocking relationship between society and state is indicated by the fact that practically all social organizations—religious, commercial, or merely recreational—also have constitutions. These, like a national constitution, establish disciplinary rules and regulations that may be, and often are, rigorously enforced within the particular association. The difference is that the disciplinary power of the social organization is always limited and seldom physically punitive.

A Red-Headed League, for instance, could properly exclude from membership anybody whose hirsute coloration fell short of a previously determined standard. But nothing would then prevent the deficient individual from forming an Auburn Association in the same community. Of course, the penalties inflicted by society may be much more serious than this fanciful illustration indicates. They do not, however, effectively constrain individual liberty. Penalties by the state are designed to do just that.[5]

---

[5] Pareto points out that "Sunday idleness is enforced by law in the name of freedom." *Op. cit.,* v. III, sect. 1554.

Society, in other words, is more fluid, more flexible, less constitutionalized, and less resolutely disciplinary than the state, which because of its supremacy possesses a power of ostracism far exceeding that of the most exclusive social organization. Between the discrimination of a governmental edict directed against Jews, and that of a social covenant with the same objective, there is a difference of kind rather than of degree. The inclusive discrimination of the state is tyrannical. The exclusive discrimination of a social group is merely offensive.

Nevertheless, it cannot be asserted that society, in any of its almost numberless groupings, is particularly interested in the enlargement of freedom. Regardless of the social institution we stop to consider—whether it be the family as the oldest known cooperative unit, or an association of atomic scientists as a modern manifestation—we see similar evidences of self-imposed restraint. Husband and wife put definite limits on their individual freedom, in order to promote certain objectives, such as the rearing of children, which they have in common. And the atomic scientists in congress assembled are making comparable individual sacrifices for their particular common end. So it seems to be the nature of human association, whether voluntary or involuntary, to limit the condition of freedom for those whose association is something more than merely casual.

But when this association for a common end is voluntary, a very interesting result is wont to ensue. Although the area of individual freedom suffers undeniable contraction from association, the act of association simultaneously permits and encourages development along the lines of deepest individual interest, to an extent that would have been impossible without association. The enlargement of personality may be as inconsequential as the pleasure afforded by a foursome of golf at the country club. It may be as momentous as a general improvement of diagnostic methods resulting from a medical conference. But whatever the case in point, ridiculous or sublime, we observe that the income derived from voluntary cooperation is expected by the participants to exceed the outlay involved in such cooperation. If that were not so, we would not have voluntary cooperation, in all its myriad forms, and man would not possess the "social instinct" to the degree that makes him "a political animal."

IV

At this point we would see a distinction arising between freedom and liberty, even if it had not already been made. Voluntary association limits freedom while it enlarges liberty. That which is limited by continuous association is the indulgence of individual appetites, passions, and animal instincts—the carnal side of man. That which is expanded by continuous association is the perfection of individual skills, ambitions, and aspirations—the spiritual side of man. Thus, continuous voluntary association may and does limit the physical condition of freedom. But it does so to enlarge the moral endowment of liberty.

During the term of earthly life, physical condition and moral endowment can never be wholly separated, for they are like body and soul. When irrevocably separated, the result is dissolution of the individual. We may suggest that this complete termination of physical freedom simultaneously brings the complete apotheosis of spiritual liberty. That would be the logical conclusion of our thought, if we were not hesitant to consider the subject of immortality in a political study already sufficiently difficult. However, we *are* concerned to point out that the quality of liberty is spiritual, and can be advanced by voluntary association, while the condition of freedom is physical, and must be limited by voluntary association. From this it follows that the individual can happily compromise with his fellows in matters of physical adjustment, but should never compromise where spiritual sacrifice is involved.

As a generality, to which many individual exceptions could be cited, man throughout his recorded history has preferred liberty to freedom. Left to himself, his natural tendency is to limit his freedom in order to enlarge his liberty. From this tendency the observant Aristotle reasoned, more than three centuries before the birth of Christ, that: "Man is by nature a political animal."

Aristotle "first brought to bear on political phenomena the patient analysis and unbiased research which are the proper marks and virtues of scientific inquiry."[6] This early political scientist concentrated on the problems of a closely integrated city-state, where it was not an impossible ideal for all the citizens to know each other. Nevertheless, in Book III of *The Politics,* Aristotle was forced to the conclusion that "a state is not a mere society," and to see further that "the good citizen need not of necessity possess the virtue which makes a good man."[7] As the state has grown in power and magnitude to become a political aggregation that certainly would have seemed dreadful to Aristotle, the contrast between state and society that he dimly discerned has

---

[6] Sir Frederick Pollock, *History of the Science of Politics,* p. 2.

[7] *Op. cit.,* pp. 106 and 119.

become increasingly clear. The contrast is also increasingly important for those who assert that their national objective is to secure the blessings of liberty.

For the purpose of this study, it is unnecessary to debate whether the origins of state and society are coeval, or whether the state in primitive form was originally imposed on pre-existent social groups in order to systematize exploitation of the weak by the strong. Certain observations on the issue will be made for what they are worth. Beyond contention, however, is the obvious fact that the nation-state has acquired characteristics that make it differ in nature as well as in degree from any voluntary social organization. The rapid extension of the authority of the state, and its increasing competence to control, discipline, and subordinate not only the individual but also all unofficial forms of social organization, was the painfully outstanding political development of the first half of the twentieth century.

V

We are now in a position to identify the components of political life as (1) the individual; (2) society, meaning every form of voluntary association directed to the self-defined benefit of individuals; (3) the state, as the dominant organization, which has gradually acquired the power to dictate both to individuals and to social groupings under its sovereignty. From his initial entrance into family organization to his final separation from those with whom he has labored, man has for centuries fulfilled his destiny within the framework of society. But there are many indications that he is now exchanging membership in society for servitude to the state.

The individual, as Aristotle pointed out, is *in* society. Regardless of his line of endeavor or interest, he fulfills himself through various forms of social organization, of which the family, giving continuity to the race, is the oldest. But a celibate brotherhood, secluded on the Tibetan side of the Himalayas, is equally a form of human society. The occasional hermit, who seeks to withdraw from society as well as from the world, is only the exception confirming the rule that "a social instinct is implanted in all men by nature."

Although the various forms of society overlap and interlock, none is naturally superior to another. The local chamber of commerce and the sandlot baseball team pursue their wholly distinct activities in happy separation, with father and son leaving it to mother to bring composition into the picture at the family table. In this separation lie both the strength and weakness of society. The division of function makes it possible for each individual to concentrate on the activity that temporarily interests or concerns him most. But the division of function also makes it necessary to have some synthetic agency that will be less transitory than every purely social unit. To achieve permanence this artificial agency must have overriding power, either seized by it or freely entrusted to it. When that effective sovereignty has been attained, this synthetic agency is called the state.[8]

---

[8] Franz Oppenheimer, in his study of *The State,* defines six distinct stages which can usually be discerned in its evolution to the modern form.

In most countries, the state has evolved slowly, acquiring its power now here, now there, going through numerous structural changes before taking form as the nation-state that came to flower in the period following the French Revolution. In the American republic, however, the federal state was created at a given moment by a concentrated effort of mind and will. We have already examined the procedure and we can even name the date on which the United States was legally established as a definite sovereign power.[9]

Because its origin was not haphazard, it was possible in this republic to establish a boundary line between the powers of the new American state and those of the antecedent American society. That boundary is drawn in the Constitution and emphasized in the Ninth and Tenth Amendments, which may again be quoted:

> The enumeration in the Constitution of certain rights shall not be construed to deny or disparage others retained by the people.
> The powers not delegated to the United States by the Constitution, nor prohibited by it to the states, are reserved to the states respectively, or to the people.

Boundaries in the field of political ideas are, and must always be, elastic. Unfortunately, the elasticity that permits improvement is equally receptive to deterioration. The Constitution makes a clear distinction between the prerogative of the state and the prerogative of society. But it also provides procedure whereby the former can be enlarged at the expense of the latter, both by open and by insidious means. In this republic it is more difficult than in most other coun-

---

[9] June 21, 1788, when the ninth state (New Hampshire) gave the ratification necessary to make the Constitution effective, under the wording of Article VII.

tries for the state to discipline and regiment society. But one need only survey the record to realize that here, as elsewhere, the development of the state has been that of constant aggrandizement. Necessarily, that aggrandizement has been at the expense of the two other components in political life—at the expense of society and of the individuals who create society because it is their nature so to do. Of course, this does not mean that the state has made no contribution to social and individual welfare.

It should be noted here that in recent years there has been concerted effort to establish what at first glance seems to be a fourth component in political life—that of official international organization. But this development, of both the League of Nations and the United Nations, has so far been one of intergovernmental cooperation. There is no right of citizenship in the United Nations, and a national of one of its member-states is not for that reason entitled even to cross the frontier of any other member-state. Like its ill-fated predecessor, the United Nations does not replace the state as a political entity and does not set up a new political entity effectively depriving the state of sovereignty. Indeed, five powers were given the right of absolute veto, precisely to prevent that development.

There was nothing accidental in the aggressive use of this veto by Soviet Russia. This Union of Soviet Socialist "Republics" does far more than the allegedly United Nations to curtail the independence of its constituent political units and of adjacent countries within the Russian sphere of influence. And from 1945 on, the endeavor of communist organization to break down the system of nation-states made the USSR a factor of transcendent political significance. To the extent that communist organization bears directly on the individual, instead of affecting him only through the medium of his national government, the "Comintern" can properly be called a wholly new component of political life. That claim could never be made for an essentially intergovernmental organization, like the United Nations.

Whether or not communism would triumph over statism, in the traditional nationalistic form of the latter, had become the outstanding political question even before the close of World War II. Communism, as an antinational political party, was able, as a result of that war, to penetrate and undermine the national organization of many states to an extent which was literally "subversive." But before considering the clash between the nation-state and the Communist Internationale, it is necessary to give thought to the antecedent struggle between the state and society.

The ascendancy of the nation-state and the breakdown of society present a pronounced coincidence. This is not fortuitous. There has been direct and causal connection between the increasing exaltation of the state and the increasing demoralization of society. It is necessary to understand how the state has everywhere weakened society, and how that process has in turn weakened the state, before one can intelligently consider the magnitude of the struggle between the American republic and its Russian antagonist.

VI

It is not surprising that the state is still regarded by some writers as nothing more than a particular form of society. In origin it was exactly that. Oppenheimer even asserts: "The concept of society, as a contrast to the concept of the state, first appears in Locke," whose philosophical influence was partly due to his skill in political diagnosis.[10]

Nobody has ever been able to isolate and identify with any precision the beginnings of the state. All we know for certain is that early in the line of human evolution people began to associate for purposes that today we would call political, rather than social or biological. At some prehistoric moment, the dwellers in some cave united, not to hunt animals or to safeguard their young, but to launch an attack against the denizens of another, more desirable, location. The hairy inmates of the preferable fastness undoubtedly cooperated in resistance. Here were two rudimentary states in conflict, without names, without flags, without anything that we would today call government—nevertheless offering the prototype of all the glorious wars that fill the pages of conventional history.

But, in these uncivilized and therefore relatively harmless scuffles, primitive society and the primitive state are all mixed up. It might be said that, at this embryonic stage, sex has not been determined. The function of society and the function of the state are indistinguishable. "Its rudimentary forms are not so much germs from which the mature state evolves as conglomerates from which it slowly frees itself. . . . It is not surprising, therefore, that contemporary enquiries into the origin of the state bear the aspect of an uncertain and inconclusive quest."[11]

As an institution, Professor Hocking further concludes, "the state certainly did not arise in a contract," though he recognizes that the American republic is exceptional in this

---

[10] *Op. cit.*, preface, p. xxxi.
[11] William Ernest Hocking, *Man and the State*, pp. 142*n* and ff.

respect. The state, he reasons, "can only arise as man, looking forward, begins with conscious awareness to build for futurity not his tombs alone but his communal life also." Thus, the state "begins together with the historical sense." This thought of a prominent American philosopher is clearly derived from Hegel, as was that of Spengler when he wrote: "State is history regarded as at the halt; history the state regarded as on the move."

The theory becomes less metaphysical, and therefore more convincing to the unphilosophic mind, if we reduce it to particulars. At some unascertainable period, the individual presumably began to reflect on what would happen after his death to the group with which he was associated. We may reasonably conclude that this thought was early prominent in the minds of those who in some way had acquired positions of leadership, and with that eminence the sense of responsibility that leadership tends to foster. Evidently this dawning individual awareness of a group future must have followed some definition of the group as such— in other words, society does antedate the state. We may guess that it was the corpse of a mate that first aroused in the mind of primitive man the fearsome thought of what would happen to the helpless offspring if the survivor also were slain by a saber-toothed tiger or falling rock.

It is important to realize that this particular form of anxiety about the future was neither narrowly selfish nor superstitious. It was, on the contrary, social and mundane. Accepting his own physical extinction as an eventual certainty, man sought some procedure whereby after his death his accomplished work could still contribute to the welfare of his group. Here was the first problem in statecraft, and its solution involved creation of the state. Moreover, the gregarious instinct that underlies society led naturally to the formation of the state.

Because of its voluntary nature, society is fluid. And because of its fluidity, society could not create the desired element of permanence. The head of a primitive group, whether patriarch or matriarch, whether warrior or magician, could do something to provide shelter, weapons, bodily covering, and even fuel and food that would be available after the individual leader's death.[12] But a nomadic organization of hunters, fishermen, or even predatory herdsmen did not have the continuity necessary for significant accumulation. Like the neighborhood "gang" of modern boyhood, the primitive group was always subject to the disintegrating processes clearly characteristic of voluntary organizations, wherever or whenever found. The condition of freedom was present, but not that sense of responsibility for the future that is a concomitant of liberty. It was not until men ceased to be wholly nomadic and began to settle down as cultivators that the means of introducing permanence into social organization became available.

The most intractable enemy of man is man himself. The seed of the modern state can be detected in the groupings of primitive man for offense or defense against his fellows. The seed could flower only for a season, however, prior to the agricultural stage of social development. Husbandry provided the condition of continuity that gives the state,

---

[12] Because irrelevant to present consideration, we intentionally evade argument as to the location of directive power in primitive society. For a scholarly and searching review of the whole subject, the reader is referred to Bertrand de Jouvenel's *Du Pouvoir,* an important study of the evolution and growth of political power. Sir James G. Frazer's *The Golden Bough* remains fundamental.

as offspring, characteristics that society, as parent, does not possess. And with the rise of the state as a permanent institution, the arts of peace and those of war alike begin that tremendous development traced by recorded history. "The roots of modern civilization are planted deeply in the highly elaborate life of those nations which rose into power over six thousand years ago, in the basin of the Eastern Mediterranean, and the adjacent regions on the east of it."[13]

VII

So the state, as a human institution, has a definite and rational objective: to offset mortality by means of an agency that can be expected to go on functioning without reference to the individual life span. This objective was always distinct from the will to personal aggrandizement, for at least a part of the underlying purpose was to make available to survivors those fruits of labor that men cannot take with them when they leave this world. But there were implications to this creation of the state that, as we look backward, are horrifying.

To achieve the objective of permanence, it was essential, in the first place, to endow the state with a collective power far beyond that which any individual, or any ephemeral social group, could hope to exercise. As Dr. Breasted says, civilization took root as the first states of which we have definite knowledge "rose into power." But evils, as well as blessings heretofore unknown to man, also rooted as this

---

[13] James Henry Breasted, *History of Egypt,* p. 3. See also Oppenheimer, *op. cit.,* ch. II.

concentration of power took place. It is suggestive that the long history of political thought is more concerned with the restraint, than with the exercise, of power entrusted to the state.

The state, in origin, was a projection of power in the field of time. Because time and space are related, the time-projection involved a projection of power in the field of space.[14] Since such spatial projections were certain to intersect on this small planet, it was foreordained that the state system would be a war system, and that the more highly developed this system, the greater the probability of friction between its units. The fact that the state system is a war system in turn made it certain that each developing state would do everything possible constantly to enlarge its power "in self-defense." As the human source of this power was the individual, state aggrandizement necessarily pointed toward human enslavement. As man enslaved the power of the beast, so the state proceeded to enslave the power of man. But some beasts cannot be enslaved, and neither can some men.

Aside from its tendency to monopolize power and to wage war with other states, the nature of the state harbors a third inherent danger to the happiness, and even the existence, of man. This third danger arises from the bestowal of artificial immortality on a human institution. Because of its permanence, the state has gradually established for itself a dubious moral authority. This spurious authority is based on the

---

[14] Political science, with its tendency toward ontological method, has given inadequate consideration to the implications of the time-space continuum. Cf. John Dewey, *Logic: The Theory of Inquiry,* pp. 482–86.

state's assumption of the divine attribute of immortality. But while man derives from his Creator a moral sense, the state, which is the creation of man, has none. Power it has, and force, and techniques to make its commands effective. Through the agency of the state, also, the moral as well as the bestial side of man can be encouraged. But with morals, *as such,* as distinct from the imposed prohibitions of man-made law, the state is not, has never been, and never will be concerned. The state is a physical and not a moral instrument. It is therefore antipodean and always latently hostile to the instrument of human conscience, which is moral and not physical.

It is, of course, true that as an instrument the state may be utilized to forward morality and to oppose immorality. It is true that administrators with the highest personal ideals may, like Marcus Aurelius, temporarily go far to meet Plato's requirement of a philosopher-king. But since the state has no conscience and is primarily a continuing mechanism of material power, the human welfare side of state activity should blind no thoughtful person to its underlying menace. And the potential of the state for "the abolition of man"—to use the telling phrase employed by C. S. Lewis—is the greater because man himself has created and directs this juggernaut that rolls over him.

Idolatry is always blind, and never more so than when it seeks to cloak a human creation with mystical significance. It was the tragedy of the German genius to carry worship of the state to the stage where Hegel could reason that: "The state is the Divine Idea as it exists on Earth."[15] If literally interpreted, this thought could lead logically to the assertion

---

[15] Introduction to lectures on *The Philosophy of History.*

of Nazi Minister Robert Ley: "Truth is whatever benefits the state; error is whatever does not benefit the state."

The monstrous perversion in this axiom was due not so much to any particular national aberration as to a general tendency to exaggerate the potential of the state for good, and to underestimate its capacity for evil. Goethe's countrymen, of all people, should have realized that it is the bargain of Faust to sell one's soul, which is one's self, for an enlargement of temporal power. Even a bargain with Mephistopheles is less surely a losing proposition than one in which the individual surrenders his soul to the state. For Satan has forbidden fruit of his own to distribute, while the state, in the last analysis, has absolutely nothing to offer that it has not already expropriated from its subjects. So, in worship of the state, men sacrifice their souls to a false god that can give them in return only what has already been placed by the worshipers themselves on this sacrilegious altar.

If this indictment seems strong, it is primarily because Americans have so largely ceased to reflect upon the implications of the unconditional surrender of power to political government. We have seen that such surrender is wholly contrary to the principles of the republic. But even without that patriotic justification, there would be good reason for men to rise in opposition to state aggrandizement. It is a case of selling the human birthright for a mess of pottage.

For the instrumentality of the state is only relatively immortal. And there is reason to believe that not only particular states are on the road to dissolution, but also the nation-state as an institution. The state is afflicted with a disease that can be called hypertrophy of function. And the germ of this disease of overgrowth appears to be inherent in its nature.

VIII

The outstanding characteristic of the state, regardless of its place in time, its location in space, its form of government, is monopolization of physical power. To endure as a political entity, the state must be in a position to enforce its laws, however adopted or decreed, on all persons and private organizations resident or operating within its boundaries or, as we say, "under its flag." While retaining social value as a symbol of fidelity and loyalty, the flag has also become increasingly emblematic of national sovereignty—of the state's possession of power and its corporate will to make that power effective.

War, in which the flag is an important emotional asset, is the classic device by which the state most rapidly augments its power. There is an exhilarating gamble in the process, because war is simultaneously a device whereby a state may be utterly destroyed. To repeat: through war, new states have frequently achieved independence; our own nation is an example. But not every attempt to establish a new state by force of arms has succeeded, as is also illustrated in American history by the failure of the Southern confederacy. The importance of war in the creation and development of states has been sadly neglected by many who have labored devotedly to secure stabilized peace within the state system. As already suggested, it is doubtful whether that system was ever really compatible with international peace.

We must also realize that the strength gained by a victorious state through war is in large part taken not from the enemy but from its own people. All of the private ele-

ments in society—the family, the church, the press, the
school, the corporation, the union and other cooperatives—
are subject to special discipline by the state in wartime.
The pressure of this discipline depends on the urgency of
the wartime emergency, which the state itself defines. The
phrase "total war" accurately expresses the evolution to its
logical conclusion of a state-building activity obviously antisocial to the extent that state and society have opposing
interests and objectives. Total war, arriving in our lifetime,
is the perfected means for building the totalitarian state.
And it is scarcely necessary to emphasize that once an
emergency control has been established by the state, all
sorts of arguments for making it permanent are forth-
coming.

That the state moves consistently to augment its power
is indicated not only by the entire course of history, but also
in everyday parlance. We speak of "great powers" and
"small powers," using the noun "power" synonymously with
"state," and evaluating the quality of the state by that single material attribute. Regardless of how the state originated, it has evidently developed into a final repository of
power, with the exercise of this overriding power its fundamental and characteristic function. Only that conclusion
can explain the pronounced unwillingness of states to yield
sovereignty, even when it is of clear social advantage that
some aspect of sovereignty, such as preventive measures
against epidemics, should be administered by a nonpolitical
international body.

Moreover, insistence on national sovereignty grows
stronger as the power of the state augments. The strong, not
the weak, nations were the ones that insisted on maintaining
a governmental veto in the work of the United Nations.

IX

The word "power," however, implies much more than physical supremacy. There is also moral power and intellectual power. Some individuals are also granted a magnetic power of personality that may have moral, intellectual, or physical bases, yet is nevertheless seemingly independent of all these attributes. But every form of human power, however exercised, involves some influence over others, whether that influence is positive or negative, for good or for evil, as defined by the standards of the period.

Intellectual power is obviously a higher form than the merely physical. It had been frequently harnessed to the service of the state long before Machiavelli advised Lorenzo the Magnificent that: "Whoever becomes the ruler of a free city and does not destroy it, can expect to be destroyed by it, for it can always find a motive for rebellion in the name of liberty. . . ."[16]

The adjective derived from Machiavelli's name reminds us that the state develops its physical supremacy with utter disregard for morality. A Machiavellian policy is simply one in which intellectual ability is wholly divorced from moral considerations. And there is no doubt that, as the state has gained in power, the inclination to follow the teachings of Machiavelli has increased. "We live today in the shadow of a Florentine, the man who above all others taught the world to think in terms of cold political power."[17]

Quite naturally, the tendency of the state to exploit intel-

---

[16] *The Prince*, ch. V.

[17] Max Lerner, introduction to *The Prince* and *The Discourses;* Modern Library ed.

ligence for its own uses has given rise to increasing official suspicion of unregimented thinking. Instances of this are seen in the effort to suppress "dangerous thoughts" in pre-war Japan, and in the disciplinary action taken in postwar Russia against writers, artists, and composers accused of "poisoning the consciousness of our people with a world outlook that is hostile to Soviet society."[18] Incidentally, this accusation identifies society with state, intimating that in Russia the state has definitely engulfed society.

It is noteworthy that conscientious objection to state supremacy is still treated somewhat more tolerantly than other forms of hostility. Undoubtedly this is because conscientious objection is negative and impartial between rival states. Objection based on material consideration may lead to active support of another government against one's own, which in war is defined as treason.

In her case study of *The Meaning of Treason,* Rebecca West asserts that: "All men should have a drop or two of treason in their veins, if the nations are not to go soft like so many sleepy pears." But this defense of the individual against the state clearly bothers Miss West, for she adds immediately: "Yet to be a traitor is to be most miserable." This generality is absurd, for there is ample evidence to show that neither George Washington nor Robert E. Lee was ever made miserable by his treason, successful in one case and unsuccessful in the other.

Miss West's rather muddled argument is nevertheless significant because of the illuminating overtones in the conclusions to which she is driven. The summation of this English writer is that the unsavory traitors whom she analyzes de-

---

[18] Quoted by Brooks Atkinson, *New York Times,* October 6, 1946.

served a certain sympathy because they "needed a nation which was also a hearth." In other words, their treason was excusable to the extent that they had not been comforted and consoled by a welfare state of their own. The suggestion is that the more maturely reasoned and self-sacrificial an act of treason, the less pardonable it becomes. We are not concerned with debating this belief pro or con, but merely with pointing out that it reflects the general European assumption that the higher the intelligence, the more imperative is its subordination to the service of a particular state.[19]

X

We owe some further consideration to the element of moral power, meaning the force that impels the individual to observe certain idealistic standards of conduct regardless of their conflict with his physical or intellectual desires. Like intellectual power, that of morality has been increasingly preempted by the state for political purposes. Thus we have reached the stage where an ill-assorted group of victorious governments can assert a moral basis for the indictment, trial, and execution of the leaders of a defeated nation who were responsible for "crimes against humanity." But the same governments placidly ignore the presumably equally criminal character of comparable actions by their own states against other human beings, or even reward such actions with decorations, when carried out under the direction of their own leadership.

In the Christian religion, as contrasted with the political

---

[19] *Op. cit., passim,* especially pp. 306–7.

life of nominally Christian countries, morality is regarded as an evenhanded force of universal applicability, one which cannot properly be nationalized or made subservient to either physical or intellectual power. Indeed, the social contribution of Jesus may be summed up by saying that in the hierarchy of values he places love first, denying merit in all forms of power centering on that hatred of other peoples which governments so often seek to stimulate.

In this Christian doctrine, of course, are found both the origin and the justification—perhaps the only valid justification—of democratic theory, dismissed by many philosophers, ancient and modern, as politically impractical. The logic of Christianity has never attempted to deny that men are unequal in their physical and mental endowments. It has emphasized that such differences do not prevent them from associating in full comradeship in many social undertakings where the solidarity of the human species is more important than its differentiations. "The idea of a Christian society," in the words of a great poet who has thought deeply on the subject, "is one which we can accept or reject; but if we are to accept it, we must treat Christianity with a great deal more *intellectual* respect than is our wont; we must treat it as being for the individual a matter primarily of thought and not of feeling."[20]

We have had occasion to note the profound, though declining, influence of Christianity on American political thought. Yet even in the various activities of private society, the exercise of ruthless power has been none too successful restrained by the moral suasion of Christianity. This inclines one to reflect on the use that would be made of the almost

---

[20] T. S. Eliot, *The Idea of a Christian Society,* pp. 4–5.

unbelievable physical power of the United States, if its control were concentrated without restriction in a strongly centralized government. Power in the hands of the state is less inhibited morally and more destructive physically than in society. The state, not society, is responsible for the design, development, and utilization of the atomic bomb.

State power, no matter how well disguised by seductive words, is in the last analysis always coercive physical power. And since the Industrial Revolution, this form of power, unlike that of mind or morals, has grown with increased physical wealth. The greater the material resources over which it can exercise absolute control, the greater the potential power of the state. From this arises the tendency to develop and pyramid governmental controls in order to augment power. As we come to recognize that the state is the repository of coercive power, and by its nature works ceaselessly to enlarge that power, much that seems shameful and senseless in the world today becomes intelligible, though not for that reason cheerful.

Freedom, Inequality, Primitivism and the Division of Labor

Murray N. Rothbard

Murray N. Rothbard is one of the outstanding leaders of libertarian thought in the United States today and is best known for his two-volume treatise on economic theory, Man, Economy, and State. *Among his other major works are* Power and Market: Government and the Economy *and* America's Great Depression.

Dr. Rothbard writes and lectures widely on subjects dealing with political economy, international relations, and contemporary social issues. In addition to being a consultant to research and educational organizations, he has contributed essays to various symposiums and has authored numerous pamphlets. His articles have appeared in a broad spectrum of professional journals and popular magazines. He has also been editor or contributing editor of a variety of publications, including Left and Right, Libertarian Forum, *and* The Individualist. *Since 1966, he has served as professor of economics at the Polytechnic Institute of Brooklyn.*

This essay was originally prepared for the Symposium on Human Differentiation, held in August 1970 at the Institute of Paper Chemistry in Appleton, Wisconsin, and sponsored by the Institute for Humane Studies. It was first published in Modern Age, *v. 15, no. 3, Summer 1971, and is reprinted by permission. Copyright © 1971 by the Foundation for Foreign Affairs, Inc. All rights reserved.*

I

If men were like ants, there would be no interest in human freedom. If individual men, like ants, were uniform, interchangeable, devoid of specific personality traits of their own, then who would care whether they were free or not? Who, indeed, would care if they lived or died? The glory of the human race is the uniqueness of each individual, the fact that every person, though similar in many ways to others, possesses a completely individuated personality of his own. It is the fact of each person's uniqueness—the fact that no two people can be wholly interchangeable—that makes each and every man irreplaceable and that makes us care whether he lives or dies, whether he is happy or oppressed. And, finally, it is the fact that these unique personalities need freedom for their full development that constitutes one of the major arguments for a free society.

Perhaps a world exists somewhere where intelligent beings are fully formed in some sort of externally determined cages, with no need for internal learning or choices by the individual beings themselves. But man is necessarily in a different situation. Individual human beings are not born or fashioned with fully formed knowledge, values, goals, or personalities; they must each form their own values and goals, develop their personalities, and learn about themselves and the world around them. Every man must have freedom, must have the scope to form, test, and act upon his own choices, for any sort of development of his own personality to take place. He must, in short, be free in order that he may be fully human. In a sense, even the most frozen and totalitarian civilizations and societies have allowed at least a modicum of scope for individual choice and development. Even the most monolithic of despotisms have had to allow at least a bit of "space" for freedom of choice, if only within the interstices of societal rules. The freer the society, of course, the less has been the interference with individual actions, and the greater the scope for the development of each individual. The freer the society, then, the greater will be the variety and the diversity among men, for the more fully developed will be every man's uniquely individual personality. On the other hand, the more despotic the society, the more restrictions on the freedom of the individual, the more uniformity there will be among men and the less the diversity, and the less developed will be the unique personality of each and every man. In a profound sense, then, a despotic society prevents its members from being fully human.[1]

If freedom is a necessary condition for the full development of the individual, it is by no means the only require-

---

[1] On the interrelations between freedom, diversity, and the development of each individual, see the classic work of Wilhelm von Humboldt, *The Limits of State Action* (Cambridge: Cambridge University Press, 1969). On freedom as necessary for the development of individuality, see also Josiah Warren, *Equitable Commerce* (New York: Burt Franklin, 1965), and Stephen Pearl Andrews, *The Science of Society* (New York, 1852).

ment. Society itself must be sufficiently developed. No one, for example, can become a creative physicist on a desert island or in a primitive society. For, as an economy grows, the range of choice open to the producer and to the consumer proceeds to multiply greatly.[2] Furthermore, only a society with a standard of living considerably higher than subsistence can afford to devote much of its resources to improving knowledge and to developing a myriad of goods and services above the level of brute subsistence. But there is another reason that full development of the creative powers of each individual cannot occur in a primitive or undeveloped society, and that is the necessity for a wide-ranging division of labor.

No one can fully develop his powers in any direction without engaging in *specialization*. The primitive tribesman or peasant, bound to an endless round of different tasks in order to maintain himself, could have no time or resources available to pursue any particular interest to the full. He had no room to specialize, to develop whatever field he was best at or in which he was most interested. Two hundred years ago, Adam Smith pointed out that the developing division of labor is a key to the advance of any economy above the most primitive level. A necessary condition for any sort of developed economy, the division of labor is also requisite to the development of any sort of civilized society. The philosopher, the scientist, the builder, the merchant— none could develop these skills or functions if he had had

---

[2] The economists Bauer and Yamey cogently define economic development as "the widening of the range of alternatives open to people as consumers and as producers." Peter T. Bauer and Basil S. Yamey, *The Economics of Underdeveloped Countries* (Cambridge: Cambridge University Press, 1957), p. 151.

no scope for specialization. Furthermore, no individual who does not live in a society enjoying a wide range of division of labor can possibly employ his powers to the fullest. He cannot concentrate his powers in a field or discipline and advance that discipline and his own mental faculties. Without the opportunity to specialize in whatever he can do best, no person can develop his powers to the full; no man, then, could be fully human.

While a continuing and advancing division of labor is needed for a developed economy and society, the extent of such development at any given time limits the degree of specialization that any given economy can have. There is, therefore, no room for a physicist or a computer engineer on a primitive island; these skills would be premature within the context of that existing economy. As Adam Smith put it, "the division of labor is limited by the extent of the market." Economic and social development is therefore a mutually reinforcing process: the development of the market permits a wider division of labor, which in turn enables a further extension of the market.[3]

If the scope of the market and the extent of the division of labor are mutually reinforcing, so too are the division of labor and the diversity of individual interests and abilities among men. For just as an ever greater division of labor is needed to give full scope to the abilities and powers of each individual, so does the existence of that very division depend upon the innate diversity of men. For there would be no scope at all for a division of labor if every person were uniform and interchangeable. (A further condition of the

---

[3] See George J. Stigler, "The Division of Labor Is Limited by the Extent of the Market," *Journal of Political Economy* (June 1951), p. 193.

emergence of a division of labor is the variety of natural resources; specific land areas on the earth are also not interchangeable.) Furthermore, it soon became evident in the history of man that the market economy based on a division of labor was profoundly *cooperative,* and that such division enormously multiplied the productivity and hence the wealth of every person participating in the society. The economist Ludwig von Mises put the matter very clearly:

> Historically division of labor originates in two facts of nature: the inequality of human abilities and the variety of the external conditions of human life on the earth. These two facts are really one: the diversity of Nature, which does not repeat itself but creates the universe in infinite, inexhaustible variety. . . .
>
> These two conditions . . . are indeed such as almost to force the division of labor on mankind. Old and young, men and women cooperate by making appropriate use of their various abilities. Here also is the germ of the geographical division of labor; man goes to the hunt and woman to the spring to fetch water. Had the strength and abilities of all individuals and the external conditions of production been everywhere equal the idea of division of labor could never have arisen. . . . No social life could have arisen among men of equal natural capacity in a world which was geographically uniform. . . .
>
> Once labor has been divided, the division itself exercises a differentiating influence. The fact that labor is divided makes possible further cultivation of individual talent and thus cooperation becomes more and more productive. Through cooperation men are able to achieve what would have been beyond them as individuals. . . .
>
> The greater productivity of work under the division of labor is a unifying influence. It leads men to regard each other as comrades in a joint struggle for welfare, rather than as competitors in a struggle for existence.[4]

---

[4] Ludwig von Mises, *Socialism* (New Haven: Yale University Press, 1951), pp. 292–95. Also *ibid.,* p. 303.

Freedom, then, is needed for the development of the individual, and such development also depends upon the extent of the division of labor and the height of the standard of living. The developed economy makes room for, and encourages, an enormously greater specialization and flowering of the powers of the individual than can a primitive economy, and the greater the degree of such development, the greater the scope for each individual.

If freedom and the growth of the market are each important for the development of each individual and, therefore, to the flowering of diversity and individual differences, then so is there a casual connection between freedom and economic growth. For it is precisely freedom, the absence or limitation of interpersonal restrictions or interference, that sets the stage for economic growth and hence of the market economy and the developed division of labor. The Industrial Revolution and the corollary and consequent economic growth of the West were a product of its relative freedom for enterprise, for invention and innovation, for mobility and the advancement of labor. Compared to societies in other times and places, eighteenth and nineteenth century Western Europe and the United States were marked by a far greater social and economic freedom—a freedom to move, invest, work, and produce—secure from much harassment and interference by government. Compared to the role of government elsewhere, its role in these centuries in the West was remarkably minimal.[5]

---

[5] Historians have been reminding us in recent decades that neither in England nor in the United States did government confine itself strictly to the ideal of laissez faire. True enough; but we must compare this era to the role of government in earlier—and later—days to see the significance of the difference. Thus, cf. Karl Wittfogel, *Oriental Despotism* (New Haven: Yale University Press, 1957).

By allowing full scope for investment, mobility, the division of labor, creativity, and entrepreneurship, the free economy thereby creates the conditions for rapid economic development. It is freedom and the free market, as Adam Smith well pointed out, that develop the "wealth of nations." Thus, freedom leads to economic development, and both of these conditions in turn multiply individual development and the unfolding of the powers of the individual man. In two crucial ways, then, freedom is the root; only the free man can be fully individuated and, therefore, can be fully human.

If freedom leads to a widening division of labor, and the full scope of individual development, it leads also to a growing population. For just as the division of labor is limited by the extent of the market, so is total population limited by total production. One of the striking facts about the Industrial Revolution has been not only a great rise in the standard of living for everyone, but also the viability of such ample living standards for an enormously larger population. The land area of North America was able to support only a million or so Indians five hundred years ago, and that at a bare subsistence level. Even if we wished to eliminate the division of labor, we could not do so without literally wiping out the vast majority of the current world population.

II

We conclude that freedom and its concomitant, the widening division of labor, are vital for the flowering of each individual, as well as for the literal survival of the vast bulk of the world's population. It must give us great concern, then, that over the past two centuries mighty social movements have sprung up which have been dedicated, at their heart, to the stamping out of all human differences, of all individuality.

It has become apparent in recent years, for example, that the heart of the complex social philosophy of Marxism does not lie, as it seemed to in the 1930s and 40s, in Marxian economic doctrines: in the labor theory of value, in the familiar proposal for socialist state ownership of the means of production, and in the central planning of the economy and society. The economic theories and programs of Marxism are, to use a Marxian term, merely the elaborate "superstructure" erected on the inner core of Marxian aspiration. Consequently, many Marxists have, in recent decades, been willing to abandon the labor theory of value and even centralized socialist planning, as the Marxian economic theory has been increasingly abandoned and the practice of socialist planning shown to be unworkable. Similarly, the Marxists of the "New Left" in the United States and abroad have been willing to jettison socialist economic theory and practice. What they have *not* been willing to abandon is the philosophic heart of the Marxian ideal—not socialism or socialist planning, concerned anyway with what is supposed to be a temporary "stage" of development, but *communism* itself. It is the communist ideal, the ultimate goal of Marxism, that excites the contemporary Marxist, that engages his most fervent passions. The New Left Marxist has no use for Soviet Russia because the Soviets have clearly relegated the communist ideal to the remotest possible future. The New Leftist admires Che, Fidel, and Mao not simply because of their role as revolutionaries and guerrilla leaders, but more because of their repeated attempts to leap into communism as rapidly as possible.[6]

Karl Marx was vague and cloudy in describing the communist ideal, let alone the specific path for attaining it. But one essential feature is the eradication of the division of labor. Contrary to current belief, Marx's now popular concept of "alienation" had little to do with a psychological sense of apartness or discontent. The heart of the concept was the individual's "alienation" from the product of labor. A worker, for example, works in a steel mill. Obviously, he himself will consume little or none of the steel he produces; he earns the value of his product in the shape of a money-commodity, and then he happily uses that money to buy whatever he chooses from the products of other people. Thus, A produces steel, B eggs, C shoes, etc., and then each exchanges them for products of the others through the use of money. To Marx this phenomenon of the market and the division of labor was a radical evil, for it meant that no one consumed any of *his own* product. The steelworker thus became "alienated" from his steel, the shoemaker from his shoes, etc.

The proper response to this "problem," it seems to me, is: "So what?" Why should anyone care about this sort of "alienation"? Surely the farmer, shoemaker, and steelworker are very happy to sell their product and exchange it for whatever products they desire; deprive them of this "alienation" and they would be most unhappy, as well as die

---

[6] The New Left, for example, ignores and scorns Marshal Tito despite his equally prominent role as Marxian revolutionary, guerrilla leader, and rebel against Soviet Russian dictation. The reason, as will be seen further below, is that Tito has pioneered in shifting from Marxism toward an individualistic philosophy and a market economy.

from starvation. For if the farmer were not allowed to produce more wheat or eggs than he himself consumes, or the shoemaker more shoes than he can wear, or the steelworker more steel than he can use, it is clear that the great bulk of the population would rapidly starve and the rest be reduced to a primitive subsistence, with life "nasty, brutish, and short."[7] But to Marx this condition was the evil result of individualism and capitalism and had to be eradicated.

Furthermore, Marx was completely ignorant of the fact that each participant in the division of labor cooperates through the market economy, exchanging for each other's products and increasing the productivity and living standards of everyone. To Marx, any *differences* between men and, therefore, any specialization in the division of labor, is a "contradiction," and the communist goal is to replace that "contradiction" with harmony among all. This means that to the Marxist any individual differences, any diversity among men, are "contradictions" to be stamped out and replaced by the uniformity of the antheap. Friedrich Engels maintained that the emergence of the division of labor shattered the alleged classless harmony and uniformity of primitive society, and was responsible for the cleavage of society into separate and conflicting classes. Hence, for Marx and Engels, the division of labor must be eradicated in order to abolish class conflict and to usher in the ideal harmony of the "classless society," the society of total uniformity.[8]

Thus, Marx foresees his communist ideal only "after the

---

[7] It is difficult, of course, to see how intangible *services* could be produced at all without "alienation." How can a teacher teach, for example, if he is not allowed to "alienate" his teaching services by providing them for his students?

[8] Thus, see Alexander Gray, *The Socialist Tradition* (London: Longmans, Green, 1947), pp. 306, 328.

enslaving subordination of individuals under division of labor, and therewith also the antithesis between mental and physical labor has vanished."[9] To Marx the ideal communist society is one where, as Professor Gray puts it, "everyone must do everything." According to Marx in *The German Ideology:*

> In communist society, where nobody has one exclusive sphere of activity but each can become accomplished in any branch he wishes, society regulates the general production and thus makes it possible for me to do one thing today and another tomorrow, to hunt in the morning, fish in the afternoon, rear cattle in the evening, criticize after dinner, just as I have a mind, without ever becoming hunter, fisherman, shepherd or critic.[10]

And the Marxist August Bebel consistently applied this dilettantish notion to the role of women:

> At one moment a practical worker in some industry she is in the next hour educator, teacher, nurse; in the third part of the day she exercises some art or cultivates a science; and in the fourth part she fulfills some administrative function.[11]

The concept of the *commune* in socialist thought takes on its central importance precisely as a means of eradicating individual differences. It is not just that the commune owns all the means of production among its members. Crucial to the communal ideal is that every man takes on every function, either all at once or in rapid rotation. Obviously, the

---

[9] Karl Marx, *Critique of the Gotha Programme* (New York: International Publishers, 1938), p. 10.

[10] Quoted in Gray, *op. cit.*, p. 328. Gray amusingly adds: "A short weekend on a farm might have convinced Marx that the cattle themselves might have some objection to being reared in this casual manner, in the evening."

[11] August Bebel, in *Women and Socialism.* Quoted in Mises, *op. cit.*, p. 190*n.*

commune has to subsist on no more than a primitive level, with only a few common tasks, for this ideal to be achieved. Hence the New Left commune, where every person is supposed to take turns equally at every task; again, specialization is eradicated, and no one can develop his powers to the full. Hence the current admiration for Cuba, which has attempted to stress "moral" rather than economic incentives in production, and which has established communes on the Isle of Pines. Hence the admiration for Mao, who has attempted to establish uniform urban and rural communes, and who recently sent several million students into permanent exile into the frontier agricultural areas, in order to eliminate the "contradiction between intellectual and physical labor."[12] Indeed, at the heart of the split between Russia and China is Russia's virtual abandonment of the communist ideal in the face of China's "fundamentalist" devotion to the original creed. The shared devotion to the commune also accounts for the similarities between the New Left, the Utopian socialists of the nineteenth century,[13] and the communist anarchists, a wing of anarchism that has always shared the communal ideal with the Marxists.[14]

---

[12] A recent news report disclosed that China has now softened its assault on intellectual labor. The policy of interchanging students and workers seems to have worked badly, and it has been found that "a lack of teachers and of technical training has hampered industrial development and production in recent years." Furthermore, "workers appear often to have been not tempered but softened by their exposure to a more sedentary life as many students, rather than finding life on the farm rewarding, fled China or killed themselves." Lee Lescase,"China Softens Attitude on Profs. School Policy," *Washington Post* (July 23, 1970), p. A12.

[13] On the Utopian socialists, see Mises, *op. cit.,* p. 168.

[14] It is probable that Mao's particular devotion to the communist ideal was influenced by his having been an anarchist before becoming a Marxist.

The communist would deny that his ideal society would suppress the personality of every man. On the contrary, freed from the confines of the division of labor, each person would fully develop *all* of his powers in every direction. Every man would be fully rounded in all spheres of life and work. As Engels put it in his *Anti-Dühring,* communism would give "each individual the opportunity to develop and exercise all his faculties, physical and mental, in all directions. . . ."[15] And Lenin wrote in 1920 of the "abolition of the division of labor among people . . . the education, schooling and training of people, with *an all-round development* and *an all-round* training, people *able to do everything.* Communism is marching and must march toward this goal, and *will reach it. . . .*"[16]

This absurd ideal—of the man "able to do everything"— is only viable if (a) everyone does everything very badly, or (b) there are only a very few things to do, or (c) everyone is miraculously transformed into a superman. Professor Mises aptly notes that the ideal communist man is the dilettante, the man who knows a little of everything and does nothing well. For how can he develop *any* of his powers and faculties if he is prevented from developing any one of them to any sustained extent? As Mises says of Bebel's utopia,

> Art and science are relegated to leisure hours. In this way, thinks Bebel, the society of the future "will possess scientists and artists of all kinds in countless numbers." These, according to their several inclinations, will pursue their studies and their arts in their spare time. . . . All mental work he regards as mere dilettantism. . . . But nevertheless we must inquire whether under

---

[15] Quoted in Gray, *op. cit.,* p. 328.

[16] Italics are Lenin's. V. I. Lenin, *Left-Wing Communism: An Infantile Disorder* (New York: International Publishers, 1940), p. 34.

these conditions the mind would be able to create that freedom without which it cannot exist.

Obviously all artistic and scientific work which demands time, travel, technical education and great material expenditure, would be quite out of the question.[17]

Every person's time and energy on the earth are necessarily limited; hence, in order to develop *any* of his faculties to the full, he must specialize and concentrate on some rather than others. As Gray writes,

That each individual should have the opportunity of developing *all* his faculties, physical *and* mental, in *all* directions, is a dream which will cheer the vision only of the simple-minded, oblivious of the restrictions imposed by the narrow limits of human life. For life is a series of acts of choice, and each choice is at the same time a renunciation . . . .

Even the inhabitant of Engels' future fairyland will have to decide sooner or later whether he wishes to be Archbishop of Canterbury or First Sea Lord, whether he should seek to excel as a violinist or as a pugilist, whether he should elect to know all about Chinese literature or about the hidden pages in the life of the mackerel.[18]

Of course, one way to resolve this dilemma is to fantasize that the New Communist Man will be a superman. The Marxist Karl Kautsky asserted that in the future society "a new type of man will arise . . . a superman . . . an exalted man." Leon Trotsky prophesied that under communism

. . . man will become incomparably stronger, wiser, finer. His body more harmonious, his movements more rhythmical, his voice more musical. . . . The human average will rise to the level

---

[17] Mises, *op. cit.,* p. 190.
[18] Gray, *op. cit.,* p. 328.

of an Aristotle, a Goethe, a Marx. Above these other heights new peaks will arise.[19]

In recent years, communists have intensified their efforts to end the division of labor and reduce all individuals to uniformity. Fidel Castro's attempts to "build communism" in the Isle of Pines, and Mao's Cultural Revolution, have been echoed in miniature by the American New Left in numerous attempts to form hippie communes and to create organizational "collectives" in which everyone does everything without benefit of specialization.[20] In contrast, Yugoslavia has been the quiet despair of the communist movement by moving rapidly in the opposite direction—toward ever-increasing freedom, individuality, and free-market operations—and has proved influential in leading the other "communist" countries of Eastern Europe (notably, Hungary and Czechoslovakia) in the same direction.[21]

---

[19] Quoted in Mises, *op. cit.,* p. 164.

[20] Thus, one of the major criticisms of the New Left journal *The Guardian,* by its rebellious split-off, *The Liberated Guardian,* was that the former functioned in the same way as any "bourgeois" magazine, with specialized editors, typists, copyreaders, business staff, etc. The latter is run by a "collective" in which, assertedly, everyone does every task without specialization. The same criticism, along with the same solution, was applied by the women's caucus which confiscated the New Left weekly *Rat.* Some of the "Women's Liberation" groups have been so extreme in the drive to extirpate individuality as to refuse to identify the names of individual members, or spokesmen.

[21] Thus, a shock to orthodox communists throughout the world was the 1958 Program of the League of Communists of Yugoslavia, which declared that the individual's "personal interest . . . is the moving force of our social development. . . . The objectivity of the category of personal interest lies in the fact that [Yugoslav] socialism . . . cannot subject the personal happiness of man to any ulterior 'goals' or 'higher aims,' for the

III

One way of gauging the extent of "harmonious" development of all of the individual's powers in the absence of
specialization is to consider what actually happened during
primitive or preindustrial eras. And, indeed, many socialists
and other opponents of the Industrial Revolution exalt the
primitive and preindustrial periods as a golden age of harmony, community, and social belonging—a peaceful and
happy society destroyed by the development of individualism, the Industrial Revolution, and the market economy. In
their exaltation of the primitive and the preindustrial, the
socialists were perfectly anticipated by the reactionaries of
the Romantic movement, those men who longed to roll back
the tide of progress, individualism, and industry, and return
to the supposed golden age of the preindustrial era. The
New Left, in particular, also emphasizes a condemnation of
technology and the division of labor, as well as a desire to
"return to the earth" and an exaltation of the commune and
the "tribe." As John W. Aldridge perceptively points out,
the current New Left virtually constitutes a generational
tribe that exhibits all the characteristics of a uniform and

---

highest aim of socialism is the personal happiness of man." From *Kom-
munist* (Belgrade), August 8, 1963. Quoted in R. V. Burks, "Yugoslavia:
Has Tito Gone Bourgeois?" *East Europe* (August 1965), pp. 2–14. Also
see T. Peter Svennevig, "The Ideology of the Yugoslav Heretics," *Social
Research* (Spring 1960), pp. 39–48. For attacks by orthodox communists,
see Shih Tung-Hsiang, "The Degeneration of the Yugoslav Economy
Owned by the Whole People," *Peking Review* (June 12, 1964), pp. 11–16;
and "Peaceful Transition from Socialism to Capitalism?" *Monthly Review*
(March 1964), pp. 569–90.

interchangeable herd, with little or no individuality among its members.[22]

Similarly, the early nineteenth century German reactionary Adam Müller denounced the

> . . . vicious tendency to divide labor in all branches of private industry. . . [The] division of labor in large cities or industrial or mining provinces cuts up man, the completely free man, into wheels, rollers, spokes, shafts, etc., forces on him an utterly one-sided scope in the already one-sided field of the provisioning of one single want. . . .[23]

The leading French conservatives of the early nineteenth century, Bonald and de Maistre, who idealized the feudal order, denounced the disruption by individualism of the preexisting social order and social cohesion.[24] The contemporary French reactionary Jacques Ellul, in *The Technological Society,* a book much in favor on the New Left, condemns "our dehumanized factories, our unsatisfied senses . . . our estrangement from nature." In the Middle Ages, in contrast, claims Ellul, "Man sought open spaces . . . the possibility of moving about . . . of not constantly colliding with other people."[25] In the meanwhile, on the socialist side, the economic historian Karl Polanyi's influential *The*

---

[22] John W. Aldridge, *In the Country of the Young* (New York: Harper & Row, 1970).

[23] Quoted in Mises, *op. cit.,* p. 304.

[24] On the strong influence of these reactionary thinkers on the anti-individualism of nineteenth century Marxists and socialists, see in particular Leon Bramson, *The Political Context of Sociology* (Princeton: Princeton University Press, 1961), pp. 12–16 and *passim.*

[25] See the critique of Ellul in Charles Silberman, *The Myths of Automation* (New York: Harper & Row, 1966), pp. 104–5.

Great Transformation makes this thesis of the disruption of a previous social harmony by individualism, the market economy, and the division of labor the central theme of the book.

For its part, the worship of the primitive is a logical extension of the worship of the preindustrial. This worship by modern sophisticated intellectuals ranges from Rousseau's "noble savage" and the lionizing of that creature by the Romantic movement, all the way to the adoration of the Black Panthers by white intellectuals.[26] Whatever other pathology the worship of the primitive reflects, a basic part of it is a deep-seated hatred of individual diversity. Obviously, the more primitive and the less civilized a society, the less diverse and individuated it can be.[27] Also part of this primitivism reflects a hatred for the intellect and its works, since the flowering of reason and intellection leads to diversity and inequality of individual achievement.

For the individual to advance and develop, reason and the intellect must be *active,* it must embody the individual's mind working upon and transforming the materials of reality. From the time of Aristotle, the classical philosophy presented man as only fulfilling himself, his nature, and his personality through purposive action upon the world. It is from such rational and purposive action that the works of civilization have developed. In contrast, the Romantic movement has always exalted the passivity of the child who,

---

[26] Thus, see the perceptively satiric article by Tom Wolfe, "Radical Chic: That Party at Lenny's," *New York* (June 8, 1970).

[27] This worship of the primitive permeates Polanyi's book, which at one point seriously applies the term "noble savage" to the Kaffirs of South Africa. Karl Polanyi, *The Great Transformation* (Boston: Beacon Press, 1957), p. 157.

necessarily ignorant and immature, only reacts passively to his environment rather than acts to change it. This tendency to exalt passivity and the young, and to denigrate intellect, has reached its present embodiment in the New Left, which worships both youth *per se* and a passive attitude of ignorant and purposeless spontaneity. The passivity of the New Left, its wish to live simply and in "harmony" with "the earth" and the alleged rhythms of nature, harks back completely to the Rousseauist Romantic movement. Like the Romantic movement, it is a conscious rejection of civilization and differentiated men on behalf of the primitive, the ignorant, the herd-like "tribe."[28]

If reason, purpose, and action are to be spurned, then what replace them in the Romantic pantheon are unanalyzed, spontaneous "feelings." And since the range of feelings is relatively small compared to intellectual achievements, and in any case is not objectively known to another person, the emphasis on feelings is another way to iron out diversity and inequality among individuals.

Irving Babbitt, a keen critic of Romanticism, wrote about the Romantic movement:

> The whole movement is filled with the praise of ignorance and of those who still enjoy its inappreciable advantages—the savage, the peasant and above all the child. The Rousseauist may indeed be said to have discovered the poetry of childhood . . . but at what would seem at times a rather heavy sacrifice of rationality. Rather than consent to have the bloom taken off things by analysis one should, as Coleridge tells us, *sink back* to the

---

[28] Both the passive and the tribal aspects of New Left culture were embodied in its ideal of the "Woodstock Nation," in which hundreds of thousands of herd-like, undifferentiated youth wallowed passively in the mud listening to their tribal ritual music.

devout state of childlike wonder. However, to grow ethically is not to sink back but to struggle painfully forward. To affirm the contrary is to proclaim one's inability to mature. . . . [The Romantic] is ready to assert that what comes to the child spontaneously is superior to the deliberate moral effort of the mature man. The speeches of all the sages are, according to Maeterlinck, outweighed by the unconscious wisdom of the passing child.[29]

Another perceptive critique of Romanticism and primitivism was written by Ludwig von Mises. He notes that "the whole tribe of romantics" have denounced specialization and the division of labor. "For them the man of the past who developed his power 'harmoniously' is the ideal: an ideal which alas no longer inspires our degenerate age. They recommend retrogression in the division of labor . . ." with the socialists surpassing their fellow Romantics in this regard.[30] But are primitives or preindustrial men privileged to develop themselves freely and harmoniously? Mises answers:

It is futile to look for the harmoniously developed man at the outset of economic evolution. The almost self-sufficient economic subject as we know him in the solitary peasant of remote valleys shows none of that noble, harmonious development of body, mind, and feeling which the romantics ascribe to him. Civilization is a product of leisure and the peace of mind that only the division of labor can make possible. Nothing is more false than to assume that man first appeared in history with an independent individuality and that only during the evolution [of society] . . . did he lose . . . his spiritual independence. All his-

---

[29] Irving Babbitt, *Rousseau and Romanticism* (New York: Meridian Books, 1955), pp. 53–54. The New Left's emphasis on passivity, primitivism, the irrational, and the dissolution of individuality may account for the current popularity of Taoist and Buddhist philosophy. See *ibid.*, pp. 297ff.

[30] Mises, *op. cit.*, p. 304.

tory, evidence and observation of the lives of primitive peoples are directly contrary to this view. Primitive man lacks all individuality in our sense. Two South Sea Islanders resemble each other far more closely than two twentieth-century Londoners. Personality was not bestowed upon man at the outset. It has been acquired in the course of evolution of society.[31]

Or we may note Charles Silberman's critique of Jacques Ellul's rhapsodies on the "traditional rhythms of life and nature" lived by preindustrial man, as compared to "dehumanized factories . . . our estrangement from nature." Silberman asks:

> But with what shall we contrast this dehumanized world? The beautiful, harmonious life being lived by, say, the Chinese or Vietnamese peasant woman, who works in the fields close to nature, for twelve hours a day—roughly the conditions under which the great bulk of women (and men) have worked . . . through all of human history? For this is the condition that Ellul idealizes.

And, as for Ellul's paean to the Middle Ages as being mobile, spacious, and uncrowded:

> This would have been startling news to the medieval peasant, who lived with his wife and children, other relatives, and probably animals as well in a one-room thatched cottage. And even for the nobility, was there really more possibility of "moving about" in the Middle Ages, when travel was by foot or hoof, than today, when steelworkers spend sabbaticals in Europe?[32]

The savage is supposed not only to be "noble" but also supremely happy. From the Rousseauans to what Erich

[31] _Ibid._, p. 305.

[32] Silberman, _op. cit._, pp. 104–5.

Fromm has called "the infantile paradise" of Norman O. Brown and Herbert Marcuse, the Romantics have extolled the happiness yielded by the spontaneous and the childlike. To Aristotle and the classic philosophers, happiness was *acting in* accordance with man's unique and rational nature. To Marcuse, any purposive, rational action is by definition "repressive," to which he contrasts the "liberated" state of spontaneous play. Aside from the universal destitution that the proposed abolition of work would bring, the result would be a profound *un*happiness, for no individual would be able to fulfill himself, his individuality, or his rational faculties. Diversity and individuality would largely disappear, for in a world of "polymorphous" play everyone would be virtually alike.

If we consider the supposed happiness of primitive man, we must also consider that his life was, in the famous phrase of Hobbes, "nasty, brutish, and short." There were few medical aids against disease; there were none against famine, for in a world cut off from interregional markets and barely above subsistence any check to the local food supply will decimate the population. Fulfilling the dreams of Romantics, the primitive tribe is a passive creature of its given environment and has no means for acting to overcome and transform it. Hence, when the local food supply within an area is depleted, the "happy-go-lucky" tribe dies *en masse*.

Furthermore, we must realize that the primitive faces a world which he cannot understand, since he has not engaged in much of a rational, scientific inquiry into its workings. *We* know what a thunderstorm is, and therefore take rational measures against it; but the savage does not know, and therefore surmises that the God of Thunder is displeased with him and must be propitiated with sacrifices and votive offerings. Since the savage has only a limited concept of a world knit together by natural law (a concept which employs reason and science), he believes that the world is governed by a host of capricious spirits and demons, each of which can only be propitiated by ritual or magic, and by a priest-craft of witch doctors who specialize in their propitiation.[33] The renaissance of astrology and similar mystic creeds on the New Left marks a reversion to such primitive forms of magic. So fearful is the savage, so bound is he by irrational taboo and by the custom of his tribe, that he cannot develop his individuality.

If tribal custom crippled and repressed the development of each individual, then so too did the various caste systems and networks of restriction and coercion in preindustrial societies that forced everyone to follow the hereditary footsteps of his father's occupation. Each child knew from birth that he was doomed to tread where his ancestors had gone before him, regardless of ability or inclination to the contrary. The "social harmony," the "sense of belonging," supplied by mercantilism, by the guilds, or by the caste system, provided such contentment that its members left the throes of the system when given an opportunity. Given the freedom to choose, the tribesmen abandon the bosom of their

---

[33] Neither is the magic used by primitive tribes any evidence of superior, "idealistic," as opposed to this worldly, "materialistic," ends. On the contrary, the magic rites were unsound and erroneous means *by which* the tribes hoped to attain such materialistic ends as a good harvest, rainfall, etc. Thus, the cargo cult of New Guinea, on observing Europeans obtaining food from overseas by sending away scraps of paper, imitated the Europeans by writing ritualistic phrases on slips of paper and sending them out to sea, after which they waited for cargoes from overseas. Cf. Ludwig von Mises, *Epistemological Problems of Economics* (Princeton: D. Van Nostrand, 1960), pp. 62–66, 102–5.

tribe to come to the freer, "atomistic" cities looking for jobs and opportunity. It is curious, in fact, that those Romantics who yearn to restore the mythical golden age of caste and status refuse to allow each individual the freedom to choose between market on the one hand, or caste and tribal commune on the other. Invariably, the new golden age has to be imposed by coercion.

Is it, indeed, a coincidence that the natives of undeveloped countries, when given a chance, invariably abandon their "folk culture" on behalf of Western ways, living standards, and "Coca-Colaization"? Within a few years, for example, the people of Japan were delighted to abandon their centuries-old traditional culture and folkways, and turn to the material achievements and market economy of the West. Primitive tribes, too, given a chance, are eager to differentiate and develop a market economy, to shed their stagnant "harmony" and replace their magic by knowledge of discovered law. The eminent anthropologist Bronislaw Malinowski pointed out that primitives use magic only to cover those areas of nature of which they are ignorant; in those areas where they have come to understand the natural processes at work, magic is, quite sensibly, not employed[34]

A particularly striking example of the eager development of a pervasive market economy among primitive tribesmen is the largely unheralded case of West Africa.[35] And Bernard Siegel has pointed out that when, as among the Panajachel of Guatemala, a primitive society becomes large and tech-

---

[34] Bronislaw Malinowski, *Magic, Science, Religion and Other Essays* (New York: Doubleday, Anchor Books, 1955), pp. 27–31. Also see Mises, *Epistemological Problems.*

[35] See the inspiring discussion in Peter T. Bauer, *West African Trade* (Cambridge: Cambridge University Press, 1954).

nologically and societally complex, a market economy inevitably accompanies this growth, replete with specialization, competition, cash purchases, demand and supply, prices and costs, etc.[36]

There is thus ample evidence that even primitive tribesmen themselves are not fond of their primitivism and take the earliest opportunity to escape from it; the main stronghold of love for primitivism seems to rest among the decidedly nonprimitive Romantic intellectuals.

Another primitivistic institution that has been hailed by many social scientists is the system of the "extended family," a harmony and status supposedly ruptured by the individualistic "nuclear family" of the modern West. Yet the extended family system has been responsible for crippling the creative and productive individual as well as repressing economic development. Thus, West African development has been impeded by the extended family concept that, if one man prospers, he is duty bound to share this bounty with a host of relatives, thus draining off the reward for his productivity and crippling his incentive to succeed, while encouraging the relatives to live idly on the family dole. And neither do the productive members of the tribe seem very happy about this

---

[36] Bernard J. Siegel, "Review of Melville J. Herskovits, *Economic Anthropology*," *American Economic Review* (June 1953), p. 402. On developing individualism among the Pondo of South Africa, see Bauer and Yamey, *op. cit.*, p. 67n. Also see Raymond Firth, *Human Types* (New York: Mentor Books, 1958), p. 122; Sol Tax, *Penny Capitalism: A Guatemalan Indian Economy* (Washington, D.C., 1953); and Raymond Firth and Basil S. Yamey, eds., *Capital, Saving and Credit in Peasant Societies* (Chicago: Aldine, 1963).

On the responsiveness of African natives to market economic incentives, see (in addition to Bauer, *West African Trade*) Peter Kilby, "African Labor Productivity Reconsidered," *Economic Journal* (June 1961), pp. 273–91.

supposedly harmonious societal bond. Professor Bauer points out that

> ... many admit in private discussion that they dread these extensive obligations. . . . The fear of the obligations of the family system is partly responsible for the widespread use of textiles and trinkets as outlets for savings, in preference to more productive forms of investment which are more likely to attract the attention of relatives.

And many Africans distrust banks, "fearing that they may disclose the size of their accounts to members of their families. They, therefore, prefer to keep their savings under the fireplace or buried in the ground."[37]

In fact, the primitive community, far from being happy, harmonious, and idyllic, is much more likely to be ridden by mutual suspicion and envy of the more successful or better-favored, an envy so pervasive as to cripple, by the fear of its presence, all personal or general economic development. The German sociologist Helmut Schoeck, in his important recent work on *Envy,* cites numerous studies of this pervasive crippling effect. Thus the anthropologist Clyde Kluckhohn found among the Navaho the absence of any concept of "personal success" or "personal achievement"; any such success was automatically attributed to exploitation of others, and, therefore, the more prosperous Navaho Indian feels himself under constant social pressure to give his money away. Allan Holmberg found that the Siriono Indian of

---

[37] Bauer, *West African Trade*, p. 8. Also see Bauer and Yamey, *op. cit.,* pp. 64–67. Similarly, Professor S. Herbert Frankel reports on how West Africans habitually wait at entrances of banks to fall upon their relatives to demand money as they leave. Any man who accumulates money must go to great lengths to deceive his relatives on his actual status. Cited in Helmut Schoeck, *Envy: A Theory of Social Behaviour* (New York: Harcourt, Brace & World, 1970), pp. 59–60.

Bolivia eats alone at night because, if he eats by day, a
crowd gathers around him to stare in envious hatred. The
result among the Siriono is that, in reaction to this pervasive
pressure, no one will voluntarily share food with anybody.
Sol Tax found that envy and fear of envy in "a small community where all neighbors watch and where all are neighbors" accounted for the unprogressiveness, the slowness of
change toward a productive economy among the Indians of
Guatemala. And when a tribe of Pueblo Indians showed the
beginnings of specialization and the division of labor, the
envy of their fellow tribesmen impelled them to take measures to end this process, including physical destruction of
the property of those who seemed in any way better off than
their fellows.

Oscar Lewis discovered an extremely pervasive fear
of the envy of others in a Mexican Indian village, a fear
producing intense secretiveness. Wrote Lewis:

> The man who speaks little, keeps his affairs to himself, and
> maintains some distance between himself and others has less
> chance of creating enemies or of being criticized or envied. A
> man does not generally discuss his plans to buy or sell or take a
> trip.[38]

Professor Schoeck comments:

> . . . it is difficult to envisage what it means for the economic
> and technical development of a community when, almost auto-
> matically and as a matter of principle, the future dimension is

---

[38] The works cited are Clyde Kluckhohn, *The Navaho* (Cambridge, Mass.,
1946) and *Navaho Witchcraft* (Cambridge, 1944); Allan R. Holmberg,
Nomads of the Long Bow: The Siriono of Eastern Bolivia (Washington,
1950); Sol Tax, "Changing Consumption in Indian Guatemala," *Economic
Development and Cultural Change* (1957); and Oscar Lewis, *Life in a
Mexican Village: Tepoztlan Restudied* (Urbana, Ill., 1951). See Schoeck,
op. cit., pp. 26–61.

banned from human intercourse and conversation, when it cannot even be discussed. Ubiquitous envy, fear of it and those who harbor it, cuts off such people from any kind of communal action directed towards the future. . . . All striving, all preparation and planning for the future can be undertaken only by socially fragmented, secretive beings.[39]

Furthermore, in this Mexican village no one will warn or tell anyone else of imminent danger to the other's property; there is no sense of human social solidarity whatsoever.

Among the Indians of Aritama in Colombia, the Reichel-Dolmatoffs reported:

> Every individual lives in constant fear of the magical aggression of others, and the general social atmosphere in the village is one of mutual suspicion, of latent danger, and hidden hostility, which pervade every aspect of life. The most immediate reason for magical aggression is envy. Anything that might be interpreted as a personal advantage over others is envied: good health, economic assets, good physical appearance, popularity, a harmonious family life, a new dress. All these and other aspects imply prestige, and with it power and authority over others. Aggressive magic is, therefore, intended to prevent or to destroy this power and to act as a leveling force.[40]

The Reichel-Dolmatoffs also noted that if one member of a group in Aritama should work faster or better than his fellows, his place of work is marked with a cross before he arrives the next morning, and his envious colleagues pray to God to make this more able worker slow and tired.

Finally, Watson and Samora (*American Sociological Review*, 1954) found that the major reason for the failure of a

---

[39] *Ibid.*, p. 50.

[40] From Gerardo and Alicia Reichel-Dolmatoff, *The People of Aritama: The Cultural Personality of a Colombian Mestizo Village* (Chicago, 1961), p. 396. Quoted in Schoeck, *op. cit.*, pp. 51–52.

group of lower-class Spanish-speaking citizens of a mountain township in southern Colorado to rise into parity with the upper-class Anglo community, was the bitter envy of the Spanish group toward any of their number who managed to rise upward. Anyone who works his way upward is regarded as a man "who has sold himself to the Anglos," "who has climbed on the backs of his people."

The anthropologist Eric Wolf (*American Anthropologist,* 1955) has even coined the term "institutionalized envy" to describe such pervasive institutions, including the practice and fear of black magic in these primitive societies. Schoeck notes:

> *Institutionalized envy* . . . or the ubiquitous fear of it, means that there is little possibility of individual economic advancement and no contact with the outside world through which the community might hope to progress. No one dares to show anything that might lead people to think he was better off. Innovations are unlikely. Agricultural methods remain traditional and primitive, to the detriment of the whole village, because every deviation from previous practice comes up against the limitations set by envy.[41]

And Schoeck aptly concludes:

> There is nothing to be seen here of the close community which allegedly exists among primitive peoples in preaffluent times— the poorer, it is held, the greater the sense of community. Sociological theory would have avoided many errors if those phenomena had been properly observed and evaluated a century ago. The myth of a golden age, when social harmony prevailed because each man had about as little as the next one, the warm and generous community spirit of simple societies, was indeed for the most part just a myth, and social scientists should have known

---

[41] *Ibid.*, p. 47.

better than to fashion out of it a set of utopian standards with which to criticize their own societies.[42]

In sum, Ludwig von Mises' strictures against Romanticism do not seem to be overdrawn:

> Romanticism is man's revolt against reason, as well as against the condition under which nature has compelled him to live. The romantic is a daydreamer; he easily manages in imagination to disregard the laws of logic and nature. The thinking and rationally acting man tries to rid himself of the discomfort of unsatisfied wants by economic action and work; he produces in order to improve his position. The romantic . . . imagines the pleasures of success but he does nothing to achieve them. He does not remove the obstacles; he merely removes them in imagination. . . . He hates work, economy, and reason.
>
> The romantic takes all the gifts of a social civilization for granted and desires, in addition, everything fine and beautiful that, as he thinks, distant times and creatures had or have to offer. Surrounded by the comforts of European town life he longs to be an Indian rajah, bedouin, corsair, or troubadour. But he sees only that portion of these people's lives which seems pleasant to him. . . . The perilous nature of their existence, the comparative poverty of their circumstances, their miseries and their toil—these things his imagination tactfully overlooks: all is transfigured by a rosy gleam. Compared with this dream ideal, reality appears arid and shallow. There are obstacles to overcome which do not exist in the dream. . . . Here there is work to do, ceaselessly, assiduously. . . . Here one must plough and sow if one wishes to reap. The romantic does not choose to admit all this. Obstinate as a child, he refuses to recognize it. He mocks and jeers; he despises and loathes the bourgeois.[43]

The Romantic, or primitivist, attitude was also brilliantly criticized by the Spanish philosopher Ortega y Gasset:

---

[42] *Ibid.,* p. 31.

[43] Mises, *Socialism,* pp. 463–64. See also José Ortega y Gasset, *The Revolt of the Masses* (New York: W. W. Norton, 1932), pp. 63–65.

> . . . it is possible to have peoples who are perennially primitive . . . those who have remained in the motionless, frozen twilight, which never progresses towards midday.
>
> This is what happens in the world which is mere Nature. But it does not happen in the world of civilization which is ours. Civilization is not "just there," it is not self-supporting. It is artificial. . . . If you want to make use of the advantages of civilization, but are not prepared to concern yourself with the upholding of civilization—you are done. In a trice you find yourself left without civilization. . . . The primitive forest appears in its native state. . . . The jungle is always primitive and, vice versa, everything primitive is mere jungle.[44]

Ortega adds that the type of man he sees rising to the fore, the modern "mass-man," "believes that the civilization into which he was born and which he makes use of, is as spontaneous and self-producing as Nature. . . ." But the mass-man, the herd-man, is also characterized by his desire to stamp out those individuals who differ from the mass: "The mass . . . does not wish to share life with those who are not of it. It has a deadly hatred of all that is not itself."[45]

IV

The Left, of course, does not couch its demands in terms of stamping out diversity; what it seeks to achieve sounds semantically far more pleasant: *equality*. It is in the name of equality that the Left seeks all manner of measures, from progressive taxation to the ultimate stage of communism.

But what, philosophically, *is* "equality"? The term must

---

[44] *Ibid.*, p. 97.

[45] *Ibid.*, pp. 84, 98. For Ortega, the great looming danger is that the mass-man will increasingly use the state "to crush beneath it any creative minority which disturbs it—disturbs it in any order of things: in politics, in ideas, in industry." *Ibid.*, p. 133.

not be left unanalyzed and accepted at face value. Let us take three entities: A, B, and C. A, B, and C are said to be "equal" to each other (i.e., A = B = C) *if* a particular characteristic is found in which the three entities are uniform or identical. In short, here are three individual men: A, B, and C. Each may be similar in some respects but different in others. If each of them is precisely 5'10" in height, they are then *equal* to each other *in height*. It follows from our discussion of the concept of equality that A, B, and C can be *completely* "equal" to each other only if they are identical or uniform in *all* characteristics—in short, if all of them are, like the same size of nut or bolt, completely interchangeable. We see, then, that the ideal of human equality *can only* imply total uniformity and the utter stamping out of individuality.

It is high time, then, for those who cherish freedom, individuality, the division of labor, and economic prosperity and survival, to stop conceding the supposed nobility of the ideal of equality. Too often have "conservatives" conceded the ideal of equality only to cavil at its "impracticality." Philosophically, there can be no divorce between theory and practice. Egalitarian measures do not "work" because they violate the basic nature of man, of what it means for the individual man to be truly human. The call of "equality" is a siren song than can only mean the destruction of all that we cherish as being human.

It is ironic that the term "equality" brings its favorable connotation to us from a past usage that was radically different. For the concept of "equality" achieved its widespread popularity during the classical liberal movements of the eighteenth century, when it meant, *not* uniformity of status or income, but freedom for each and every man, without exception. In short, "equality" in those days meant the libertarian and individualist concept of full liberty for all persons. Thus, the biochemist Roger Williams correctly points out that the " 'free and equal' phrase in the Declaration of Independence was an unfortunate paraphrase of a better statement contained in the Virginia Bill of Rights . . . 'all men are by nature equally free and independent.' In other words, men can be *equally free* without being *uniform*."[46]

This libertarian credo was formulated with particular cogency by Herbert Spencer in his "Law of Equal Liberty" as the suggested fundamental core of his social philosophy:

> . . . man's happiness can be obtained only by the exercise of his faculties. . . . But the fulfillment of this duty necessarily presupposes freedom of action. Man cannot exercise his faculties without certain scope. He must have liberty to go and to come, to see, to feel, to speak, to work; to get food, raiment, shelter, and to provide for each and all the needs of his nature. . . . To exercise his faculties he must have liberty to do all that his faculties actually impel him to do. . . . Therefore, he has a *right* to that liberty. This, however, is not the right of one but of all. All are endowed with faculties. All are bound to . . . [exercise] them. All, therefore, must be free to do those things in which the exercise of them consists. That is, all must have rights to liberty of action.
>
> And hence there necessarily arises a limitation. For if men

---

[46] Roger J. Williams, *Free and Unequal: The Biological Basis of Individual Liberty* (Indianapolis: LibertyPress, 1979), pp. 25–26. Williams adds: "Does not our love of liberty, which seems to be inherent in all of us, rest squarely upon our *in*equalities? If at birth we all possessed the same potential tastes . . . would we care about being free to pursue them as we individually desire? . . . It seems to me clear that the idea of freedom arose directly out of this human variability. If we were all alike there would seem to be no reason for wanting freedom; 'living my own life' would be an empty, meaningless expression." *Ibid.,* pp. 26, 38.

have like claims to that freedom which is needful for the exercise of their faculties, then must the freedom of each be bounded by the similar freedom of all. . . . Wherefore we arrive at the general proposition, that every man may claim the fullest liberty to exercise his faculties compatible with the possession of like liberty by every other man.[47]

Thus, only the specific case of equality of *liberty*—the older view of human equality—is compatible with the basic nature of man. Equality of *condition* would reduce humanity to an antheap existence. Fortunately, the individuated nature of man, allied to the geographical diversity on the earth, makes the ideal of total equality unattainable. But an enormous amount of damage—the crippling of individuality, as well as economic and social destruction—could be generated in the attempt.

Let us turn from equality to the concept of inequality, the condition that exists when every man is *not* identical to every other in all characteristics. It is evident that inequality flows inevitably out of specialization and the division of labor. Therefore, a free economy will lead not only to diversity of occupation, with one man a baker, another an actor, a third a civil engineer, etc., but specific *in*equalities will also emerge in monetary income and in status and scope of control within each occupation. Each person will, in the free-market economy, tend to earn a monetary income equal to the value placed upon his productive contribution in satisfying the desires and demands of the consumers. In economic terminology each man will tend to earn an income

---

[47] Herbert Spencer, *Social Statics* (London: John Chapman, 1851), pp. 76–78. In the remainder of the book, Spencer spins out the concrete implications of his basic principle. For a critique of the "Law of Equal Liberty," see Murray N. Rothbard, *Power and Market* (Menlo Park, Calif.: Institute for Humane Studies, 1970), pp. 159–60.

equal to his "marginal productivity," to his particular productivity in satisfying consumer demands. Clearly, in a
world of developed individual diversity, some men will be
more intelligent, others more alert and farsighted, than the
remainder of the population. Still others, meanwhile, will be
more interested in those areas reaping greater monetary
gain; those who succeed at wildcatting of crude oil will
reap greater monetary rewards than those who remain in
secretarial jobs.

Many intellectuals are wont to denounce the "unfairness"
of the market in granting a far higher monetary income to a
movie star than, say, a social worker, in that way rewarding
"material" far more than "spiritual" values and treating
"better" people unfairly. Without going into the peculiar
usage of such terms as "spiritual" and "material," it strikes
one that if the social worker's alleged "goodness" indeed resides in her "spirituality," then it is surely inappropriate and
inconsistent to demand that she receive more of the "material" amenities (money) *vis à vis* the movie star. In the free
society, those who are capable of providing goods and
services that the consumers value and are willing to purchase, will receive precisely what the consumers are willing
to spend. Those who persist in entering lower-priced occupations, either because they prefer the work or because they
are not sufficiently capable in the higher-paid fields, can
scarcely complain when they earn a lower salary.

If, then, *in*equality of income is the inevitable corollary of
freedom, then so too is inequality of control. In *any* organization, whether it be a business firm, a lodge, or a bridge
club, there will always be a minority of people who will rise
to the position of leaders and others who will remain as
followers in the rank and file. Robert Michels discovered

this as one of the great laws of sociology, "The Iron Law of Oligarchy." In every organized activity, no matter the sphere, a small number will become the "oligarchical" leaders and the others will follow.

In the market economy, the leaders, being more productive in satisfying the consumers, will inevitably earn more money than the rank and file. Within other organizations, the difference will only be that of control. But, in either case, ability and interest will select those who rise to the top. The best and most dedicated steel producer will rise to the leadership of the steel corporation; the ablest and most energetic will tend to rise to leadership in the local bridge club; and so on.

This process of ability and dedication finding its own level works best and most smoothly, it is true, in institutions such as business firms in the market economy. For here every firm places itself under the discipline of monetary profits and income earned by selling a suitable product to the consumers. If managers or workers fall down on the job, a loss of profits provides a very rapid signal that something is wrong and that these producers must mend their ways. In non-market organizations, where profit does not provide a test of efficiency, it is far easier for other qualities extraneous to the actual activity to play a role in selecting the members of the oligarchy. Thus, a local bridge club may select its leaders, not only for ability and dedication to the activities of the club, but also for extraneous racial or physical characteristics preferred by the membership. This situation is far less likely where monetary losses will be incurred by yielding to such external factors.

We need only look around us at every human activity or organization, large or small, political, economic, philan-

thropic, or recreational, to see the universality of the Iron
Law of Oligarchy. Take a bridge club of fifty members and,
regardless of legal formalities, half-a-dozen or so will really
be running the show. Michels, in fact, discovered the Iron
Law by observing the rigid, bureaucratic, oligarchic rule
that pervaded the Social Democratic parties in Europe in
the late nineteenth century, even though these parties were
supposedly dedicated to equality and the abolition of the
division of labor.[48] And it is precisely the obviously frozen
inequality of income and power, and the rule by oligarchy,
that has totally disillusioned the equality-seeking New Left
in the Soviet Union. No one lionizes Brezhnev or Kosygin.

It is the egalitarian attempt by the New Left to escape the
Iron Law of inequality and oligarchy that accounts for its
desperate efforts to end elite leadership within its own organizations. (Certainly there has been no indication of any
disappearance of the power elite in oft-heralded Cuba or
China.) The early drive toward egalitarianism in the New
Left emerged in the concept of "participatory democracy."
Instead of the members of an organization electing an elite
leadership, so the theory ran, each person would participate
equally in all of the organization's decision-making. It was,
by the way, probably this *sense* of direct and intense participation by each individual that accounted for the heady
enthusiasm of the masses in the very early stages of the revolutionary regimes in Soviet Russia and Cuba—an enthusiasm that quickly waned as the inevitable oligarchy began to
take control and mass participation to die.

---

[48] Robert Michels, *Political Parties* (Glencoe, Ill.: Free Press, 1949). See
also the brilliant work by Gaetano Mosca, *The Ruling Class* (New York:
McGraw-Hill, 1939), which focuses on the inevitability of a minority
"ruling class" wielding power in government.

While the would-be participatory democrats have made keen criticisms of bureaucratic rule in our society, the concept itself, when applied, runs rapidly against the Iron Law. Thus, anyone who has sat through sessions of any organization engaged in participatory democracy knows the intense boredom and inefficiency that develop rapidly. For if each person must participate equally in all decisions, the time devoted to decision-making must become almost endless, and the processes of the organization *become* life itself for the participants. This is one of the reasons why many New Left organizations quickly begin to insist that their members live in communes and dedicate their entire lives to the organization—in effect, to merge their lives with the organization. For if they truly live and pursue participatory democracy, they can hardly do anything else. But despite this attempt to salvage the concept, the inevitable gross inefficiency and aggravated boredom ensure that all but the most intensely dedicated will abandon the organization. In short, if it can work at all, participatory democracy can work only in groups so tiny that they are, in effect, the "leaders" shorn of their following.

We conclude that, to succeed, any organization must eventually fall into the hands of specialized "professionals," of a minority of persons dedicated to its tasks and able to carry them out. Oddly enough, it was Lenin who, despite his lip service to the ultimate ideal of egalitarian communism, recognized that a revolution, too, in order to succeed, must be led by a minority, a "vanguard," of dedicated professionals.

It is the intense egalitarian drive of the New Left that accounts, furthermore, for its curious theory of education—a theory that has made such an enormous impact on the contemporary student movement in American universities in recent years. The theory holds that, in contrast to "old-fashioned" concepts of education, the teacher knows *no more* than any of his students. All, then, are "equal" in condition; one is no better in any sense than any other. Since only an imbecile would actually proclaim that the student knows as much about the content of any given discipline as his professor, this claim of equality is sustained by arguing for the abolition of content in the classroom. This content, asserts the New Left, is "irrelevant" to the student and hence not a proper part of the educational process. The only proper subject for the classroom is not a body of truths, not assigned readings or topics, but open-ended, free-floating participatory discussion of the student's feelings, since only his feelings are truly "relevant" to the student. And since the lecture method implies, of course, that the lecturing professor knows more than the students to whom he imparts knowledge, the lecture too must go. Such is the caricature of "education" propounded by the New Left.

One question that this doctrine calls to mind, and one that the New Left has never really answered, of course, is *why* the students should then be in college to begin with. Why couldn't they just as well achieve these open-ended discussions of their feelings at home or at the neighborhood candy store? Indeed, on this educational theory, the school as such has no particular function; it *becomes,* in effect, the local candy store, and it, too, merges with life itself. But then, again, why have a school at all? And why, in fact, should the students pay tuition and the faculty receive a salary for their nonexistent services? If all are truly equal, why is the faculty alone paid?

In any case, the emphasis on feelings rather than rational

content in courses again ensures an egalitarian school; or rather, the school as such may disappear, but the "courses" would surely be egalitarian, for if only "feelings" are to be discussed, then surely everyone's feelings are approximately "equal" to everyone else's. Once allow reason, intellect, and achievement full sway, and the demon of inequality will quickly raise its ugly head.

If, then, the natural inequality of ability and of interest among men must make elites inevitable, the only sensible course is to abandon the chimera of equality and accept the universal necessity of leaders and followers. The task of the libertarian, the person dedicated to the idea of the free society, is not to inveigh against elites which, like the need for freedom, flow directly from the nature of man. The goal of the libertarian is rather to establish a free society, a society in which each man is free to find his best level. In such a free society, everyone will be "equal" only in liberty, while diverse and unequal in all other respects. In this society the elites, like everyone else, will be free to rise to their best level. In Jeffersonian terminology, we will discover "natural aristocracies" who will rise to prominence and leadership in every field. The point is to allow the rise of these natural aristocracies, but not the rule of "artificial aristocracies"— those who rule by means of coercion. The artificial aristocrats, the *coercive* oligarchs, are the men who rise to power by invading the liberties of their fellow-men, by denying them their freedom. On the contrary, the natural aristocrats live in freedom and harmony with their fellows, and rise by exercising their individuality and their highest abilities in the service of their fellows, either in an organization or by producing efficiently for the consumers. In fact, the coercive oligarchs invariably rise to power by suppressing the natural elites, along with other men; the two kinds of leadership are antithetical.

Let us take a hypothetical example of a possible case of such conflict between different kinds of elites. A large group of people voluntarily engage in professional football, selling their services to an eager consuming public. Quickly rising to the top is a natural elite of the best—the most able and dedicated—football players, coaches, and organizers of the game. Here we have an example of the rise of a natural elite in a free society. Then, the power elite in control of the government decides in its wisdom that all professional athletics, and especially football, are evil. The government then decrees that pro football is outlawed and orders everyone to take part instead in a local eurythmics club as a mass-participatory substitute. Here the rulers of the government are clearly a coercive oligarchy, an "artificial elite," using force to repress a voluntary or natural elite (as well as the rest of the population).

The libertarian view of freedom, government, individuality, envy, and coercive *versus* natural elites has never been put more concisely or with greater verve than by H. L. Mencken:

> All government, in its essence, is a conspiracy against the superior man: its one permanent object is to oppress him and cripple him. If it be aristocratic in organization, then it seeks to protect the man who is superior only in law against the man who is superior in fact; if it be democratic, then it seeks to protect the man who is inferior in every way against both. One of its primary functions is to regiment men by force, to make them as much alike as possible and as dependent upon one another as possible, to search out and combat originality among them. All it can see in an original idea is potential change, and hence an invasion of its prerogatives. The most dangerous man to any government is

the man who is able to think things out for himself, without regard to the prevailing superstitions and taboos.[49]

Similarly, the libertarian writer Albert Jay Nock saw in the political conflicts between Left and Right "simply a tussle between two groups of mass-men, one large and poor, the other small and rich. . . . The object of the tussle was the material gains accruing from control of the state's machinery. It is easier to seize wealth (from the producers) than to produce it; and as long as the state makes the seizure of wealth a matter of legalized privilege, so long will the squabble for that privilege go on."[50]

Helmut Schoeck's *Envy* makes a powerful case for the view that the modern egalitarian drive for socialism and similar doctrines is a pandering to envy of the different and the unequal, but that the socialist attempt to eliminate envy through egalitarianism can never hope to succeed. For there will always be personal differences, such as looks, ability, health, and good or bad fortune, which no egalitarian program, however rigorous, can stamp out, and on which envy will be able to fasten its concerns.

---

[49] H. L. Mencken, *A Mencken Crestomathy* (New York: Alfred A. Knopf, 1949), p. 145.

[50] Albert Jay Nock, *Memoirs of a Superfluous Man* (New York: Harper, 1943), p. 121.

Essay Four

Egalitarianism and Empire

William Marina

William Marina earned his AB in American Studies from the University of Miami, and his MA and PhD in that area from the University of Denver. He taught for two years at the University of Texas at Arlington before joining the faculty of Florida Atlantic University, where he is presently Professor in Business, Communications, and History at the Boca Raton campus.

Dr. Marina is coauthor of American Statesmen on Slavery and the Negro (New Rochelle, N.Y.: Arlington House, 1971) and associate editor of the revised edition of News of the Nation (Englewood Cliffs, N.J.: Prentice-Hall, 1975). Among his other papers and articles, "Surviving in the Interstices," Reason, v. 7, no. 2 (June 1975), relates to the subject discussed in this pamphlet.

This essay was adapted from a longer paper Dr. Marina presented at the Second Symposium on Human Differentiation, sponsored by the Institute for Humane Studies and held at Gstaad, Switzerland, September 10–14, 1972. A different version, entitled "The 'E' Factors in History," appeared in Modern Age, v. 18, no. 2 (Spring 1974). Copyright © 1975 by the Institute for Humane Studies, Inc. Reprinted by permission. All rights reserved.

Almost a century and a half ago Alexis de Tocqueville predicted that the belief in "the principle of equality," which he saw as the most fundamental and significant feature of American life, eventually would spread throughout the world. That age of egalitarianism, which he believed was primarily motivated by envy, has dawned.[1]

In concepts such as "the revolt of the masses," "the herd," "the will to power," "the cheerful robot," "sensate culture," "centralization," "bureaucratization," and "Caesarism," a number of diverse social thinkers have grasped some of the contours of the current egalitarian epoch.[2] The most accurate term, however, to describe the developing historical paradigm in which we find ourselves, and which encompasses the above ideas, is *empire.*

The preoccupation of many twentieth century intellectuals with the phenomenon of imperialism, once a secondary

---

[1] Sanford A. Lakoff, *Equality in Political Philosophy* (Cambridge, 1964), pp. 166–67.

[2] The references, in order, are to the terms employed by José Ortega y Gasset. Friedrich Nietzsche, C. Wright Mills, Pitirim Sorokin, Brooks Adams, Max Weber, and Oswald Spengler.

definition of empire, has obscured the original meaning of the latter. As Western civilization retreats from imperialism, it is confronted in its maturity, as have been civilizations such as Rome and China, with the dilemma of empire as a stifling, centralized, bureaucratic statism, which threatens, despite considerable material abundance and leisure, to rob life of freedom, creativity, and, ultimately, meaning itself.

Equality, envy, egalitarianism, and *empire*—referred to here as the "E" factors—are, therefore, key aspects of a historical syndrome within which civilizations have tended to evolve.

It is difficult to discover exactly what some writers have meant by the terms *equality* and *egalitarianism.* Sir James Fitzjames Stephen, a nineteenth-century critic of equality, complained that "equality is a word so wide and so vague as to be by itself almost unmeaning." And even a defender of the idea, R. W. Tawney, admitted that the word had more than one meaning.[3]

Although both words are often employed as if they were synonymous, two concepts are actually involved, and the two terms should be used in such a way as to make that distinction clear. In the literature on the subject, even its critics tend not to oppose *equality* when applied in two areas: of opportunity, in the sense that a society be without castes, and before the law. Opposition centers around the effort to extend the idea into other areas, such as income, property, and status. Some writers have tried to differentiate

---

[3] Sir James Fitzjames Stephen, *Liberty, Equality, Fraternity* (London, 1873), p. 201; R. H. Tawney, *Equality* (London, 1952), p. 35.

by referring to this extension of the concepts as "radical" or "strict" egalitarianism.[4]

Rather than use *equality* and *egalitarianism* interchangeably, or add qualifying adjectives, a basic conceptual distinction is made here between equality—of opportunity and before the law—which assumes that differences in income, property, and status may still exist; and egalitarianism—the desire to level and thus to eradicate such distinctions.[5]

The confusion that can result from a failure to distinguish clearly between these two concepts is demonstrated in *A Theory of Justice,* by philosopher John Rawls. He ended a section on envy with an attack on "conservative writers" and suggested that a desire for equality is not based upon envy, but a sense of justice. Rawls then observed, "To be sure there may be forms of equality that do spring from envy. Strict egalitarianism, the doctrine that insists upon an equal distribution of all primary goods, conceivably springs from this propensity."[6]

To concede this point, however, weakened Rawl's argument; the only example he cited for "many conservative writers" was Helmut Schoeck. Schoeck, however, appeared to agree with the relationship of envy to what Rawls called "strict egalitarianism." And although Schoeck saw envy as a factor in the demand for equality of opportunity and before the law, it operated as a "positive and constructive func-

---

[4] Hugo A. Bedau, "Radical Egalitarianism," in Bedau (ed.), *Justice and Equality* (Englewood Cliffs, N.J., 1969), pp. 168–80; and John Rawls, *A Theory of Justice* (Cambridge, 1971), section 81.

[5] Tocqueville's work becomes clearer if one understands that he is talking about both concepts under the term *equality.*

[6] Rawls, *Justice,* section 81.

tion" of which he obviously approved. While he did not explicitly make the distinction made here between equality and egalitarianism, Schoeck came close in speaking of "an increasingly fervent egalitarianism, the misunderstanding and exaggeration of the idea of equality." Thus he found a sense of justice, an aspect of which is a desire for equality of opportunity and before the law, as based upon legitimate "indignation-envy," in contrast to egalitarianism, which derives from "vulgar envy."[7]

Egalitarianism often has a negative connotation even among advocates of equality, as can be seen, for example, in Rawls' comment above. Whether this arises from an awareness of a relationship to envy and leveling, or, in the minds of Americans, the association of *equality* with the Declaration of Independence and *égalité* with the violence of the French Revolution, is difficult to establish. It is simply something that one "senses" in surveying the literature, often by the absence of *egalitarianism* as, for example, in the *Encyclopedia of the Social Sciences,* or the newer, massive, *International Encyclopedia of the Social Sciences,* both of which discuss only *equality.*

If this analysis is correct, and given the historical American commitment to equality, of opportunity and before the law, one can expect advocates of egalitarianism to continue to talk of *equality,* implying that their program is not radically different from, but merely a fulfillment of, traditional American notions of equality. And, quite expectedly, "inequality," with its strong moral implication that "social jus-

---

[7] Helmut Schoeck, *Envy, A Theory of Social Behavior* (New York, 1969), p. 227.

tice" has been violated, is preferred by egalitarians to the neutral word "difference."[8]

Envy is a part of the human condition. As a factor in social and historical development, it is only now beginning to receive the attention it has long deserved.[9] Although he never made an extended analysis of envy, Tocqueville, in a number of separate comments, came to view it as the driving force behind the egalitarian impulse. Sanford A. Lakoff has emphasized the same somewhat overlooked point:

> He tried to separate the experience of violent hatred in the [French] revolutionary period from democracy itself, but he was not very successful. . . . Democracy was conceived out of envy and in Tocqueville's view it was to be forever tainted with the marks of its birth. From the standpoint of aristocratic ethics the revolution was justified; but, for the mobs which carried it out, the principal motivation was naked envy. . . . In attacking the holders of privileges. . . . the populace sought not to protest an imbalance but to despoil the favored few; to gain for themselves the marks of privilege they professed to find intrinsically unjust.[10]

In this context envy can be defined as a deep hatred and resentment of another person because of something that he possesses but the envier does not, as opposed to jealousy—a

---

[8] I am indebted to Peter T. Bauer of the London School of Economics for pointing out that in many instances an objective observer would use the term "difference" rather than "inequality." See, for example, Christopher Jencks, *et al., Inequality, A Reassessment of the Effect of Family and Schooling in America* (New York, 1972).

[9] See especially Schoeck, *Envy,* and also George M. Foster, "The Anatomy of Envy: A Study in Symbolic Behavior," *Current Anthropology,* XIII, no. 2 (April 1972), pp. 165–202.

[10] Lakoff, *Equality,* p. 167.

concern to guard that which one possesses. This may vary from physical characteristics such as beauty, which the envier can probably never possess, to wealth, status, and power, which the envier may argue ought to be redistributed, but which he often wishes merely to obtain for himself.

Envy of differences created by equality is a significant factor in the demand for egalitarianism, which is the harbinger of empire—that is, the need for a strong, bureaucratic, centralized state to carry out the egalitarian program.

In its original definition, *empire* referred to a "centralized bureaucratic" state. As S. N. Eisenstadt noted, "Its basic connotation, as manifest in the Latin *Imperium,* is the existence of a relatively strong center . . . diffusing its authority over broad territorial contours."[11] A second definition, however, has gained ascendancy, associated with a policy of imperialism, in which a powerful state exercises control of various kinds over a weaker state.

Some years ago, William Langer commented upon the "loose" use and "bad repute" of the word *imperialism.* In stressing the second definition, he acknowledged that in the past the term had been "associated with ideas of dictatorial power, highly centralized government, arbitrary methods of administration, and in general with ideas of Caesarism and Bonapartism." Unfortunately, Langer concluded that this definition was "now almost obsolete."[12]

As the era of imperialism, of Western control over weaker nations and peoples, draws to a close, it is time to return

---

[11] "Empire," in *International Encyclopedia of the Social Sciences* (New York, 1968), V, p. 41.

[12] William Langer, *The Diplomacy of Imperialism* (New York, 1935), I, p. 67.

once again to the original definition of empire, and to recognize it as one of the most persistent problems in history.

An awareness of this problem among the more perceptive American thinkers preceded the Revolution. It is, of course, well known that the Founding Fathers read Montesquieu, whose ideas on the separation of power was one source for the incorporation of that idea into the American Constitution. Somewhat less known than *The Spirit of the Laws* is his *Considerations on the Causes of the Greatness of the Romans and Their Decline,* first published in 1734. It was not only widely read, but had a strong impact on Edward Gibbon and his *The Decline and Fall of the Roman Empire.*[13]

Fundamentally, the problem revolved around the possibility of creating a free society with sufficient power to defend itself without developing the centralizing, bureaucratic tendencies which plagued the civilizations of the ancient world. Although the Founding Fathers were committed to the idea of a republic, at the same time they feared that the dissolution toward empire, which had occurred in Rome, was historically inevitable.[14]

As early as 1775, in the *Novanglus* papers, John Adams was concerned with an analysis of empire. Citing Aristotle, Livy, and Harrington, he noted that:

> [T]he British Constitution is more like a republic than an empire. They define a republic to be a government of laws, and not of men. . . . An empire is a despotism, and an emperor is a despot, bound by no law or limitation but his own will; it is a stretch of

---

[13] David P. Jordan, *Gibbon and His Roman Empire* (Urbana, 1971), p. 183 and *passim.*

[14] See Richard W. Van Alstyne, *The Rising American Empire* (Chicago, 1965), especially chapter one.

tyranny beyond absolute monarchy. For, although the will of an absolute monarch is law, yet his edicts must be registered by parliaments. Even this formality is not necessary in an empire.[15]

The debate over empire continued throughout the early years of the American republic, but with perhaps less intellectual rigor than had been displayed by the generation of the Founding Fathers. Enemies of Andrew Jackson saw the general as a dictatorial Caesar, while his political opponents, Henry Clay and John Quincy Adams, were compared to Cicero. This analogy proved embarrassing, however, when the Whig party also ran generals for the presidency in the 1830s.[16]

The rise of the issue of slavery tended to obscure the debate over empire. After the Civil War, Alexander Stephens, the former Vice President of the Confederacy and a political theorist and historian whose insights have not received the attention they deserve, called attention to the war as an example of the trend toward empire and centralization:

> If centralism is ultimately to prevail; if our entire system of free institutions as established by our common ancestors is to be subverted, and an empire is to be established in their stead; if that is to be the last scene of the great tragic drama now being enacted: then, be assured, that we of the South will be acquitted, not only in our own consciences, but in the judgment of mankind, of all responsibility for so terrible a catastrophe, and from all guilt of so great a crime against humanity.[17]

---

[15] In S. E. Morison (ed.), *Sources and Documents Illustrating the American Revolution, 1764–1788* (London, 1962), pp. 131–32.

[16] See R. W. Van Alstyne, *Genesis of American Nationalism* (Waltham, 1970), and Edwin A. Miles, "The Whig Party and the Menace of Caesar," *Tennessee Historical Quarterly*, XXVII, no. 4 (1968), pp. 361–79.

[17] Alexander Stephen, *A Constitutional View of the Late War Between the States* (Philadelphia, 1868–70), II, p. 669, quoted in Richard M. Weaver, *The Southern Tradition at Bay* (New Rochelle, N.Y., 1968), p. 128.

When the debate was opened again in the 1890s, it was essentially in terms of American overseas imperialism. It was this shift in meaning to which Langer had referred in his discussion of the term imperialism. Only a few of the antiimperialists saw the debate over American overseas imperialism as an aspect of the larger problem of empire.[18]

Thus empire, as a description of the process of "bureaucratic centralization," has received relatively little attention throughout most of the twentieth century. Yet, although they employed different terminology, several of our most perceptive social critics were in essence describing the fundamental process of empire. Robert A. Nisbet has called attention to this converging of thinking:

> The relationship between Tocqueville's "administrative centralization" and what Weber was to call "rationalization" is, of course, very close. Both saw conflict between bureaucracy and the democratic impulses that had helped to produce it. Tocqueville's depiction of the sort of despotism democratic nations have to fear is almost indistinguishable in tenor from that found two generations later in Weber's melancholy ruminations on administrative rationalization. For both men, any future despotism would emerge not primarily from individuals or groups but from the bureaucratic system per se.[19]

The terms used by both Tocqueville and Weber were precisely those that historically had been employed as a

---

[18] See William Marina, "Opponents of Empire: An Interpretation of American Anti-Imperialism, 1898–1921," doctoral dissertation, University of Denver, 1968.

[19] Robert A. Nisbet, "Alexis de Tocqueville," in *Int. Ency. Soc. Sci.* XVI, p. 91. Nisbet further noted that: "Democracy inevitably has an accelerative influence on bureaucracy. . . . Tocqueville saw the relationship between bureaucratic centralization and social egalitarianism not only as historical but also as functional. All that erodes social hierarchy, regionalism, and localism is bound to intensify centralization in the state. Conversely, all that furthers the development of political centralization—war, dynastic ambition, and revolution—is bound to accelerate social leveling."

classic description of empire. The thinker who perhaps saw this process most clearly was the German philosopher of history Oswald Spengler. In his view, "civilization," "Caesarism," and "imperialism" were all virtually synonymous concepts, or as he stated it, "Imperialism is civilization unadulterated."[20] It is one of the ironies of history that the West in its increasing sense of power should reject Spengler's concept of "decline" as hopelessly in error. Only a society literally "hooked" on power could fail to comprehend what is revealed by the most cursory reading of Spengler: that the decline is in freedom and creativity, while the degree of power inherent in "civilization" is enormous.[21]

Accompanying the development of the "E" factors syndrome is a corresponding shift in the source of value or law. In his effort to understand the source of the drive toward equality, for example, and what in this paper has been called egalitarianism, "Tocqueville did not begin from the premise that equality was an irreducible principle."[22]

Equality, egalitarianism, and democracy, for instance, however they are defined, are all secondary or derivative values. That is, they are justified as aspects of a more fundamental system of value or law. There are only three sources from which concepts of value or law can ultimately be derived. The first of these is supernaturalism or supernatural law. A value or law is so because it is a part of God's plan, communicated to the rest of mankind through his specially chosen instruments among them. A second source is natural

---

[20] Oswald Spengler, *The Decline of the West* (New York, 1972), p. 38.

[21] John F. Fennelly, *Twilight of the Evening Lands: Oswald Spengler—A Half Century Later* (New York, 1972), especially the last part.

[22] Lakoff, *Equality*, p. 166.

law, or the laws of nature. Something is so because using reason, experience, and experimentation, it appears to be in the nature of things, that is, in conformity with nature as man understands it. Thirdly, there is positive law, or the law of the state. A law or value is so simply because the state says so. In republican or democratic societies such decisions rest upon the will of the majority, which is regarded as the final arbiter as to what is right. This is often linked to both utilitarianism and pragmatism by suggesting that what is right is what seems to "work" for the majority, or provides the greatest happiness for the greatest number.

While all three concepts of value have existed in societies, and some thinkers have attempted to combine them in a coherent hierarchy, they tend to emerge into prominence in an order related to the "E" factors. Societies begin their development with a basic value system derived from supernatural law. The breakdown of feudalism and the growth of equality is accomplished by the development of natural law.

Egalitarianism and empire are characterized by a growing acceptance of positive law and a belief in the state as the ultimate source of all value and law.[23]

An understanding of the "E" factors and their relationship to the sources of value provides a basis from which to observe the development of that syndrome historically. The desire for equality has been a major factor leading to the breakdown of feudal relationships and the growth of more open, mobile social structures, which have characterized the emergence of the great civilizations throughout history.

---

[23] A succinct example of this view is Stephen Decatur's famous toast, "my country, right or wrong." A criticism of that view is in J. Q. Adams to John Adams, August 1, 1816, in J. Q. Adams, *Writings* (New York, 1913–17), VI, p. 62.

Functionally, such equality has meant development of a relatively free market within which individuals could freely exchange ideas, goods, and services. Talent and intelligence do not, however, necessarily correlate with wealth and status, and not everyone is able to rise to the top of society. Although the overall increase in abundance raises the average considerably, the distance between the top and bottom may widen.

The egalitarianism latent within the thrust for equality now begins to be asserted. The egalitarian argument for "social justice" articulated by some religious leaders, secular intellectuals, and politicians to the rest of society is essentially a program for leveling income, property, and status, and is fundamentally in conflict with the idea of equality. The continued demand for greater equality often serves as a convenient issue behind which egalitarians can disguise the real nature of their program.

The quest for justice is given impetus by the existence of many economic and social privileges derived from earlier and, in many cases, continued access to the state apparatus by various interests within the society. Some advocates of egalitarianism are probably sincere in their belief that a more equitable society will emerge from a state-enforced program of leveling, rather than through the curtailment of the power of the state. For many of its advocates, however, egalitarianism simply masks an envious desire to replace those at the top, regardless of whether their position stems from privlieges granted by the state, or is the result of superior ability and/or hard work. At best, the egalitarian may concede that such success is due only to "luck."[24]

---

[24] This is the explanation of success in Jencks, *Inequality*. Schoeck, *Envy*, discusses "luck" as a protective device in societies dominated by envy. This

The significant question is: Why do a large number of people come to believe that only through increased state intervention can justice be achieved? To a great extent this belief is due to the overwhelming acceptance of the state as the source of value and law. Society not only looks for solutions within the paradigm defined by the state, but also finds it difficult to consider the view that statism is at the heart of the problem.

The idea of the state emerges, as do certain aspects of the market economy, with the breakdown of feudalism. Statists develop a policy that in the West has been called mercantilism; that is, a policy under which the state allows private property but those in control of the state use their power to regulate and direct the economy for the general welfare of the whole society. With or without monopolies, such a system is inherently unstable and tends toward corporate syndicalism, in which various economic interests utilize the state for their own ends. Criticism of the system emanates from three sources: those who wish to reform the system by returning to a responsible mercantilism; those who want to replace the system by going one step beyond mercantilism to the abolition of private ownership in many areas of the economy, thus instituting socialism; and those who advocate the principles of the free market and who view the increased power of the state as the basic problem.

The four political economies discussed above can perhaps be better understood if we imagine the economy, or the market, as a black billiard ball, and the state as a white one. In the free-market model, the state is not involved in the economy, and its main function is to maintain the rule of law.

---

is, of course, the central meaning of the well-known story of "Columbus and the Egg."

In the mercantilist model, the thrust (represented as an arrow in the diagram below) is from the white political ball seeking to utilize the economy for the "general welfare." The area of interpenetration (shaded area), whatever its size, is under the control of the state. In the long run, power tends to flow toward the bureaucracy administering the state, and away from the politicians. In the corporate syndicalist model, the economic interests increasingly define the system. It should be noted, however, that the system is dominated by those interests within the area of interpenetration, and not by those still in the market area, though in this model the market area appears on top. In the final model, socialism, the market has been eliminated, and is under the complete control of the political authority.[25]

Democracy obviously lends itself to mass egalitarianism, while representative government leads to the development of corporate syndicalism, for the election of representatives offers an easy opportunity for the economic interests to bring their influence and money to bear on the legislative process. This explains the persistent appeal to the would-be reformers of a "Caesarian" figure who will place himself above and beyond such interests. The ability of the economic interests to "buy" the mercantilist regulatory apparatus drives the reformers increasingly toward a socialist position.

The tendency of the system is thus toward empire. Centralized state power is viewed as essential to cope with the

---

[25] I have used the terminology, especially "corporate syndicalism," of William Appleman Williams. The concept is similar to Theodore Lowi's "interest group liberalism," or Gabriel Kolko's "political capitalism." The billiard ball idea, much extended here, appears in W. A. Williams, *The Tragedy of American Diplomacy* (New York, 1962), pp. 71–72.

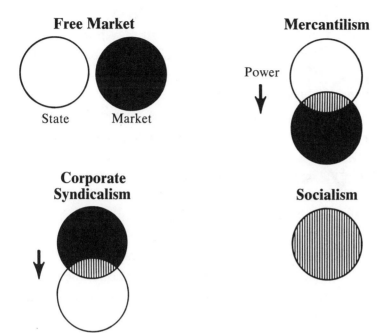

Free Market

State   Market

Mercantilism

Power

**Corporate
Syndicalism**

Socialism

"evils" of the existing system. This in turn suggests a bureaucracy to run the increasingly complex society. Both the
politicians and the intellectuals (the large number of the
latter a direct result of the great affluence) see such a rationalized bureaucracy based upon merit as the way to control
the power of the "vested interests." In the final analysis,
however, the aim of every bureaucracy is to protect itself
above all else. A power struggle is generated between the
ruler, the bureaucracy, the economic interests, and the people as a whole, often complicated by the military as a separate and distinct group within the state apparatus.

A crisis is reached when the economy can no longer
produce enough to meet the voracious appetites of those
groups that have access to the state. The classic case is
agrarian China, where the "squeeze" system led to crisis,

revolt, and the initiation of a new cycle. The incredible abundance produced by industrialization may postpone the crisis, but it does not alter the fundamental contours of the process.

Intellectuals and politicians enjoy the idea of power and control. Like the mandarin, whose long fingernails demonstrated his distaste for, and ability to evade, physical labor, many politicians and intellectuals have an inherent dislike of the market economy with its emphasis on work, entrepreneurial risk, and money. Utilizing economic regulation, the rationalized bureaucracy promises not only security and an end to injustice, but also curtailment of the "brutish" and "antisocial" competitiveness, which accompanies the free market. One of the great appeals of a rational bureaucracy is that, in eliminating competition, it also promises to eradicate envy. But, in cutting itself loose from the creativity of the free market, the bureaucracy has no way to define merit. At best a system of irrelevant symbols is established, as, for example, the Confucian examination or the Western doctorate. Such increasingly artificial elites either remain exclusive, denying equality and generating envy, or they lower whatever standards remain in response to the continued egalitarian pressures. While bureaucracy ostensibly is initiated to promote equality, it must inevitably lead to egalitarianism.

The contours of empire are thus inexorably interwoven with envy and egalitarianism. We can observe the entire "E" factor syndrome as it developed in ancient Greece, Rome, China, and the modern West, especially in the United States.

The idea of equality permeated the whole fabric of Greek society. As Alfred E. Zimmern noted, "Equal lands and equal rights were deeply rooted and persistent traditions of

Greek life. . . . But equal lands never remain equal for long—least of all in a society in which the tradition of equality is strongly developed."[26] While the supernaturalism derived from the gods never died out completely, it was subordinated or combined in the writings of the great philosophers and dramatists with the idea of natural law. Equality was tied to natural law in, for example, *The Trojan Women,* where Jaeger points out that Euripides "describes equality, the foundation of democracy, as the law, manifest a hundredfold in nature, which man himself cannot escape."[27]

The putative author Pseudo-Xenophon provided a fascinating glimpse of the process whereby equality was extended even within the institution of slavery. "Slaves . . . enjoy an extreme degree of license at Athens, where it is illegal to assault them and where the slave will not make way for you. . . . The free proletariat . . . are no better dressed than the slaves . . . and . . . they allow the slaves to live in luxury and in some instances to keep up an imposing establishment."[28]

The expanding equality led to increasing differences of condition, which in turn provided the basis for a strong egalitarianism, in which envy was a significant factor.[29] The movement culminated in a series of "shadowy" lawgivers who emerged throughout Greece; Lycurgus of Sparta and Solon of Athens are the best known. "One feature we can

---

[26] *The Greek Commonwealth* (London, 1931), pp. 88–89.

[27] Werner Jaeger, *Paideia* (New York, 1945), I, pp. 323–24.

[28] Arnold Toynbee, *Greek Civilization and Character* (New York, 1953), p. 43.

[29] S. Ranulf, *The Jealousy of the Gods and Criminal Law at Athens* (Copenhagen, 1933), I, p. 117, cited in Schoeck, *Envy,* p. 119.

trace in the work of all these lawgivers—an attempt to restore the unity of the state by restricting the use of wealth." And while Sparta's elaborate egalitarian formula prescribed the style of life even to the kind of meals to be eaten, Athens also had a rather rigorous code. Furthermore, "the aim in both cases was the same—to redress the inequalities of wealth . . . not merely . . . [through laws] . . . but by causing the rich to *look* as much like the poor as possible."[30]

Lycurgus's egalitarian solution was a monumental effort to turn back the clock of history. The measure of his success was that Sparta became the prototype of the economically stagnant military state. He believed the principal cause of Sparta's disorder "was the fact that the land was concentrating in the hands of the rich." Lycurgus proposed to do away with "competitive money making . . . greed, and luxury." All land was thus turned over to the polis for redistribution and each Spartan given an equal share. As money was the root of all evil, "he caused all gold and silver coin to be withdrawn and he issued in its place a clumsy iron money, too heavy and of too little value to invite hoarding or other misuse" such as any extensive commercial activity.[31]

Under such circumstances, any meaningful equality before the law or of opportunity in a relatively free market was severely curtailed. Even in Athens the supposed aristocracy defended by Plato and Aristotle was not a traditional one, "but temporary oligarchies having risen chiefly in reaction to democracies." They were simply "the wealthy who had seized the polis in self-defense. Oligarchs of this kind tried to

---

[30] Zimmern, *Commonwealth,* pp. 130–31.
[31] Stringfellow Barr, *The Will of Zeus* (Philadelphia, 1961), pp. 57 and 67.

keep the burden of the state on others and to keep for themselves its dignities and its profits."[32] "Equality before the law," the slogan of the oligarchs, was an empty statement to mask their control of the state for their own interests.[33]

In *The History of the Peloponnesian War,* Thucydides brilliantly recounted how the war was interwoven with the crisis of empire and the egalitarian thrust of the masses and their expansionistic, demagogic leaders. There is no more fitting description of the degradation of Athens, and of the arrogance of power and statist, positive law that characterizes empire, than the speech of the Athenians to the Melians before conquering them, exterminating all the males, selling into slavery the women and children, and resettling the area themselves:

> For ourselves, we shall not trouble you with specious pretences—either of how we have a right to our empire . . . or are now attacking you because of wrong that you have done us—and make a long speech which would not be believed; . . . since you know as well as we do that right, as the world goes, is only in question between equals in power, while the strong do what they can and the weak suffer what they must.[34]

In a real sense freedom was destroyed in the fractionalized world of the Greeks long before their conquest by the

---

[32] Jacob Burckhardt, *History of Greek Culture* (London, 1963), pp. 55–56.

[33] Zimmern, *Commonwealth,* pp. 92–93.

[34] Book V, paragraph 89, many editions. The great egalitarian communist experiments, of course, were in the Hellenistic world under such leaders as King Agis IV. These were after leadership in the ancient world clearly had passed to Rome.

Macedonians. Alexander's empire was a military expansion made possible by a long-developing internal process.

The long span of Roman history offers an even better example of the "E" factors in operation. In the ancient world, Rome was noted very early in its history for the emphasis it placed upon the concept of law. By the late Hellenistic Age, this had resulted in a metamorphosis in the position of women. Equality for women extended beyond politics into economic life, and in some occupations such as plumbing they came to dominate. The rate of divorce increased enormously, and the power "of the *pater familias* was shaken to its foundations and eventually swept away altogether." "The meek and henpecked Roman husband was already a stock comedy figure in the great days of the Second Punic War." This changing relationship led Cato the Censor to protest bitterly, "All other men rule over women; but we Romans, who rule all men, are ruled by our women."[35] Equality had progressed to the point that by the late empire a woman who married retained her property, "and, legally, the man had not even the right to enjoy the income from it."[36]

As in the case of Greece, the burgeoning equality led to great differentials in wealth. In the long struggle between the plebeians and the aristocrats for control of the state, an egalitarian program began to take shape. Over the years various efforts were made, such as the Licinian-Sextian Laws

---

[35] The quotes are found in Amaury de Riencourt, *The Coming Caesars* (New York, 1957), pp. 288–89, 367–68. See also "Kinship and Political Power in First Century Rome," in Robert A. Nisbet, *Tradition and Revolt, Historical and Sociological Essays* (New York, 1968), pp. 203–24.

[36] Martin P. Nilsson, *Imperial Rome* (New York, 1966), pp. 217–18.

of 367 B.C., to limit the possessions of the wealthy but these were "disregarded and evaded in the same way that sumptuary laws trying to limit personal luxury in clothes, food, carriages, and jewelry were always disregarded."[37]

Writing in 150 B.C. after the conclusion of the Punic Wars, the historian Polybius made a pessimistic assessment which was prophetic in the light of the almost century-long civil war which ensued. He observed that a nation, "after warding off many great dangers" and arriving "at a high pitch of prosperity and undisputed power," often develops an "ostentation and extravagance of living," which "prove the beginning of a deterioration." The people "become convinced that they are being cheated by some from avarice," and "in their passionate resentment . . . will refuse to obey any longer, or to be content with equal powers with their leaders, but will demand to have all or far the greatest themselves."[38]

The crisis was brought to a head by the efforts of Tiberius Gracchus in 133 B.C. to reassert the Licinian-Sextian Laws. The story of the violent civil war unleashed by the actions of the Gracchi and extending on-and-off to the triumph of Augustus Caesar is, of course, well known. At issue was who would control the state and to what purpose? In the long run, victory went to those who coupled a policy promising booty from expansionist wars with an egalitarian welfare program at home. Thus, Julius Caesar, for example, "helped the debtors in 49 B.C. by canceling the interests in arrears, and the creditors had to accept payment of property

---

[37] F. R. Crowell, *The Revolutions in Ancient Rome* (New York, 1943), p. 83.

[38] *Ibid.*, pp. 75–76.

as it was valued before the inflation." As Theodor Mommsen commented, "Caesar did what he could to repress permanently the fearful omnipotence of capital."[39]

In the empire, while the emperor attempted to link himself to the gods, and thus to supernatural law, it was apparent to the more perceptive thinkers that "right" rested ultimately with Caesar, the power of the army, and the state apparatus.[40] In a sense the empire can best be understood as an effort to stem the long era of violence generated by the egalitarian impulse. The emperor sought to balance the egalitarian desire for leveling by the masses and the rapacious quest to use the state to acquire and protect great wealth by various economic interests through a policy of opposing these forces with the army and the civilian bureaucracy. Despite the enormous tensions created within such a system, and the failure of positive law to provide an adequate social cement, the structure held together for an incredibly long time. In the end it fell because the crisis was exacerbated by pressures from outside the empire.

In the current debate over the desirability of a volunteer army, the Roman experience offers some possible insights. In an extended analysis of Rome's army, Martin P. Nilsson pointed out that, "Ancient states were like all republics, in that they had a system of universal compulsory service." Furthermore:

> The transition of the Roman army from an army based upon compulsory service to a professional army, a few generations before the appearance of Augustus, was the prelude to the transition

---

[39] Quoted in Riencourt, *Caesars,* p. 249.

[40] All of the aspects mentioned here are brilliantly discussed in Chester Starr, *Civilization and the Caesars* (New York, 1965).

of the Roman constitution from a republic to a monarchy. . . .
The army no longer had any sentiment for the State and its
citizens, but only for the profession and its profits, and the com-
mander who knew how to exert his personal influence over it.[41]

The growth of the "centralized bureaucracy" also explains something of the crisis of the empire. W. C. Beyer
has concluded that:

[T]he Roman civil service finally became oppressive and burdensome. It, too, engaged in excessive regulation of the economic life
of the people and subjected them to heavy taxation to support a
growing number of imperial agents. Under this dual frustration,
the Roman citizenry suffered the same breakdown of spirit as did
their Egyptian predecessors under the Ptolemies. Industry and
agriculture languished, population declined, even the army became so weakened that it could no longer hold back the bar-
barians who were pressing upon the nation's borders. In a real
sense, the Roman civil service, which at the outset had been the
empire's chief instrument for bringing peace and prosperity to the
Roman world, in its latter stages became one of the principal
causes of the empire's fall.[42]

The "E" factors and the changing sources of values mesh
with the interpretations of the fall of Rome offered by
scholars such as M. Rostovtzeff and Chester G. Starr. Rostovtzeff began his analysis by observing that "One of the
most striking phenomena in economic life was the rapid
depreciation of the currency and a still more rapid increase
in prices." If silver depreciated, gold literally disappeared.
A system of "fiduciary" money was introduced. It had almost no value, and was accepted only because the state

---

[41] Nilsson, *Rome,* pp. 282–83.
[42] W. C. Beyer, "The Civil Service in the Ancient World," in S. N. Eisenstadt, ed., *The Decline of Empires* (Englewood Cliffs, N. J., 1967), p. 50.

forced people to do so. "The depreciation of money was closely connected with the rise in the prices of products of prime necessity."[43]

Taxation and confiscation bore down especially on the cities where economic development was centered. "Naturally the main sufferers . . . were those who belonged to the class of well-to-do, but not very rich, men and those who were comparatively honest." In a passage that reminds one of the plot of *Atlas Shrugged,* written later by another Russian *émigré,* Ayn Rand, Rostovtzeff noted that "Such men [the upper middle class] lost their property, were degraded, and took flight, living in hiding all over the country." Those who succeeded within such a system "were the rich and unscrupulous men who had the means and cunning to bribe the officials and to found their prosperity on the misfortune of their poorer and more honest colleagues."[44] About the only glimmer of hope was that by the fourth century the police and state apparatus had become so inept that it was fairly easy to "hide" and to return from exile.[45]

The state used the army, increasingly composed of half-barbarian peasants, to crack down on the urban, entrepreneurial class which was responsible for much of the economic productivity. Unfortunately, however, the egalitarian army itself became difficult to manage. "The driving forces," Rostovtzeff held, "were *envy* [italics added] and hatred, but the army had no positive program." The army came to feel it shared little in the wealth often acquired and defended through its efforts and the deaths of many of its sol-

---

[43] M. I. Rostovtzeff, *Social and Economic History of the Roman Empire* (Oxford, 1953), I, pp. 470–71.

[44] *Ibid.*

[45] Starr, *Caesars,* p. 368.

diers. As a result, "the dull submissiveness which had for centuries been the typical mood" of the peasant-soldier "was gradually transformed into a sharp feeling of hatred and envy" toward the urban inhabitants. When brought in to quell an urban riot, the army often created more havoc than it prevented.

"Envy and hatred" of the city were the ultimate causal factors in Rostovtzeff's "thesis that the antagonism between the city and the country was the main driving force of the social revolution of the third century," which destroyed the internal structure of the empire.[46] Such an analysis, minus any reference to envy and favoring a victory of the forces of the countryside, is put forward today by many revolutionaries in the poor nations and was especially evident in a well-publicized speech of some years ago by the Chinese leader Marshal Lin Piao.

The excesses of the Roman peasant-soldier did not lead to the triumph of that inchoate group. The system established by the Emperor Diocletian, who "raised himself from slavery to the purple at thirty-nine," returned some semblance of order.[47] If, however, the republic was the first act in the Roman drama, and the empire the second, although the term empire was still employed, this third act was structurally different, and can perhaps best be described as an "oriental despotism." The new ruling bureaucracy very soon established close relations with "the strongest and richest" part of the upper class. "The class that was disappearing was the middle class, the active and thrifty citizens of the thou-

[46] Rostovtzeff, *Empire,* I, pp. 495–97.

[47] Brooks Adams, *The Law of Civilization and Decay* (New York, 1955), p. 29.

sand cities in the empire, who formed the link between the upper and lower classes." Little else is heard of this class except that "[i]t became more and more oppressed and steadily reduced in numbers." Thus "[a] movement which was started by envy and hatred and carried on by murder and destruction," Rostovtzeff concluded, "ended in such depression of spirit that any stable conditions seemed to the people preferable to unending anarchy."[48] There were many who accepted the final collapse of the empire "without heartfelt regret," and others who had visited among the Huns and considered their society "far better" than that of Rome.[49]

Even China, a society some have thought devoid of such notions as equality and egalitarianism, was not exempt from the development of the "E" factor syndrome. By the time of the Ch'in dynasty the old feudal aristocracy had been eliminated. Confucianism, Legalism, and Taoism were all efforts to cope with the breakdown of the old order.

The pressure for equality of opportunity and before the law was a factor in this process. While both Confucianism and Legalism accepted the state, "they disagreed . . . on the question of raising the law to universality [the Legalist view]. . . . It was not legality itself which divided the two parties, but equality before the law."[50] Both systems had moved beyond a value orientation based upon supernatural law. Confucianism was close to natural law in its emphasis on living in "harmony" with nature, while Legalism was the

---

[48] Rostovtzeff, *Empire,* I, p. 501.

[49] Starr, *Caesars,* p. 365.

[50] Etienne Balazs, *Chinese Civilization and Bureaucracy* (New Haven, 1964), xiv.

epitome of positive law. Both these statist philosophies were
opposed to Taoism, which, although it also functioned
within a framework of natural law in stressing the idea of
"the way," rejected the idea of the state. Etienne Balazs has
described the thinking of Taoists like Pao Ching-yen as
"libertarian anarchism." Unfortunately, the enormous
power exerted by the state pushed the best of the Taoist
thinkers toward an increasingly nihilistic outlook.[51]

The equality before the law promised by the Legalists was
an important factor in the triumph of that idea and the
unification of the country and establishment of the empire
under Shih Huang Ti. A constant demand at the founding of
a new dynasty, as the cycle was repeated over the centuries,
was that the land be redistributed to the farmers.

To whatever extent this redistribution was carried out,
differences soon became apparent as some men managed to
accumulate more wealth than others, either through their
own efforts or through access to the state apparatus. The
resulting envy also reflected the tension between the city and
the countryside, which can be seen in other civilizations as
well. The agrarian orientation of the Confucian emphasized
his "gentlemanly" dislike for a free-market economy. This
dislike was especially true of a radical reformer such as
Wang An Shih, whose massive program of state regulation
was a response to the urbanization and growing market
economy of the eleventh century.

In his famous "Ten Thousand Word Memorial," Wang
attacked the increasing materialism and affluence of the
society. Unfortunately, not only did the poor "envy" the
rich, but they also sought to "emulate" them. His solution,

---

[51] *Ibid.,* p. 347.

which was never fully carried out, would have meant a managed economy far beyond the already extensive state control, monopolies, and ownership. In a massive plan for egalitarian leveling, Wang wanted to inspect all goods and to punish those persons producing "articles of a useless, extravagant or immoral character." Through increased taxation, many artisans and merchants engaged in making and exchanging such articles would "be forced into the fields," and there would thus "be no lack of food."[52]

One is impressed not only by the sheer time span of the Chinese empire, but the manner in which the Confucian bureaucracy kept control, despite the cyclical rise and fall of dynasties and barbarian incursions. The complexity of China's riverine civilization was one factor in this continuity, and the examination system was another. In theory, the examination system offered equality of opportunity for all those with sufficient ability to enter into the ruling hierarchy. In practice, this was not true because it took years of subsidized study to master the literary classics that formed the core of the examination. Egalitarian pressure was probably the major factor in the gradual watering down of standards and the eventual introduction of a procedure whereby degrees could simply be purchased.

The Confucian leadership, however, was not without its divisions, which approximate views in the West. Radicals such as Wang used the envy and egalitarianism present in the society as a means to move toward a virtually complete state socialism. A second element reflected a typically mercantilist desire to control the economy for the good of the

---

[52] Quoted in H. R. Williamson, *Wang An Shih* (London, 1935), II, pp. 114–17.

bureaucracy itself. A third group resembled the corporate syndicalist politician as the representative of an economic interest: its members sought to use their positions to advance the fortune of the larger family clan that had supported the study necessary for the examination.

Balazs has demonstrated the extent to which, beneath a rhetoric of humanism, the Confucian bureaucracy functioned as a system of power. The bureaucracy took a large portion of the economic wealth produced from an essentially agrarian base and, in the process, helped to hasten the crisis that usually resulted in the establishment of a new dynasty and a new cycle. An enormous network of informers and police was necessary to control the society.[53] Under such conditions, as in Rome, freedom and creativity languished. In despair, the great historian Ssu-ma Ch'ien, in his last will and testament, "denounced the autocratic state for the humiliations inflicted upon its subjects, and discussed with great lucidity the problem of whether to commit suicide under a despotism."[54]

From this perspective of the history of China, the present regime is not a departure from the past, but rather a continuation with heavier emphasis upon the Legalist tradition.[55]

The contours of Western civilization demonstrate this same tendency. The society began its development around a value system based upon Christianity and supernatural law. The gradual rise of cities and a market economy offered an

---

[53] Balazs, *Bureaucracy,* p. 18.
[54] *Ibid.,* p. 14.
[55] Amaury de Riencourt, *The Soul of China* (New York, 1958).

increased equality of opportunity and before the law. Such changes were uneven, and did not extend into the countryside where feudalism continued, as is evidenced in the numerous peasant uprisings of the thirteenth and fourteenth centuries, many of which were fomented by religious leaders who advocated a program of egalitarian leveling. Within the church, men such as Thomas Aquinas developed a synthesis of natural law and supernatural law. The rise of science greatly stimulated the development of a secular natural law, while the emergency of the national state aided the growth of positive law, and the three sources were found in various combinations.

Both a desire for equality and egalitarianism can be observed among the groups pressing for social change from the peasant rebellions of the late medieval period to the revolutions of the modern era. To some extent the crisis was postponed by the discovery of America, and what Walter Prestcott Webb called "the great frontier."[56] Land and opportunity were thus available to those motivated to avail themselves of the chance to better their situation. Henry Bamford Parkes has pointed out that the common denominator of all those who came to the New World was a psychological one: their willingness to leave the Old World rather than accept the existing system of continued inequalities, attempt to reform it, or revolt against it.[57] Elsewhere I have suggested that within America those who chose the "safety-valve" of the frontier were representative of the types of persons and groups who, according to theories of

---

[56] W. P. Webb, *The Great Frontier* (New York, 1964), especially chapter one.

[57] Henry Bamford Parkes, *The American Experience* (New York, 1959), p. 7.

the sociology of revolution, would be most likely to revolt if no frontier of opportunity were open to them.[58]

Tocqueville's major insight was the recognition that equality was the central feature of American life. The abundance of land and the relative inability of the European states to re-create feudalism in America opened up considerable opportunity.[59] The vast wealth flowing in from the New World also opened up some measure of equality of opportunity in the Old World, but it did so within the existing system of privilege. If a large number of those willing to leave Europe were advocates of equality, among those who remained, apart from the beneficiaries of the system, there was likely a disproportionately large number of proponents of egalitarianism. Thus, a polarization developed in Europe between those who wished to use the state to protect their privileges, and those who wished to use the state to institute an egalitarian socialism. It is within these parameters that the course of modern European history has moved, culminating in the bureaucratic welfare state or socialism, which now characterizes that continent.

In America, the revolution eliminated many of the vestiges of feudalism, which had been transported to this side of the Atlantic. The birth of an American state, however, meant there would be a struggle among several groups for control of the state apparatus in order to utilize it for their program. Thus, a number of leaders wished to replace British mercantilism with an American version of that policy. The decentralization, or mercantilism at the level of the in-

---

[58] William Marina, "Turner, the Safety-Valve, and Social Revolution," in D. Koenig, ed., *Historians and History: Essays in Honor of Charlton W. Tebeau* (Coral Gables, 1967), pp. 23–32.

[59] Webb, *Great Frontier, passim.*

dividual state, which followed the revolution, they found not at all to their liking. The adoption of the Constitution greatly facilitated the tendency toward centralization and a number of court decisions also aided the process. The high mark of this early period was reached in the presidency of John Quincy Adams. As William Appleman Williams has noted:

> Indeed, by 1826 the government was the largest single economic entrepreneur in the country. It handled more funds, employed more people, purchased more goods, and borrowed more operating and investment capital than any other enterprise. For generations that are reputed to have believed in weak and minimal government, the Founding Fathers and their first offspring created a rather large and active institution. . . . And the principle of government assistance to private companies was to know no greater application than in the pattern of land grants to railroads unless, perhaps, it was in the direct and indirect subsidies to corporation enterprises during World War I and World War II.[60]

The Jacksonians never fully reversed this process, nor was their so-called *laissez nous faire* policy very internally consistent since many of them were quite willing to use the power of the state to control their slaves and to take land from the Indians. In any event the coming of the Civil War greatly enhanced the centralizing tendencies, and the dominant group within the Republican party was composed of many of those economic interests that had supported Henry Clay's whiggish "American System." The alliance of government and various business interests was thus formalized by the late nineteenth century. Abuse of centralized power and disregard for law and the constitutional process were

[60] W. A. Williams, *The Contours of American History* (Chicago, 1966), p. 211.

evident in William McKinley's handling of the Cuban Revolution, the coming of the war with Spain, and our intervention in the Philippines in the late 1890s.[61] Certainly, these actions were illustrative of the definition of empire which John Adams had put forward in 1775.

As the area of the free market diminished, the American political economy, since late in the nineteenth century, has become increasingly corporate syndicalist. Gabriel Kolko, among others, has pointed out that the efforts of the progressive reformers to use government to regulate business (what here would be termed a mercantilist solution) was primarily aided by those segments of business that were threatened by the competition of smaller, more efficient entrepreneurs. The failure of trusts and mergers to create monopolistic protection led to the development of regulation as a means of curtailing competition.[62]

The reformers were frustrated that business came to dominate the regulatory apparatus. Some had hoped to use government to restore competition (equality of opportunity), while others had hoped to use increased governmental intervention for purposes of egalitarian redistribution.

The late nineteenth century was thus a watershed for American reform. It could have been argued from a libertarian standpoint that the worst abuses of the system were the result of government's support or creation of privilege, which regulation would formalize and perpetuate. Such a position would have worked within the natural-law tradition to stress the dynamic aspect of evolution rather than its

---

[61] Marina, "Opponents," *passim.*

[62] Gabriel Kolko, *The Triumph of Conservatism: A Re-Interpretation of American History, 1900–1916* (Chicago, 1967), conclusion.

static qualities. So-called Social Darwinists usually argued for the status quo and "the survival of the fittest," when it was clear that progress had come through the evolving "unfit"; the organism that was not fitted to a given environment and had developed something "new" for survival. Dynamic change and adaption rather than the status quo were fundamental. The great body of American reformers, however, rejected the idea of the free market and natural law, and turned instead to government regulation and positive law.[63]

The growth of centralized, bureaucratic government (empire) was aided by parts of three groups: the reformers, the businessmen, and the politicians. To regulation and welfare were added the needs of an increasingly imperial foreign policy. Each new crisis, whether global war or internal economic stress engendered by the system, added to the size of the structure. The present economic crisis is the result of the incredible growth of the government in the 1960s and the expenditures in domestic and foreign policies. Had the government been able to tie most of the world to the dollar, the system might have been able to sustain itself longer, but that effort failed.[64] The United States has begun to realize that the cost of keeping "order" throughout the world is more than it can afford in money, or in the opposition of the young men who refuse to be drafted for such a cause.

The egalitarian, garrison-welfare state is increasingly characterized by a continuing battle among economic interests, politicians, and the bureaucracy to dominate and benefit from the imperial system. We are witnessing the

---

[63] See Sidney Fine, *Laissez Faire and the General-Welfare State: A Study of Conflict in American Thought, 1865–1901* (Ann Arbor, 1956).

[64] Michael Hudson, *Super Imperialism* (New York, 1972).

beginning rounds in the battle that was played out over many years in Rome and China.

There is not space here to examine the many ways in which egalitarianism has affected the development of American society. Some of these are quite subtle, as, for example, the relationship of egalitarian thinking to success in business and education, and the increasing violence in our society. Commenting on the assassination of President James Garfield in 1881, Alexander Stephens attributed it to a growing belief that everyone had a right to succeed in business and education. The "ambitions" of many had been "stimulated in excess" of their capacity. Failure often resulted in a resort to violence and a desperate search for notoriety as a partial substitute for success.[65] Arthur Bremer, who shot Governor George Wallace of Alabama in 1972, is a rather pathetic example of this frustrated egalitarianism. From his diary, we learn that it mattered little to Bremer whom he shot; a more important person simply meant more publicity. Throughout the diary are four-letter words and a constant reference to "failure." The degree of self-hatred is overpowering.[66] It seems likely in this epoch of egalitarianism that increasing frustration and violence can only result when many individuals find they cannot achieve the success that egalitarians promised as everyone's "right."

In an area such as education, failure can be averted by simply lowering standards. This debasement lies at the heart of the present crisis in American education, but is seldom commented upon. At the university level, poor schools,

---

[65] Alexander Stephens, *A Pictorial History of the United States* (New Orleans, 1882), I, p. 975.

[66] Arthur H. Bremer, "An Assassin's Diary," *Harper's Magazine,* CCXLV (January 1973), pp. 52–66.

often state-supported and easily subjected to egalitarian political pressure, drive out good schools in a kind of application of Gresham's law in the area of education. Egalitarian pressures from students who demand the right to evaluate their teachers, and from peers who evaluate one another, push the system toward bureaucratization in which free thought and creativity are undermined. In the United States, governmental pressure for increased egalitarianism has resulted in quota formulae for various "minority" groups such as women and blacks. Such policies are a denial of traditional American notions of equality of opportunity and before the law.

The arbitrary power of the centralized governmental bureaucracy permeates American life at all levels, stifling freedom and initiative. The director of the Patent Office, for example, recently reported that for the first time there has been a marked drop in the rate at which Americans are patenting new ideas and inventions.[67] One suspects this decline is due not to Americans suddenly becoming less intelligent, but to the structure of governmental regulation having grown so great that it is discouraging the development and application of new ideas. Unfortunately, this trend comes at a time when government has created or exacerbated problems such as pollution, solutions to which will demand freedom and creativity unfettered by a rigid, bureaucratic statism.

Those epochs in other civilizations characterized by the emergence of positive law and the rise of the state have

---

[67] *Miami Herald,* May 18, 1973. In conjunction with this development on January 27, 1975, NBC news noted that the federal government had announced that American productivity per man hour had declined for the first time since records began to be kept on this statistic.

frequently experienced a breakdown of values and the family, and a turn toward drugs and sex in a rather desperate search for meaning. Suicide comes increasingly into prominence, especially among some of the more perceptive thinkers, such as the Stoics in Rome.[68] It is obvious that our own civilization already manifests aspects of this growing cultural sterility and bureaucratic blockage.[69]

Can the historical drift toward egalitarianism and empire, which has plagued other civilizations, be reversed in the West? Ironically, perhaps the best hope lies in the gathering economic crises of advanced nations whose economies are staggering under the heavy weights of subsidy, defense, welfare, and bureaucracy. The continued inability of government to solve such problems may yet lead to a reassessment of the whole situation in which natural law and a free market would take on new relevance in the struggle for human freedom.

---

[68] Starr, *Civilization,* pp. 271–72.

[69] A recent, insightful study of some of the problems raised by the end of "the great frontier," by one of the students of Walter Prescott Webb, is Forrest McDonald, *The Phaeton Ride: The Crisis of American Success* (New York, 1974).

Essay Five

The New Despotism

Robert A. Nisbet

Robert A. Nisbet, Albert Schweitzer Professor Emeritus at Columbia University, received his doctorate in social institutions from the University of California in 1939. He has held numerous teaching and administrative positions in California and Arizona during the course of his distinguished career, and is currently a Resident Scholar with the American Enterprise Institute in Washington, D.C. He has authored or coauthored twelve books, among which are The Quest for Community *(1953),* The Sociological Tradition *(1966),* Social Change and History *(1969), and* Twilight of Authority *(Oxford University Press, 1975).*

Reprinted here in a revised version, this essay originally appeared in Commentary *magazine (June 1975) and later was a chapter in* Twilight of Authority. *Reprinted by permission.*

When the modern political community was being shaped at the end of the eighteenth century, its founders thought that the consequences of republican or representative institutions in government would be the reduction of political power in individual lives.

Nothing seems to have mattered more to such minds as Montesquieu, Turgot, and Burke in Europe and to Adams, Jefferson, and Franklin in the United States than the expansion of freedom in the day-to-day existence of human beings, irrespective of class, occupation, or belief. Hence the elaborate, carefully contrived provisions of constitution or law whereby formal government would be checked, limited, and given root in the smallest possible assemblies of the people. The kind of arbitrary power Burke so detested and referred to almost constantly in his attacks upon the British government in its relation to the American colonists and the people of India and Ireland, and upon the French government during the revolution, was foremost in the minds of all the architects of the political community, and they thought it could be eliminated, or reduced to insignificance, by ample use of legislative and judicial machinery.

What we have witnessed, however, in every Western country, and not least in the United States, is the almost incessant growth in power over the lives of human beings—power that is basically the result of the gradual disappearance of all the intermediate institutions which, coming from the predemocratic past, served for a long time to check the kind of authority that almost from the beginning sprang from the new legislative bodies and executives in the modern democracies. The eighteenth century hope that people, by their direct participation in government, through voting and officeholding, would be correspondingly loath to see political power grow, has been proved wrong. Nothing seems so calculated to expand and intensify the power of the state as the expansion of electorates and the general popularization of the uses of power.

Even so, I do not think we can properly explain the immense power that exists in modern democracies by reference solely to the enlargement of the base of government or to the kinds of parliaments Sir Henry Maine warned against in his *Popular Government.* Had political power remained *visible,* as it largely did down until about World War I, and the manifest function of legislature and executive, the matter would be very different. What has in fact happened during the past half century is that the bulk of power in our society, as it affects our intellectual, economic, social, and cultural existences, has become largely *invisible,* a function of the vast infragovernment composed of bureaucracy's commissions, agencies, and departments in a myriad of areas. And the reason this power is so commonly invisible to the eye is that it lies concealed under the humane purposes that have brought it into existence.

The greatest single revolution of the last century in the political sphere has been the transfer of effective power over human lives from the constitutionally visible offices of government, the nominally sovereign offices, to the vast network that has been brought into being in the name of protection of the people from their exploiters. It is this kind of power that Justice Brandeis warned against in a decision nearly half a century ago: "Experience should teach us to be most on guard to protect liberty when the governments' purposes are beneficent. Men born to freedom are naturally alert to repel invasion of their liberty by evil-minded rulers. The greatest dangers to liberty lurk in insidious encroachments by men of zeal, well-meaning but without understanding."

What gives the new despotism its peculiar effectiveness is indeed its liaison with humanitarianism, but beyond this fact is its capacity for entering into the smallest details of human life. The most absolute authority, wrote Rousseau, "is that which penetrates into a man's inmost being and concerns itself no less with his will than with his actions." The truth of that observation is in no way lessened by the fact that for Rousseau genuinely legitimate government, government based upon the general will, *should* so penetrate. Rousseau saw correctly that the kind of power traditionally exercised by kings and princes, represented chiefly by the tax collector and the military, was in fact a very weak kind of power compared with what a philosophy of government resting on the general will could bring about. Tocqueville, from a vastly different philosophy of the state, also took note of the kind of power Rousseau described. "It must not be forgotten that it is especially dangerous to enslave men in the minor details of life. For my part, I should be inclined to think freedom less necessary in the great things than in the little ones, if it were possible to be secure of the one without the other."

Congresses and legislatures pass laws, executives enforce them, and the courts interpret them. These, as I have said, are the bodies on which the attentions of the Founding Fathers were fixed. They are the visible organs of government to this day, the objects of constant reporting in the media. And I would not question the capacity of each of them to interfere substantially with individual freedom. But of far greater importance in the realm of freedom is that invisible government created in the first instance by legislature and executive but rendered in due time largely autonomous, is often nearly impervious to the will of elected constitutional bodies. In ways too numerous even to try to list, the invisible government—composed of commissions, bureaus, and regulatory agencies of every imaginable kind—enters daily into what Tocqueville calls "the minor details of life."

Murray Weidenbaum, in an important study of this invisible government, *Government Mandated Price Increases,* has correctly referred to "a second managerial revolution" that is now well under way in American society. The first managerial revolution, described originally by A. A. Berle and Gardiner C. Means in their classic book *The Modern Corporation and Private Property* and given explicit identity by James Burnham, concerned, as Weidenbaum points out, the separation of management from formal ownership in the modern corporation. The second managerial revolution is very different. "This time," writes Weidenbaum, "the shift is from the professional management selected by the corporation's board of directors to the vast cadre of government regulators that influences and often controls the key decisions of the typical business firm." Weidenbaum concerns himself almost entirely with the business sector—pointing out incidentally that this whole cadre of regulation is a by now deeply embedded cause of inflation—but the point he makes is just as applicable to other, nonbusiness areas of society.

In the name of education, welfare, taxation, safety, health, environment, and other laudable ends, the new despotism confronts us at every turn. Its effectiveness lies, as I say, in part through liaison with humanitarian rather than nakedly exploitative objectives but also, and perhaps most significantly, in its capacity to deal with the human will rather than with mere human actions. By the very existence of one or another of the regulatory offices of the invisible government that now occupies foremost place, the wills of educators, researchers, artists, philanthropists, and enterprisers in all areas, as well as in business, are bound to be affected: to be shaped, bent, driven, even extinguished.

Of all the social or moral objectives, however, which are the taking-off points of the new despotism in our times, there is one that stands out clearly, that has widest possible appeal, and that at the present time undoubtedly represents the greatest single threat to liberty and social initiative. I refer to equality, or, more accurately, to the New Equality.

"The foremost, or indeed the sole, condition required in order to succeed in centralizing the supreme power in a democratic community is to love equality or to get men to believe you love it. Thus, the science of despotism, which was once so complex, has been simplified and reduced, as it were, to a single principle."

The words are Tocqueville's, toward the end of *Democ-*

racy in America, in partial summary of the central thesis of
that book, which is the affinity between centralization of
power and mass equalitarianism. Tocqueville yielded to no
one in his appreciation of equality before the law. It was, he
thought, vital to a creative society and a free state. It was
Tocqueville's genius, however, to see the large possibility of
the growth in the national state of another kind of equality,
more akin to the kind of leveling that war and centralization
bring to a social order. It is only in our time that his words
have become analytic and descriptive rather than prophetic.

There is a great deal in common between military collectivism and the kind of society that must be the certain result
of the doctrines of the New Equalitarians, whose aim is not
mere increase in equality before the law. In fact this historic
type of equality looms as an obstacle to the kind of equality
that is desired: *equality of condition, equality of result.*
There is nothing paradoxical in the fondness of equalitarians
for centralized power, the kind that the military best evidences, and the fondness of centralizers for equality. The
latter, whatever else it may signify, means the absence of the
kinds of centers of authority and rank that are always
dangerous to despotic governments.

Equality of condition or result is one thing when it is set
in the utopian community, the commune, or the monastery.
The Benedictine Rule is as good a guide as we need for the
administration of this kind of equalitarian order, small
enough, personal enough to prevent the dogma of equality
from extinguishing normal diversity of strength and talent.
For countless centuries, everywhere in the world, religion
and kinship have been contexts of this kind of equality; they
still are in theme.

Equality of result is a very different thing, however, when

it becomes the guiding policy of the kind of national state that exists in the West today—founded in war and bureaucracy, its power strengthened by these forces throughout modern history, and dependent from the beginning upon a degree of leveling of the population. We may have in mind the ideal of equality that the monastery or family represents, but what we will get in actual fact in the modern state is the kind of equality that goes with uniformity and homogeneity —above all, with war society.

Tocqueville was by no means alone in his perception of the affinity between equality and power. At the very end of the eighteenth century, Edmund Burke had written, in *Reflections on the Revolution in France,* of the passion for leveling that exists in the militant and the military: those, he wrote, "who attempt to level, never equalize." The French Revolution, Burke believed correctly, was different from any revolution that had ever taken place before. And the reason for this difference lay in its combination of eradication of social diversity on the one hand and, on the other, the relentless increase of military-political power that expressed itself in the timeworn fashion of such power. All that ended toward the destruction of the intermediate authorities of social class, province, church, and family brought simultaneously into being, Burke noted, a social leveling and a transfer to the state alone of powers previously resident in a plurality of associations. "Everything depends upon the army in such a government as yours," he wrote; "for you have industriously destroyed all the opinions and prejudices, and, as far as in you lay, all the instincts which support government." In words prophetic indeed, since they were written in 1790, Burke further declared that the crisis inherent in "military democracy" could only be resolved by the rise of "some popular general who understands the art of conciliating the soldiery, and who possesses the true spirit of command." Such an individual "shall draw the eyes of all men upon himself."

The theme of military democracy, of the union of military and social equality, was strong in certain nineteenth century critics. We see it in some of Burckhardt's writings, where he refers to the future rise of "military commandos" in circumstances of rampant equality. We see it, perhaps most profoundly, in James Fitzjames Stephen's *Liberty, Equality, and Fraternity,* though what is most evident in that remarkable work is much less the military, save by implication, than the implacable conflict Stephen discerned between equality and liberty. There were others—Henry Adams in America, Taine in France, Nietzsche in Germany—who called attention to the problem equality creates for liberty in the modern democratic state. Nor were such preceptions confined to the pessimists. Socialists such as Jaurès in France saw in the citizen army, based upon universal conscription, an admirable means of instilling in Frenchmen greater love for equality than for the liberty associated with capitalist society.

It is evident in our day how much more of a force the ethic of equality has become since these nineteenth century prophecies and prescriptions were uttered. Two world wars and a major depression have advanced bureaucracy and its inherent regimentations to a point where the ideology of equality becomes more and more a means of rationalizing these regimentations and less and less a force serving individual life or liberty.

No one will question the fact that a higher degree of equality now exists in Western countries than at any time in the past. This is true not only of equality of opportunity and legal equality, each of which became a burning issue by the early nineteenth century, but of the more generalized equality of economic, political, and social *condition*. It is condition or result, not opportunity, that is today the central perspective in equalitarianism; and that ideological fact is itself part of the larger reality of an extraordinary achievement of equality of condition or result, at least by the standard given us by history. Nor is there anything strange in the intensification of equalitarianism in such an age as ours, for, on the evidence of the history of social movements, powerful agitation in behalf of some social or moral value comes only when the surrounding social order can be seen to reflect that value in at least some degree, commonly only recently accomplished.

Equality has the great advantage of being able to draw upon both religious and political energies. It is only in the religious and political realms indeed that the cry for equality has been heard historically—much more often in the former than the latter, prior to the age of the French Revolution. Whatever else equality is, it is a spiritual dynamic. Major social movements require such a dynamic, irrespective of whether they are primarily religious or political at the core. It is not so much the surrounding material conditions as this inner spiritual dynamic that in the long run determines, though by means that are complex and still inadequately understood, what the outcome of an issue will be. I think it would be hard to exaggerate the potential spiritual dynamic that lies in the idea of equality at the present time. One would have to go back to certain other ages, such as imperial Rome, in which Christianity was generated as a major historical force, or Western Europe of the Reformation, to find a theme endowed with as much unifying, mobilizing power, especially among intellectuals, as the idea of equality carries now.

Equality has a built-in revolutionary force lacking in such ideas as justice or liberty. For once the ideal of equality becomes uppermost, it can become insatiable in its demands. It is possible to conceive of human beings conceding that they have enough freedom or justice in a social order; it is not possible to imagine them ever declaring they have enough equality—once, that is, equality becomes a cornerstone of national policy. In this respect it resembles some of the religious ideals or passions that offer, just by virtue of the impossibility of ever giving them adequate representation in the actual world, almost unlimited potentialities for continuous onslaught against institutions.

Affluence is a fertile ground for the spread of equalitarian philosophy, for the pains of affluence manifestly include in our age the pain of guilt over the existence of any and all inequalities. It is not enough, as we have been discovering, to create equality before the law—at least to the degree that this is ever possible—and to seek legal equality of opportunity. Vast systems labeled affirmative action or open admissions must be instituted. And then, predictably, it is discovered that even these are not enough.

The reason for this is plain enough. Equality feeds on itself as no other single social value does. It is not long before it becomes more than a value. It takes on all the overtones of redemptiveness and becomes a religious rather than a secular idea.

Like other historic religious ideas and also ideas of political character, equality has an inherent drive that carries it well beyond national boundaries. The proper abode of equality, like any other redemptive idea, is all mankind, not simply this or that parochial community. We are already in the presence of this universalizing state of mind in discussions of equality. It is not enough that classes and groups in the United States, or in the West, should become equal. The entire world, especially the Third World, must be brought in. Yet simple arithmetic suffices to prove the impossibility of either the United States or the West extending its resources to this Third World—particularly in light of the population increases which would become inexorable and, also, the present spread in these countries of an ideology, Russian or Chinese in source, that, as the present record makes only too clear, reduces what productive power is presently in existence.

But it is the nature of providential ideas like equality that they are stayed by neither fact nor logic. They acquire a momentum of their own, and I can think of few things more probable than the spread of equalitarianism in the West— not despite but because of its manifest irrationality as the sovereign objective of national and world policy.

The significance of equalitarianism in our day is made all the greater by the profound affinity that exists, and has existed for many centuries, between equality and the distinctive nature of the Western state from the time of the Cleisthenean reforms at the end of the sixth century B.C. Those revolutionary changes put an end to the inequalities of traditional kinship society in Athens and ushered in the polis. Excepting only, as we are obliged to here, the class of slaves, a high degree of equality was instituted among the Athenian citizens. This equality was, of course, in part a function of the central power that was also inaugurated in the polis, a power that cut, often destructively, through all the intermediate loyalties that had been handed down from the most ancient times. Athenian equality, in sum, is comprehensible only in light of the leveling that resulted from political extermination of the traditional kinship diversity of Athenian society.

Neither Plato nor Aristotle liked equalitarianism, though there is assuredly an equality of sorts within the class of guardians that Plato creates to govern his utopian Republic. But like it or not, both Plato and Aristotle perforce gave equality a higher place than could be imagined in the minds of earlier Greek thinkers such as Heraclitus or statesmen such as Solon. Aristotle, who intensely disliked Platonic communism, nevertheless thought that some degree of equality of wealth was a prerequisite for political stability.

With rare exceptions, the Western philosophy of the political state has carried from that time to ours an imposing emphasis on the desirability of equality. The reason for this lies, in the first instance, in the nature of the power that has gone with the Western state since the Greeks. This power—sovereignty, as it is commonly called—seeks to go directly to the individual. The great difference between the Western state during the past twenty-five hundred years and the traditional state of Asia—as Karl Marx was one of the first to note—lies in the contrasting relation they have to the individual. In China, India, and other Eastern societies prior to the present century, governments reigned, as it were, but did not rule. Their claimed powers were at times certainly as centralized and bureaucratized as anything to be found in the West, but these powers almost never touched individual lives directly. Between the power of the government and the life of the individual lay strata of membership and authority —clan, village, caste, temple—which were almost never penetrated by the ruler or his bureaucracy. It was possible, in short, for the Asiatic state to exist for thousands of years in the presence of, as a superstructure of, a nonpolitical society founded on kinship and locality that was the real center of human life in matters of authority, function, and responsibility.

Very different has been the Western state. Omitting only the Middle Ages—and even then the *idea* of the centralized state remained vivid to those acquainted with Greek and Latin—the Western structure of political power has been a process of almost permanent revolution against the social groups and authorities that lay intermediate between individual and state. By virtue of its inherent centralization, its definition in terms of territory rather than social or religious function, its prized doctrine of sovereignty through which the state's power is declared superior and supervening to all other powers, the Western state's very existence in the ancient world and in the modern since the Reformation has represented a kind of built-in war against traditional society and its ingrained authorities.

In its struggle for individual allegiance, the Western state has, in a very real sense, actually manufactured individualism. It has done this not merely as a result of the negative attitude political rulers since Cleisthenes have taken toward social, religious, and economic groups that seemed to be competing with the state, but, perhaps more crucially, in the positive creation of individual rights, freedoms, and benefits. Say what one will of the unique power of the state and of its all-too familiar capacity for extending this power bureaucratically into the lives of countless human beings, creating coercions and invasions of autonomy all the way, the fact remains that the central power of the state has also been associated with some resplendent gains in liberty and welfare. It is no exaggeration to say that from the time of Pericles, through Alexander the Great, the Caesars, and down to the Cromwells and Napoleons of modern history and also the more centralizing of American Presidents from Andrew Jackson to Lyndon Johnson, a great many such gains have come directly from the use of central power. It was after all the central power of the American government, not the local or regional powers of communities and states, that brought about first the abolition of slavery in the United States and then, slowly but surely, increased civil rights for blacks and other minorities.

It is for this reason, no doubt, that the state in the West has attracted to itself what can only be called a clerisy of power. I refer to the long succession of philosophers and intellectuals from Greek and Roman times to our own who have made the political state the temple, so to speak, of their devotion. Religion is the only other value system that has had its clerisy—older than the political clerisy but, in modern Western civilization, possessed of much less power and influence. No other institution comes to mind that has won itself a clerisy as have religion and politics. Not until the early nineteenth century did economists come into existence in their own right, and it is hard to find in economic writings any of the sense of redemptive passion that is so common in religious and political works. It is possible, though I am skeptical, that technology today has a clerisy in the sense in which I use the word here. There is surely no other.

Through most of the history of Western civilization the political clerisy has given itself to the needs and values of the state, just as its great rival, the religious clerisy, has to those of the church. Each clerisy has produced its titans—St.

Augustine, Aquinas, Luther, on the one side; Plato, Hobbes, Rousseau, on the other—as well as its vast ranks of lesser minds, its ordinary intellectuals and technicians. The political state can be seen to be a temple in Rousseau quite as much as the church is a temple in Augustine.

It is Tocqueville who, so far as I know, first made the relation between equality and power a principle not only of political sociology but of the philosophy of history. "In running over the pages of our history," Tocqueville writes in the introduction to *Democracy in America,* "we shall scarcely find a single great event of the last seven hundred years that has not promoted equality of condition." The Crusades, the introduction of firearms, the rise of the infantry, the invention of movable type in printing, the Protestant Reformation, the opening of gates to the New World—all of these, Tocqueville notes, had been attended by a leveling of medieval ranks and a spreading equality of economic, political, and intellectual condition.

But equality is only half the story that Tocqueville gives us, not only in *Democracy in America* but also in his classic study of the old regime and the French Revolution. The other half of the story is, of course, centralization of power. In the same introduction he writes: "I perceive that we have destroyed those individual powers which were able, single-handed, to cope with tyranny; but it is the government alone that has inherited all the privileges of which families, guilds, and individuals have been deprived. . . ."

Centralization and equality—these are for Tocqueville the two dominant tendencies of modern Western history, with the relationship between them functional. All that has magnified equality of condition has necessarily tended to abolish or diminish the buffers to central power that are constituted by social classes, kindreds, guilds, and other groups whose virtual essence is hierarchy. As Tocqueville—and before him Burke—perceived, some degree of inequality is the very condition of the social bond. Variations among individuals, in strength, intelligence, age, aspiration, ability of whatever kind, and aptitude, will always tend toward the creation of inequality of result. Only through operation of a single, centralized structure of power that reaches all individuals in a community, that strives to obliterate all gradations of power, rank, and affluence not of this power's own making, can these variations and this inequality be moderated.

This is clearly the reason that all the great modern revolutions, with the single and mixed exception of the American, have presented the by now often described spectacle of enormous increases in governmental authority. Never mind the motivational value of the catchwords freedom and justice; the unfailing result of European revolutions, culminating in the communist and Nazi revolutions of this century, has been immensely greater use of political power.

Not least of the reasons for this has been, of course, the role equalitarianism has played in these revolutions. For all European revolutions have been founded upon assault against the kinds of inequality that are the lineal products of the Middle Ages. The real issue was not capitalism but the lingering remnants of feudalism, even for the revolutions in this century that have taken place in the name of socialism. But the thrust toward equalitarianism inevitably led to a disintegration of old social unities, and only the power of the state was left to fill this vacuum.

The conditions for the spread of equality as a motivating value have been very fertile during the past two or three centuries. Populations have grown hugely; local and regional boundaries have eroded away in large measure, thus exposing many inequalities which have been concealed behind these boundaries. Industrialism, with its own machine-based disciplines, has done much, as Marx realized more vividly than anyone before him, to diminish inequalities, to concentrate them, as it were, into the single inequality between capitalist and worker. The immense spread of consumer goods, their cheapness of price, has also done much to bring about a generalized equality of patterns of living, at least as measured against earlier patterns in the West. And finally, as I have noted, there has been the incessant spread of centralized power, whether in the hands of king, military, or the people, during the past two centuries, to spread further equality by virtue of this power's destructive effects upon social and economic differentiation.

In one of his excellent essays, the British political scientist Kenneth R. Minogue refers to the "suffering-situations" which modern history so abundantly reveals. These either are in fact or can be rendered into a fairly widespread, standardized kind of situation calling for sudden and heroic action, invariably political action. I think inequality will prove to be the single greatest suffering-situation of our age. As one thinks of it, one sees that feudalism and capitalism were regarded in earlier times as suffering-situations by large numbers of intellectuals concerned with political power. The word "feudal" did not come into existence until the seventeenth century, and when it did it took on almost immediate pejorative significance. By almost all of the key minds of the seventeenth and eighteenth centuries, feudalism was regarded as infamous; its localisms, decentralizations, and divisions of power were made tantamount to anarchy and evil. We would not, surely, have seen the central power of the national state increase as greatly as it did in these two centuries had there not been something large and evil, by designation at least, for the state to cope with. The *philosophes'* common liking for highly centralized political power had behind it in great part their loathing of everything "feudal."

In the nineteenth century, "capitalism" replaced feudalism as the important suffering-situation. Modern radicalism was to a great extent formed around hatred of capitalism, and while not all radicals, by any means, gravitated toward the national state as the means of redemption, we find just about all of them, save only some of the anarchists, profuse in their appreciation of revolutionary centralization of power. If any single thing identifies the modern radical mind, it is the invariably negative reaction to private enterprise, profit, and competition. And just as the national state aggrandized itself in the seventeenth and eighteenth centuries at the expense of authorities that could be labeled feudal, so has the national state in the nineteenth and twentieth centuries further aggrandized itself, in powers claimed and in bureaucracy, by virtue of the controls and restraints it has placed upon capitalist enterprise. That the controlling boards and agencies quickly become dominated by representatives of the very industries and channels of commerce they are supposed to regulate, leading to even greater exploitation of consumer and public, is a fact well attested by this time, but not one that ever enters the minds of legislators and others when some alleged suffering-situation leads to the creation of still another regulatory agency.

I am inclined to think that "capitalism" is in our time becoming as moribund, as archaic, a term as "feudalism." What is surely succeeding these is "inequality," though there are some serious observers of the present scene who believe that "technology" comes very close in this respect. There is no doubt that the powers of government have become greatly increased in very recent years on the basis of un- doubtedly well-intentioned proposals for the regulation of technology, which so many of poetic or romantic disposition have seen as suffocating to the human spirit. Even so, the evidence is clear, I think, that inequality is the great suffer- ing-situation of the late twentieth century. In its name power will increase drastically; it already has!

Something more must be said about the mind that above any other I can think of exerts profound influence upon the New Equalitarians in the present age. Rousseau is, as con- servatives and anarchists alike came to realize in the early nineteenth century, the representative of the special kind of power that is inherent in the modern, centralized national state. He is, I believe, the single most radical political mind in the West after Plato—whom Rousseau adored and re- garded as the first of his intellectual masters. Only Marx exerts the kind of effect Rousseau has today upon the radical mind.

Rousseau's influence is more than political in the ordinary sense. He is the real source of that subjectivism of political and social consciousness that has been growing steadily ever since the appearance of his major writings in the late eighteenth century. Not only in radical ideology, but in large sectors of education, psychology, literature, philosophy, and the social sciences, his distinctive blend of worship of self and of power conceived as community is all too apparent.

What gives Rousseau currency in so many areas of thought on man and the state is his extraordinary combination of emphasis upon the ego and power—the power that lies in the General Will. This is the will of the people, but only of a people that has been cleansed, so to speak, of all the corruptions and prejudices that lie in the historic social order. Equality is the very essence of Rousseau's political community; but it is the kind of equality that exists when every form of association and every social value that could possibly rival the General Will have been exterminated. Equality of result is the great and overarching aim of Rousseau's political writings. Freedom too, if we like; but, as nearly all commentators have stressed, Rousseau's is a very special kind of freedom that is virtually indistinguishable from the equalitarian political community. No other knew better than Rousseau the intensity of political power that would be required to create equality in the political order. It is in this light that one of the New Equalitarians, Christopher Jencks, writes in our day:

> If we want substantial redistribution we will not only have to politicize the question of income equality but alter people's basic assumptions about the extent to which they are responsible for their neighbors and their neighbors for them . . . . As long as egalitarians assume that public policy cannot contribute to economic equality directly but must proceed by ingenious manipulations of marginal institutions like the schools, progress will be glacial. If we want to move beyond this tradition, we will have to establish political control over the economic institutions that shape our society.

In actuality, however, such control will almost certainly have to go beyond strictly economic institutions and values, which are the express concerns of most proposals today for equality of condition. For, as Rousseau realized so prophetically, once equality has been made the dominant value of a social order, it must, and will, reach toward cultural, social, educational, even psychological spheres of human life, for it is in these that the real consequences of economic inequality are most deeply felt. We have Rousseau's *Confessions* as witness of the fact that, in his own life, it was less the occasional poverty he experienced that gnawed at him than the subtler gradations of prestige, influence, and power he encountered in the Paris of the Sorbonne, in the glittering salons where brilliance of conversation was so much prized, and among the *philosophes,* whose intellectual superior Rousseau was in most respects but whose general love of the *haute monde* he found repugnant.

Moreover, Rousseau realized, and stated eloquently in his *Discourse on the Arts and Sciences,* that the springs of egoism, ambition, and desire for social eminence lie deep in human nature as it has been formed over the long period of man's history following the original instituting of private property and the rise of the agricultural and mechanical arts. All of man's ills, his torments and subjections to oppression, originated, Rousseau tells us in the second *Discourse,* with inequality, when with private property there appeared "social interdependences" which made inequality of status fixed and inevitable. Given the length of mankind's history since the early "fatal departure" from natural equality, it is evident that corrective measures must be encompassing and powerful. Men may want equality, once its virtue is made evident to them, but more than simple popular desire by majorities is required to root equality securely in human nature. Hence Rousseau's call, in the *Social Contract,* for a Legislator, as Rousseau calls him, who will not hesitate to remake human nature itself in the pursuit of equality:

> He who dares to undertake the making of a people's institutions ought to feel himself capable, so to speak, of changing human nature, of transforming each individual who is by himself a complete and solitary whole, into part of a greater whole from which he in a manner receives his life and being. . . . He must, in a word, take away from man his own resources and give him instead new ones alien to him, and incapable of being made use of without the help of other men.

Elsewhere Rousseau tells us with the candor that is so typical of his political writings that "if it is good to know how to deal with men as they are, it is much better to make them what there is need that they should be. The most absolute authority is that which penetrates into a man's inmost being, and concerns itself no less with his will than with his actions."

How well Rousseau knew! He records in his *Confessions* that from an early age he had become aware of the fact that men are entirely what their form of government makes them. Hence there must be no reluctance in the uses of power, the power, especially, that lies at the core of the absolute, total, and unremitting General Will. If we would have virtue, Rousseau wrote electrically in his *Discourse on Political Economy,* we must be willing to *establish* it!

Western society is rarely lacking in those who, in one way or other, religious or political usually, are obsessed by the mission of establishing virtue. Most clearly, the West is not lacking now in such individuals. And in our time, by a rising number of persons, chiefly intellectuals and politicians, virtue is defined solely and exclusively as equality; again, let it be emphasized, equality of condition or result.

And there is no want either of ingenuity or cleverness in demonstrating that virtue is equality—nothing less, nothing more. Undoubtedly the most highly praised work in philosophy of the past decade or two is John Rawls' *Theory of Justice*. Although there is excellent reason to believe that the almost ecstatic response to it will shortly abate among professional philosophers, it is certain that this book will be for a long time to come the central work in moral philosophy for the clerisy of power. It is tailor-made for the needs of those to whom equalitarianism and central power are but two sides of the same coin.

Justice, we discover, is for Rawls "fairness," which is surely a reasonable definition. What is a good deal less reasonable is the author's further conclusion that justice and fairness are—equality! And for John Rawls, as for all others in the cult of equality, equality has little to do with historic equality before the law. Through two dubious rhetorical techniques, which he labels "the original position" and "the veil of ignorance," Rawls seeks to demonstrate that all men of reason and good will, when liberated from the misconceptions and prejudices of the social order they live in, will easily reach the conclusion that society is built on the rock of equality; that is, equality of "social primary goods," the economic, cultural, political, and even psychological attributes that are so variously distributed in society as the result of equality of opportunity and equality before the law. Social primary goods, which may be stretched to include even "bases of self-respect," are to be made equal, or at least equitable, through what he calls "the difference principle."

This principle means simply that there shall be no in-equalities of "social primary goods" in society unless it can be demonstrated that such inequalities are in the interest of the less advantaged. There must be no differences among individuals in social position, the fruits of knowledge, talent, and enterprise, as well as in income and property, except insofar as superior possession among some can be demon-strated to redound to the welfare of others. This, succinctly stated, is Rawls' difference principle.

The mind boggles at the thought of the political apparatus necessary to give expression to and to enforce such a principle. Rawls seems not to have heard of political bureaucracy, but even if he had, he would no doubt take refuge in his stated principle that the "liberty" of each indi-vidual is primary, not to be violated by interests of utility or expediency. Liberty, however, turns out to be for Rawls very much what it is for Rousseau: mere equal shares of something *called* liberty, which bears little relation to the autonomies and immunities that are the true hallmarks of liberty. Equality is the dominant value in Rawls.

The New Equalitarians of our day seem to detest the central elements of the social bond quite as much as Rousseau did. I refer to the whole tissue of interdependences —interactions, conflicts, coercions, conformities, protec-tions, and disciplines—which are the molecules of social order. It is with good reason that our equalitarians detest such interdependences, for, in whatever degree or form, inequality is the essence of the social bond. The vast range of temperaments, minds, motivations, strengths, and desires that exists in any population is nothing if not the stuff of hierarchy. When associations are formed for whatever purpose, cooperation and mutual aid included, inequality is immediately apparent. Even the New Equalitarians would presumably balk at the thought of holding all musical talents to the same limits; and no doubt they would feel the same way with respect to academic and intellectual talents. It is the "economic" realm that they have in mind. But, as I have said, it is cultural, psychological, and social inequality that galls once equality is declared the ascendant ideal. Rousseau detested the arts and sciences, just as he did all social interdependences, seeing correctly that in these areas inequality is impossible to contain.

Inevitably there is opposition to kinship. The family, final enclave of political and economic privacy, is correctly perceived by the New Equalitarians as the most powerful barrier to the redistribution of goods and statuses which is called for in their strategy. In this they are also in harmony with Rousseau, who did not hesitate, in the final pages of the *Discourse on Political Economy,* to recommend virtual abolition of the family, chiefly as a means of separating the children from what Rousseau described as the "prejudices" of the fathers. There were a number of radical equalitarian movements in the late eighteenth and early nineteenth centuries that frankly proposed that children be separated from their families at a very early age and brought up in state-operated schools. Only thus, it was believed, could the family's inherently destructive effect upon the ideal of the accomplishment of mass equality be offset.

There is much less awareness of this vital necessity among present-day New Equalitarians, or, if there is in fact awareness, much less courage and forthrightness in recommending abolition of the family. It is much easier to concentrate upon private property as the target, not giving emphasis to the well-attested fact that wherever there is private property there will be a strong family system. After all, the origins of private property lie in clan and kindred; and even after the conjugal family, the household, became the chief element of kinship, its relationship to property remained very close. As Joseph Schumpeter noted in his *Capitalism, Socialism, and Democracy,* it was not the isolated individual, so dear as an abstract concept to the classical economists, but the household that was the main engine of modern capitalist development. It is not economic man, but quite literally, the head of the household—working for the present and future of the members of his family, and hence saving and investing, in however small degree—who is the central figure in the capitalist drama, as in all earlier forms of economy.

Unquestionably it is this fact that will offer the New Equalitarians their greatest single challenge. For, although equality is a prestige-laden word in contemporary Western society, it is largely the more traditional types of equality—in law and economic opportunity—which are the referents. Individuals at all levels may at times burn with the sense of injustice where the multiple rewards of social life are involved—social and cultural as well as economic—but it is far from certain that a mandatory redistribution would only issue in choice, would wish for a generalized policy of equality, whether of income or anything else. The realization is too strong that, given the immense range of aptitudes, desires, aspirations, strengths, and motivations in any population, any genuine effort to offset this range by a national policy of mandatory redistribution would only issue in novel forms of inequality: those which result when differently endowed human beings are obliged to submit to a single measure of result. Ordinary majority will in democracy, then, can hardly be counted upon, certainly at the present time, to support and give acquiescence to the kind of equality that is dreamed of by those members of the clerisy of power who have result and condition, not law, in their minds.

All of this is true, but we are living in strange and frightening times. Whereas majority will, merely polled by Roper or Gallup, might very well even today register strong opposition to the New Equality, the blunt fact is that an operating and motivated majority will shows clear signs of becoming one of the casualties of the decline of the political habit of mind, of the revolt against politics in any and all of its forms.

The politics of virtue, from Plato to Bentham, has rarely if ever corresponded with emphasis on majority will any more than it has with emphasis on historic individual rights and immunities before the law. Plato thought majority will in the good state as absurd as in matters of mathematical truth. Rousseau made a careful and absolutely vital distinction between majority will as such, which he termed the mere "will of all," and the General Will, which might or might not, Rousseau candidly states, be congruent with what a simple majority might wish at any given time. It is interesting to note that in *Theory of Justice,* while not actually abrogating majority will in a democracy, John Rawls has given it a somewhat lower status among the crucial verities than certain other elements of his just society.

I have perhaps paid too much attention to the writings of the New Equalitarians, for, ascendant though they assuredly are at the present time in the intellectual world, and fertile though they will undoubtedly prove to be in the preparing of political manifestos and platforms, there is no more reason to believe they will be crucially responsible for egalitarian tendencies in the future than their intellectual forerunners—socialists, social democrats, progressives—have been in the past.

If we plot the development of social equality in Western society over the past few centuries, we find that it follows almost perfectly the development of centralization and bureaucratization in the political sphere. Even more strikingly, the development of equality follows the trajectory of war. It is in periods of national, mass warfare that we observe the greatest advances of the egalitarian ethic in many areas. The point is that even if no egalitarian ethic existed, if there were not the vein of equality in the modern Western mind that there so plainly is, the mere existence of political and military centralization in the modern world would have brought about pretty much the same patterns of equality we see around us.

My own estimate is that a good seventy-five percent of all the national programs that have been instituted in Western countries during the past two centuries to equalize income, property, education, working conditions, and other aspects of life have been in the first instance adjuncts of the war state and of the war economy. Equality is far from least among the qualities that go with social and economic programs of nationalization during times of war.

"Every central power which follows its natural tendencies," wrote Tocqueville, "courts and encourages the principle of equality; for equality singularly facilitates, extends, and secures the influence of a central power." And it was Thomas Jefferson who observed that the state with power to do things *for* people has the power to do things *to* them.

I do not say that the ethic of equality necessarily leads to the demand for absolute power. Philosophers, like the rest of us, are entitled to be taken at their word, and, however naive the New Equalitarians may be in their common indifference to problems of political power, we cannot justly accuse them of wishing to bring about either military socialism or political absolutism. Moreover, there are ages in history when diffuseness of power, fragmentation, and the concomitant forms of local oppression and inequality are so great that even the most ardent libertarian could properly wish for an increase in central political power and the leveling of ranks in society that goes with it. The West has seen such ages. Nor will we soon forget the morally repugnant inequality of legal right imposed upon the blacks right down to very recent times. I do not see how anyone who prizes a free and creative culture could oppose the extension of the forms of equality which have been, over and over, the crucial circumstances within which long-oppressed minorities have broken free and given their talents to the arts, the sciences, politics, and other areas of leadership.

But the evidence is clear enough that we are looking well beyond legal equality in many circles today, and a very different kind of equality is becoming ever more widely prized. With it, or with such achievements of this kind of equality as have been thus far a part of the social order, goes a degree of political power and of political intrusion into once autonomous areas that a rising number of persons will, I am convinced, find odious. Ongoing experience with certain programs of equalitarianism—affirmative action, mandatory busing to achieve ethnic quotas, open admissions, among others—certainly suggests this. All other things being equal, it is more likely that popular opposition to such programs would increase and even become successful.

Alas, all other things are not equal. For the equalitarianism of such programs is only one facet of a much larger reality: the existence of a bureaucratized welfare state that prizes uniformity above all other things and that, as a large number of recent instances suggest, will stop at nothing to enforce this uniformity. Uniformity is prized by all bureaucracies, political or other, simply because it saves bureaucrats from the always agonizing responsibility of dealing with the individuality and the complexity of real life.

There is a measure of equality without which any community must suffer. And although I would not rank equality among the very highest of the West's moral values—not as high, assuredly, as liberty and justice—its ethic is no mean one. The tragedy in our time is that what is good in the ethic of equality is fast becoming swamped by forces—of power above all—which aim not, really, at equality in any civilized sense but at uniformity, leveling, and a general mechanization of life.

There is, obviously, inevitable conflict with liberty. I mean the kind of liberty that goes with differentiation, variety, individuality, and a very wide spectrum of social and psychological traits; the kind of liberty that is involved in all creative work, whether in the arts and sciences or in the economic sphere. It is nonsense to say that the pupil in public school today has the same freedom to learn that was once present before uniform programs took command in the country as the result of the ever-greater penetration of the school system by the federal government and its central bureaus of education. Given these conditions and also the constantly increasing emphasis upon equal grading, or upon no grading at all, with differences between the bright and dull wiped out symbolically, how could there possibly be the freedom to learn that is always stimulated by visible incentive?

There is, to be sure, another kind of freedom that does not suffer from the spread of equalitarianism: the kind best seen in totalitarian societies; the kind that is divisible into equal shares irrespective of the talents and motivations of those holding these shares. The Russian and Chinese governments are scrupulous in their attention to this kind of mass freedom, for there is nothing to worry about in the way of consequences. What such governments do have to worry about is the kind of freedom that is simply impossible to divide equally among a people: the freedom to be creative. The problem of the intellectual, the artist, and the scientist in contemporary Russia is evidence enough of the strain presented to a social order by this kind of freedom, which is inherently incompatible with any kind of equality except equality before the law and of opportunity.

It is extremely unlikely that political power could be as encompassing of life, as penetrating of privacy, were it not for certain changes in the nature of power. If I were to seize upon a single phrase for these changes, it would be "the softening of power." The power of the state is no less—indeed it is far greater—than it was even during the divine-right monarchies. But where the exercise of power over individual life was then nakedly coercive, commonly brutal in infliction, and above all direct and personal, the same exercise of governmental power is today blander, more indirect, engaged in the immobilization of the human mind when possible rather than in the infliction of corporal punishments. A great deal that is commonly ascribed to popular welfare, to humanitarianism, even to an increase in individual freedom, might better be ascribed to the softening of power, through organization, technology, social work, psychiatry, equalitarianism, and various other techniques and values whereby the impact of government upon human life has been lessened in the experiencing, all the time that political control of human life has vastly increased.

We have been recently made aware of profound changes in the nature of power in Soviet Russia. Rare today are the brutality, torture, and terror that were so manifest in the age of Stalin. Rare too are the public trials before state tribunals that in the 1930s were means not only of exterminating declared enemies of the state but of terrorizing the public at large. I think it is exceedingly unlikely that we shall see again in the world the kind of direct, naked use of force on large numbers of persons that the governments of Stalin and Hitler brought to such heights. Very probably Stalinist and Nazi concentration camps, torture chambers, and death camps represent a watershed in the history of the use of power by government over individual lives. For it is notable that even the Nazi government felt it necessary so to organize the torture and destruction of Jews and others as to conceal so far as was possible these enormities from the German public. To a lesser extent, that was true of Stalin's Russia as well. Once, in almost all nations of the world, such torture and execution, far from being in any degree concealed, would have been flaunted before the public. I am inclined to think that the advances of humanitarianism during the past century or two, together with advances in technology which have made possible a liberation, through drugs and machinery, from the incidence of pain our ancestors knew, have combined to give people a very different attitude toward the visible infliction of cruelty and brutality.

"Not many people," writes Sir Dennis Gabor in *The Mature Society,* "could stand the sight of a tumbril moving slowly through the streets, with the delinquent tied to a stake, and the executioner with the brazier next to him digging the red hot poker into the screaming wretch." Indeed they could not; not today. Yet a surprisingly short time separates us from ancestors who not only could stand it, but who solemnly regarded such spectacles, along with public hangings and floggings, as indispensable to the maintenance of order. We do not have to go very far back in Western history to find otherwise humane and gentle minds in perfect composure at the sight of floggings, drawings and quarterings, and flayings which it is unlikely that more than a tiny handful of the pathological could today bear the knowledge —much less the sight—of as public policy.

In substantial part, as Sir Dennis observes, the changed attitude toward the more brutal uses of power by government has come from the changed place of physical pain in almost all human lives. It is difficult, in our age of pain preventives and pain-liberators, to realize the extent to which physical pain was once commonplace. It is rather horrifying today to read of the agony that was once the unavoidable accompaniment of a long list of diseases, not to mention injuries and disabilities of one kind or other. And, as Sir Dennis well notes, in a society in which physical pain is the common lot, there is not likely to be the same reaction to, the same perception of, pain deliberately inflicted upon individuals either for amusement's sake or for the protection of society. A social order that could, in its lower classes, find diversion in the frequent spectacle of bloody, knockdown, eye-gouging, nose- or ear-mutilating fights—among women as well as men, we read of the English eighteenth century— would not be likely to react as we do to the torturing, flogging, and hanging of miscreants.

That kind of society has almost wholly disappeared in our time, and with it the shape of punishment and of power. But such transformation of police or governmental power in no way means that such power has lessened. It can mean actual increase, especially if power is disguised as a form of therapy. The relative absence of Stalinist torture and mass murder in Russia does not mean that a power vacuum now exists. No doubt the memory in the older generation of Stalinist terror is sufficient to restrain dissident impulses, but, as we have recently been made aware, the art and technology of therapy, so-called, have become in present-day Russia the commonest guise of power over the unruly or dangerously creative. Techniques lumped in the public mind under the label "brainwashing" have manifestly assumed far greater use in the totalitarian countries than would once have been thought either desirable or necessary by their rulers.

It is not as though such uses of power had not been foreseen—by Huxley, or Orwell, or before both by Samuel Butler in *Erewhon,* a utopia in which the delinquent and criminal were put in hospitals. It is a commentary on the time we ourselves live in that we are less likely to find Erewhon as humanitarian as our Victorian ancestors might have, for we are too well aware of the employment today of hospitals and other contexts of therapy for the express purposes of punishment and overt behavior control.

It would be comforting if power-as-therapy were confined to the totalitarian societies, but it is not. As I write, there has just been released a 651-page report by Senator Sam Ervin's subcommittee on constitutional rights which describes in great detail the number and variety of projects, mostly sponsored by the Department of Health, Education, and Welfare, whose essence is the control of behavior through drugs and related means. Alcoholics, shoplifters, child molesters, and homosexuals are, the report states, but a few of those on whom therapy is being used, often in clear violation of constitutional rights, as a means of alteration of mind and behavior. "There is a real question," Senator Ervin is quoted as saying in connection with release of the report, "whether the government should be involved at all in programs that potentially pose substantial threats to our basic freedoms."

Dr. Thomas Szasz has been writing eloquently for years now on the extent to which legal pleas of insanity and mental inadequacy, with consequent commitment of individuals to asylums rather than jails, have intruded into the once sacrosanct area of individual ethical responsibility. Our villains have vanished along with our heroes, and each disappearance is related to a spreading state of mind that sees less and less responsibility devolving upon the individual for his acts. The same overall set of mind that snatches the chronic rapist or the mass murderer from the ranks of villainy and places him among the mentally disturbed is likely to remove the occasional great man or woman from the ranks of heroism and subject this individual instead to relentless examination of private life and to public exposure. Not a Washington or a Lincoln, surely, would have been able to maintain the image of greatness in circumstances such as those the media, the social sciences, governmental investigative agencies and committees have created.

The greatest power, as major political theorists from Plato to Rousseau have declared, is that which shapes not merely individual conduct but also the mind behind that conduct. Power that can, through technological or other means, penetrate the recesses of culture, of the smaller unions of social life, and then of the mind itself, is manifestly more dangerous to human freedom than the kind of power that, for all its physical brutality, reaches only the body. We shrink today from the infliction of physical pain upon our contemporaries—except, that is, in time of war, and even then we prefer the kind that is dealt out at thirty-thousand feet in bombs to the kind revealed at My Lai—but we do not shrink from projects in government, in the social and behavioral sciences, and in the media by which mind and spirit are invaded and thus affected by power, in how-ever soft a form.

Privacy is an excellent litmus test, it woud seem, for the actual state of freedom in a culture. I do not think many people would argue seriously that the extent of individual privacy today is even close to what it was a few decades ago. The exposure that Governor Rockefeller was required to make of economic, family, and personal life—and, I think, much more could have been required without serious outcry—during the consideration that followed his nomina-tion to the Vice Presidency would have once been utterly inconceivable. So gross a violation of privacy would surely have converted our political heroes of the past, from Wash-ington to FDR, into beings of somewhat less than heroic mold. I am aware that a strong case can be made for the propriety and safety (to public weal) of detailed penetrations of economic and political privacy. But we shall, I think, find that an equally strong case will shortly be made in justification of identical invasions of sexual and other equally intimate recesses of privacy.

Large-scale government, with its passion for equalitarian uniformity, has prepared our minds for uses of power, for invasions of individual privacy, and for the whole bureaucratization of spirit that Max Weber so prophetically identified as the disease of modernity. We do indeed see, and take a measure of comfort in, certain liberties of an individual kind in the realms of the theater, publishing, and public speech that our ancestors did not know. Rights to obscenity, pornography, public display of body and mind, and others of related character exist that were once absent. If these are in some way connected with the larger structure of freedom, especially political freedom, and might even be reckoned forces in the long run toward ending the kinds of invasion of privacy that governmental, military, and paramilitary agencies now represent, we can perhaps overlook the crudities and vulgarities that such rights so plainly carry with them.

It is well to be reminded, though, that more often than not in history, license has been the prelude to exercises of extreme political coercion, which shortly reach all areas of a culture. That is one observation that history makes possible. Another and related one is that very commonly in ages when civil rights of one kind are in evidence—those pertaining to freedom of speech and thought in, say, theater, press, and forum, with obscenity and libel laws correspondingly loosened—very real constrictions of individual liberty take place in other, more vital, areas: political organization, voluntary association, property, and the right to hold jobs, for example.

I believe it was Napoleon who first sensed the ease with which, in modern society, the illusion of freedom can be created by strategic relaxation of regulations and law on individual thought, provided it is *only* individual, while all the time *fundamental economic and political liberties* are being circumscribed. The barriers to the kind of power Napoleon wielded as emperor are not *individual* rights so much as the kinds of rights associated with autonomy of local community, voluntary association, political party. These are the real measure of the degree to which central political power is limited in a society. Neither centralization nor bureaucratized collectivism can thrive as long as there is a substantial body of local authorities to check them. But on the other hand, there is no reason why a considerable degree of individual freedom cannot exist with respect to such matters as sexual conduct, speech, writing, and religious belief without serious impact upon the structure of political power. There are, after all, certain freedoms that are like circuses. Their very existence, so long as they are individual and enjoyed chiefly individually as by spectators, diverts men's minds from the loss of other, more fundamental, social and economic and political rights.

A century ago, the liberties that now exist routinely on stage and screen, on printed page and canvas, would have been unthinkable in America—and elsewhere in the West, for that matter, save in the most clandestine and limited of settings. But so would the limitations upon economic, professional, educational, and local liberties, to which we have by now become accustomed, have seemed equally unthinkable a half century ago. We enjoy the feeling of great freedom, of protection of our civil liberties, when we attend the theater, watch television, buy paperbacks. But all the while we find ourselves living in circumstances of a spread of military, police, and bureaucratic power that cannot help but have, that manifestly does have, profoundly erosive effect upon those economic, local, and associative liberties that are by far the most vital to any free society. From the point of view of any contemporary strategist or tactician of political power, indulgence in the one kind of liberties must seem a very requisite to diminution of the other kind. We know it seemed that way to the Caesars and Napoleons of history. Such indulgence is but one more way of softening the impact of political power and of creating the illusion of individual freedom in a society grown steadily more centralized, collectivized, and destructive of the diversity of allegiance, the autonomy of enterprise in all spheres, and the spirit of spontaneous association that any genuinely free civilization requires.

Politization and
Political Solutions

Jacques Ellul

Jacques Ellul was born in Bordeaux, France, in 1912. He studied at the University of Bordeaux and the University of Paris, and holds the degree of Doctor of Laws. Since 1946, he has been associated with the University of Bordeaux as professor of the history of law and of social history. Among his books are The Technological Society, Propaganda, The Political Illusion, A Critique of the New Commonplaces, *and* The Ethics of Freedom.

It is a stereotype in our day to say that everything is political. We were reminded only recently that politization
is "denounced by both official moralists and the good
people."[1] But what is politization? We have been given two
of its dimensions: Politization is represented by the importance and growing frequency of ideological debates; and it
is manifested by the tendency to treat all social problems in
the world according to patterns and procedures found in
the political world.

Though these two characteristics are indeed part of the
phenomenon of politization, they are much too limited and
specific to provide a full description. It is quite true that one
of the aspects of politization in our society is the volume of
ideological debate, doctrinal conflict, systematic argumen-
tation along certain lines. But politization also exists in
countries where ideological debates do not occupy an important place; what is more, we must ask *why* these ideological debates have increased and what attitude people assume

---

[1] François Bourricaud, *Esquisse d'une théorie de l'autorité* (Paris: Plon,
1961), p. 326.

with regard to political matters, and not just to one or another doctrine. On the other hand, it is also true that there is a tendency to treat all social problems within the procedural framework of politics, that is, with debates, conferences, and so on. But this is an extremely narrow and limited view of politization, for it must be stated first that *all* problems *have,* in our time, become political. It is not just a question of accepted political procedures being applied to questions that at first glance do not seem political. The point is that these questions *are* by now in the political realm, and political procedures are applied to them because they have become part and parcel of political affairs.[2]

The essential element that must be taken into consideration if we want to understand the *total* phenomenon of politization is a fact that is, if not the cause at least the moving force of this phenomenon. The fact is the growth of the state itself. Governmental action is applied to a constantly growing number of realms. The means through which the state can act are constantly growing. Its personnel and its functions are constantly growing. Its responsibilities are growing. All this goes hand in hand with inevitable centralization and with the total organization of society in the hands of the state.

The nation-state is the most important reality in our day. It is much more fundamental in our world than economic reality. Nowadays the state directs the economy. To be sure, the state must take economic factors into account. The economy is not an inert object in the hands of an arbitrary

---

[2] We have not spoken here of the country's high standard of living that has permitted the development of a true democracy, the establishment of a stable government, and the development of sociopolitical techniques.

and capricious ruler. But the ruler versed in economic techniques determines the economy much more than the economy determines the state. The state is not just a super-structure. Marxist analysis was valid only in the nineteenth century, when the emergence of uncontrolled, explosive economic power relegated a weak, liberal, and unclearly delineated state to the shadows and subjugated it. But today the major social phenomenon is the state, becoming ever more extended, ever more assured, and everywhere standing in the limelight. Of course, Lenin knew well that every revolution must be political, but in his last letter (his "Testament") he admitted that the emergence, evolution, and persistence of the Soviet state was for him a surprising and disturbing phenomenon. It was not as a result of a crisis, accident, or a disagreeable necessity in the pursuit of the highest objectives that the Soviet state has never ceased becoming stronger, despite its illusory reduction in power since the days of Khrushchev. Only the believers can still accept the dogma of the state's "withering away"; it seems clear today that the Soviet state's concern with the administration of all things by no means signifies its decline but rather its having become absolute. This development could take place only as a result of man's need to conform, which is the aim of all propaganda. In this confirmation of its power, the Soviet state is not fulfilling a special destiny. Soviet society is not evolving according to special laws, and the transition to socialism has not modified general socio-political trends. What we see in Soviet society is the general development of the state in our world, its growth and structure. To be sure, we are aware of all the differences that may exist between the Soviet state and the American state, the British state, or the French state. There are juridical and constitutional differences, differences of practice and intention. They exist, but are of little consequence compared with the similarities, and particularly with the general trend. There are more differences between the American state of 1910 and that of 1960 (despite the constitutional sameness) than between the latter and the Soviet state (despite the constitutional differences).

The idea that the state has become a phenomenon in itself—the most important in our society—is still expressed by certain Marxists in the well-known analysis of the emergence of a third class (the bureaucracy, the great cadres, the major technicians)—the class of those constituting the real political power. The fact that this political power eventually produced its own class is probably the most telling sign of society's takeover by the state.[3] And in our days the individual's seizure by the political powers is much graver and more decisive than economic alienation. The substitution of political slavery for economic slavery is the current fraudulent exchange.

At present the greatest problem is the citizen in the clutches of political power. In one sense we can feel reassured, for here we return to well-known problems always debated by political men and philosophers: the relation of man to state power? Let us call upon Plato and Montesquieu for assistance. The danger of the individual being absorbed by the state? Let us appeal to Hobbes and Rousseau. But I want to stress that aside from the customary reflections on the nature of power (to which insufficient attention is being paid in our day), the uniqueness of our situation must be

---

[3] Milovan Djilas, *The New Class* (New York: Frederick A. Praeger, 1957).

taken into account. The given facts of the problem have changed and past political philosophy can be of little help. It seems to me that there is an entire, so far little explored, *intermediary* zone between the zone studied by political scientists, who often remain at the surface of the events, and the zone of pure political thought—I could almost say political metaphysics—that has a certain permanence. I shall try to keep myself in the zone between the two.

The other element (the growth of the state is the first) that conditions and determines the politization of society is the growth of the individual's participation in political life. It is a doctrinal offshoot of democracy—of various arrangements in different republican states, of demographic growth that brings the masses closer to the seat of power, of speedier communications, development in education, and, finally, of the fact that the state's decisions increasingly concern everybody, and that the state does not feel assured of its legitimacy except by the expressed support of the people. These are the reasons for and symptoms of this growing participation.[4]

All this forms a solid body of evidence. But one neglected fact must be stressed. It is accepted that since the eighteenth century the individual's participation in political affairs has increased. But while this is generally admitted (before the eighteenth century there was little such participation in the West), the corollary is generally omitted: except on rare occasions, political affairs in and by themselves, and in the eyes of man, formerly had little importance. In view of the fact that *we* judge everything in relation to political affairs, this seems unbelievable. How can we admit that in those

---

[4] Jacques Ellul, *Propaganda* (New York: Alfred A. Knopf, 1964), ch. iv.

past centuries political affairs were not a subject of interest, of passion—that lack of public participation was much less the result of the autocratic character of the prevailing regimes than of great indifference on the part of the public itself? Nevertheless, it seems that for centuries political affairs, except for rare moments, produced little activity, were the care of specialists in a specialized domain, or a princes' game that affected a very limited number of individuals. True political revolutions were palace revolutions, and when they took place the masses were rarely more than extras or stage decorations. However that may be, even if this claim does not ring quite true, active participation in political affairs by the masses is a new phenomenon.

To think of everything as political, to conceal everything by using this word (with intellectuals taking the cue from Plato and several others), to place everything in the hands of the state, to appeal to the state in all circumstances, to subordinate the problems of the individual to those of the group, to believe that political affairs are on everybody's level and that everybody is qualified to deal with them— these factors characterize the politization of modern man and, as such, comprise a myth. The myth then reveals itself in beliefs and, as a result, easily elicits almost religious fervor. We cannot conceive of society except as directed by a central omnipresent and omnipotent state. What used to be a utopian view of society, with the state playing the role of the brain, not only has been ideologically accepted in the present time but also has been profoundly integrated into the depths of our consciousness. To act in a contrary fashion would place us in radical disagreement with the entire trend of our society, a punishment we cannot possibly accept. We

can no longer even conceive of a society in which the political function (on the part of the governmental authority)
would be limited by external means: we have arrived at the
monistic idea of power that stops power. We can no longer
conceive of a society with autonomous "in-between" groups
or diverging activities. The primary role of political affairs
is one of the common sociological presuppositions shared
by all and growing in all countries.

We consider it obvious that everything must be unre-
servedly subjected to the power of the state; it would seem
extraordinary to us if any activity should escape it. The
expansion of the state's encroachment upon all affairs is
exactly paralleled by our conviction that things *must* be that
way. Any attempt on the part of any enterprise, university,
or charitable enterprise to remain independent of the state
seems anachronistic to us. The state directly incarnates the
common weal. The state is the great ordainer, the great
organizer, the center upon which all voices of all people
converge and from which all reasonable, balanced, impartial—i.e., just—solutions emerge. If by chance we find
this not so, we are profoundly scandalized, so filled are we
with this image of the state's perfection. In our current consciousness no other center of decision in our social body can
exist. To repeat: it is not just the fact of the state being at
the center of our lives that is crucial, but our spontaneous
and personal acceptance of it as such. We believe that for
the world to be in good order, the state must have all the
powers.

Conversely, we find a rather curious attitude among
certain social psychologists who regard every phenomenon
of authority, at whatever level, in whatever groups, or in
whatever way it manifests itself, as never anything but an

accident whose paradigm is the state. If a leader emerges in a group, or if a father exercises his authority in the family, or if a technician imposes himself upon a corporation, the phenomenon of authority is taken out of its proper context and traced back conceptually to approximate that of the state, so that *all* instances of authority are microcosms of central authority.

The place we accord in our hearts to the state and political activity leads us to an interpretation of history which we regard primarily as political history. For a long time only events concerning empires and nations, only wars and conquests, only political revolutions were taken into account. Undoubtedly that conception of history is obsolete: it has been replaced by the importance attributed to political and administrative structures. A society has no reality for us except in its political institutions, and those institutions take precedence over all others (despite the importance assumed by economic and social history). Above all, we cannot escape the strange view that history is ultimately a function of the state. Only where the state is, is history worth the name. The Merovingian times are so dark only because the state was inconsequential. The "Middle Ages" are merely an intermediary age, a period without name, only because they unfolded between two periods when the state was glorious: the Roman and the Monarchistic. Between the two there was this regrettable interlude in which the historian must look at society as unformed because it was not directed from a summit, animated by a single will, or centrally organized. Fortunately the kings restored the state with iron hand. France again became a property of value and the superiority of that restoration was contrasted to the disorderly dissolution of the Holy Roman Empire. To

be sure, because we are democrats, we are against Louis
XIV's monarchic authoritarianism. But he retains our secret
affection because he was The State.

And we are profoundly irritated with de Gaulle because
he promised—but failed to produce—the centralized, impartial, all-powerful state, so powerful that it would have
only to show its power without exercising it: the unchallenge-
able and sure state that would have given us pride and
peace of mind. How many times have we read and heard of
efforts that would finally give the state all the needed authority! We are poor, lost children who seem no longer to
remember what the means and the price of that would be!
This aspiration, this unconscious assigning of the supreme
role to the state leads us immediately to the consideration
that everything is now its business. The question returns
again and again, like some evidence that it would be absurd
to protest: "But after all, what is there that is *not* political?"

To be sure, if we begin by conceiving society as a whole
made up of dead pieces without autonomy, receiving an
active place only in a coherent system, and obtaining life
only from the supreme impetus of political power, then we
must accept the suggested answer as evident. And it *is*
evident for us contemporaries. But one should be aware of
the fact that it is based on a prejudice, on adherence to a
preconception. What we see here is the result of the process
of politization in our selves: the penetration into our unconscious of the "truth" that an ultimately political process
rules our lives. As a result we are lead to render all questions
political. Those which are not must then be politicized
because our frame of mind dictates that ultimately everything is political. This is not only fixed in the minds of the
masses but is stated to be so—and justified—by the intellec-

tuals. Take Talcott Parsons: "Political affairs are the center of integration of all analytical elements of the social system, and not one of these particular elements."[5]

If art is not part of this, that is only because we do not notice it. To notice it more clearly one need only encourage attributing political sense or value to art—make the artist feel that his efforts are vain if he is not "engaged" or does not manufacture doves that can be plastered on all the walls. This constant confusion between political affairs and society is a new phenomenon in history. Undoubtedly there were some earlier models: the Aztec Empire, Egypt, perhaps China, and, to some extent, Rome. But there we must make two major reservations: in those days the state did not have the means to execute its intentions. The mass of the people did not spontaneously—or, one might say, ontologically— offer its faith and ideology to the state. If there was a religion sanctioned by the state, there was not, ordinarily, a *religion* of state (worship of the state). In other eras, a man could be regarded as being committed by being involved in the structure and the collective life of his society—in the arts, science, religion, etc. He is no longer considered "committed," however, unless the implications of his activity are directly political.[6] To participate in non-political activities

---

[5] Talcott Parsons, *The Social System* (Glencoe, Ill.: The Free Press, 1951), p. 126.

[6] The term "political" must be taken here in its precise and restricted sense, i.e., with relation to the state and not to just any power, or just any social activity. Max Weber's definition is both classic and excellent: "Politics is the leadership by a political body called the state, or any influence exerted in that direction." I also agree with Weber that the state can be defined sociologically only by its specific means, which is force. Obviously, force is not the state's only normal means, but it is its specific and exclusive means. The definition of politics by François Goguel and Alfred Grosser

that are nevertheless definitely related to our society is regarded as without value. A poet restricting himself to being a poet without signing petitions or manifestos would immediately be accused of retiring to his ivory tower. Nowadays we prefer Aristophanes' political pieces to Aeschylus. As the renowned and very politicized French actress Simone Signoret said: "We want to bring a message to the world."

In this general trend, values are also being politicized. As Jean Barets has said, all values have a political connotation —in fact, a political content—in our eyes. Liberty? We jump with both feet from the haziest metaphysical discussion to the concept of political regimes, and from this to a political definition of freedom, which in our eyes is negligible unless it is officially incorporated in a regime, or the fruit of a constitution, or represented by the participation of a citizen in state power. To say that freedom simply means that the individual can escape the power of the state and decide for himself on the sense of his life and his works seems in our day a simplistic, ridiculous, and adolescent reaction. Similarly, justice no longer exists as a personal virtue or as the more or less attained result of the law. When we take it seriously, justice unfortunately must be endowed with some adjective, particularly the adjective "social," i.e., it is ultimately regarded as political. It is up to the state to make justice prevail: there is only *collective* justice, and the difficult questions by legal philosophers of past centuries make no more sense to us now than does the Christian affirmation that justice is the individual's miracu-

---

is also acceptable (see *La Politique en France* [Paris: A. Colin, 1964]): "It is the whole of behavioral patterns and institutions concerning public affairs which help create power, control actions through such power, and ultimately try to replace those who exert it."

lous transformation by the grace of God. In our day values that cannot be given political content or serve some political activity are no longer taken seriously.

In fact, values no longer serve us as criteria of judgment to determine good or evil: political considerations are now the pre-eminent value, and all others must adjust to them. Politics and its offspring (nationalism, for example) have become the cornerstone of what is good or represents progress. Political concerns are thought to be inherently excellent. Man's progress in today's society consists in his participation in political affairs. How many articles and declarations have we not read on that subject! For example, women finally become human beings because they receive "political rights." To say that woman, mother of the family, exerting a profound effect on the development of her children, was the true creatress in the long run, the true force from which all politics originated, is now just reactionary talk. A person without the right (in reality magical) to place a paper ballot in a box is nothing, not even a person. To progress is to receive this power, this mythical share in a theoretical sovereignty that consists in surrendering one's decisions for the benefit of someone else who will make them in one's place. Progress is to read newspapers. The political scientist Rivet meant it seriously when he said: "A man who cannot read a newspaper [Rivet was talking about Africa] to be informed is not a man." What a strange conception of manhood. This is the political trinity: "Information—Participation—Action." That is now the order of the day and the nature of progress.

People fight for economic democracy, which is expected to give them an opportunity to express their desires on affairs that touch them most closely, and this economic democracy, concerned with working conditions, distribution channels, plan requirements, prices and tariffs—all things that are infinitely concrete—is now contrasted with the political democracy of a former time, which is today regarded as merely abstract and theoretical. But let us turn the clock back two hundred years. What did those who clamored for this political democracy have in mind? To attain direct and effective control over the police; not to pay taxes except those one had agreed upon (which then seemed like a voluntary contribution); not to go to war except when the people themselves wanted it; to be able to express one's ideas freely and publicly; for each and every person to be able to affect and form public opinion. Were these abstract matters? By no means. They were terribly precise and concrete. We know how important such things are. But, except for ideologists who only see things in their dreams and imagination, we also know that economic democracy is in the process of failing now, at the very moment when it is being built, and that the power attributed to the "toilers" in Yugoslavia, the Soviet Union, or France is only theoretical and apparent. The process by which, in the nineteenth century, political decisions became a mere abstraction is being repeated in identical form, before our eyes, in connection with economic decisions now allegedly entrusted to the individual. The same farce takes place in the economic realm, always under the pretense of giving man powers in relation to the state. But it should be understood first that in the case of the modern state, powers granted to the individual are never anything but innocuous concessions, mere powers to endorse what is good for the state—the latter being the sum of all the social good.

However, the masses, who do not actually participate in political affairs, firmly believe that they do; and, in addition, make their illusory participation their principal criterion of dignity, personality, liberty. Colonial people finally become civilized people because they join the United Nations; Africans finally attain dignity because they share political power; and, solemnly, the thinkers tell us: "They are entering into History." For those thinkers no history exists where there is no politics. Who can fail to be struck by such profound politization! To claim that the complex social organization of the Bantus or the transformation of a continent by the Manchus are not part of our history would be ridiculous. Yet it is the most profound conviction of our time that such peoples enter into history only when they begin to adapt their state structures and political life to the Western model. The reference to *political* affairs is what really counts. Now, finally, these people will "make their voices heard."

This judgment, only mildly exaggerated, has its corollary: the severe condemnation of "apolitical people." In our society anyone who keeps himself in reserve, fails to participate in elections, regards political debates and constitutional changes as superficial and without real impact on the true problems of man, who feels that the war in Algeria deeply affects him and his children, but fails to believe that declarations, motions, and votes change anything will be judged very severely by everybody. He is the true heretic of our day. And society excommunicates him as the medieval church excommunicated the sorcerer. He is regarded as a pessimist, a stupid fellow (for he fails to see the very deep and secret mores in the political game), a defeatist who bows his head to fate, a bad citizen: surely, if things go badly, it is his fault, for if he were more civic minded, the vote would turn out differently (it is not enough to have eighty percent of the voters cast their vote; no, we need 100 percent!), and democracy would be more effective. Negative judgments rain down on him; his effectiveness and his morality are judged; even his psychic health is questioned (the unpolitical man is obviously a little paranoid or schizophrenic!). Finally the ultimate condemnation of our day and age is hurled at him: he must be a reactionary.

This shows us that man in his entirety is being judged today in relation to political affairs, which are invested with ultimate value. In our judgment everything has become political and political affairs are the ultimate guidepost. Beyond them there is nothing. And political affairs can be judged only by political considerations. One may say, of course, that politics should be in the service of man or of the economy, but that does not detract from the fact that the greatness of the state, its power to organize, and man's participation in the collective *via political channels* are the ultimate value symbols and criteria of our time, substituted for the religious symbols and criteria of the past.

One must reach the same conclusions if one considers not just the presuppositions, prejudices, and unconscious motivations of modern man, but his conscious emotional attitude. As soon as this man involves himself in politics he is animated by a passion without measure. In our day political conflict has definitely become the decisive and ultimate form of conflict. It is enough to have been in contact with the fascists in 1934, the communists, or the Gaullists to understand to what extent disagreements nowadays over forms of government, or the European Defense Community, or other limited concerns are more fundamental than disagreements over the ultimate ends of man. It is celebrated as a victory of the spirit when anti-Christian materialists and fervent Christians collaborate, when bourgeois intellectuals and factory workers sit on the same committees, when fascists and Mohammedans, or Christians and Mohammedans work in fraternal harmony. But it should first be asked, what *is* this powerful cement that permits men to overcome race and class differences and eliminates the most violent metaphysical and religious differences? There is only one: politics. Compared to a similarity of views for or against a decision regarding some war, how significant can differences be on the meaning of life? It should also be asked whether this beautiful accord, celebrated with such enthusiasm, is not dearly paid for by concomitant divisions. In fact, such accords can be established only at the price of designating a common enemy—a political enemy—and the accord will be all the closer as the hatred against "the other" becomes more violent. As a result, Christians will drive Christians from the church and Mohammedans will kill Mohammedans. Political disputes today are what disputes between Christians were in the sixteenth century. But perhaps to know whether it really is Christ who saves us is ultimately much less important than the conclusion of a treaty or the choice between permanent revolution and other ways of doing things.

But do not the lives of millions depend on such political decisions? They do because our political passion creates such dependence. But this dependence need not exist. For political conflicts, political solutions, political problems, political forms are ultimate, not in themselves or by the nature of things, but by the glory we attribute to them, by the importance assigned to them by every one of us, by the frantic trembling exhibited each time the political sacrament —the flag, the chief, the slogan—comes near us. We may say that the basis for this is the factual situation of the expanding state. That is true. But this state has no powers except those recognized by its subjects. I do not say it exists by virtue of what we yield; much rather, it exists by virtue of our loyalties and our passions. But the remedy Marx considered a cure for political alienation no longer applies. It is no longer sufficient that man deny the state his confidence or reject its authority (as observed already by Father Suarez) for the state to appear clearly as an empty phantom. Nowadays the crystallization of political structures, the growth of means of actions on the part of the state, and the creation of a new political class are irreversible phenomena to the extent that they exist; in any case, one's feelings cannot change them.

Thus our passions can only reinforce political affairs, and never weaken them. Traveling along this road, we are, in order to survive without an internal split, forced to attribute great good sense to political conflicts and, proceeding in the reverse direction from what was always man's course in such matters, to jump from the expanded political sphere into metaphysics, from politicized history into metahistory that knows no miracle, no ends. Moreover, instead of the consoling presence—that experience so much desired by religious people—man now experiences faith and religious conversion thanks to his participation in politics. What was lost by the church has been found by the parties, at least those worthy of the name. Faith in attainable ends, in the improvement of the social order, in the establishment of a just and peaceful system—by political means—is a most profound, and undoubtedly new, characteristic in our society. Among the many basic definitions of man, two are joined together at this point: *homo politicus* is by his very nature *homo religiosus*. And this faith takes shape in active virtues that can only arouse the jealousy of Christians. Look how full of devotion they are, how full of the spirit of sacrifice, these passionate men who are obsessed with politics. But people never ask whether all this is worthwhile. Because these witnesses are so devoted, they invest the object of their service with their passion. In this fashion a nation becomes a cult by virtue of the millions of dead who were sarcrificed for it. It must all be true, as so many agreed (did they?) to die for it. The same goes for the state, or national independence, or the victory of a political ideology.

Those who are thus devoted do not remain without compensation or profit: here they find the communion that escaped them everywhere else. On the level of political action, or in the Resistance, or in the well-known solidarity of parliamentarians among themselves, or in communist cells or OAS groups, or in great, solemn, vibrant meetings in defense of the republic man can experience the communion that he absolutely needs but no longer finds in his family, his neighborhood, or his work—a common objective, some great popular drive in which he can participate, a camaraderie, a special vocabulary, an explanation of the world. Politics offers him these joys and symbols, these indispensable expressions of communion.

These are, it seems to me, the various aspects of politization, constituting a whole. But we still must find out whether man, once politicized, is not victim of a hoax or trapped in a *cul de sac*.

Contrary to what we have just said, some speak nowadays of modern man's *de*politization. By merely looking at the distress displayed by the political scientists and essayists who analyze this depolitization, we can measure to what extent politics have become value. If man were depolitized, what a disaster; it is as though he should cease being an artist, intelligent, or sensitive. Depolitized? An entire dimension of man would disappear. Surely, political affairs are neither a game nor a useful, only moderately important, pragmatic activity: they represent a genuine value and appear to give man control over his destiny. But, it seems to me, if it is true that depolitization is only a temporary and local phenomenon, it must be understood in any case that it can be discerned only in relation to politization. Because modern man is politicized as he presumably never was before, any retreat from political affairs becomes very noticeable and visible, and we experience it as a retrogression. But it is not only with regard to the general movement of politization that we can discern depolitization; it is also within the compass of the former that the latter takes place. Depolitization is not a phenomenon of similar magnitude: it is more limited than politization, affects only certain areas, certain forms of behavior, and certain attitudes. Politization, on the other hand, affects the whole conception of actual life and even gives depolitization a significance different than it seems to have at first glance.

In order to judge the nature of depolitization more specifically, some observations must be made: on the one hand, there really is a certain depolitization in the form of "*de*participation," "*de*ideologization," "*de*partisanization," and a certain reluctance to vote. On the other hand, there is apolitization of new groups that take the place of weakening older political groups, and a growing interest in political problems. S. M. Calvez has said it very well: "A politicized mind is not the opposite of a depoliticized mind. A politicized mind is an invaded, crushed, passively submissive mind, even where this submission provokes agitation and violence."[7]

On the other hand, we cannot assume the presence of just any depolitization. Most authors wrestling with the problem (many of whom are convinced, a priori, that there is depolitization) admit that the term covers variable realities (with the Left complaining of the growing apathy of its militant members, parties of the loss of adherents, and so on), but ultimately depolitization is seen as a decline of political participation in its older and more traditional forms, not as the refusal of all participation (Calvez). This is true even when there is some skepticism or indifference with regard to political activity (Merle), a "relativization of political affairs" (André Philip), or an "empirical political existence that is ambiguous, prudent, and a little facetious" (Georges Lavau). All this does not imply genuine depolitization, and above all does not signify a breach in the phenomenon of politization as we have described it earlier. Depolitization as discussed by most political scientists is really concerned only with actual participation of a democratic nature. Yet, for example, to put oneself in the hands of the state not by default but because of loyalty is the height of politization (Alfred Grosser); similarly, in a democracy politization in the general concept of social life is more important than participation in election meetings. There can be, simultaneously, a disinterest in politics and an overevaluation of political affairs. There can be a "*de*ideologization" of controversies by the surrender of old

---

[7] Taken from an article by S. M. Calvez in Georges Vedel (ed.), *La Dépolitisation: Mythe ou réalité* (Paris: A. Colin, 1962).

doctrines, and at the same time a "mythization" of the state and an emotionalization of its problems. In such instances depolitization is superficial and, as soon as circumstances change, a violent and massive "*re*politization" will appear on the very level of activity which seemed to have been abandoned.[8]

The point is to try to penetrate to a certain reality of political affairs within, but also outside of, the philosophy of politics, outside the "framework of a positive conception of history, that imaginary shelter to which we are led equally by the theory of the proletariat as the universal class, and by the religious idea of the 'becoming of the spirit,' " in Clement Lefort's remarkable formula.[9] Here the point is to reject at the same time the conviction that the ultimate questions are answered and the conviction that there is nothing except questions of fact. Besides, these two orientations lead to the same result, as was noted by Lefort: "Political reflection takes place within a limited horizon . . . Political science and Marxist ideology have come to be two examples of contemporary conservatism."

Politics as General Solution

One more aspect of the political illusion resides in the conviction, anchored in the heart of modern Western man, that ultimately all problems are political, and solvable

---

[8] In this connection, see David Riesman, "Criteria for Political Apathy," who thinks that visible participation in elections and public expression of political opinions can hide deep political indifference and an absence of political engagement.

[9] Clement Lefort, "La Pensée de la politique," *Lettres nouvelles* (1963).

only along political lines. Without repeating what I have already said on this belief held by modern man, or on the influence of Leninist thinking in this direction, let us just look at one example: We all feel that when a man is "bad," it is "society's fault."

Studies on criminals and other antisocial elements have no other aim but to demonstrate that "it is not *their* fault." Guilt and responsibility rest with the milieu, the social body, the parents, housing, the cinema, circumstances. With all of us. We are all murderers. Conversely, people are convinced that if society only were what it should be, there would be no criminals or other antisocial elements. And who, according to the average modern man, should reorganize society so that it would finally become what it should be? The state, always the state. In this fashion the entire problem of morality is thrown back upon the state, even by non-Marxists. Morality, like values, resides in the political realm. We want to attain justice, liberty, and even— through science and information—truth. But what is the average man's attitude toward these goals? In his mind there is no doubt but that the state can and must accomplish all this. The state must ensure social justice, guarantee truth in information, protect freedom (which leads to Tito's admirable abbreviation: the more powerful the state, the more freedom). The state as creator and protector of values —that is the business of politics.

Yet in all these domains we are facing the most tragic illusion of our day. It is certain that politics can solve administrative problems, problems concerning the material development of a city, or general problems of economic organization—which is a considerable accomplishment. But politics absolutely cannot deal with man's personal problems, such as good and evil, or the meaning of life, or the responsibilities of freedom. Of course we also know that all these things are of no importance in the eyes of most people. So be it. But then they should not be discussed, and our ears should not be continuously assailed with stories of tortures, the seizure of newspapers, democracy—for all that is significant only if good and evil, the true and the just, or the meaning of life and responsibility have personal value. Without it, the torturer and the tortured are entirely impersonal, and there is not the slightest sense in protesting, condemning, or glorifying anything. Those who discuss the use of torture presuppose that it has a personal and not just a collective meaning. But if that is the case, no solution can be found through political channels, political action, or a transformation of the state. In fact, if one disregards the mythological explanations in the post-Marxist style or the unconscious Marxist style, the enthusiasm with which everybody has reached for this convenient solution—existentialist intellectuals, reactionary businessmen, and petty bourgeois radicals—shows one common preoccupation: to escape personal responsibility in such matters. The conviction that the individual's inner conflicts, like the external realization of values, are a collective and social affair and will find their solutions in the political realm is only the mystifying aspect of every man's personal surrender with respect to his own life. Because I am incapable of doing good in my own life, I insist that the state must do it in my place, by proxy. Because I am incapable of discerning the truth, I ask the government to discern it for me; I thus free myself of an onerous task and get my truth ready-made. Because I cannot dispense justice myself, I expect a just organization to exist which I only have to join to safeguard justice.

Paul Johann Feuerbach's perfectly convincing proof of God can today be transferred to the subject that has taken God's place in modern man's conscience, i.e., the state. The motives, the processes, the mysteries that made man accept religion and expect God to accomplish what he was unable to do, lead him nowadays into politics and make him expect those things from the state. "But," it will be said, "in politics man is prompted to act for himself; he commits himself, sacrifices himself, takes his destiny into his own hands." It is easily forgotten that in religion, too, man was by no means passive; he acted a great deal, sacrificed himself even more, and engaged himself to the limit. And, looking at contemporary politics, we already have seen how little man really attains influence over his own destiny through it. In reality, he does not expect to accomplish this from politics, or from any person, but from a mysterious and superior power, invested with indefinable qualities such as sovereignty—a power which, by a sort of magic, transforms the citizen's poor efforts into something efficient, good, and absolute. As prayer will release transcendental forces, the voting ballot will move the sovereign will. But the latter assumption is no more reasonable than the former. We are all agreed that the sovereign will is not simply a sum of individual wills. This is really a religious phenomenon. Political engagement is thus comparable to a religion. Moreover, both terms have the same general tenor of "tying the individual" (*in vadiam, religare*). This becomes a true flight from oneself, from one's own destiny, one's personal responsibilities. On the one hand, we assume personal, collective, and social responsibilities; but they are never anything but vicarious and secondary, external, even if the individual completely submerges himself in them. They are never anything but a distraction and are taken seriously only by those concerned with the behavioral sciences. On the other hand, in the confrontation with ourselves, we reject, hide, and flee all immediate responsibility, vis-à-vis our neighbor. We find here the same mystification, but in the reverse sense, as when Marxism rightly said that personal virtue allowed men to forget their collective responsibilities or that charity allowed them to forget justice. Such criticism was justified in the nineteenth century. Today this is no longer the problem, for the same phenomenon takes place under our eyes, but in reverse. To charge the social organism with the solution of all one's personal problems and the realization of all one's values is to absent oneself from the problems of the human condition.

This mechanism, resulting from politization, presents two aspects: first of all, it means that nobody is truly responsible or has any real obligation with respect to justice, truth, and freedom, which are the affair of organizations—a collective affair. It is not "I do," but "one does." If our values are not attained, if things go badly, it means that the organization is bad or that there is a saboteur, a devil who prevents me from being just, in accord with society's objective justice. We will then accuse this Enemy, and also the state power, because state power must provide all just organization and the elimination of the pernicious enemy. This strenuous flight from the personal obligation to accomplish, oneself, what is good and just is often accompanied, in the case of intellectuals and Christians, by a corollary vice, that of insisting on universal responsibility. To consider oneself responsible for the tortures in Algeria while actually being a professor in Bordeaux, or for all hunger in the world, or for racist excesses in various countries is exactly the same thing as to reject all responsibility. What characterizes this attitude is impotence in the face of reality: I really cannot do anything about these things except sign manifestos and make declarations or claim that I act through political channels and establish a just order with the help of some abstraction. To say that we are all murderers means, translated, that nobody is individually a murderer, i.e., that I am not a murderer. To admit that I am co-responsible for all the evil in the world means to assure a good conscience for myself even if I do not do the good within my own reach. To admit that I am a dirty dog because, being French, I am involved in the acts of all Frenchmen in Algeria, means to free myself of the slightest efforts to cease being a dirty dog personally and to do so, moreover, at the cheapest price, namely by joining a political party or shouting in the streets; in addition, I am assured of being on the right side of those who want "the French" to cease being dirty dogs. Clearly, the demands made on us by religion were more severe, and all these proclamations of scruples, bad conscience, and divided responsibility quickly resolve into the claim that the villain is on the other side—in the FLN, or the OAS, or the Communist Party. And the same people proclaim both, without seeing the contradiction. This contradiction reveals that we are dealing here with a myth.

The second mythic element inherent in the politization of problems and values springs from the facility with which all things are relegated to tomorrow or the day after tomorrow. Because justice is a political matter, and will eventually be brought about as a result of some new organization, why not wait until tomorrow? People say: "Today we are only in a state of preparation, in search of means; we are following tortuous roads, but the direction is surely right. Injustices happen, but only pending the achievement of greater justice.

We are destroying freedoms, but we are preparing the ultimate freedom. We are asking you, today, right now, you, the militant, to lie, kill, jail; but you will be absolved of your deed by the grandiose results.

"You yourself will never see those results, as one, or two, or three generations must be sacrificed, but be reassured, your sacrifice will not have been in vain, your injustice will be compensated by the great justice to come." Here we have the individual, moral, and psychological aspect of the general ethical problem of ends and means. And with admirable facility everybody avoids the personal question of his own conduct by politicizing it. The more the solution is in the future, the more *everything* is permissible today.

Jouvenel[10] properly reminds us that "the myth that there is a solution obscures our understanding of politics, and in all such matters only precarious settlements can be reached by political means." A problem is composed of precise and known facts and can therefore be solved: for any arithmetical problem there must be a solution. But a political situation is not of that order; what makes it political is "precisely the fact that the frame of reference in which it exists does not permit any solution in the exact sense of that term. A true political problem arises only when the given facts are contradictory, i.e., when it is insoluble." A political problem permits only an accommodation, never a solution. There can be compromise, evolution, conciliation, various methods of using authority, and so on. But these are not solutions. Yet modern man increasingly demands solutions. Increasingly, the technicians insist on formulating problems

---

[10] Bertrand de Jouvenel, *De la politique pure* (Paris: Calmann-Lévy, 1963), pp. 248 *ff*.

of society as though they were exact problems permitting exact solutions. The growing myth of "solutions" progressively removes from our conscience the sense of the relative, i.e., limited, nature of all true political effort.

There is one final aspect: the politization of a genuine, existing problem permits us to avoid its reality, its depth, its human aspects.[11] On the political level, what one says and does may be just, even though one pays no attention to individual or human values. But any attempt to consider the individual as a human value makes it impossible to think of the problem in political terms. The Third Reich had no doubt that the Jewish problem had to be "solved." In the eyes of the Nazi chiefs it was a political problem. Therefore they could give an abstract order for the massacre. But all historians of the Third Reich report that Himmler fainted when he saw a few dozen Jews shot. At that point, the matter had suddenly become brutally human again. But in the ordinary course of the political process, the human aspects are generally hidden. Celebrating the Don Canal helped it hide the fact that it cost 100,000 human lives to build. The war in Algeria clearly demonstrated this function of politization.

Actually, the political point of view allows people today to escape values, to obliterate the reality of human situations which are individual situations and therefore no longer of interest. What is true and real is hidden under politics; people carry posters and in a leisurely way discuss future plans and revolutions. Political considerations permit us to think

---

[11] How true in this connection is Rubel's formula: "The conquest of political power is a bait and a trap: it is the death of the labor movement." (*Arguments,* No. 25.)

that we have the "general solution" because they permit us to do away at one stroke with all human reality and the search for truth.

Politics as Attainment of Values

Concerning the problem of justice,[12] it is an illusion to think that justice can be attained by a political organization of any kind. First of all, concepts of justice and its content vary greatly among civilizations and even individual points of view. Communists insist that bourgeois justice is only class justice. But it can be demonstrated that the same class aspects prevail in justice as conceived in the Soviet Union or China. Let us therefore leave aside the problem of juridical justice and even that of social justice, the ambiguities of which are well known. Let us deal only with two aspects of justice that fall within the purview of politics: justice of opinion and justice of decision. These obviously only delineate "periods" in political affairs, but if we give up the idea that someday, in unexpected fashion, the state will create a finished society including absolute justice (which is the vision of all utopians and most militants—proof that they have been propagandized), we must also admit that in political affairs justice is in reality expressed in fragmentary, and in some way prophetic, fashion, *here and now,* in *one*

---

[12] We could also take other values: freedom, for example. Among the innumerable treatises on freedom, I cannot resist referring to R. Ikor's, which is accurate but shows a remarkable ignorance as to the nature of the modern, or the more recent, state. Does Ikor believe that since 1789 freedom has ever been anything but a revocable favor? And can he imagine a modern, technological state structure in which freedom would not be exactly that? What innocence!

just decision, in *one* just opinion. That is the justice which, effectively and at best, politics might attain.

Let us begin by taking a perhaps extreme example of the justice of opinion. How can justice be administered to the Hitler regime? To be sure, all that was said against him was true and entirely deserved. But let us ask what would have happened if Hitler had won. We then would never have heard anything of Hitler's concentration camps, the massacres, or the experiments on human beings. Instead, Stalin's crimes of 1945 would have been discovered, and he would have been considered a war criminal. The Russians would have been charged with genocide because of their concentration camps, their massacres in the Baltic countries, the Ukraine, and Rumania. (Let us remember that of the 100,000 German soldiers captured at Stalingrad and deported from there, less than 5,000 returned—all the rest died in Russian camps!) In victory, Hitlerism would have softened progressively, after having liquidated all the elements to be liquidated—such as communism. And ten years later the moderation of the chiefs, who by then would have relaxed their hold, would have been admired. Historically, the struggle between races rather than the class struggle would have then taken first place. The Nazi doctrine would have been deepened and broadened, eminent philosophers such as Heidegger would have made their contribution to it. and Marxism would have ceased to preoccupy the intellectuals. Christians, after having been violently opposed to the Nazi doctrine, would have progressively doubted the need to oppose Hitlerism, in the same way they came to doubt the need to oppose Marxism, which surely no longer ruffles the Christian conscience. And, thanks to propaganda, because people would have known little of communism except its crimes—nothing of its love of justice, nothing of economic progress in the Soviet Union—and because people would have been submersed perpetually in National Socialist ideology, the latter would have appeared perfectly just at the end of ten years, and the well-known Nazi crimes would have been forgotten.

This extreme example—and the changes in attitude toward communism between 1939 and 1950 are probably sufficient to make such description reasonable—reminds us that the concept of justice in public opinion is subject to extreme fluctuation, indecision, and variation according to circumstances, even while giving itself the strongest doctrinal assurances. It was exactly this vacillation that was apparent during the distressing years of the Algerian war. The justice of one's cause, invoked by both camps, was nothing but a pretext to cover up political opinions.[13]

We are dealing here not only with the fluctuating character of public opinion, but also with the strange mixture of ideas, influences, prejudices, justifications, and irrational learnings which we call "our" opinions. The *same* people were opposed to the personalization of power in de Gaulle's case in 1962 and in favor of such personalization in Ben Bella's case. People will immediately exclaim: "That has nothing to do with it! Such personalization is reactionary in de Gaulle's case, and progressive in Ben Bella's case." These are just words. Was personalization of power reactionary in Stalin's case? It is being condemned by the same people who condemn it in de Gaulle's. And *objectively* speaking it was not reactionary, despite all the talk on the subject, because exactly that personalization of power permitted the Soviet

---

[13] See the excellent issue of *Esprit* on the subject.

Union to advance along the road toward socialism and attain a situation considered by Khrushchev as approaching communism. What justice of judgment is there in these opinions? As a corollary we can confirm that a just opinion in the political domain is necessarily partisan and therefore cannot be just by itself, whatever definition one might want to give to the word.

With regard to the second aspect of political justice, i.e., just political decisions, in political affairs, justice is not a matter of objectives or situations but a matter of moments. The possibility of a political solution or decision being in fact just or unjust depends on the moment when it is made, and not on the concept of justice of those making it or on their good will or political inclinations. Let us assume, for example, that a just solution for some delicate political problem can be found at the beginning, when the problem begins to emerge, and the matter is in the process of becoming twisted—before it has burst forth full-blown, before the contest has really begun, before the entire procedure is caught up in an inexorable mechanism. A decision must be made before irreparable acts have been committed or public opinion has come into play. In the former case, the matter would have moved into an area of force and of demands that will be either refused or unsatisfactory; in the latter case, public opinion's demand for justice will have made its appearance and political passion will have entered; from that very moment all just solution will have been rendered impossible. An example of the first: the Hitler regime could have been eliminated without much trouble in 1934–35, and a subsequent well-weathered crisis would have permitted a cleansing of Germany's political life and, probably, a reconstitution of the country.[14] But after 1936 no just solution was possible. An example for the second case is the relationship between the Western and Arab worlds. In 1918 it would have been possible to find a sensible situation and to establish true justice in the Near East. But after 1919 that was no longer possible. The same goes for the war in Algeria; in 1954–55 a just and generally satisfactory solution was definitely possible, but after 1956 no just solution could be found. From then on, either the FLN had to be crushed and millions of Arabs murdered or the European population had to be sacrificed because of the *de facto* victory by the FLN (which is what actually happened). Partition would not have been any more just, as the Mohammedans would have been pushed back into economically inferior regions.

But if this diagnosis is correct, under what conditions can a just solution be applied from the beginning, as soon as a political problem makes its appearance? There seem to be three conditions. Firstly, the existence of the intellectual capacity to anticipate the problem long before it emerges, to predict what threatens to become a problem from a mass of often minor indications. Such foresight need be neither prophetic nor superhuman. A good and well-informed political scientist can predict certain developments accurately. But continually less attention appears to be being paid to such efforts.

Secondly, a just solution would require the capacity to engage in actions not required here and now. In effect, it would not be *necessary* to intervene in a developing situa-

---

[14] After the ravages of war and political aberrations.—tr.

tion; intervention would, in fact, seem gratuitous (whereas our attitude now dictates that a hundred urgent events press in on us and demand attention). But a just solution can be found only if there is a considerable range of solutions. If, as a result of some development, choices have been progressively eliminated and, eventually, only one solution remains, inexorably imposing itself, such a solution will always be an expression of the strongest power supporting it, and *never* can be just. A solution imposed by necessity in political affairs cannot be just.

A third condition for any just solution is generosity. He who feels master of a situation must act generously with regard to the weakest party. A just solution can only be found if the strongest will give full consideration to the true situation of the weaker party, not in order to dominate him, but to help him to his feet. The elimination of the Hitler regime in 1935 would have been just only if the rest of Europe had helped provide Germany with a better economic and political life. The solution at that point would probably have been a united Europe.

But these three conditions seem impossible to meet. The more the technicians' power grows, the more technological and, to a lesser degree, economic foresight grows with it—but always at the expense of political foresight. There seems to be a contradiction between the technological order and the proper methods of political prediction. For example, the sterility of all studies concerned with political statistics is striking. Nonmathematical prediction is held in low esteem nowadays: it is allegedly nonscientific and therefore chancy. This is considered a deadly criticism. It implies in turn that genuine political thought is no longer appreciated.

Because of the attention that must be paid to public opinion, the second condition is even less possible to fulfill than the other two. Could any just solution have been found in 1934 with respect to Hitler? Indeed, but the French Right would have cried injustice; the Left did not want to risk war at any price; and French public opinion as a whole wanted no excitement, only comfort and quiet. Under such conditions, why mix into something that did not concern us? Could a just solution have been found in Algeria in 1954? Indeed, but the European Algerians did not want to make any concessions and most Frenchmen in France did not see why "these people" should be taken seriously. Actually, because of the curious role played by public opinion in political affairs, public opinion's *inertia* impedes all possible just efforts at the *beginning* and *once public opinion is aroused,* it immediately turns partisan and insists on unjust solutions. On the whole, partly because people are deluged with information and current events, any matter that has not yet been blown up and become irreversible cannot be taken seriously. People cannot take seriously the indications revealing an emerging drama; they will not be interested in it, will not accept any sacrifices in order that justice prevail. They will not accept a sacrifice while they are free to do so. The people will make any sacrifice demanded of them, but only when the drama has descended upon them fully, when the monster is at their doorstep, when straight and simple necessity demands it, and when they are completely propagandized, i.e., after a just solution can no longer emerge.

The problem of whether certain values can be realized through politics may be approached in another way. A fundamental contradiction exists between politics and justice. Politics, as said before, can act only with material or psychological force—with spiritual, ideological, or police constraint. A well-conducted political move can never produce anything but power—the institutions created by it are only ends or instruments of such power. But, it might be objected, is the politically interested citizen not eager to see this power controlled, rather than see its growth further promoted? This is a great illusion. The more an individual has become politicized, the more he will see and think about all problems as political problems, the more importance will he attach to political action, and consider it the only possible course and, by his attitude, endow that course with a maximum of power and effectiveness. At the same time, the more politicized he is, the more will he be focused on and oriented toward that basic political force and form: the state. The more he takes recourse to the state, the more power he gives it. For him the *only* problem is: *who* will control the state? Will it be *his* party? All will then be perfect. Will it be another party? Then things will be bad. But he never thinks of reducing the state *itself*—on the contrary. All he thinks of is to replace the incumbents. No minority wants to reduce the state's power. The last fifty years have shown that each minority attaining power increases the state's power in order to prevent its defeated opponents from using the same means it used to gain power. At each step, state power is increased. The people under the spell of politics seek less and less to control the state; politicizing everything, they consider it normal that the state should constantly expand its area of action and use ever more instruments of power. This is legitimate in their eyes, as they believe that all will be solved by political action.

All the phenomena already described can be seen here: the autonomy of political affairs with regard to moral values; the conflict between values and increasing state power; the

connection between means and ends. This combination reveals the tragically illusory character of the belief that any
justice, truth, or freedom can be attained by entrusting these
values to the state.

It might be objected that my examples are partial, my
approximations too rough, and that political activities are
not everywhere or always of this kind, that they are more
differentiated, that excesses should not be taken as examples, and that, in any event, American and British democracy is entirely different. That is true. But the *significant*
facts all point in the same direction. It also is a sign of our
present political development that a growing number of
military governments that are neither dictatorships nor
democracies are being established in a growing number of
countries. We must evaluate the facts that bear upon the
future; that is what counts, not the current precarious maintenance of parliamentary democracies and liberal traditions.

Essay Seven

Liberty and Law

Giovanni Sartori

The Italian scholar Giovanni Sartori holds doctoral degrees in political and social science. He has served as Dean of the Faculty of Political Science and Director of the Institute of Political Science at the University of Florence, as Director of the Center of Comparative Politics in Florence, and as visiting professor at Harvard and Yale universities. In 1976 he was appointed professor of political science at Stanford University, and he is presently Albert Schweitzer Professor in the Humanities at Columbia University.

Since 1971 Professor Sartori has been editor of the quarterly Rivista Italiana di Scienza Politica. *He also serves on the boards of the* American Political Science Review, Comparative Politics, Comparative Political Studies, Government and Opposition, *and* Political Theory. *His publications include nine books and numerous articles in European and American scholarly journals.*

The more corrupt the Republic, the more the laws.
—Tacitus*

1. Freedom and Freedoms

When we talk of liberalism, people find it difficult to understand exactly what is being discussed; when we speak of democracy, they think they do. The notion of popular power is almost tangible, while the idea of liberty is hard to grasp—at least so long as we are free. And whereas democracy has a descriptive meaning (although, owing to historical change, a misleading one), liberty or freedom has not. For the word "freedom" and the declaration "I am free to" can be used whenever we refer to the realm of action and will, and consequently can stand for the infinite scope and variety of human life itself.

However, and fortunately, it will be sufficient for us to consider this chameleonlike, all-embracing word from one specific angle: political freedom. For this purpose our main problem is to introduce some order, since the major complications arise because we seldom separate the specific issue of political freedom from general speculations about the nature

---

* *Annals*, III, 27.

of true freedom. For instance, Lord Acton introduced his *History of Freedom in Antiquity* with the following remark: "No obstacle has been so constant, or so difficult to overcome, as uncertainty and confusion touching the nature of true liberty. If hostile interests have wrought much injury, false ideas have wrought still more."[1] While I agree very much with Lord Acton's diagnosis—the harm brought about by uncertain, confused, and false ideas—I wonder whether his therapy is sound. For the problem before us is not to discover "the nature of true liberty" but, on the contrary, to remove all the extraneous incrustations that prevent us from examining the question of political freedom by itself, and as one empirical question among others.[2]

We must put some order, to begin with, in the contexts out of which we speak of psychological freedom, intellectual freedom, moral freedom, social freedom, economic freedom, legal freedom, political freedom, and other freedoms as well.[3] These are related to one another, of course, for

---

[1] *Essays on Freedom and Power,* p. 53.

[2] On the problem of freedom in general, Mortimer J. Adler's work, *The Idea of Freedom* (Garden City, 1958), is a precious mine of information (see also the bibliography, pp. 623–63). I disagree, however, both with the classification and the method, which he calls "dialectical." The concepts of each author are treated in a historical vacuum, independently of the circumstances and motives that prompted them. Thus in Adler's presentation one misses both the fact that different theses were held for the same reason, and that many differences are due to the fact that the same thing is being said under different circumstances. For further reference to the general problem consult esp. the following collections containing excellent contributions: *Freedom, Its Meaning,* ed. R. N. Anshen; and *Freedom and Authority in Our Time,* ed. Bryson, Finkelstein, MacIver, and McKeon (New York, 1953).

[3] I do not use the current labels of freedom from fear, from want, from need, or the formula "freedom as self-expression," since it is seldom clear in what context they belong. With the exception of freedom from need

they all pertain to a same man. However, we have to distinguish between them because each one is concerned with examining and solving a particular aspect of the overall question of freedom. Hence the first clarification to be made is that political freedom *is not* of the psychological, intellectual, moral, social, economic, or legal type. It presupposes these freedoms—and it also promotes them—but it is not the same as these.

The second clarification has to do with the level of discourse. In this connection the error is to confuse the political with the philosophical problem of freedom. Philosophers have very often speculated about political freedom, but only rarely have they dealt with it as a practical problem to be approached as such. Aristotle, Hobbes, Locke, and Kant are among the few exceptions, that is, among the small number of philosophers who have not made the mistake of offering a philosophical answer to a practical question. Locke, particularly, had this virtue, and this explains why he has played such an important part in the history of political thought. His treatment of the problem of freedom in the *Essay Concerning Human Understanding* is different from, and unconnected with, the one we find in the second of the *Two Treatises on Government*. In the former he defines liberty as acting under the determination of the self, whereas in the latter he defines it as not being "subject to the inconstant, uncertain, unknown, arbitrary will of another man."[4]

(which is clearly economic), freedom from fear and from insecurity can be understood as instances of psychological freedom, but also as related to political freedom. Still worse, freedom as self-expression can be just as much a psychological freedom as a moral and/or intellectual one.

[4] Cf. *Essay Concerning Human Understanding,* esp. v. I, bk. II, ch. 21 *passim;* and *Two Treatises on Government,* bk. II, ch. 4, sect. 22.

However, most philosophers have not been concerned with the problem this way. As philosophers, they are concerned with True Liberty, or with the Essence of Liberty, meaning by this either the problem of the freedom of the will, or the question of the supreme form of liberty (conceived variously as self-expression, self-determination, or self-perfection). This is exactly what philosophers are supposed to do, and nobody is reproaching them for having done it. But they should be reproached when they project their metaphysics of liberty into the political sphere and, unlike Locke, do not notice that in this context we are no longer discussing the same problem. And this point is still far from being accepted. In reviewing the relationship between political philosophy and the science of politics, Carl J. Friedrich—after having rightly criticized the mixing of philosophical questions and "the empirical realm of government and politics"—concludes by accepting a relation that I still consider much too close. He asserts: "Any discussion of freedom and of liberalism must, if it takes its argument seriously, confront the issue of 'freedom of the will.' "[5] Frankly, I do not see why. Of course any discussion about the freedom cherished by the West is based on a *Weltanschauung*—on a conception of life and values. To be more exact, it presupposes that we somehow believe in the value of individual liberty. But I am reluctant to consider the connection any closer than that.

In the first place, I do not see what difference it would make in practice if we were to ascertain that man is not a free agent, and that he is not really responsible for his actions. Should we suppress penal legislation? Should we

---

[5] In *Approaches to the Study of Politics,* ed. R. Young, pp. 174 and 184.

further give up a social order that is regulated by norms accompanied by sanctions? I do not see how we could. The only thing that would change, I am afraid, is the meaning of penalty, which would lose its value as a deterrent and its justification as punishment. The convict would become a martyr of society, paying for offenses that he was not responsible for. But he would still be condemned, since all societies have to remove from circulation murderers, thieves, lunatics, and all others who, being incapable of submitting to rules, constitute a danger to their neighbors.

The second reason for keeping the philosophical problem separate from the others is that, unless we do, we cannot even understand what the philosophers themselves have been saying. Whoever has had philosophical training knows in what sense Spinoza maintained that liberty was perfect rationality, or Leibniz that it was the spontaneity of the intelligence, or Kant that it was autonomy, or Hegel that it was the acceptance of necessity, or Croce that it was the perennial expansion of life. All these definitions are valid if they are understood in their context. But their validity has to do with a "nuclear meaning," with the search for a freedom that is essential, final, or as Kant said, transcendental. On the other hand, let it be noted, none of these conceptualizations refers to a "relational" problem of freedom. It follows from this that if we try to use the aforesaid concepts to deal with the problem of political bondage—which is a relational problem—we distort their meaning without solving our problem. As soon as the ideas on freedom of Spinoza, Leibniz, Kant (as a moral philosopher), Hegel, or Croce are lowered to an empirical level for the purpose of dealing with problems that these conceptualizations did not consider, they become false and dangerous. Even dangerous because, if the question of political freedom has been submerged over and over again in a sea of confusion, it is by virtue of the false witnessing that these philosophers have arbitrarily been called upon to bear. So, the second point I wish to make is that political liberty *is not* a philosophical kind of liberty. It is not the practical solution to a philosophical problem, and even less the philosophical solution to a practical problem.

Finally, we must deal with the question of the stages of the process of freedom. The phrase "I am free to" can have three different meanings or can be broken up into three phases. It can mean I *may,* or I *can,* or I *have the power to.* In the first sense freedom is permission; in the second sense it is ability; and in the third sense it is a substantive condition. The third meaning is the newest, the last of the series, and for the purpose of the present discussion it can be put aside. I shall therefore confine myself to the two primary meanings of freedom: I may, and I can.

Clearly, freedom as permission and freedom as ability are very closely connected, since permission without ability and ability without permission are equally sterile. Yet they should not be confused, because no one type of liberty can by itself fulfill both these functions. Certain kinds of liberty are designed primarily to create the *permissive conditions* of freedom. Political freedom is of this kind, and very often so are juridical freedom and economic freedom (as understood in a market system). In other contexts the emphasis is instead placed primarily, if not exclusively, on the roots and sources of freedom—on freedom as *ability.* This is notably the case of the philosophical approach to the problem of freedom; and it is also true of the notions of psychological, intellectual, and moral freedom.

The distinction between I may, and I can, corresponds to the difference between the external sphere and the internal sphere of freedom. When we are interested in the externalization of liberty, that is, in free action, it takes the form of permission. When on the other hand there is no problem of external freedom—as in the case of psychological, intellectual, and moral freedom—then we are concerned with freedom as ability. Thus terms like "independence," "protection," and "action" are generally used to indicate *external liberty*, i.e., permission. Whereas the notions of "autonomy," "self-realization," and "will" usually refer to the freedom that exists *in interiore hominis*. And this leads us to a third and final clarification: Political liberty is not an internal freedom, for it is a permissive, instrumental, and relational freedom. In sum, it is a liberty whose purpose is to create a situation of freedom—the conditions for freedom.

2. Political Freedom

Cranston has remarked that "the word liberty has its least ambiguity in political use in times of centralized oppression."[6] This is so true that I suggest we should always approach the problem as if we were being oppressed, that is, assuming that we find ourselves subject to tyrannical rule. And my contention is that the concept of political freedom is not at all ambiguous, provided that (i) we eliminate the confusions of the *alienum genere* kind, (ii) we make clear that it raises a practical, not a speculative issue, and (iii) we specify that it aims at the creation of an external situation of liberty.

---

[6] In *Freedom, op. cit.,* p. 11.

Actually, what I find striking in the history of the idea of political freedom is not variety of meaning, but rather continuity of meaning. For whenever the aforesaid provisos are complied with, we always meet with this basic connotation of the concept: Political freedom is "absence of opposition,"[7] absence of external restraint, or exemption from coercion. Whenever man asks or has asked for political liberty (outside of a small community like the *polis*), he means that he does not like constraint, and specifically the forms of constraint associated with the exercise of political power.[8] In other words, political freedom is characteristically freedom *from,* not freedom *to.* People are accustomed to say that it is a "negative" freedom, but since this adjective is often used in a derogatory sense, or at least to present political freedom as an inferior kind of liberty, I prefer to say, more accurately, that it is a defensive or protective freedom.

Critics have repeated to the point of saturation that this idea of freedom comes from an erroneous individualistic

---

[7] This is Hobbes's well-known definition in ch. XXI of *Leviathan,* which reads in full: "Liberty, or freedom, signifieth, properly, the absence of opposition; by opposition I mean external impediments of motion." This definition was—according to Hobbes himself—the "proper, and generally received meaning of the word" in England. (For the sake of exactness the definition is placed by Hobbes in the context of "natural liberty"; but it overlaps also into the context of civil liberty, of the "liberty of subjects.") I assume that even Adler would agree with my statement about the basic continuity of the concept of political freedom, since he writes in his conclusion: "In the course of identifying political liberty . . . we found that *exemption from* the arbitrary will of another was commonly present in the understanding of all freedoms" (*The Idea of Freedom,* pp. 611–12).

[8] Of course, economic and religious as well as social constraints (as the Tocquevillian type of tyranny of the majority) may also be a concern of public authorities, but they are not necessarily an aspect of political liberty.

philosophy based on the false assumption that the individual is an atom or a monad. In the first place, I would question the charge that this notion has a philosophical origin, if we mean by this that only a small number of intellectuals are really interested in the individual. If we consider, for instance, the French Revolution (an event that, admittedly, escaped from the control of the *philosophes*), its entire parabola took on the meaning of a vindication of liberty *against* power. During the years 1789–1794, the Third and the Fourth Estates were asking for individual and political liberty in opposition to the state, and not for a social and economic liberty to be achieved by means of the state. The idea that it is a purpose and a concern of the state to promote liberty would have appeared extravagant, to say the least, to the French people of the time. It would have appeared that way to them not because of their philosophical individualistic beliefs, but for the much simpler reason that they had been crushed for centuries by monarchs, lords, and the meticulous and paralyzing interference of the corporate economic system.

In truth, I think that we need not always call upon monads and the atomistic philosophy of man in order to explain why political freedom tends to be understood at all times—at least when oppression occurs—as freedom *from,* i.e., as a defensive freedom. It is much more important to realize, I believe, that the question of political freedom arises only when we approach the relation between citizen and state *from the point of view of the citizen*. If we consider this relation from the point of view of the state, we are no longer concerned with the problem of political freedom. To say that the state is "free to" is meaningless, unless we wish to introduce the question of arbitrary power. The tyrannical state is free *to* rule at its pleasure, and this means that it deprives its subjects of freedom.[9]

Let this point be very clear: (i) To speak of political freedom is to be concerned with the power of subordinate powers, with the power of the power-addressees, and (ii) the proper focus to the problem of political freedom is indicated by the question: How can the power of these minor and potentially losing powers be safeguarded? We have political liberty, i.e., a free citizen, so long as conditions are created that make it possible for his lesser power to withstand the greater power that otherwise would—or at any rate could—easily overwhelm him. And this is why the concept of political freedom assumes an adversative meaning. It is freedom *from,* because it is the freedom *of* and *for* the weaker.

Of course, the formula "absence of external impediments"[10] should not be taken literally, lest it bring to mind an anarchic ideal. The absence of restriction is not the absence of all restriction. What we ask of political freedom is protection against arbitrary and absolute power. By a situation of liberty we mean a situation of protection that permits the governed effectively to oppose abuse of power by the governors. It might be objected that this clarification still does not clarify much. For what is meant by "abuse" of

---

[9] It does not seem to me, therefore, as H. J. Morgenthau maintains, that political freedom is confronted with a dilemma: freedom for the holder, or for the subject of political power? The concept of political freedom is associated with the latter problem, not with freedom of domination. I agree very much with Morgenthau's conclusions, but I would not say, as he suggests, that there is a case of unfreedom when a power holder is not allowed unrestricted power. See "The Dilemmas of Freedom," in *American Political Science Review,* III (1957), pp. 714 ff.

[10] This is Hobbes's shorthand. See *Leviathan,* ch. XIV.

power? Where does the legitimate exercise of power end, and the illegitimate begin? If we review the literature on freedom, we shall find considerable disagreement on this point. But we should not fail to perceive that much of the disagreement can be accounted for by the difference in historical situations. The answers to the questions "Protected from what?" and "Unrestricted to what extent?" depend on what is at stake at any given time and place, and on what is most valued (and how intensely it is valued) in a specific culture. "Coercion" does not apply to every kind and degree of restraint. Nor does "protection" imply defense against everything. In the first place, people must feel that what is involved is worth protecting (the threat of constraint has to be directed against something that they value); and secondly, nobody worries about protecting what is not in danger. Therefore we can be specific only if we examine a specific situation and know what is being threatened, which threat is feared the most, and which is considered most imminent.

A more difficult issue is raised by the question: Is freedom *from* an adequate concept of freedom? To answer this query we must refer to a broader picture. Clinton Rossiter has summed up the general idea we have of liberty today as consisting of four notions: independence, privacy, power, and opportunity. *"Independence* is a situation in which a man feels himself subject to a minimum of external restraints. . . . *Privacy* is a special kind of independence which can be understood as an attempt to secure autonomy . . . if necessary in defiance of all the pressures of modern society." However, says Rossiter, at this point we have only mentioned "one-half of liberty, and the negative half at that. . . . Liberty is also a positive thing . . . and we must therefore think of it in terms of *power* . . . and also in terms of *opportunity*."[11] Perhaps there is one slight imperfection in Rossiter's analysis, in that when he says "power" he seems to mean "ability to," in the sense of capacity. To avoid ambiguity, I will include the concept of capacity in our list and place the concept of power at the end. Thus complete freedom, as we understand it, implies the following five traits: independence, privacy, capacity, opportunity, and power.

Now we can frame our question more accurately: What is the relation between the first half of liberty (independence and privacy) and the second half (ability, opportunity, and power)? The answer seems to me to be clear: It is a relation between condition and conditioned, between means and ends. It is, therefore, also a *procedural relation*. It is no accident that these concepts are generally presented in an order in which the notion of independence (and not that of opportunity or of power) comes first. Unfortunately, this point is seldom made sufficiently clear. Rossiter is by no means an exception to this rule when, in putting his "pieces back together into a unity," not only does he pass over the fact that it is an ordered unity, or rather, an irreversible succession, but, if anything, he tends to stress the opposite. He concludes: "The emphasis of classical liberalism, to be sure, is on the negative aspects of liberty. Liberty is thought of almost exclusively as a state of independence and privacy. But this is precisely one of those points at which classical liberalism no longer serves, if ever it did serve, as a wholly adequate instrument for describing the place of the free man

[11] See "The Pattern of Liberty," in *Liberty,* ed. M. R. Konvitz and C. Rossiter (Ithaca, 1958), pp. 16–18.

in the free society.''[12] That statement is not incorrect; it only omits what is essential.

Political freedom is by no means the only kind of freedom. It is not even the most important kind, if by important we mean the one that ranks highest in the scale of values. It is, however, the primary liberty, as far as procedure goes; that is, it is a preliminary condition, the *sine qua non* of all other liberties. So, to speak of "independence from" as an inadequate notion of liberty—as people often tend to do— is very misleading. The other liberties as well, if they are considered singly, are just as inadequate. For adequacy is provided by the whole series, and by the whole series *arranged in a particular order*. It is not sufficient that our minds be free, for instance, if our tongues are not. The ability to direct our own lives is of very little use if we are prevented from doing so. How, then, are the so-called positive liberties adequate if they cannot materialize? It seems to me, therefore, that when we assert that negative liberty is not sufficient we are stating an obvious platitude, while we are not stating what is most important of all; that we need freedom *from* in order to be able to achieve freedom *to*.

It can be argued that political freedom has also a positive aspect (and this might seem to be a reply to those who consider it insufficient and incomplete). Now, there is no doubt that political freedom cannot be inert, that it postulates some activity; in other words that it is not only freedom *from* but also *participation in*. No one denies this. But we must not overstress this latter aspect, for we must remember that participation is made possible by a state of indepen-

---

[12] *Ibid.*

dence, and not vice versa. Even our subjective rights, as Jhering wrote in his famous pamphlet *Der Kampf um's Recht,* are reduced to nothing if we do not exercise them, if we do not avail ourselves of them.[13] However, it is clearly useless to speak of exercising rights if they do not already exist. And the same holds good for political freedom. It is pointless to speak of "exercise" if there is not already independence. Totalitarian dictatorships require and promote a great deal of activity and participation. But so what?

My feeling is, therefore, that we ought to resist the temptation to treat political freedom as if it were, in itself, a complete liberty. Those who inflate it by speaking of it as "participation" are disfiguring its basic feature.[14] If we have so often failed in our search for more liberty, the main reason is that we have expected from participation more than it can give. Of course, liberty as nonrestraint is not an end in itself, and political freedom requires action, active resistance,[15] and positive demands. Where there are lifelessness and apathy there cannot be liberty. But we must not forget that the relation of forces between citizens and state is unequal; that in comparison with the state their power is destructible; and therefore that their freedom is typified not

---

[13] Thus Jhering reminds us that "law is not a logical concept but an energetic and active one" (*Der Kampf um's Recht,* 1st ed., 1873, ch. I). Compare with note 15 below.

[14] Or otherwise they are following the formula of ancient liberty discussed in sections 5 and 6.

[15] "Les libertés sont des résistances" (liberties are resistances), Royer-Collard, the doctrinaire of the French Restoration, used to say. It is symptomatic how in an author so far removed as Laski one should find a connotation so closely related. Cf. Harold J. Laski, *Liberty in the Modern State* (New York, 1949), p. 172: "Liberty cannot help being a courage to resist the demands of power at some point that is deemed decisive."

by its positive aspects but by the presupposition of defense mechanisms. In relation to the state the citizens are the weaker party, and therefore the political concept of freedom is to be pinpointed as follows: Only if I am not prevented from doing what I wish, can I be said to have the power to do it.[16]

There is no reason to be oversensitive when we are told that this conception is incomplete. So it is. Or, rather, it is incomplete in the obvious sense that each specific form of freedom can only amount to a partial freedom, because it concerns only the specific problem that it attempts to solve. Therefore, what really matters is to realize that, despite its incompleteness, political liberty is *preliminary* to the other brands, and this means that it cannot be bypassed. We cannot pass over freedom in the negative sense, if we want to achieve freedom in the positive sense. If we forget for one instant the requirement of not being restrained, our entire edifice of liberties is worthless.

Once we have assessed the question of the procedural importance of political freedom, we may well raise the question of its historical importance to us today. The assertion that political freedom is not enough, meaning that "real freedom" is something else, is totally beside the mark. But the question as to the relation, here and now, between political

---

[16] It should be clear that in the expression "political liberty" I include also the so-called civil liberties (freedom of speech, of press, of assembly, etc.). Civil liberties, too, are liberties that come under the category of freedom *from,* since they delimit the sphere of action of the state and mark the boundary between the use and abuse of political power. Our political rights stem from civil liberties both as their prosecution and above all as their concrete guaranty. That is to say, political rights are civil liberties that have been extended and protected, and civil liberties are the *raison d'être* (even if not the only one) for the existence of political rights.

and other kinds of freedom is, of course, pertinent. Every epoch has its urgencies and particular needs. So we may well maintain, in this context, that since today political freedom is assured, it requires less attention than other liberties—such as economic freedom, or freedom from want. However, this is a question that can be dealt with only after having reviewed historically the nature of the problems that confront us.[17]

3. Liberal Freedom

It will be noted that so far I have spoken of political freedom and not of the liberal conception of freedom. It is true that the two concepts have become closely linked. However, since the liberal idea of freedom is often considered antiquated nowadays, it is wise to keep the problem of political freedom separate from the liberal solution of it. For it is easy to demonstrate that the freedom of liberalism, being a historical acquisition, is bound to come to an end. But are we prepared to make the same assertion about political freedom? Can we say that even this is a transitory need? If so, let us say so openly. What is more difficult, let us try to demonstrate it. Political freedom and liberal freedom cannot be killed with one stone. Rather, it is at the very moment that we reject the liberal solution of the problem of freedom that this problem again demands, more pressingly than ever, a solution.

What we ask of political freedom is protection. How can we obtain it? In the final analysis, from the time of Solon to the present day, the solution has always been sought in

---

[17] See below, section 7.

obeying laws and not masters. As Cicero so well phrased it, *legum servi sumus ut liberi esse possimus,*[18] we are servants of the law in order that we might be free. And the problem of political freedom has always been interwoven with the question of legality, for it goes back to the problem of curbing power by making it impersonal.[19]

There is, then, a very special connection between political freedom and juridical freedom. But the formula "liberty under law," or by means of law, can be applied in different ways. The idea of protection of the laws has been understood, by and large, in three ways: the Greek way, which is already a legislative interpretation; the Roman way, which approaches the English rule of law;[20] and the way of liberalism, which is constitutionalism.

The Greeks were the first to perceive the solution, for they well understood that if they did not want to be ruled tyrannically they had to be governed by laws.[21] But their idea of law oscillated between the extremes of sacred laws, which were too rigid and immutable, and conventional laws, which were too uncertain and shifting. In the course of their

---

[18] *Oratio pro Cluentio,* 53.

[19] The exceptions are not probatory, for as M. J. Adler has aptly noted, although there are "(i) authors who maintain that freedom consists in exemption from legal regulations or restrictions and (ii) authors who maintain that freedom consists in obedience to law . . . they are not talking about the same freedom. Though they may appear to be giving opposite answers to the question 'How is law related to liberty?' they are really not taking that question in the same sense" (p. 619). Cf. below, note 73.

[20] The similarity of development between Roman and English constitutionalism was perceived by Rudolf von Jhering in his *Geist des römischen Rechts,* and also by Bryce in his *Studies in History and Jurisprudence.*

[21] See e.g. Aristotle: "Men should not think it slavery to live according to the rule of the constitution; for it is their salvation" (*Politics* 1310a).

democratic experience, the *nomos* soon ceased to mirror the nature of things (*physis*), and the Greeks were unable to stop at the golden mean between immobility and change. As soon as law lost its sacred character, popular sovereignty was placed above the law, and by that very act government by laws was once again confused with government by men. The reason for this is that the legal conception of liberty presupposes the rejection of the Greek *eleuthería*—of a freedom that is turned into the principle *quod populo placuit legis habet vigorem* (what pleases the people is law). Looking at the Greek system from the vantage point of our knowledge, we see that what their conception of law lacked was precisely the notion of "limitation"—a notion that, as was discovered later, is inseparable from it.

That is the reason why our juridical tradition is Roman, not Greek. The experience of the Greeks is important precisely because it shows us how *not* to proceed if we want liberty under law. The Romans, it is true, posed for themselves a more limited problem. As Wirszubski remarks, "The Roman republic never was . . . a democracy of the Athenian type; and the *eleuthería, isonomía* and *parrhesía* that were its chief expressions, appeared to the Romans as being nearer *licentia* than *libertas*."[22] Actually, Roman jurisprudence did not make a direct contribution to the specific problem of political freedom. But it did make an essential indirect contribution by developing the idea of legality whose modern version is the Anglo-Saxon rule of law.

The third juridical solution to the problem of political freedom is that of liberalism—which was developed in English constitutional practice, found its most successful

---

[22] Wirszubski, *Libertas* (Cambridge, 1950), p. 13.

written formulation in the Constitution of the United States, and is expounded in the theory of "constitutional *garantisme*" and, in this sense of the *Rechtsstaat,* the state based on law.[23] What did liberalism specifically contribute to the solution of the problem of political freedom? It was not the originator of the modern idea of individual freedom, although it added something important to it.[24] Nor, as we have seen, was it the inventor of the notion of liberty in the law. But it did invent the way to guarantee and institutionalize a balance between government by men and government by laws.

The originality and value of the approach of classical liberalism can be seen if we compare it with previous attempts to solve the problem. Basically, the legal solution to the problem of freedom can be sought in two very different directions; either in rule by legislators or in the rule of law.[25] In the first approach, law consists of written rules that are enacted by legislative bodies; that is, law is legislated law. In the second, law is something to be discovered by judges: It is

[23] However, I prefer to say "constitutional *garantisme*" instead of state based on law (*Rechtsstaat*) because the latter can also be understood in a restrictive sense as a mere system of administrative justice. In fact, the administrative notion of *Rechtsstaat* has prevailed upon the constitutional notion (at least in the Italian and German juridic doctrine). See the pertinent remarks of Giuseppino Treves, "Considerazioni sullo stato di diritto," in *Studi in onore di E. Crosa* (Milano, 1960), v. II, pp. 1591–94.

[24] Notably the externalization and generalization of the principle that every man has the right to live according to his own conscience and principles.

[25] Dicey's *The Law of the Constitution* (1885), Part II, still remains the classic exposition of the rule of law theory. For the precedents that escaped Dicey, and in particular the contribution of the Italian communes to the elaboration of the principle of the rule of law, see the detailed study of Ugo Nicolini, *Il principio di legalità nelle democrazie Italiane* (Padova, 2nd ed., 1955).

judicial law. For the former approach, law consists of statutory, systematic lawmaking; for the latter, it is the result of piecemeal law finding (*Rechtsfindung*) by means of judicial decisions. From the first viewpoint, law may be conceived as the product of sheer will; from the second it is the product of theoretical inquiry and debate. The danger of the legislative solution is that a point may be reached in which men are tyrannically ruled by other men in spite of laws (as happened in Greece), i.e., in which laws are no longer a protection. On the other hand, the second solution may be inadequate because the rule of law does not, per se, necessarily safeguard the political aspect of freedom (e.g., the Roman rule of law concerned the elaboration of the *jus civile,* not of public law). And while the Greek approach was too dynamic and thereby destroyed the certainty of law, the other is, or may be, too static.

Liberal constitutionalism is, we may say, the technique of retaining the advantages of the earlier solutions while eliminating their respective shortcomings. On the one hand the constitutional solution adopts rule by legislators, but with two limitations: one concerning the method of lawmaking, which is checked by a severe *iter legis;* and one concerning the range of lawmaking, which is restricted by a higher law and thereby prevented from interfering with the rights of man, that is, with the fundamental rights affecting the liberty of the citizen. On the other hand, the constitutional solution also sees to it that the rule of law is retained in the system. Even though this latter component part of the constitutional rule has been gradually set aside by the former, it is well to remind ourselves that the framers of the liberal constitutions did not conceive of the state as being a *ma-*

chine à faire lois, a lawmaking machine, but conceived of the role of legislators as being a complementary role according to which parliament was supposed to integrate, not to replace, judicial law finding. However, an essential feature of the rule-of-law principle is retained: that aspect of the principle of the separation of powers which provides for the independence of the judiciary. (Incidentally, this is actually what the ill-famed principle of the separation of powers demands. *Pace* Montesquieu, English constitutionalism separated the power to rule from the power to ascertain and declare the law, but never separated the exercise of power between parliament and government, for in this case what is required is a shared, not a divided, exercise of power.)

There are, to be sure, many significant differences among our constitutional systems. If we refer to the origins, the unwritten English constitution was largely built upon, and safeguarded by, the rule of law; the American written constitution formalized and rationalized British constitutional practice, thereby still leaning heavily on the rule of law; whereas written constitutions in Europe, for want of common law, were based from the outset on the legislative conception of law. But these initial differences have been gradually reduced, since there is at present a general trend—even in the English-speaking countries—in favor of statutory law. Despite this trend, however, we cannot say as yet that present-day constitutions have lost their *raison d'être* as the solution that combines the pros and obviates the cons of both the rule-of-law and the rule-of-legislators techniques. Even though our constitutions are becoming more and more unbalanced on the side of statutory lawmaking, so long as they are considered a higher law, so long as we have judicial review, independent judges, and, possibly, the due process of law;[26] and so long as a binding procedure establishing the method of lawmaking remains an effective brake on the bare will-conception of law—so long as these conditions prevail, we are still depending on the liberal-constitutional solution of the problem of political power.

Constitutional systems, both past and present, are therefore, historically speaking, liberal systems. One might say that liberal politics is constitutionalism.[27] And constitutionalism is the solution to the problem of *political* freedom in terms of a *dynamic* approach to the legal conception of freedom. This explains why we cannot speak of political freedom without referring to liberalism—liberalism, I repeat, not democracy. The political freedom that we enjoy today is the freedom of liberalism, the liberal kind of liberty; not the precarious, and, on the whole, vainly sought liberty of the ancient democracies. And this is the reason why, in recalling the typical guiding principles of the democratic deontology, I have mentioned equality, isocracy, and self-government, but—and perhaps this was noted—never the idea of liberty.

---

[26] I say "possibly" because "due process of law" as understood in the United States has no equivalent in Europe and in substance considerably surpasses not only the *lex terrae* of the old English law, but the English interpretation of the rule of law as well.

[27] Duverger reminds us that "when Laboulaye gave the title *Cours de politique constitutionelle* to a collection of Benjamin Constant's works, he meant to say in substance *Course in liberal politics.* 'Constitutional' regimes are liberal regimes." See M. Duverger, *Droit constitutionelle et institutions politiques* (Paris, 1955), p. 3. To be precise Constant himself had collected those writings in 1818–19, saying that "they constitute a sort of course in constitutional politics. . . ."

Of course, it is also possible to derive the idea of liberty from the concept of democracy. But not directly. It must be derived indirectly, in the sense that it does not follow from the notion of popular power, but from the concept of isocracy. It is the assertion "We are equal" that can be interpreted: "Nobody has the right to command me." Thus, it is from the postulate of equality that we can deduce the demand for a "freedom from." However, we should note that this inference is made by modern rather than by ancient thinkers. In the Greek tradition, democracy is much more closely associated with *isonomía* (equal law) than with *eleuthería* (liberty), and the idea of popular power is by far preponderant in the inner logic of development of the Greek system. Moreover, as we have already seen, when the Greeks did speak about liberty it meant something different from what it means today, and they were confronted with a problem of liberty that was the reverse of the modern one.

Therefore, to avoid a historical falsification, which also has a vital practical bearing, we must stress that neither our ideal nor our techniques of liberty pertain, strictly speaking, to the line of development of the democratic idea. It is true that modern liberal democracies have incorporated the ideal of a liberty of Man, which includes the liberty of each man. But originally this concept was not democratic; it is an acquisition of democracy, not a product of it—which is very different. And we must keep this fact in mind in order to avoid the mistake of believing that our liberty can be secured by the method that the Greeks tried. For our liberties are assured by a notion of legality that constitutes a *limit* and a *restriction* on pure and simple democratic principles. Kelsen, among others, sees this very clearly when he writes that a democracy "without the self-limitation represented by the principle of legality destroys itself."[28] Although modern democracy has incorporated the notions of liberty and legality, these notions, as Bertrand de Jouvenel rightly points out, "are, in terms of good logic, extraneous to it"[29]— and I should like to add, in terms of good historiography as well.

4. The Supremacy of Law in Rousseau

I have mentioned three ways of seeking legal protection for political freedom: the legislative way, the rule-of-law way, and the liberal or constitutional way. But it is held that there is another relationship (which would be the fourth in my list) between liberty and law: "autonomy," i.e., giving ourselves our own laws. And since liberty as autonomy is supposed to have Rousseau's *placet,* many people take for granted that this is the democratic definition of liberty, and contrast, on this basis, a *libertas minor* with a *libertas major*—that is to say, the minor liberty of liberalism (as freedom *from*) with the greater democratic liberty, autonomy. Personally, I question whether those who equate liberty with autonomy are justified in associating this notion with Rousseau. In the second place, which is the supposedly minor liberty: political freedom or the liberal solution of it? The two are evidently, albeit erroneously, being treated as if they were the same thing. In the third place, I wonder whether it is correct to contrast freedom *from* with autonomy, for it is hard to see in what sense autonomy can be

---

[28] *Vom Wesen und Wert der Demokratie,* ch. VII.
[29] B. de Jouvenel, *Du pouvoir,* p. 290.

conceived of as a political kind of freedom. However, these questions deserve attention, and we shall start by ascertaining exactly what Rousseau thought and said.

We can have doubts about Rousseau's solutions, but not about his intentions. The problem of politics, Rousseau affirmed, "which I compare to the squaring of the circle in geometry [is] to place law above man."[30] This was for him *the* problem, because—he said—only on this condition may man be free: when he obeys laws, not men.[31] And Rousseau was more sure of this certainty than on any other. "Liberty," he confirmed in *Letters from the Mountain*, "shares the fate of laws; it reigns or perishes with them. There is nothing of which I am surer than this."[32] And, as he said in the *Confes-*

---

[30] He added: "[Otherwise] you can be sure that it will not be the law that will rule, but men" (*Considérations sur le gouvernement de la Pologne*, ch. 1).

[31] It is the constant thesis in all of Rousseau's writings. In the *Discours sur l'économie politique*, compiled probably in 1754 for the *Encyclopédie*, he wrote: "Law is the only thing to which man owes his freedom and the justice he receives." In the dedicatory letter to the *Discours* on *Quelle est l'origine de l'inégalité parmi les hommes* he wrote: "No one of you is so little enlightened as not to realize that where the vigor of the law and the authority of its defenders end, there can be no safety or freedom for anyone." In the first draft of the *Contrat social* (1756), law was described as "the most sublime of all human institutions." In the "brief and faithful" condensation of his *Contrat social* in the *Lettres écrites de la montagne* Rousseau repeated: "When men are placed above the law . . . you have left only slaves and masters" (pt. I, no. 5).

[32] Pt. II, no. 8. Rousseau had said before: "There is . . . no freedom without laws, nor where there is anyone who is above the law. . . . A free nation obeys the law, and the law only; and it is through the power of the law that it does not obey men. . . . People are free . . . when they see in whoever governs them not a man, but an organ of the law" (*ibid.*). And in pt. II, no. 9 he wrote: "All that the citizen wants is the law and the obedience thereof. Every individual . . . knows very well that any exceptions will not be to his favor. This is why everyone fears exceptions; and those who fear exceptions love the law."

sions, the question he constantly asked was: "Which is the form of government which, by its nature, gets closer and remains closer to law?"[33]

This was a problem that Rousseau had every reason to liken to the squaring of the circle.[34] Whereas in *Letters from the Mountain* he observed that when "the administrators of laws become their sole arbiters . . . I do not see what slavery could be worse,"[35] in the *Social Contract* his question was: "How can a blind multitude, which often does not know what it wills, because only rarely does it know what is good for it, carry out for itself so great and difficult an enterprise as a system of legislation?"[36] For Rousseau this question had only one answer: to legislate as little as possible.[37] He had been coming to this conclusion with more and more conviction for some time, for already in the dedication of his *Discourse on Inequality* he had stressed the fact that the Athenians lost their democracy because everybody proposed laws to satisfy a whim, whereas what gives laws their sacred and venerable character is their age.[38] And this is precisely the point: The laws that Rousseau referred to were Laws

---

[33] *Les Confessions,* bk. IX. It is a rephrasing of this question: "What is the nature of a government under which its people can become the most virtuous, most enlightened, most wise, in short the best that can be expected?"

[34] Rousseau enjoys this comparison, which is also found in a letter to Mirabeau dated July 26, 1767.

[35] Pt. II, no. 9.

[36] *Contrat social,* II, 6.

[37] Cf. B. de Jouvenel in the *Essai sur la politique de Rousseau* which introduces his ed. of the *Contrat social* (Genève, 1947), pp. 123–26. See also *Du pouvoir,* pp. 295–304.

[38] The criticism against the legislative fickleness of the Athenians is resumed in the *Contrat social,* II, 4. See also III, 11, *ibid.*

with a capital *L*—that is, few, very general, fundamental, ancient, and almost immutable supreme Laws.[39]

Rousseau held that the people are the judges and custodians of the Law, not the makers and manipulators of laws. He by no means had in mind the idea of a legislating popular will.[40] On the contrary, he proposed to liberate man by means of an impersonal government of Laws placed high above the will from which they may emanate, that is, related to a will that acknowledges them rather than creates them, sustains them rather than disposes of them, safeguards them rather than modifies them. Whoever appeals to the authority of Rousseau must not forget that his Laws were not at all the

---

[39] The state, says Rousseau, "needs but a few laws" (*Contrat social,* IV, 1). And let us remember that his model was Sparta, that is, the static constitution by antonomasia. Addressing the citizens of his favored Geneva he wrote: "You have good and wise laws, both for themselves, and for the simple reason that they are laws. . . . Since the constitution of your government has reached a definite and stable form, your function as legislators has terminated: to assure the safety of this building it is necessary that you now find as many obstacles to keep it standing as you found aids in building it. . . . The building is finished, now the task is to keep it as it is" (*Lettres écrites de la montagne,* pt. II, no. 9). The exhortation to "maintain and reestablish the ancient ways" is found also throughout the *Considérations sur le gouvernement de la Pologne* (see ch. III). One must also keep in mind that Rousseau's concept of law is based on custom, which he judges as the most important aspect of law (see *Contrat social,* II, 12).

[40] In the dedicatory letter to the *Discours on L'inégalité parmi les hommes* Rousseau states that the republic he would have chosen is the one in which "individuals are happy to accept the laws." In the *Considérations sur le gouvernement de la Pologne* (ch. II), Rousseau distinguishes between the common "lawmakers" and the "Legislator," laments the absence of the latter, and recalls as examples Moses, Lycurgus, and Numa Pompilius. See also *Contrat social,* II, 7, where he invokes the Legislator, "an extraordinary man in the state" who must perform "a particular and superior function which has nothing in common with the human race," for "it would take gods to make laws for human beings."

laws with a small *l* which, by virtue of our formal definition of law, are fabricated with ever increasing speed and magnitude by legislative assemblies in the name of popular sovereignty. His Laws were substantive, i.e., laws by reason of their content. As far as their model is concerned, they were very similar to the notion of law expressed in the theory of natural law.[41] And to appreciate Rousseau's difficulties we must realize that they sprang from the fact that he tried to make immanent the same concept of law that the school of natural law considered transcendent.

He tried to do this by invoking the *volonté générale*,[42] a concept that turns out to be less mysterious than it seems—notwithstanding all the fluctuations to which it is subject—if we remember that it is an expression of the crisis of natural law and, at the same time, of the search for an *Ersatz,* for something to take its place. In the shift from Grotius's *ius naturale* to the Law sanctioned and accepted by the general will, the foundations are different, but the new protagonist (the general will) has the same functions and attributes as the old (nature). Rousseau's general will is not the will of all, that is, it is not "the sum of individuals wills";[43] nor is it a *sui generis* individual will freed of all selfishness and egotism. It is somewhere between the two.[44] And to better ap-

---

[41] The relationship between Rousseau and natural law is studied in detail by R. Derathé, *Jean-Jacques Rousseau et la science politique de son temps* (Paris, 1950).

[42] The wording is not Rousseau's, in fact the expression was common enough. See the careful and intelligent reconstruction of the concept in Jouvenel's *Essai sur la politique de Rousseau,* pp. 105–20, 127–32.

[43] *Contrat social,* II, 3.

[44] We should not look at Rousseau's general will through romantic glasses or for how it has reached us after the idealistic mediation. Also because, as Derathé points out, "the general will is essentially a juridic notion which

preciate its mysterious nature, it is worthwhile recalling Diderot's definition in the *Encyclopédie:* "The general will is in each individual a pure act of understanding, reasoning in the silence of the passions."[45] Rousseau did not accept that definition. Why?

I do not think that what disturbed Rousseau was the rationalistic flavor of Diderot's definition, i.e., his reducing the general will to "a pure act of understanding, reasoning in the silence of the passions." For, although Rousseau's general will is nourished and strengthened by love and by feelings, it is guided by reason.[46] That is, it is still a rational will—"will" as it could be conceived before the romantic outburst, certainly not that voluntaristic will of our time, which precedes and dominates reason.[47]

---

can be understood only through the theory of the moral personality which had been formulated by Hobbes and Pufendorf" (*J. J. Rousseau,* etc., pp. 407–10).

[45] *Encyclopédie,* "Droit naturel," sect. 9.

[46] Rousseau is just as much a rationalist when, e.g., he declares that in the civil society man must "consult his reason before listening to his inclinations" (*Contrat social,* I, 8), and that to submit to the civil society means to be subject to a "law dictated by reason" (*ibid.,* II, 4). Consider also the following passage in the *Contrat,* II, 6: "Private citizens see the good which they repudiate; the public wants the good which it does not see. . . . It is necessary to compel the first to make *their will conform with their reason;* one must teach the other to *know what it wants*" (my italics).

[47] See in this connection A. Cobban's *Rousseau and the Modern State* (London, 1934) and Derathé's *Le Rationalisme de Rousseau* and *Jean-Jacques Rousseau et la science politique de son temps.* Cassirer goes as far as maintaining that "Rousseau's ethics is not an ethics of sentiment, but it is the purest and most definite ethics of the law ever formulated before Kant" ("Das Problem Jean Jacques Rousseau," Italian tr., p. 84). Which is going too far. My deviation from Masson's thesis does not imply that I disregard his fundamental work, i.e., his classic book, *La Religion de J. J. Rousseau* (Paris, 1916, 3 vols.); nor do I wish to deny that Rousseau's political thought is a continuation of his ethics. But I do not

No, what he could not accept was Diderot's answer to the question *Où est le dépôt de cette volonté générale?*—where is the general will located? He could not accept the location of the general will "in each individual." Rousseau could not settle for this approach because he had to rebuild somehow, within society itself, an equivalent of the transcendence that was formerly placed above and outside the realm of human affairs. In other words, the general will had to be the anthropomorphic substitute for the order of nature and for the natural reason that mirrored that order. So much so that in Rousseau the laws were derived from the general will just as they were previously derived from natural law. He wrote: "Whenever it becomes necessary to promulgate new ones

---

see how one can pile together *Émile* (and along with it the *Discours,* the *Confessions,* the *Réveries,* or even the *Nouvelle Héloïse*) with Rousseau's political writings. Whether Rousseau's sentiment has a romantic character or not, the point is that the "ethics of the sentiment" and the "ethics of politics" belong to radically different contexts: in *Émile* Rousseau educates man "according to nature," in the *Contrat* he "denatures" him into a citizen. As Rousseau himself points out in *Émile* (I), "Whoever wants to preserve in a society the priority of the natural sentiments does not know what he wants."

This is to say that Rousseau considers two hypotheses. When society is too large and corrupt only the individual can be saved. Therefore in *Émile,* Rousseau proposes to abolish even the words "country" and "citizen," and exalts love for one's self. In this hypothesis man must devote his attention entirely to himself. But when the city and society are small and still patriarchal—this is the second hypothesis—then one must save the community: This is the problem of the *Contrat.* In the latter case the citizen must cancel the man, the patriot must collectivize his love for himself, and the individual must give his self to the whole; he dies as a "particular" and is reborn as a moral member of the collective body. Rousseau is coherent, but his hypotheses are discontinuous, or better, alternative. In the "nature man" the sentiment dominates, but in the denatured" one (the citizen) passion and love become a catalyst that helps in the production of a society that acts according to reason; and the general will is the very *deus ex machina* of a purely logical construction.

[laws], this necessity is perceived universally. He who proposes them only says what all have already felt."[48] This is like saying that laws are not produced *ex homine,* but are recognized and proclaimed *ex natura:* The general will does not, strictly speaking, make them and want them, but bears them within itself. If it were really a will, when inert it would not exist, and when mute it would not will; while for Rousseau the general will is "always constant, unchangeable, and pure" and cannot be annihilated or corrupted.[49] Which comes back to saying that it is an entity of reason that does not suffer the vicissitudes of human will, or of particular wills.[50]

The general will can be compared, as far as the function Rousseau assigned to it, to the "spirit of the people," to what this historical school of law later called the *Volksgeist:* not because the two concepts are similar, but because they both attempt to fill the void left by natural law. Both these notions were motivated by the need to discover objectivity in subjectivity, something absolute and stable in what is relative and changeable—in short, a fixed point of reference. The romantics sought transcendence within immanence by locating the former in History (with a capital *H*), in the collective, anonymous, and fatal flux of events; Rousseau tried to find transcendence in Man by placing it in a common ego that unites all men. And just as the romantics of the historical school of law contradicted themselves when, in order

---

[48] *Contrat social,* IV, 1.

[49] *Ibid.*

[50] It is true that in Rousseau there is also a "subjective" position through which the will can decide about the laws (see *Contrat,* II, 12); but that admission is always accompanied by the position that reason discovers their "objective" necessity (see *Contrat,* II, 11).

to insert their transcendent *Volksgeist* in the orbit of immanence, they had to rely on a privileged interpreter,[51] in the same way and for the same reason Rousseau contradicted himself (thereby revealing the weak point of his system) when, in his search for a link between the general will and what the citizens want, he allowed the majority to be the interpreter of the *volonté générale*.

The contradiction lies in the fact that the majority's will is subjective and merely stems from the will of all, whereas Rousseau's general will is an objective moral will made up of qualitative elements, for it must be "general" in essence, at its origin, and for its objective.[52] Although Rousseau kept his general will in the orbit of calculable qualities—he even indicated that it is derived from a sum of the differences, i.e., after the pluses and minuses of individual will are canceled out[53]—counting can only reveal the general will, it cannot produce its essence.[54] The popular will is additive,

---

[51] The analogy holds true even in this respect: because for Rousseau too the legislator is a "revealer," as Groethuysen has pointed out in his work *Jean-Jacques Rousseau* (Paris, 1949), p. 103.

[52] See esp. *Contrat*, II, 4 and 6.

[53] *Contrat*, II, 3. Here one can perceive the distance between Rousseau and Hegel, between the philosopher of the eighteenth century and the romantics. In Rousseau's conceptualization we do not find, for there could not be, any of those ingredients used by the romantics for building their organismic, collective entities; we do not find the "soul" or the "spirit" of the people. For this reason Rousseau had to keep his general will proximate to something numerical and computable.

[54] In fact Rousseau hastens to specify: "Often there is quite a difference between the will of all (*la volonté de tous*) and the general will" (*Contrat*, II, 3). That "often" reveals Rousseau's difficulties and oscillations. On the one hand he was concerned to find a passage between Law and Sovereign, but on the other hand Rousseau was not at all resigned to accept this consequence: that "a people is always free to change its laws, even the best ones: for if it wants to harm itself, who has the right to stop it?" (*ibid.*, II, 12).

the general will is one and indivisible. Even if we grant that in the process of popular consultations an interplay of compensations eliminates individual passions, in order to achieve the quality of general will we need much more: *bonne volonté* (good will), patriotism, and enlightened popular judgment.[55] These are demanding conditions which amount to a very severe limitation on popular sovereignty.[56]

If the general will "is always good and always tends to the public interest," it does not follow—Rousseau added—"that the deliberations of the people are always right."[57] He later explains: "The people always desire the good, but do not always see it. The general will is always in the right, but the judgment which guides it is not always enlightened."[58] The people would like the good, but that does not mean that they recognize it. Therefore, it is not the general will that resolves itself into popular sovereignty, but vice versa, the popular will that must resolve itself into the general will. Rousseau did not ask whether the people rejected or accepted a bill,

---

[55] B. de Jouvenel has rendered the distinction very well. He states: "The will of all can bind everyone juridically. That is one thing. But it is quite another thing to say that it is good. . . . Therefore, to this will of all which has only a juridic value he counterposes the general will which is always correct and always tends toward public welfare" (*Essai sur la politique de Rousseau*, p. 109).

[56] Note in passing that Rousseau's "people" is completely different from the *populace*. The people consists of the "citizens" and the "patriots" only. Both in the project of the Constitution of Poland as in the one of Corsica, Rousseau foresees a meticulous *cursus honorum* which amounts to a qualification for sovereignty. And from the *Lettres écrites de la montagne* one can see very clearly that equality for Rousseau is an intermediate condition between the beggar and the millionaire represented by the bourgeoisie. Between the rich and the poor, between the rulers and the *populace,* Rousseau's "people" is not far removed from Hegel's "general class."

[57] *Contrat*, II, 3.

[58] *Ibid.,* II, 6.

but whether it did or did not express the general will.[59] In substance, his system hangs on a general will that supplants popular power.

Ironically enough, Rousseau was the proponent of a most unadventurous type of immobile democracy, which was supposed to legislate as little as possible and could survive only on condition that it kept its actions to a minimum. He devoted all his ingenuity and the most meticulous attention to controlling the forces that his ideal would have let loose. His democracy was intended to be defensive rather than aggressive, cautious, and wary; not Jacobin and omnivorous.[60] It is no paradox to assert that his democracy was a watchdog democracy, to the same extent that the liberal

---

[59] *Ibid.,* IV, 2.

[60] Rousseau not only did not have a revolutionary temperament, he was not even a political reformer. See Groethuysen's concise statement: "Rousseau's ideas were revolutionary; he himself was not" (*J. J. Rousseau,* p. 206). In his second *Discours,* Rousseau declares: "I would have liked to have been born under a democratic government, wisely tempered" (Dedicatory letter). In the third *Dialogue,* he stresses that he "had always insisted on the preservation of existing institutions." In 1765 he wrote to Buttafoco: "I have always held and shall always follow as an inviolable maxim the principle of having the highest respect for the government under which I live, and to make no attempts . . . to reform it in any way whatever." The project on the reform of Poland is throughout a reminder of the use of prudence in carrying out reforms. One of the most sarcastic refutations of revolutionary medicines is found in this text: "I laugh at those people . . . who imagine that in order to be free all they have to do is to be rebels" (*Considérations sur le gouvernement de la Pologne,* ch. VI). Only Corsica, Rousseau believed, could be reformed through legislation alone, for in his judgment it was the only state young enough to gain by it (*Contrat,* II, 10). For the rest he warned, "After customs are established and prejudices become deeply set, it is a vain and dangerous enterprise to change them" (*ibid.,* II, 8). And referring to changes of regime he admonished that "those changes are always dangerous . . . and one should never touch a government that is established except when it becomes incompatible with the common weal" (*ibid.,* III, 18).

state of the nineteenth century was nicknamed the watchdog state. He rejected representatives, wanted a direct and, as far as possible, a unanimous democracy, and required that the magistrates should have no will of their own but only the power to impose the general will. The result was, clearly, a static body, a democracy that was supposed to restrict, rather than encourage innovation. It is true that Rousseau spoke of "will," but he did not mean by it a *willing will;* he thought of it as a brake, rather than an accelerator. The general will was not a *dynamis,* but the infallible instinct that permits us to evaluate the laws, and to accept as Law only the Just, the True Law. Rousseau's aim was to free man from his bonds by inventing a system that would obstruct and curb legislation. And this was because he felt that the solution of the problem of securing freedom lay exclusively in the supremacy of law, and, furthermore, in a supremacy of law concerned with avoiding the legislative outcome of the Athenian democracy, that is, the primacy of popular sovereignty over the law.

Rousseau, then, did not present a new conception of freedom. He enjoyed going against the current and contradicting his contemporaries on many scores, but not on this one point: the legalitarian concept of liberty that had found fresh nourishment and support in the natural rights of the natural law revival of the seventeenth and eighteenth centuries.[61] Rousseau never for a minute had the idea of freeing

---

[61] One must discern at least three phases in the evolution of the idea of natural law. Until the Stoics the law of nature was not a juridic notion, but a term of comparison which denoted the uniformity and the normality of what is natural. With the Stoics, and the Romans above all, one can already speak of a theory of natural law. But the Roman conceptualization did not contain the idea of "personal rights," which is at the base of our idea of constitutional legality and which belongs to the third phase.

man by means of popular sovereignty, as is maintained by those who have evidently read little of him. The assertion that liberty is founded by law and in law, found in Rousseau, if anything, its most intransigent supporter. Rousseau was so uncompromising about it that he could not even accept the legislative conception of law within a constitutional framework proposed by Montesquieu; for this solution, after all, allowed for changing laws, while Rousseau wanted a basically unchanging Law.

5. Autonomy: A Criticism

It may be asked: Did not Rousseau speak of liberty as autonomy at all? Actually we do find in the *Social Contract* this sentence: "Obedience to laws that we have imposed on ourselves is liberty."[62] But when he declared that everybody is free because in obeying the laws that he himself has made he is submitting to his own will, Rousseau was by no means speaking of the autonomy of which we speak today as if it were his discovery.

In the first place, Rousseau related his idea of autonomy to the Contract, that is, to the hypothesis of an original pact in which ideally each party to the contract submits to norms that he has freely accepted. The fact that Rousseau had in mind a democracy that was not in the least inclined to change its Laws shows how important it was for him to keep this liberty tied to its original legitimacy, and indicates that he did not mean this idea to be used as a basis for mass legislation, which is the way we are using it. There is an essential condition that qualifies Rousseau's formula,

---

[62] *Contrat social,* I, 8. See also *ibid.,* I, 6.

namely that the people are free so long as they do not delegate the exercise of their sovereignty to legislative assemblies.[63] So his conception has very little to do with obedience to laws that are made for us by others.

In the second place, Rousseau's thesis is closely related to the notion of a small democracy in which everybody participates. His state was the city, and he never thought that his democracy could be applied to large republics.[64] He had in mind Spartans and Romans, and his projects concerned Geneva. Now it is plausible to maintain that the citizens of a small city who govern themselves directly submit only to the rules that they have accepted, and therefore obey nothing but their own wills; but when self-government is no longer possible, when the citizens are dispersed over a vast territory, when they do not participate in the legislative output, does the assertion still make sense? Certainly not for Rousseau.

In the third place, by tracing to Rousseau the concept of liberty as autonomy, we take the premise from which he started and forget the conclusion that he reached. When Rousseau went back to a liberty that is submission to laws we have prescribed ourselves, his problem was to legitimize

---

[63] *Ibid.,* III, 15.

[64] One could quote at length, for this is a very firm point in Rousseau. Even in the *Considérations sur le gouvernement de la Pologne,* that is to say in a context in which Rousseau has to soften and adjust his conception to a large state, he maintains that the "grandeur of nations, the extension of states" is the "first and principal source of human woes. . . . Almost all small states, whether republics or monarchies, prosper for the very reason that they are small, that all the citizens know each other. . . . All the large nations, crushed by their own masses, suffer whether . . . under a monarchy or under oppressors" (ch. V). Also see *Contrat social:* "The larger a state becomes, the less freedom there is" (III, 1); "the larger the population, the greater the repressive forces" (III, 2).

Law. If man renounces his natural liberty in order to achieve a superior civil liberty, he does so because the society he enters subjects him to norms he has accepted, that is, to just Laws, which liberate not oppress him. But once Law is legitimized and true Law is established, Rousseau's liberty is liberty under Law. Man is free because, when Laws and not men govern, he gives himself to no one. In other words, he is free because he is not exposed to arbitrary power. This was Rousseau's concept of liberty. And so it was understood by his contemporaries. Even in the Declaration of Rights of 1793, Article Nine stated: "The law must protect public and individual liberty against the oppression of those who govern." This article has a strange ring if we recall that the Terror was under way. Yet, what we have read in Rousseau's definition of liberty.

The truth is that "autonomy" originated with Kant, and that it was Kant who called attention to the concept. Except that for the author of the *Critique of Practical Reason,* the notion of autonomy had nothing to do with democratic liberty or any other kind of political or even juridical liberty. Kant distinguished very clearly between "external" and "internal" freedom. And the prescription by ourselves of our own laws is in Kant the definition of moral liberty, that is, of our internal freedom—a completely different matter from the question of external coercion. In the moral sphere we are concerned with the question of whether man is free in the interior forum of his conscience, while in politics we are concerned with ways of preventing man's exterior subjugation. Thus, if we are interested in the problem of man's political freedom, Kant's ethic is of no use to us. And this explains why the word "autonomy" rebounded from Kant to Rousseau as soon as it took on a political meaning. But the question is: To which Rousseau? To the real Rousseau, or to the one remodeled by the romantics and subsequently by the idealistic philosophers?

With the assurance that is characteristic of him, Kelsen flatly asserts that "political freedom is autonomy."[65] But it seems to me that Kelsen, as well as many other scholars, has adopted this thesis too lightly. For the autonomy about which especially German and Italian theory talks so much is a concept of a speculative-dialectical nature, which stems from a philosophy that has indeed little to do with liberalism and democracy.[66] I can understand that many democrats have been fascinated by the idea of autonomy, implying, as it does, a high valuation of the *demos*. But it is a concept that political theory has endowed with the very different function of justifying and legitimizing obedience. This is a perfectly respectable usage, except when we want autonomy for the solution of a problem not its own, namely the problem of safeguarding, maintaining, and defending our liberties.

The truth is that if we may speak of autonomy as a concrete expression of political freedom, this autonomy ended with ancient democracies. The formula of the Greek liberty

---

[65] *General Theory of Law and State* (New Haven, 1945), pt. II, ch. IV, B. a2.

[66] Hegelian idealism, to be precise. These infiltrations have been so deep that De Ruggiero's *Storia del liberalismo europeo* (tr. Collingwood, *History of European Liberalism* [London, 1927]) raises Hegel to the central figure of liberal thought, and following the Kant-Hegel line reaches the conclusion that "the state, the organ of compulsion par excellence, has become the highest expression of freedom" (p. 374, Italian ed.); this being, according to De Ruggiero, a typically liberal position, in fact the essential conquest of liberalism (see pp. 230–53 and pp. 372–74, Italian ed.).

was—we read in Aristotle—"To govern and to be governed alternately, . . . to be under no command whatsoever to any-one, upon any account, any otherwise than by rotation, and that just as far only as that person is, in turn, under his also."[67] Now, this self-government can be interpreted as a situation of autonomy—even though somewhat arbitrarily, since in Aristotle's description the problem of a *nomos,* and therefore of a liberty related to law, is not raised. However, if it pleases us to speak of autonomy in this connection, then we come to the conclusion that the supposedly new and most advanced conception of liberty advocated by present-day progressive democrats is none other than the oldest and most obsolete formula of liberty. For clearly only a *micropolis,* and indeed a very small one, can solve the problem of political freedom by having—I am again citing Aristotle— "all to command each, and each in its turn all." Certainly our ever growing megalopolis cannot.

Coming back from this very distant past to the present time, we meet with the expression "local autonomy." But let us not delude ourselves: Local autonomies result from the distrust of concentrated power and are, therefore, an ex-pression of freedom *from* the centralized state. The liberty connected with administrative decentralization, with the Germans' *Selbstverwaltung,* or with self-government of the Anglo-Saxon type, does not mean what Rousseau or Kelsen had in mind. Situations of local auotnomy are in effect "autarchies"[68] and serve as safeguards of liberty chiefly

---

[67] *Politics,* 1317b (W. Ellis tr.).

[68] For the difference between self-government, *Selbstverwaltung* (which German scholarship wrongly equated with self-government) and autarchy, see Giuseppino Treves, "Autarchia, autogoverno, autonomia," in *Studi in onore di G. M. De Francesco* (Milano, 1957), v. II, pp. 579–94.

because they allow a polycentric distribution of political power.

It may be said that the notion of autonomy in its political application must be interpreted in a looser and more flexible way, and that it is in this sense that it helps to connote the democratic brand of liberty. Norberto Bobbio observes that "the concept of autonomy in philosophy is embarrassing, but . . . in the context of politics the term indicates something easier to understand: It indicates that the norms which regulate the actions of the citizens must conform as far as possible to the desires of the citizens."[69] This is true—but why use the word autonomy? Orders that "conform as far as possible to the desires of the citizens" are assented orders, which means that the problem in question is one of consensus. And it is important to be precise on this matter, since the intrusion of "autonomy" is causing a great deal of confusion nowadays.

Bobbio rightly points out that while a state of liberty in the sense of nonrestriction has to do with action, a state of autonomy has to do with will.[70] This is indeed the point. For the sphere of politics concerns volitions *insofar as they are actions,* and not pure and simple will. In politics what matters is whether I am empowered to do what my will wants. The internal problem of freedom of will is not the political problem of freedom, for the political problem is the external problem of freedom of action. Politics concerns, as Hegel would say, the "objective sphere" in which the will has to externalize itself. Therefore, as long as we interpret liberty as autonomy, we do not cross the threshold of poli-

---

[69] N. Bobbio, *Politica e cultura,* p. 176.

[70] *Ibid.,* pp. 173, 272.

tics; not because autonomy is not essential, but because it is a subjective presupposition of political freedom.

The concept of autonomy is of so little use in the objective sphere, that here an antithesis of it does not exist. We can be coerced and still remain autonomous, that is, inwardly free. And this is the reason why it is said that force can never extinguish in man the spark of liberty. Likewise, we can be safe from any coercion and yet remain sleepwalkers because we are not capable of internal self-determination. Autonomy and coercion are by no means mutually exclusive concepts. My will can remain free (autonomous), even if I am physically imprisoned (coerced) just as it can be inactive and passive (heteronomous) even when I am permitted to do anything I wish (noncoerced). The antithesis of autonomy is heteronomy. And heteronomy stands for passivity, anomie, characterlessness, and the like—all of which are notions that concern not the subject-sovereign relationship but the problem of a responsible self. In short, they are all concepts that have to do with internal, not external liberty, with the power to will, not the power to do; and this goes back to saying that our vocabulary makes it impossible for us to employ the word "autonomy" in connection with the question of political freedom.

But why should we find it necessary? After all, in politics we are concerned with the practical problem of achieving a state of liberty in which state compulsion be curbed and based on consent. And this is just as much the democratic problem of liberty as it is the liberal problem of liberty. In either case we do not make the laws, but we help to choose the legislators. And that is a very different matter. Furthermore, we are free not because we actually wanted the laws that those legislators enacted, but because we limit and control their power to enact them. If the liberty that we enjoy lay in our personal share in lawmaking, I fear that we would be left with very few liberties, if any. For, as John Stuart Mill very nicely put it, "The self-government spoken of is not the government of each by himself, but of each by all the rest."[71]

The reply may be that the formula liberty-autonomy is only an ideal. So we are not actually maintaining that somewhere there are people who are free by virtue of their own lawmaking, or that some place exists where liberty actually consists in the rule of oneself by oneself. What we are expressing is only a prescription. It is only in this sense, therefore, that we put forth an ideal of political freedom that is specifically a democratic ideal. Be this as it may, on substantial grounds I am already satisfied with making the point that "liberty from" and "liberty as autonomy" are not alternatives that can be substituted for each other *in actual practice,* even though, in terms of principle, I must confess that I am still not convinced, for I doubt whether the ideal of self-obedience is really adaptable to the democratic creed, and whether it really reinforces it.

Democratic deontology is authentically expressed in the ideal of self-government, not of autonomy. To the extent that the notion of autonomy takes the place of the notion of self-government, it obscures and weakens it. It obscures it because after having been manipulated among Kant, Rousseau, and Hegel, the idea of autonomy can easily be used to demonstrate (in words, of course) that we are free when we are not. Whoever has lived under a dictatorship knows only too well how easily autonomy can be turned into a practice

---

[71] *On Liberty* (Oxford, 1947), pp. 67–68.

of submission that is justified by high-level explanations about true freedom. And not only does autonomy easily become a self-complacent exercise in obedience: there is more. For in helping people to mistake a nominal self-government for real self-government it ends up by keeping them from actually seeking the latter. I mean that when we speak of self-government, we can ascertain whether it exists, and we know what we have to do in order to approach it; whereas when we speak of autonomy, empirical verification is bypassed, and we can stay peacefully in bed and think of ourselves as free.

The rationalistic democracies have, then, been ill-advised in adopting an ambiguous philosophical concept that distracts our attention from concrete, what-to-do problems, and that comes dangerously near to being a sham construction behind which lurks the figure of liberty understood as passive conformity and subservience. In the realm of politics, autonomy is an untrustworthy interpretation of liberty, and its revival indicates how seriously the democratic *forma mentis* as such lacks political sensitivity. Having reappeared on the stage of history after liberalism, that is, in a situation of established political freedom, this *forma mentis* reveals, by the very adoption of the notion of autonomy, that it has not actually suffered the trials and lessons that political oppression imposes.

There is, of course, a type of autonomy that could be considered a *libertas major* even in the sphere of politics; but it would be found in a society that functions by spontaneous self-discipline wherein internalized self-imposed rules would take the place of compulsory laws emanating from the state. We can keep this concept in reserve for a time when the state will have withered away; but as long as the state is growing, let us not be duped into believing in a superior democratic liberty conceived of as autonomy. So long as the state grows, let us bear in mind that even though I may succeed in governing myself perfectly, this autonomy does not protect me from the possibility of being sent to a concentration camp—and the problem is just that. It amounts to saying that I believe in the notion of autonomy as moral freedom, in the sense indicated by Kant, but certainly not in autonomy as a fourth type of political freedom.

6. The Principle of Diminishing Consequences

I have wanted to discuss the concept of autonomy fully because this notion is a typical example of that verbal over-straining which tends to jeopardize—among other things—the difficult and precarious conquest of political freedom. Many scholars treat the question of liberty as if it were a logical rather than an empirical problem. That is, they ignore the principle that I call the law of diminishing consequences, or, as we may also say, of the dispersion of effects.

Thus, from the premise that we all (as infinitesimal fractions) participate in the creation of the legislative body, we boldly evince that it is *as if* we ourselves made the laws. Likewise, and in a more elaborate way, we make the inference that when a person who allegedly represents some tens of thousands contributes (he himself acting as a very small fraction) to the lawmaking process, then he is making the thousands of people whom he is representing free, because the represented thereby obey norms that they have freely chosen (even though it might well be that even their representative was opposed to those norms). How absurd!

Clearly this is nothing more than mental gymnastics in a frictionless interplanetary space. Coming back to earth, these chains of acrobatic inferences are worthless, and this for the good reason that the driving force of the causes (premises) is exhausted long before it reaches its targets. In empirical terms, from the premise that I know how to swim it may follow that I can cross a river, but not that I can cross the ocean. The "cause," ability to swim, cannot produce everlasting effects. And the same applies in the empirical realm of politics to the "cause," participation and elections.

There are at times no limits to the services that we ask of political participation. Yet from the premise that effective, continuous participation of the citizens in the self-government of a small community can produce the "result" liberty (precisely a liberty as autonomy), we cannot draw the conclusion that the same amount of participation will produce the same result in a large community; for in the latter an equally intense participation will entail diminishing consequences. And a similar warning applies to our way of linking elections with representation. Elections do produce representative results, so to speak; but it is absurd to ask of the "cause," elections, infinite effects. Bruno Leoni made the point lucidly when he wrote: "The more numerous the people are whom one tries to 'represent' through the legislative process and the more numerous the matters in which one tries to represent them, the less the word 'representation' has a meaning referable to the actual will of actual people, other than the persons named as their 'representatives'. . . . The inescapable conclusion is that in order to restore to the word 'representation' its original, reasonable meaning, there should be a drastic reduction either in the number of those 'represented' or in the number of matters in which they are allegedly represented, or both."[72]

I do not know whether we can go back to the "drastic reduction" suggested by Leoni. But there is no doubt that if we keep on stretching the elastic (but not infinitely so) cord of political representation beyond a certain limit—in defiance of the law of the dispersion of effects—it will snap. For the more we demand of representation, the less closely are the representatives tied to those they represent. Let us therefore beware of treating representation as another version of the formulas that make us believe (by logical demonstration) that we are free when we actually are not. The fable that autonomy makes for *the* true political liberty is, per se, sufficiently stupefying.

7. From Rule of Law to Rule of Legislators

There are two reasons for my having made a particular point of the connection between liberty and law. The first one is that I am under the impression that we have gone a little too far in the so-called informal approach. Nowadays, both political scientists and philosophers are very contemptuous of law. The former, because they believe that laws can do very little, or in any case much less than had previously been deemed possible; and the latter because they are usu-

---

[72] Bruno Leoni, *Freedom and the Law* (New York, 1961), pp. 18, 19. Professor Leoni was kind enough to allow me to consult in advance the text of his lectures, and I am indebted to him for many of the issues discussed in sect. 7.

ally concerned with a higher liberty that will not be hampered by humble, worldly obstacles.[73] Benedetto Croce unquestionably shared this attitude. Yet, philosophers also have a store of common sense, and it is highly significant that an antijuridical thinker such as Croce himself said: "Those who build theories attacking law, can do so with a light heart because they are surrounded by, protected by, and kept alive by laws; but the instant that all laws begin to break down they would instantly lose their taste for theorizing and chattering."[74] This is indeed a sound warning that should always be kept in mind. After all, if Western man for two and a half millennia has sought liberty in the law, there must have been a good reason for this. Our forefathers were not more ingenuous than we are. On the contrary.

We must nevertheless admit that the widespread skepticism about the value of the juridical protection of liberty is not unjustified. The reason for this is that our conception of law has changed, and that, as a consequence, law can no longer give us the guarantees that it did in the past. This is

---

[73] There are also philosophers who maintain that freedom and law are mutually exclusive. This thesis does not apply, however, to the political problem of liberty, but to freedom understood as self-realization or self-perfection. I would go as far as saying that no author who has clearly isolated the problem of political freedom holds the view of "liberty against law," provided that some qualifications are made about what is meant by law. The thesis that law infringes individual liberty, held, e.g., by Hobbes, Bentham, and Mill, does not really contradict Locke's statement that "where there is no law there is no freedom" (*Two Treatises of Government,* ch. VI, sect. 27). It is different either because they envisaged a different problem, or because they referred to the case of the unjust law (but in such a case that denial completes the sense of the thesis of liberty under law). See note 19 above.

[74] *Filosofia della pratica* (Bari, 1909, 4th ed., 1932), p. 333.

no reason for leaving, or creating, a void where law used to be, but it is certainly a reason for staying alert, and not letting ourselves be lulled by the idea that the laws stand guard over us while we sleep twenty-four hours a day. And this is my second motive for paying a great deal of attention to the relationship between law and political liberty.

Montesquieu, who was still relying on the protection of natural law, could very simply assert that we are free because we are subject to "civil laws."[75] But our problem begins exactly where this statement terminates. For we are obliged to ask the question that Montesquieu (as well as Rousseau) could ignore: Which laws are "civil laws"?

To begin with, what is law? In the Roman tradition, *ius* (the Latin word for law) has become inextricably connected with *iustum* (what is just);[76] and in the course of time the

---

[75] See *L'Esprit des lois,* bk. XXVI, ch. XX: "Freedom consists above all in not being compelled to do something which is not prescribed by law; and we are in this situation only as we are governed by civil laws. Therefore we are free because we live under civil laws."

[76] The Greek had no real equivalent of the Latin *ius.* The Greek *diké* and *dikaiosúne* render the moral but not the legal idea of justice; this means they are not equivalent to the *iustum* (just) that derives from *ius.* On the meanings and etymology of *ius* as well as of the later term *directum* (from which come the Italian *diritto,* the French *droit,* the Spanish *derecho,* etc., which are not the same as the English "right," since the latter is concrete and/or appreciative, whereas the former concepts are abstract and neutral nouns indicating the legal system as a whole), see Felice Battaglia, "Alcune osservazioni sulla struttura e sulla funzione del diritto" in *Rivista di diritto civile,* III (1955), esp. pp. 509–13; and W. Cesarini Sforza, *'Ius' e 'directum,' Note sull'origine storica dell'idea di diritto* (Bologna, 1930). From a strictly glottological point of view the origin of *ius* is not too clear. Let us just note that the associations of *ius* with *iubeo* (to order), *iuvo* (to benefit), *iungo* (to link), and *iustum* (just) all appear at a relatively late stage. See G. Devoto, "Ius—Di là dalla grammatica," *Rivista italiana per le scienze giuridiche* (1948), pp. 414–18.

ancient word for law has become the English (and the Italian and French) word for justice. In short, *ius* is both "law" and "right." That is to say, law has not been conceived as any general rule which is enforced by a sovereign (*iussum*), but as that rule which embodies and expresses the community's sense of justice (*iustum*). In other words, law has been thought of not only as any norm that has the "form" of law, but also as a "content," i.e., as that norm which also has the value and the quality of being just.

That has been the general feeling about the nature of law until recently.[77] Yet, on practical grounds we are confronted with a very serious problem, for law is not given, it has to be made. Only primitive or traditionalistic societies can do without deliberate and overt lawmaking. Thus, we have to answer the questions: Who makes the law? How? And, furthermore, Who interprets the laws? In order for us to be governed by laws, or rather by means of laws, the lawmakers themselves must be subject to law. But this is obviously a formidable, strenuous enterprise. The problem has been solved within the constitutional state by arranging the legislative procedure in such a way that the "form of law" also constitutes a guarantee and implies a control of its content.[78] A large number of constitutional devices are, in

---

[77] That is of course a very broad generalization. For a more detailed but swift historical analysis, see the survey of C. J. Friedrich, *The Philosophy of Law in Historical Perspective* (Chicago, 1958).

[78] As can be easily gathered from the whole context of this essay, I use "constitution" in the light of its political *telos* and *raison d'être,* and therefore in the perspective that conceives constitutional law—as Mirkine-Guetzévitch said—as a "technique of freedom" (see *Nouvelles tendances du droit constitutionelle* [Paris, 1931], pp. 81 ff.) and defines a constitution as "the process by which governmental action is effectively restrained" (C. J. Friedrich, *Constitutional Government and Democracy,* p. 131).

effect, intended to create the conditions of a lawmaking process in which the *ius* will remain tied to *iustum,* in which law will remain the right law. For this reason legislation is entrusted to elected bodies that must periodically answer to the electorate. And for the same reason we do not give those who are elected to office *carte blanche,* but we consider them power-holders curbed by and bound to a representative role.

But this solution, or let us say situation, has reacted upon our conception of law. As I have said, we now have a different feeling about the nature of law. For the analytical jurisprudence (that calls up the name of John Austin) on the one hand, and the juridical positivism (of the Kelsen type) on the other, have ended by giving law a purely formal definition, that is, identifying law with the form of law. This shift is actually a rather obvious consequence of the fact that the existence of the *Rechtsstaat*[79] appears to eliminate the very possibility of the unjust law, and thereby allows that the problem of law be reduced to a problem of form rather than of content. Unfortunately, however, the formalistic school

---

For the other loose meaning of constitution (but hardly of "constitutionalism" as a body of doctrine related to the constitutional function) see note 81 below.

[79] I am of course referring to the original meaning: *Rechtsstaat* as a synonym of constitutional *garantisme* (see note 23 above). If the notion of state based on law is conceived in strictly formal terms, it becomes—as Renato Treves has rightly observed—purely tautologic: "If we start with the preconception that our point of view must be exclusively juridic, on what other basis could the state based on law be founded except on law? What else could the state realize except law? And what is the significance of saying that the state must find its limits in law, given the fact that law is in itself always a limit and a position of rights and duties which are reciprocally corresponding?" (R. Treves, "Stato di diritto e stati totalitari," in *Studi in onore di G. M. De Francesco* [Milano, 1957], p. 61).

of jurisprudence completely overlooks this dependence, that is, the fact that the formal definition of law presupposes the constitutional state. Therefore the high level of systematic and technical refinement achieved by this approach cannot save it from the charge of having drawn conclusions without paying attention to the premises, and of having thus erected a structure whose logical perfection is undermined by its lack of foundations.[80]

The implication of this development, with regard to the political problem that constitutional legality tries to solve, is is that Austin, Kelsen, and their numerous following have created, albeit unwittingly, a very unhappy state of affairs. Today we have taken to applying "constitution" to any type of state organization,[81] and "law" to any state command expressed in the form established by the sovereign himself. Now, if law is no longer a fact that is qualified by a value

---

[80] It is well known that to Kelsen any state is by definition a *Rechtsstaat,* since according to the "pure doctrine of law" all state activity is by definition a juridical activity that brings about an "order" that cannot be regarded as anything but juridical. See his *General Theory of Law and State, passim.*

[81] That is, simply to designate any "political form," or better any way of "giving form" to any state whatever. This loose meaning of constitution is not unprecedented (for example, the translators of Aristotle erroneously render *politeía* by "constitution," since *politeía* is the ethico-political system as a whole, not its higher law). However, today it has found a technical justification in the formal definition of law, which consecrates, willy-nilly, the existence of what Loewenstein calls "semantic constitutions," so-called because their "reality is nothing but the formalization of the existing location of political power for the exclusive benefit of the actual power holders" (*Political Power and Government Process,* p. 149). I have taken it (see "Constitutionalism: A Preliminary Discussion," *American Political Science Review,* December 1962) that the all-embracing and purely formal use of "constitution" is an unwarranted misuse of the concept.

(an *ius* that is *iustum*), and if the idea of law is on the one hand restricted to the commands that bear the mark of the will of the sovereign, and on the other extended to any order that the sovereign is willing to enforce, then it is clear that a law so defined can no longer solve our problems. According to the purely formal definition, a law without righteousness is nonetheless law. Therefore, legislation can be crudely tyrannical and yet not only be called legal but also be respected as lawful. It follows from this that such a conception of law leaves no room for the idea of law as the safeguard of liberty. In this connection even "law" becomes, or may be used as, a trap word.

If the analytic-positivistic approaches of modern jurisprudence are not reassuring—at least for those who are concerned about political freedom—it must be added that the de facto development of our constitutional systems is even less so. What the founding fathers of liberal constitutionalism[82] had in mind—in relation to the legislative process—was to bring the rule of law into the state itself, that is, to use Charles H. McIlwain's terms, to extend the sphere of *iurisdictio* to the very realm of *gubernaculum* (government).[83] English constitutionalism actually originated in

---

[82] I say "liberal constitutionalism" where American authors are inclined to say "democratic constitutionalism" on account of the peculiar meaning that "liberal" has acquired in the United States. The latter label, however, has two disadvantages: One is that it is historically incorrect, for it is difficult to understand in what sense English constitutionalism belongs in the orbit of the development of the idea of democracy; the other is that it is confusing in terms of the present-day constitutional debate as well, since the democratic component of our system tends nowadays to erode liberal constitutions.

[83] See Charles H. McIlwain, *Constitutionalism: Ancient and Modern* (Ithaca, 1940), ch. IV. *Iurisdictio* and *gubernaculum* were the terminology used by Bracton toward the middle of the thirteenth century.

this way, since the *garantiste* principles of the English constitution are generalizations derived from particular decisions pronounced by the courts in relation to the rights of specific individuals. And since English constitutional practice—even if it has always been misunderstood—has constantly inspired the Continental constitutionalists, the theory of *garantisme* as well as of the *Rechtsstaat* (in its first stage) had precisely this in mind: to clothe the *gubernaculum* with a mantle of *iurisdictio*. No matter how much the Anglo-Saxon notion of the rule of law has been misinterpreted,[84] there is no doubt that liberal constitutionalism looked forward to a government of politicians that would somehow have the same flavor and give the same security as a government of judges. But after a relatively short time had elapsed, constitutionalism changed—although less rapidly and thoroughly in the English-speaking countries—from a system based on the rule of law to a system centered on the rule of legislators. And there is no point in denying the fact that this transformation per se modifies to a considerable extent the nature and concept of law.

Bruno Leoni summarizes this development very clearly:

> The fact that in the original codes and constitutions of the nineteenth century the legislature confined itself chiefly to epitomizing non-enacted law was gradually forgotten, or considered as of little significance compared with the fact that both codes and constitutions had been enacted by legislatures, the members of which were the "representatives" of the people. . . . The most important consequence of the new trend was that people on the Continent and to a certain extent also in the English-speaking

---

[84] This misunderstanding has been well singled out by Bruno Leoni, *Freedom and the Law,* esp. ch. III.

countries, accustomed themselves more and more to conceiving of the whole of law as *written law,* that is, as a single series of enactments on the part of legislative bodies according to majority rule. . . . Another consequence of this . . . was that the law-making process was no longer regarded as chiefly connected with a theoretical activity on the part of the experts, like judges or lawyers, but rather with the mere will of winning majorities inside the legislative bodies.[85]

It seems to us perfectly normal to identify law with legislation. But at the time when Savigny published his monumental *System of Actual Roman Law* (1840–1849), this identification still was unacceptable to the chief exponent of the historical school of law. And we can appreciate its far-reaching implications today very much more than was possible a century ago. For when law is reduced to state lawmaking, a "will conception" or a "command theory" of law gradually replaces the common-law idea of law, i.e., the idea of a free lawmaking process derived from custom and defined by judicial decisions.

There are many practical disadvantages, not to mention dangers, in our legislative conception of law. In the first place, the rule of legislators is resulting in a real mania for lawmaking, a fearful inflation of laws. Leaving aside the question as to how posterity will be able to cope with hundreds of thousands of laws that increase, at times, at the rate of a couple of thousand per legislature, the fact is that the inflation of laws in itself discredits the law. Nor is it only the excessive quantity of laws that lessens the value of law; it is also their bad quality. Our legislators are poor lawmakers, and this is because the system was not designed to

---

[85] *Ibid.,* pp. 147–49.

permit legislators to replace jurists and jurisprudence. In this connection it is well to remember that when the classical theory of constitutionalism entrusted the institutional guarantee of liberty to an assembly of representatives, this assembly was being assigned not so much the task of changing the laws, as that of preventing the monarch from changing them unilaterally and arbitrarily. As far as the legislative function is concerned, parliaments were not intended as technical, specialized bodies; and even less as instruments devised for the purpose of speeding up the output of laws.

Furthermore, laws excessive in number and poor in quality not only discredit the law; they also undermine what our ancestors constructed, a relatively stable and spontaneous law of the land, common to all, and based on rules of general application. For, inevitably, "legislative bodies are generally indifferent to, or even ignorant of, the basic forms and consistencies of the legal pattern. They impose their will through muddled rules that cannot be applied in general terms; they seek sectional advantage in special rules that destroy the nature of law itself."[86] And it is not only a matter of the generality of the law. Mass fabrication of laws ends by jeopardizing the other fundamental requisite of law—certainty. Certainty does not consist only in a precise wording of laws or in their being written down; it is also the long-range certainty that the laws will be lasting. And in this connection the present rhythm of statutory lawmaking calls to mind what happened in Athens, where "laws were certain (that is, precisely worded in a written formula)

---

[86] See T. R. Adam in *Aspects of Human Equality*, p. 176.

but nobody was certain that any law, valid today, could last until tomorrow."[87]

Nor is this all. In practice, the legislative conception of law accustoms those to whom the norms are addressed to accept any and all commands of the state, that is, to accept any *iussum* as *ius*. Legitimacy resolves itself in legality, and in a merely formal legality at that, since the problem of the unjust law is dismissed as meta-juridical.[88] It follows from this that the passage from liberty to slavery can occur quietly, with no break in continuity—almost unnoticed. Once the people are used to the rule of legislators, the *gubernaculum* no longer has to fear the opposition of the *iurisdictio*. The road is cleared for the legal suppression of constitutional legality. Whoever has had the experience of observing, for example, how fascism established itself in power knows how easily the existing juridical order can be manipulated to serve the ends of a dictatorship without the country's being really aware of the break.

I shall not go so far as to say that decay of constitutional government—understood as the habit of considering laws in terms of the state, and not the state in terms of laws—has already deprived us of the substance of juridical protection. But I do wish to stress that we have arrived at a point where such protection depends exclusively on the survival of a system of constitutional guarantees. For our rights are no longer safeguarded by our conception of law. We are no longer protected by the rule of law but (in Mosca's terminology) only by the devices of "juridical defense." And since

[87] B. Leoni, *op. cit.*, p. 79.

[88] See A. Passerin d'Entrèves, *Dottrina dello stato* (Torino, 1959), pp. 170–71.

very few people seem to be fully aware of this fact,[89] it is important that we call attention to it. Everywhere, but especially in the rational democracies, there is a call for the democratization of constitutions. Now, this demand indicates nothing other than the steady erosion of the techniques of *garantisme*. The ideal of these reformers is to transform law into outright legislation, and legislation into a rule of legislators freed from the fetters of a system of checks and balances. In short, their ideal is constitutions that are so democratic that they are no longer, properly speaking, constitutions. This means that they, and unfortunately most other people, fail to realize that the more the achievements of liberal constitutionalism are undermined by so-called democratic constitutionalism, the closer we are to the solution at which the Greeks arrived and which proved their downfall: that man was subject to laws so easily changed that they became laws unable to assure the protection of the law.

There are then, as we can see, innumerable reasons for alarm. Whereas law, as it was formerly understood, effectively served as a solid dam against arbitrary power, legislation, as it is now understood, may be, or may become, no guarantee at all. For centuries the firm distinction between *iurisdictio* and *gubernaculum,* between matters of laws and matters of state, has made it possible for legal liberty to

---

[89] Among the few notable exceptions see *The Public Philosophy* of Walter Lippmann (Boston, 1955), p. 179; and Charles Howard McIlwain, *Constitutionalism: Ancient and Modern,* which concludes with this pertinent appeal: "If the history of our constitutional past teaches anything, it seems to indicate that the mutual suspicions of reformers and constitutionalists . . . must be ended" (p. 148). In the same line of thinking, that is, in defense of the arguments for a *garantiste* constitutionalism, see also Giuseppe Maranini, *Miti e realtà della democrazia.*

make up for the absence of political freedom in many respects (even if not all). But nowadays the opposite is true: It is only political freedom that supports the legal protection of individual rights. For we can no longer count on a law that has been reduced to statutory law, to a *ius iussum* that is no longer required to be (according to the formal conception) a *ius iustum*. Or, rather, we can rely on it only insofar as it remains tied to the constitutional state in the liberal and *garantiste* meaning of the term.

Today, as yesterday, liberty and legality are bound together, because the only way that we know to construct a political system that is not oppressive is to depersonalize power by placing the law above men. But this bond has never been as precarious and tenuous as it is at present. When the rule of law resolves itself into the rule of legislators, the way is open, at least in principle, to an oppression "in the name of the law" that has no precedent in the history of mankind. It is open, I repeat, unless we return to the constitutional state with renewed vigor and awareness.

And there is nothing legalistic in this thesis. I believe in law as an essential instrument of political freedom, but only to the extent that political freedom is the foundation and condition of everything else. In other words, what protects our liberties today are "rights," and not the law-as-form on which so many jurists seem to rely. And our rights are the institutionalization of a freedom *from,* the juridical garb of a liberty conceived of as absence of restraint.[90] It is in this

---

[90] See Harold Laski, who was right in repeating an ancient but by no means antiquated truth: "Liberty . . . is a product of rights. . . . Without rights there cannot be liberty, because, without rights, men are the subject of law unrelated to the needs of personality" (*A Grammar of Politics,* p. 142).

sense, and strictly under these conditions, that I have stressed that only liberty under law (not liberty as autonomy), and only a constitutional system as an impersonal regulating instrument (not popular power as such), have been, and still are, the guardians of free societies.

We asked at the beginning what place in the scale of historical priorities the principle of political freedom has for us today. If my diagnosis is correct, the answer is: to the extent that *iurisdictio* becomes *gubernaculum* and legality supplants legitimacy, to the same extent political liberty becomes paramount and the need for freedom *from* again becomes a primary concern. Only a few decades ago it might have seemed that the political and liberal notions of liberty had become obsolete. But now it is important to realize that the new freedoms about which we were so keen not long ago are becoming old freedoms, in the sense that the political freedom that we have been taking for granted is the very liberty for which we must again take thought. The pendulum of history goes back and forth. Accordingly, those who are still advocating a greater democratic liberty at the expense of the despised liberal liberty, are no longer in the forefront of progress. They resemble much more a rearguard that is still fighting the previous war than a vanguard that is facing the new enemy and present-day threats.

By this I do not mean in the least that the question of freedom is exhausted by the liberal solution of the political problem of liberty, or that it is not important to supplement a liberty envisaged as nonrestriction by adding a freedom *to* and a substantive power *to*. But it is equally important to call attention again to the proper focus of the problem of political freedom: For it is freedom *from* and not freedom *to* that marks the boundary between political freedom and political oppression. When we define liberty as "power *to*," then the power *to* be free (of the citizens) and the power *to* coerce (of the state) are easily intermingled. And this is because so-called positive liberty can be used in all directions and for any goal whatsoever.

Therefore the so-called democratic, social, and economic freedoms presuppose the liberal technique of handling the problem of power. And I wish to stress *liberal* because it has become important not to confuse the liberal notion of liberty—which is perfectly clear—with the manifold and obscure notions that can be drawn from the much-abused formula "democratic freedoms." It is true that democratic ideals put pressure on the liberty of liberalism, in that they expand a "possibility to" into a "power to," adding to the right of being equal the conditions of equality. But no matter how much democracy permeates liberalism and molds it to its goals, I do not see how we can distinguish and enucleate from the need of liberty as nonrestriction a second form of *sui generis* political freedom. To the question as to whether we can oppose to the freedom *from* other and more tangible forms of liberty, I would answer: other freedoms, Yes, of course; but another kind of *political* freedom, No, since it does not exist.

The Masses in
Representative Democracy

Michael Oakeshott

Michael Oakeshott has been a fellow of Gonville and Caius College, Cambridge University, since 1924, and professor of political science at the London School of Economics since 1951. He has also served as a visiting professor at Harvard University, and was editor of the Cambridge Journal from 1947 to 1953. He is the author of Experience and Its Modes and Rationalism in Politics, and Other Essays.

I

The course of modern European history has thrown up a character whom we are accustomed to call the "mass man." His appearance is spoken of as the most significant and far-reaching of all the revolutions of modern times. He is credited with having transformed our way of living, our standards of conduct and our manners of political activity. He is, sometimes regretfully, acknowledged to have become the arbiter of taste, the dictator of policy, the uncrowned king of the modern world. He excites fear in some, admiration in others, wonder in all. His numbers have made him a giant; he proliferates everywhere; he is recognized either as a locust who is making a desert of what was once a fertile garden, or as the bearer of a new and more glorious civilization.

All this I believe to be a gross exaggeration. And I think we should recognize what our true situation is in this respect, what precisely we owe to this character, and the extent of his impact, if we understood more clearly who this "mass man" is and where he has come from. And with a view to answering these questions, I propose to engage in a piece of historical description.

It is a long story, which has too often been made unintelligible by being abridged. It does not begin (as some would have us understand) with the French Revolution or with the industrial changes of the late eighteenth century; it begins in those perplexing centuries which, because of their illegibility, no historian can decide whether they should properly be regarded as a conclusion or a preface, namely the fourteenth and fifteenth centuries. And it begins, not with the emergence of the "mass man," but with an emergence of a very different kind, namely, that of the human individual in his modern idiom. You must bear with me while I set the scene for the entry of the character we are to study, because we shall mistake him unless we prepare ourselves for his appearance.

II

There have been occasions, some of them in the distant past, when, usually as a consequence of the collapse of a closely integrated manner of living, human individuality has emerged and has been enjoyed for a time. An emergence of this sort is always of supreme importance; it is the modification not only of all current activities, but also of all human relationships from those of husband, wife and children to those of ruler and subject. The fourteenth and fifteenth centuries in western Europe were an occasion of this kind. What began to emerge then were conditions so preeminently favorable to a very high degree of human individuality, and human beings enjoying (to such a degree and in such numbers) the experience of "self-determination" in conduct and belief, that it overshadows all earlier occasions of the sort.

Nowhere else has the emergence of individuals (that is, persons accustomed to making choices for themselves) modified human relationships so profoundly, or proved so durable an experience, or provoked so strong a reaction, or explained itself so elaborately in the idiom of philosophical theory.

Like everything else in modern Europe, achievement in respect of human individuality was a modification of medieval conditions of life or thought. It was not generated in claims and assertions on behalf of individuality, but in sporadic divergences from a condition of human circumstance in which the opportunity for choice was narrowly circumscribed. To know oneself as the member of a family, a group, a corporation, a church, a village community, as the suitor at a court or as the occupier of a tenancy, had been, for the vast majority, the circumstantially possible sum of self-knowledge. Not only were ordinary activities, those concerned with getting a living, communal in character, but so also were decisions, rights and responsibilities. Relationships and allegiances normally sprang from status and rarely extricated themselves from the analogy of kinship. For the most part anonymity prevailed; individual human character was rarely observed because it was not there to be observed. What differentiated one man from another was insignificant when compared with what was enjoyed in common as members of a group of some sort.

This situation reached something of a climax in the twelfth century. It was modified slowly, sporadically and intermittently over a period of about seven centuries, from the thirteenth to the twentieth century. The change began earlier and went more rapidly in some parts of Europe than in others; it penetrated some activities more readily and more profoundly than others; it affected men before it touched women; and during these seven centuries there have been many local climaxes and corresponding recessions. But the enjoyment of the new opportunities of escape from communal ties gradually generated a new idiom of human character.

It emerged first in Italy: Italy was the first home of the modern individual who sprang from the breakup of medieval communal life. "At the close of the thirteenth century," writes Burckhardt, "Italy began to swarm with individuality; the ban laid upon human personality was dissolved; a thousand figures meet us, each in his own special shape and dress." The *uomo singolare,* whose conduct was marked by a high degree of self-determination and a large number of whose activities expressed personal preferences, gradually detached himself from his fellows. And together with him appeared, not only the *libertine* and the *dilettante,* but also the *uomo unico,* the man who, in the mastery of his circumstances, stood alone and was a law to himself. Men examined themselves and were not dismayed by their own want of perfection. This was the character which Petrarch dramatized for his generation with unmatched skill and unrivaled energy. A new image of human nature appeared —not Adam, not Prometheus, but Proteus—a character distinguished from all others on account of his multiplicity and of his endless power of self-transformation.

North of the Alps, events took a similar course, though they moved more slowly and had to contend with larger hindrances. In England, in France, in the Netherlands, in Spain, in Switzerland, in Poland, Hungary and Bohemia, and particularly in all centers of municipal life, conditions favorable to individuality, and individuals to exploit them, appeared. There were few fields of activity untouched. By the middle of the sixteenth century they had been so firmly established that they were beyond the range of mere suppression: not all the severity of the Calvinist *régime* in Geneva was sufficient to quell the impulse to think and behave as an independent individual. The disposition to regard a high degree of individuality in conduct and in belief as the condition proper to mankind and as the main ingredient of human "happiness," had become one of the significant dispositions of modern European character. What Petrarch did for one century, Montaigne did for another.

The story of the vicissitudes of this disposition during the last four centuries is exceedingly complex. It is a story, not of steady growth, but of climaxes and anti-climaxes, of diffusion to parts of Europe at first relatively ignorant of it, of extension to activities from which it was at first excluded, of attack and defense, of confidence and of apprehension. But, if we cannot pursue it in all its detail, we may at least observe how profoundly this disposition imposed itself upon European conduct and belief. In the course of a few hundred years, it was magnified into an ethical and even into a metaphysical theory, it gathered to itself an appropriate understanding of the office of government, it modified political manners and institutions, it settled itself upon art, upon religion, upon industry and trade and upon every kind of human relationship.

In the field of intellectual speculation the clearest reflection of this profound experience of individuality is to be seen in ethical theory. Almost all modern writing about moral conduct begins with the hypothesis of an individual human being choosing and pursuing his own directions of activity. What appeared to require explanation was not the existence of such individuals, but how they could come to have duties to others of their kind and what was the nature of those duties; just as the existence of other minds became a problem to those who understood knowledge as the residue of sense experience. This is unmistakable in Hobbes, the first moralist of the modern world to take candid account of the current experience of individuality. He understood a man as an organism governed by an impulse to avoid destruction and to maintain itself in its own characteristic and chosen pursuits. Each individual has a natural right to independent existence: the only problem is how he is to pursue his own chosen course with the greatest measure of success, the problem of his relation to "others" of his kind. And a similar view of things appeared, of course, in the writings of Spinoza. But even where an individualistic conclusion was rejected, this autonomous individual remained as the starting point of ethical reflection. Every moralist in the seventeenth and eighteenth centuries is concerned with the psychological structure of this assumed "individual": the relation of "self" and "others" is the common form of all moral theory of the time. And nowhere is this seen more clearly to be the case than in the writings of Kant. Every human being, in virtue of not being subject to natural necessity, is recognized by Kant to be a Person, an end in himself, absolute and autonomous. To seek his own happiness is the natural pursuit of such a person; self-love is the motive of the choices which compose his conduct. But as a rational human being he will recognize in his conduct the universal conditions of autonomous personality; and the chief of these conditions is to use humanity, as well in himself as in others, as an end and never as a means. Morality consists in the recognition of individual personality whenever it appears. Moreover, personality is so far sacrosanct that no man has either a right or a duty to promote the moral perfection of another: we may promote the "happiness" of others, but we cannot promote their "good" without destroying their "freedom," which is the condition of moral goodness.

In short, whatever we may think of the moral theories of modern Europe, they provide the clearest evidence of the overwhelming impact of this experience of individuality.

But this pursuit of individuality, and of the conditions most favorable to its enjoyment, was reflected also in an understanding of the proper office of government and in appropriate manners of governing and being governed, both modifications of an inheritance from the Middle Ages. We have time only to notice them in their most unqualified appearance, namely, in what we have come to call "modern representative democracy." This manner of governing and being governed appeared first in England, in the Netherlands and in Switzerland, and was later (in various idioms) extended to other parts of Western Europe and the United States of America. It is not to be understood either as an approximation to some ideal manner of government, or as a modification of a manner of government (with which it has no connection whatever) current for a short while in certain parts of the ancient world. It is simply what emerged in western Europe where the impact of the aspirations of individuality upon medieval institutions of government was greatest.

The first demand of those intent upon exploring the intimations of individuality was for an instrument of government capable of transforming the interests of individuality into rights and duties. To perform this task government required three attributes. First, it must be single and supreme; only by a concentration of all authority at one center could the emergent individual escape from the communal pressures of family and guild, of church and local community, which hindered his enjoyment of his own character. Secondly, it must be an instrument of government not bound by prescription and therefore with authority to abolish old rights and create new: it must be a "sovereign" government. And this, according to current ideas, meant a government in which all who enjoyed rights were partners, a government in which the "estates" of the realm were direct or indirect participants. Thirdly, it must be powerful—able to preserve the order without which the aspirations of individuality could not be realized; but not so powerful as itself to constitute a new threat to individuality. In an earlier time, the recognized methods of transforming interests into rights had been judicial; the "parliaments" and "councils" of the Middle Ages had been preeminently judicial bodies. But from these "courts of law" emerged an instrument with more emphatic authority to recognize new interests by converting them into new rights and duties; there emerged legislative bodies. Thus, a ruler, and a parliament representative of his subjects, came to share the business of "making" law. And the law they made was favorable to the interests of individuality: it provided the detail of what became a well-understood condition of human circumstance, commonly denoted by the word "freedom." In this condition every subject was secured of the right to pursue his chosen directions of activity as little hindered as might be by his fellows or by the exactions of government itself, and as little distracted by communal pressures. Freedom of movement, of initiative, of speech, of belief and religious observance, of association and disassociation, of bequest and inheritance; security of person and property; the right to choose one's own occupation and dispose of one's labor and goods; and over all the "rule of law"; the right to be ruled by a known law, applicable to all subjects alike. And these rights, appropriate to individuality, were not the privileges of a single class; they were the property of every subject alike. Each signified the abrogation of some feudal privilege.

This manner of governing, which reached its climax in the "parliamentary" government which emerged in England and elsewhere in the late eighteenth and early nineteenth centuries, was concurrently theorized in an understanding of the proper office of government. What had been a "community" came to be recognized as an "association" of individuals: this was the counterpart in political philosophy of the individualism that had established itself in ethical theory. And the office of government was understood to be the maintenance of arrangements favorable to the interests of individuality, arrangements (that is) which emancipated the subject from the "chains" (as Rousseau put it) of communal allegiances, and constituted a condition of human circumstance in which the intimations of individuality might be explored and the experience of individuality enjoyed.

Briefly, then, my picture is as follows. Human individuality is an historical emergence, as "artificial" and as "natural" as the landscape. In modern Europe this emergence was gradual, and the specific character of the individual who emerged was determined by the manner of his generation. He became unmistakable when the habit appeared of engaging in activities identified as "private"; indeed, the appearance of "privacy" in human conduct is the obverse of the desuetude of the communal arrangements from which modern individuality sprang. This experience of individuality provoked a disposition to explore its own intimations, to place the highest value upon it, and to seek security in its enjoyment. To enjoy it came to be recognized as the main ingredient of "happiness." The experience was magnified into an ethical theory; it was reflected in manners of governing and being governed, in newly acquired rights and duties and in a whole pattern of living. The emergence of this disposition to be an individual is the preeminent event in modern European history.

III

There were many modest manners in which this disposition to be an individual might express itself. Every practical enterprise and every intellectual pursuit revealed itself as an assemblage of opportunities for making choices: art, literature, philosophy, commerce-industry and politics each came to partake of this character. Nevertheless, in a world being transformed by the aspirations and activities of those who were excited by these opportunities, there were some people, by circumstance or by temperament, less ready than others to respond to this invitation; and for many the invitation to make choices came before the ability to make them and was consequently recognized as a burden. The old certainties of belief, of occupation and of status were being dissolved, not only for those who had confidence in their own power to make a new place for themselves in an association of individuals, but also for those who had no such confidence. The counterpart of the agricultural and industrial *entrepreneur* of the sixteenth century was the displaced laborer; the counterpart of the *libertine* was the dispossessed believer. The familiar warmth of communal pressures was dissipated for all alike—an emancipation which excited some, depressed others. The familiar anonymity of communal life was replaced by a personal identity which was burdensome to those who could not transform it into an individuality. What some recognized as happiness, appeared to others as discomfort. The same condition of human circumstance was identified as progress and as decay. In short, the circumstances of modern Europe, even as early as the sixteenth century, bred, not a single character, but two obliquely opposed characters: not only that of the individual, but also that of the "individual *manqué*." And this "individual *manqué*" was not a relic of a past age; he was a "modern" character, the product of the same dissolution of communal ties as had generated the modern European individual.

We need not speculate upon what combination of debility, ignorance, timidity, poverty or mischance operated in particular cases to provoke this character; it is enough to observe his appearance and his efforts to accommodate himself to his hostile environment. He sought a protector who would recognize his predicament, and he found what he sought, in some measure, in "the government." From as early as the sixteenth century the governments of Europe were being modified, not only in response to the demands of individuality, but in response also to the needs of the "individual *manqué*." The "godly prince" of the Reformation and his lineal descendant, the "enlightened despot" of the eighteenth century, were political inventions for making choices for those indisposed to make choices for themselves; the Elizabethan Statute of Laborers was designed to take care of those who were left behind in the race.

The aspirations of individuality had imposed themselves upon conduct and belief and upon the constitutions and activities of governments, in the first place, as demands emanating from a powerful and confident disposition. There was little attempt to moralize these demands, which in the sixteenth century were clearly in conflict with current moral sentiment, still fixed in its loyalty to the morality of communal ties. Nevertheless, from the experience of individuality there sprang, in the course of time, a morality appropriate to—a disposition not only to explore individuality but to approve of the pursuit of individuality. This constituted a considerable moral revolution; but such was its force and vigor that it not only swept aside the relics of the morality appropriate to the defunct communal order, but left little room for any alternative *to itself*. And the weight of this moral victory bore heavily upon the "individual *manqué*." Already outmaneuvered in the field (in conduct), he now suffered a defeat at home, in his own character. What had been no more than a doubt about his ability to hold his own in a struggle for existence, became a radical self-distrust; what had been merely a hostile prospect, disclosed itself as an abyss; what had been the discomfort of ill-success was turned into the misery of guilt.

In some, no doubt, this situation provoked resignation; but in others it bred envy, jealousy and resentment. And in these emotions a new disposition was generated: the impulse to escape from the predicament by imposing it upon all mankind. From the frustrated "individual *manqué*" there sprang the militant "anti-individual," disposed to assimilate the world to his own character by deposing the individual and destroying his moral prestige. No promise, or even offer, of self-advancement could tempt this "anti-individual"; he knew his individuality was too poorly furnished to be explored or exploited with any satisfaction whatever. He was moved solely by the opportunity of complete escape from the anxiety of not being an individual, the opportunity of removing from the world all that convicted him of his own inadequacy. His situation provoked him to seek release in separatist communities, insulated from the moral pressure of individuality. But the opportunity he sought appeared fully when he recognized that, so far from being alone, he belonged to the most numerous class in modern European society, the class of those who had no choices of their own to make. Thus, in the recognition of his numerical superiority the "anti-individual" at once recognized himself as the "mass man" and discovered the way of escape from his predicament. For, although the "mass man" is specified by his disposition—a disposition to allow in others only a replica of himself, to impose upon all a uniformity of belief and conduct that leaves no room for either the pains or the pleasures of choice—and not by his numbers, he is confirmed in this disposition by the support of others of his kind. He can have no friends (because friendship is a relation between individuals), but he has comrades. The "masses" as they appear in modern European history are not composed of individuals; they are composed of "anti-individuals" united in a revulsion from individuality. Consequently, although the remarkable growth of population in western Europe during the last four hundred years is a condition of the success with which this character has imposed itself, it is not a condition of the character itself.

Nevertheless, the "anti-individual" had feelings rather than thoughts, impulses rather than opinions, inabilities rather than passions, and was only dimly aware of his power. Consequently, he required "leaders"; indeed, the modern concept of "leadership" is a concomitant of the "anti-individual," and without him it would be unintelligible. An association of individuals requires a ruler, but it has no place for a "leader." The "anti-individual" needed to be told what to think; his impulses had to be transformed into desires, and these desires into projects; he had to be made aware of his power; and these were the tasks of his leaders. Indeed, from one point of view, "the masses" must be regarded as the invention of their leaders.

The natural submissiveness of the "mass man" may itself be supposed to have been capable of prompting the appearance of appropriate leaders. He was unmistakably an instrument to be played upon, and no doubt the instrument provoked the *virtuoso*. But there was, in fact, a character ready to occupy this office. What was required was a man who could at once appear as the image and the master of his followers; a man who could more easily make choices for others than for himself; a man disposed to mind other people's business because he lacked the skill to find satisfaction in minding his own. And these, precisely, were the attributes of the "individual *manqué*," whose achievements and whose failures in respect of individuality exactly fitted him for this task of leadership. He was enough of an individual to seek a personal satisfaction in the exercise of individuality, but too little to seek it anywhere but in commanding others. He loved himself too little to be anything but an egoist; and what his followers took to be a genuine concern for their salvation was in fact nothing more than the vanity of the almost selfless. No doubt the "masses" in modern Europe have had other leaders than this cunning frustrate who has led always by flattery and whose only concern is the exercise of power; but they have had none more appropriate—for he only has never prompted them to be critical of their impulses. Indeed, the "anti-individual" and his leader were the counterparts of a single moral situation; they relieved one another's frustrations and supplied one another's wants. Nevertheless, it was an uneasy partnership: moved by impulses rather than by desires, the "mass man" has been submissive but not loyal to his leaders: even the exiguous individuality of the leader has easily aroused his suspicion. And the leader's greed for power has disposed him to raise hopes in his followers which he has never been able to satisfy.

Of all the manners in which the "anti-individual" has imposed himself upon western Europe two have been pre-eminent. He has generated a morality designed to displace the current morality of individuality; and he has evoked an understanding of the proper office of government and manners of governing appropriate to his character.

The emergence of the morality of the "anti-individual," a morality, namely, not of "liberty" and "self-determination," but of "equality" and "solidarity," is of course, difficult to discern; but it is already clearly visible in the seventeenth century. The obscurity of its beginnings is due in part to the fact that its vocabulary was at first that of the morality of the defunct communal order; and there can be little doubt that it derived strength and plausibility from its deceptive affinity to that morality. But it was, in fact, a new morality, generated in opposition to the hegemony of individuality and calling for the establishment of a new condition of human circumstance reflecting the aspirations of the "anti-individual."

The nucleus of this morality was the concept of a substantive condition of human circumstance represented as the "common" or "public" good, which was understood, not to be composed of the various goods that might be sought by individuals on their own account, but to be an independent entity. "Self-love," which was recognized in the morality of individuality as a legitimate spring of human activity, the morality of the "anti-individual" pronounced to be evil. But it was to be replaced, not by the love of "others," or by "charity" or by "benevolence" (which would have entailed a relapse into the vocabulary of individuality), but by the love of "the community."

Around this nucleus revolved a constellation of appropriate subordinate beliefs. From the beginning, the designers of this morality identified private property with individuality, and consequently connected its abolition with the condition of human circumstance appropriate to the "mass man." And further, it was appropriate that the morality of the "anti-individual" should be radically equalitarian: how should the "mass man," whose sole distinction was his resemblance to his fellows and whose salvation lay in the recognition of others as merely replicas of himself, approve of any divergence from an exact uniformity? All must be equal and anonymous units in a "community." And, in the generation of this morality, the character of this "unit" was tirelessly explored. He was understood as a "man" *per se,* as a "comrade," a "citizen." But the most acute diagnosis, that of Proudhon, recognized him as a "debtor"; for in this notion what was asserted was not only the absence of distinction between the units who composed the "community" (all are alike "debtors"), but also a debt owed, not to "others" but to the "community" itself: at birth he enters into an inheritance which he had played no part in accumulating, and whatever the magnitude of his subsequent contribution, it never equals what he has enjoyed: he dies necessarily insolvent.

This morality of the "anti-individual," the morality of a *solidarité commune,* began to be constructed in the sixteenth century. Its designers were mostly visionaries, dimly aware of their purposes, and lacking a large audience. But a momentous change occurred when the "anti-individual" recognized himself as the "mass man," and perceived the power that his numerical superiority gave him. The recognition that the morality of the "anti-individual" was, in the first place, the morality not of a sect of aspirants, but of a large ready-made class in society (the class, not of the "poor," but of those who by circumstance or by occupation had been denied the experience of individuality), and that in the interests of this class it must be imposed upon all mankind, appears unmistakably first in the writings of Marx and Engels.

Before the end of the nineteenth century, then, a morality of "anti-individualism" had been generated in response to the aspirations of the "mass man." It was, in many respects, a rickety construction: it never achieved a design comparable to that which Hobbes or Kant or Hegel gave the morality of individuality; and it has never been able to resist relapse into the inappropriate concepts of individuality. Nevertheless it throws back a tolerably clear reflection of the "mass man," who by this means became more thoroughly acquainted with himself. But we are not concerned with its merits or defects, we are concerned only to notice it as evidence of the power with which the "mass man" has imposed himself on modern Europe over a period of about four centuries. "Anti-individuality," long before the nineteenth century, had established itself as one of the major dispositions of the modern European moral character. And this disposition was evident enough for it to be recognized unequivocally by Sorel, and to be identified by writers such as Nietzsche, Kierkegaard and Burckhardt as the image of a new barbarism.

From the beginning (in the sixteenth century) those who exerted themselves on behalf of the "anti-individual" perceived that his counterpart, a "community" reflecting his aspirations, entailed a "government" active in a certain manner. To govern was understood to be the exercise of power in order to impose and maintain the substantive condition of human circumstance identified as "the public good"; to be governed was, for the "anti-individual," to have made for him the choices he was unable to make for himself. Thus, "government" was cast for the role of architect and custodian, not of "public order" in an "association" of individuals pursuing their own activities, but of "the public good" of a "community." The ruler was recognized to be, not the referee of the collisions of individuals, but the moral leader and managing director of "the community." And this understanding of government has been tirelessly explored over a period of four and a half centuries, from Thomas More's *Utopia* to the Fabian Society, from Campanella to Lenin. But the leaders who served the "mass man" were not merely theorists concerned to make his character intelligible in a moral doctrine and in an understanding of the office of government; they were also practical men who revealed to him his power and the manner in which the institutions of modern democratic government might be appropriated to his aspirations. And if we call the manner of government that had been generated by the aspirations of individuality "parliamentary government," we may call the modification of it under the impact of the "mass man," "popular government." But it is important to understand that these are two wholly different manners of government.

The emergent individual in the sixteenth century had sought new rights, and by the beginning of the nineteenth century the rights appropriate to his character had, in England and elsewhere, been largely established. The "anti-individual" observed these rights, and he was persuaded that his circumstances (chiefly his poverty) had hitherto prevented him from sharing them. Hence the new rights called for on his behalf were, in the first place, understood as the means by which he might come to participate in the rights won and enjoyed by those he thought of as his better placed fellows. But this was a great illusion; first, because in fact he had these rights, and secondly because he had no use for them. For the disposition of the "mass man" was not to become an individual, and the enterprise of his leaders was not to urge him in this direction. And what, in fact, prevented his enjoying the rights of individuality (which were available to him as to anyone else) were not his "circumstances" but his character—his "anti-individuality." The rights of individuality were necessarily such that the "mass man" could have no use for them. And so, in the end, it turned out: what he came to demand were rights of an entirely different *kind,* and of a kind which entailed the abolition of the rights appropriate to individuality. He required the right to enjoy a substantive condition of human circumstance in which he would not be asked to make choices for himself. He had no use for the right to "pursue happiness"—that could only be a burden to him: he needed the right to "enjoy happiness." And looking into his own character he identified this with security—but again, not security against arbitrary interference in the exercise of his preferences, but security against having to make choices for himself and against to meet the vicissitudes of life from his own resources. In short, the right he claimed, the right appropriate to his character, was the right to live in a social protectorate which relieved him from the burden of "self-determination."

But this condition of human circumstances was seen to be impossible unless it were imposed upon all alike. So long as "others" were permitted to make choices for themselves, not only would his anxiety at not being able to do so himself remain to convict him of his inadequacy and threaten his emotional security, but also the social protectorate which he recognized as his counterpart would itself be disrupted. The security he needed entailed a genuine equality of circumstances imposed upon all. The condition he sought was one in which he would meet in others only a replica of himself: what he was, everybody must become.

He claimed this condition as a "right," and consequently he sought a government disposed to give it to him and one endowed with the power necessary to impose upon all activities the substantive pattern of activity called "the public good." "Popular government" is, precisely, a modification of "parliamentary government" designed to accomplish this purpose. And if this reading is correct, "popular government" is no more intimated in "parliamentary government" than the rights appropriate to the "anti-individual" are intimated in the rights appropriate to individuality: they are not complementary but directly opposed to one another. Nevertheless, what I have called "popular government" is not a concrete manner of government established and practiced; it is a disposition to impose certain modifications upon "parliamentary government" in order to convert it into a manner of government appropriate to the aspirations of the "mass man."

This disposition has displayed itself in specific enterprises, and in less specific habits and manners in respect of government. The first great enterprise was the establishment of universal adult suffrage. The power of the "mass man" lay in his numbers, and this power could be brought to bear upon government by means of "the vote." Secondly, a change in the character of the parliamentary representative was called for: he must be not an individual, but a *mandataire* charged with the task of imposing the substantive condition of human circumstances required by the "mass man." "Parliament" must become a "workshop," not a debating assembly. Neither of these changes was intimated in "parliamentary government"; both, in so far as they have been achieved, have entailed an assembly of a new character. Their immediate effect has been twofold: first, to confirm the authority of mere numbers (an authority alien to the practice of "parliamentary government"); and secondly, to give governments immensely increased power.

But the institutions of "parliamentary government" proved to have only a limited eligibility for conversion into institutions appropriate to serve the aspirations of the "mass man." And an assembly of instructed delegates was seen to be vulnerable to a much more appropriate contrivance—the *plébiscite.* Just as it lay in the character of the "mass man" to see everyman as a "public official," an agent of "the public good," and to see his representatives not as individuals but instructed delegates, so he saw every voter as the direct participant in the activity of governing: and the means of this was the *plébiscite*. An assembly elected on a universal adult suffrage, composed of instructed delegates and flanked by the device of the *plébiscite* was, then, the counterpart of the "mass man." They gave him exactly what he wanted: the illusion without the reality of choice; choice without the burden of having to choose. For, with universal suffrage have appeared the massive political parties of the modern world, composed not of individuals but of "anti-individuals." And both the instructed delegate and the *plébiscite* are devices for avoiding the necessity for making choices. The "mandate" from the beginning was an illusion. The "mass man," as we have seen, is a creature of impulses, not desires; he is utterly unable to draw up instructions for his representative to follow. What in fact has happened, whenever the disposition of "popular government" has imposed itself, is that the prospective representative has drawn up his own mandate and then, by a familiar trick of ventriloquism, has put it into the mouth of his electors: as an instructed delegate he is not an individual, and as a "leader" he relieves his followers of the need to make choices for themselves. And similarly, the *plébiscite* is not a method by which the "mass man" imposes his choices upon his rulers; it is a method of generating a government with unlimited authority to make choices on his behalf. In the *plébiscite* the "mass man" achieved final release from the burden of individuality: he was told emphatically what to choose.

Thus, in these and other constitutional devices, and in less formal habits of political conduct, was generated a new art of politics: the art, not of "ruling" (that is, of seeking the most practicable adjustments for the collisions of "individuals"), nor even of maintaining the support of a majority of individuals in a "parliamentary" assembly, but of knowing what offer will collect most votes and making it in such a manner that it appears to come from "the people"; the art, in short, of "leading" in the modern idiom. Moreover, it is known in advance what offer will collect the most votes: the character of the "mass man" is such that he will be moved only by the offer of release from the burden of making choices for himself, the offer of "salvation." And anyone who makes this offer may confidently demand unlimited power: it will be given him.

The "mass man," as I understand him, then, is specified by his character, not by his numbers. He is distinguished by so exiguous an individuality that when it meets a powerful experience of individuality it revolts into "anti-individuality." He has generated for himself an appropriate morality, an appropriate understanding of the office of government, and appropriate modifications of "parliamentary government." He is not necessarily "poor," nor is he envious only of "riches"; he is not necessarily "ignorant," often he is a member of the so-called *intelligentsia;* he belongs to a class which corresponds exactly with no other class. He is specified primarily by a moral, not an intellectual, inadequacy. He wants "salvation"; and in the end will be satisfied only with release from the burden of having to make choices for himself. He is dangerous, not on account of his opinions or desires, for he has none: but on account of his submissiveness. His disposition is to endow government with power and authority such as it has never before enjoyed: he is utterly unable to distinguish a "ruler" from a "leader." In short, the disposition to be an "anti-individual" is one to which every European man has a propensity; the "mass man" is merely one in whom this propensity is dominant.

IV

Of the many conclusions which follow from this reading of the situation the most important is to dispose of the most insidious of our current political delusions. It has been said, and it is commonly believed, that the event of supreme importance in modern European history is "the accession of the masses to complete social power." But that no such event has taken place is evident when we consider what it would entail. If it is true (as I have contended) that modern Europe enjoys two opposed moralities (that of individuality and that of the "anti-individual"), that it enjoys two opposed understandings of the office of government, and two corresponding interpretations of the current institutions of government, then, for the "mass man" to have won for himself a position of undisputed sovereignty would entail the complete suppression of what, in any reading, must be considered the strongest of our moral and political dispositions and the survival of the weakest. A world in which the "mass man" exercised "complete social power" would be a world in which the activity of governing was understood *solely* as the imposition of a single substantive condition of human circumstance, a world in which "popular government" had altogether displaced "parliamentary government," a world in which the "civil" rights of individuality had been abrogated by the "social" rights of anti-individuality—and there is no evidence that we live in such a world. Certainly the "mass man" has emerged and has signified his emergence in an appropriate morality and an appropriate understand-

ing of the office of government. He has sought to transform
the world into a replica of himself, and he has not been entirely unsuccessful. He has sought to enjoy what he could
not create for himself, and nothing he has appropriated
remains unchanged. Nevertheless, he remains an unmistakably derivative character, an emanation of the pursuit of
individuality, helpless, parasitic and able to survive only in
opposition to individuality. Only in the most favorable circumstances, and then only by segregating him from all alien
influences, have his leaders been able to suppress in him an
unquenched propensity to desert at the call of individuality.
He has imposed himself emphatically only where the relics
of a morality of communal ties survived to make plausible
his moral and political impulses. Elsewhere, the modifications he has provoked in political manners and moral beliefs
have been extensive, but the notion that they have effaced
the morality of individuality and "parliamentary government" is without foundation. He loves himself too little to be
able to dispose effectively of the only power he has, namely,
his numerical superiority. He lacks passion rather than
reason. He has had a past in which he was taught to admire
himself and his antipathies; he has a present in which he is
often the object of the ill-concealed contempt of his "leaders"; but the heroic future forecast him is discrepant with
his own character. He is no hero.

On the other hand, if we judge the world as we find it
(which includes, of course, the emergence of the "mass
man"), the event of supreme and seminal importance in
modern European history remains the emergence of the
human individual in his modern idiom. The pursuit of individuality has evoked a moral disposition, an understanding
of the office of government and manners of governing, a

multiplicity of activity and opinion and a notion of "happiness," which have impressed themselves indelibly upon European civilization. The onslaught of the "mass man" has shaken but not destroyed the moral prestige of individuality; even the "anti-individual," whose salvation lies in escape, has not been able to escape it. The desire of "the masses" to enjoy the products of individuality has modified their destructive urge. And the antipathy of the "mass man" to the "happiness" of "self-determination" easily dissolves into self-pity. At all important points the individual still appears as the substance and the "anti-individual" only as the shadow.

Essay Nine

History as Force

Donald M. Dozer

Donald M. Dozer is professor emeritus of history at the University of California, Santa Barbara. After completion of his doctoral studies at Harvard University in 1936, he began his teaching career at the University of Maryland and resumed it following World War II at American University in Washington, D.C. As a specialist in diplomatic history, he worked for several government agencies during the war and then served in the Latin American Division of the Department of State and, later, in the Historical Division, prior to his appointment to the faculty at the University of California, Santa Barbara, in 1959.

Over the years Professor Dozer has contributed numerous articles and reviews on foreign affairs and higher education to historical and legal journals, and his writings have also appeared in several anthologies. Among his major works are two books on American foreign policy, Are We Good Neighbors? Three Decades of Inter-American Relations, 1930–1960 *(University of Florida, 1959) and* The Monroe Doctrine: Its Modern Significance *(Knopf, 1965), and a popular text,* Latin America: An Interpretive History *(McGraw-Hill, 1962), which was also published in a Portuguese edition.*

This essay is reprinted from Pacific Historical Review, *v. 34, no. 4, pages 375–95, by permission. Copyright © 1965 by the Pacific Coast Branch of the American Historical Association. All rights reserved.*

The role of the historian in American life has been
steadily declining. John Spencer Bassett noted this decline in 1926 when he wrote:

> Fifty years ago historians like Bancroft and Prescott stood side
> by side with the great poets at the top of the world of letters. . . .
> They lived like proconsuls over provinces of literary expression.
> Today the historian's influence has waned. He is no longer to be
> compared with the lordly proconsul, but rather to the hard-
> working centurion, whose labors held together the military units
> on which rested the Roman authority in the province.[1]

As a result, history guides our judgments less than it used
to do. As our society takes on more and more the characteristics of the society of George Orwell's *1984,* it becomes a
society without history or rather a society in which history
is considered to be serviceable mainly as a tool of political
action. Henry Ford proclaimed that "history is bunk." Carl
Sandburg has cynically declared, "The past is a bucket of
ashes." Senator Homer Ferguson has called it only "spilled

---

[1] Jean Jules Jusserand, Wilbur C. Abbott, Charles W. Colby, and John S.
Bassett, *The Writing of History* (New York, 1926), pp. vi–vii.

milk." Another has described history as only "an attic stuffed with dolls."

We are passing through an era of historical nihilism. "The past does not exist," cries one of the characters in Jean-Paul Sartre's *La Nausée*. "The world we are living in is totally new," pontificates Robert M. Hutchins. We are, as it were, in flight from history. We have ignored the fact, familiar to us in earlier, more sober times, that only history can explain how the present has come to be what it is. We no longer see the present as part of a living and rational whole, and we seem either unable or indisposed to relate the past creatively to the present. We have come to feel that today has sprung unexpectedly out of a void of yesterday and that we are consequently called upon to deal with problems that have never before confronted mankind. A society such as our own that has abandoned its sense of historical continuity is ripe for social innovation, even revolution.

A sense of history is an acquired characteristic of man. Perhaps it is an unnecessary encumbrance. Friedrich Nietzsche argued in his earliest philosophical work that the historic sense only inhibits the genius of man and paralyzes his will to action. A nation obsessed with a sense of the past may, for that reason, lack a sense of presentness and may fail to develop its potential greatness in the present. Communities and families that live on their history stagnate. Only when man throws off the shackles of the past, it is argued, only when, as in George Santayana's sonnet, he ceases to ponder "the ruin of the years and groan beneath the weight of boasted gain" can he fully liberate his energies and fashion a satisfactory present for himself.

History is the whole of human experience in time. It is the study of all that man has ever done, or thought, or felt. It is

the biophysical record of his experience preserved and related in sequence. History is the minutes of previous meetings. It is the recorded "tut-tut." It is the nagging counterfoil
to rashness. It is, if you please, the line that forms on the
right. In history we travel backward in time to learn the
interaction of men and events in the past that created our
present world. Men and women long since dead who lived in
a world that seemed modern to them acted or were acted
upon in ways that vitally affect our lives today. If we know
what they did, we will be better able to understand our problems today and will not have to approach each problem as
if it were unique. We shall also have a clearer vision of
prospects and possibilities as we travel forward into an unknown future.

Nietzsche's dramatic challenge to history, like other
similar criticisms of the value of history, assumes a fundamental conflict between action and thought. This assumption
is easily refuted, for thought of some kind, as modern psychology has shown, always precedes action. The question
then is whether it will be merely impulsive thought or informed thought and whether the action that it produces will
be hasty, ill-considered action or intelligent action based
upon experience. Mere actionists who have had no sense of
history have strewn man's past with their follies.

But what is more dangerous, historical nihilism denies
the idea of progress derived from experience which underlies
the empiricism of our age, at least in the field of the physical
sciences. As it rejects empiricism, it also rejects intellectual-
ism. An appeal to history in moments of crisis is an appeal
to reason—the accumulated reason of the past. When the
citizens of a state are ignorant of history, they will become
victims of ambition and intrigue, they will accept illusions as

reality, they will mistake license for liberty, they will identify treachery with patriotism. They can easily be converted into a blind instrument of their own destruction. On the other hand, if we absorb history and at the same time retain our critical faculties, we shall know better how to introduce reason into man's career as it unfolds in the future. And we shall be able to do so without emotionalism, without prejudice, and without revolution. Historians cannot be revolutionists. They know that it is impossible for any people, in Alfonso Reyes's words, "to live skipping epochs" (*vivir saltando épocas*). The secular pressures of history will ultimately prevail, and changes that are too abruptly undertaken do not solve problems but only create new inequities.

History itself is a record of a long tug-of-war between man's logic and man's experience. All of his efforts at rational living are subsumed in his historical experience. Those who attempt to impose their own dialectical systems upon society, therefore, must reckon with the alarms of the past. Without these echoed warnings, their logic can become too logical; it may become a systematic way of going wrong with confidence. Both reason and experience together are needed to produce the fullest logic, the highest pragmatism. History, in other words, supplies its own dialectics.

History is the legislation of the past. The cumulative experiences of mankind may not seem as real as the experiences of any single individual, but they are more conclusive even for that individual than anything in his own experience. This is not to say, however, that the lives of individuals are ruled by a rigid historical determinism, for history is a record of actions by individuals. But in history man only proposes and acts; he does not fix the ultimate pattern.

History is inseparable from chronology. Now, a sense of

chronology, like the sense of history itself, is an acquired characteristic. Time as a concept is unfamiliar to very young children and to the senile aged. Not until a child has advanced several years from birth does he begin to differentiate between the present and the past. To him, his parents were contemporary with all that happened before he was born, and all times are embraced in the concept of "olden times." What makes a child an ineffective member of society is his inability to see the relatedness of things in time. Similarly, the principal factor that makes the senile aged incompetent and unable to contribute to social progress is that they have lost their sense of chronology. The time sequences in their own lives have become meaningless. To them, all time is one as they begin to merge with the eternal. The grandmother talks as if her own grandfather and grandmother, her uncles and aunts, are still living on the old farm.

Only mature individuals, therefore, are able to particularize about the past, to see the sequences and consequences in history and to relate them to present living. It is our consciousness of this relatedness between the past and the present that makes us adults. Lacking it, we remain half men or children, and our actions both as individuals and as members of society are impulsive, short-range, and blundering.

History may be thought of as a union of memory and intelligence. When we acquaint ourselves with history, when we learn why our predecessors acted as they did, and when we study the outcome of their actions, we alert ourselves to all the elements in new situations that may confront us, and we face the unpredictable with a greater wealth of experience than we had before. An understanding of the past, explains Ernst Cassirer, "gives us a freer survey of the present and strengthens our responsibility with regard to the future."[2] It frees us to be more vigorously contemporary. History, it is true, may not furnish specific guidance for each daily crisis, yet it will enable us better to meet these crises by enlarging our perspective, by making us wiser. It is a means, concludes George H. Sabine, "by which society is enabled to understand what it is doing, in the light of what it has done and of what it hopes to do."[3]

How difficult it is for a man to view objectively the times in which he lives! Current history is an anomaly, for if it is current it is not history. And yet only by viewing our own times *sub specie aeternitatis* or in the perspective of past and future can we hope to relate ourselves wisely to our world. The historian, if he conceives his function thus, can become, in Friedrich Schlegel's phrase, "a retrospective prophet." If historians are not fulfilling this exalted role today, it is in part because they have yielded to the blandishments of political power. History has its political uses, and during the past generation these have been discovered and flagrantly exploited. No more than passing reference needs to be made here to the historians of Germany who prostituted their craft to the Nazi political power or to the historians of Soviet Russia who first exalted Joseph Stalin and then, at the command of his successor, Nikita Khrushchev, obligingly dropped from their histories all mention of the former Russian leader. Historians in every country dominated by the communist totalitarian ideology find it impossible to follow a course of scholarly independence. They are required to

---

[2] *An Essay on Man: An Introduction to a Philosophy of Human Culture* (New York, 1944), p. 227.

[3] George H. Sabine, in Introduction to Phil L. Snyder, ed., *Detachment and the Writings of History: Essays and Letters of Carl Becker* (Ithaca, N.Y., 1958), p. xv.

adapt their history to the cult of the personality which is dominant at the moment. A Czechoslovak scholar, writing in the organ of the Slovak Writers' Union, *Kulturny Zivot,* on March 23, 1963, complained that

> The cult of personality, and the dogmatism closely connected with it, limited and restricted creative work. . . . The tendency to juggle historical facts also became apparent. . . . A scheme of black-and-white pigeonholes was made up in historiography, too, and these were clung to. Dogmatism hampered initiative, a creative approach, and scientific analysis. Apart from this, quite a number of documents were not accessible; and in those which were available, facts of one or the other color were ferreted out to fit into the preestablished black-and-white scheme. . . . It was natural that this gave rise to the system of self-censorship, keeping writers from talking about administrative tamperings with manuscripts by the authorities.[4]

"Historians" who thus prostitute their science place themselves in fundamental conflict with historicism, indeed with history itself. They are no longer men thinking. They are only man defending. They push a servile pen. The only coherence which their "history" possesses is imposed upon them by authority, which subordinates originality to conformity, ideas to details, substance to shadow, free inquiry to a new scholasticism. They place history at the service of what they regard as a cause, namely, the preservation of the reputation of men whom their contemporaries call great.

When history is declared to be only what the ruling clique, that is, the bureaucracy in any country, says it is, it ceases to be history in any terms that free men understand. This kind of history becomes only a fiction agreed upon among the

---

[4] *East Europe: A Monthly Review of East European Affairs,* Free Europe Committee, XII (May 1963), 14–15.

principal participants. As the official truth is thus promulgated, history stops. The aim is, in Orwell's words, to "freeze history at a chosen moment." It is only one further step for the historian, who thus selectively construes his facts, to insist that we must only fall in step with history and become completely decisionless before its inexorable futurity.[5]

This is the type of lore that meets the need of certain societies that lack a written objective history. For example, Pachacuti, the great leader of the completely socialized Inca empire of Peru in the fifteenth century, seeing the need for an official organization of the history of his people and of his royal house, suppressed some of the existing lore, elaborated those parts of it which supported his house, and declared it treason to depart from this official corpus of belief. As the latest chronicler of Incan history, Burr Brundage, tells us, "this falsified Pachacutean view of history is a historical fact of major importance, for it served to steer the course of future events." Thus the history of the nation, continues Brundage, was "totally taken over as a royal prerogative." Upon his coronation, an emperor named three or four "bards as his official historians who were to compose and record in lay form each great action of his reign as it occurred. . . . On his death, his successor ordered the totality sung to him and had those he approved added to the canon. Popular history, probably in prose form, there must have been, contradicting in many ways the glorified state presentation, but these were of course driven underground."[6]

---

[5] See K. R. Popper, *The Open Society and Its Enemies* (London, 1949), II, ch. 25, "Has History Any Meaning?"

[6] Burr C. Brundage, *Empire of the Inca* (Norman, Okla., 1963), pp. 176–78.

History that is thus preserved only by the "official" re-memberers is at best a compound of fiction, legend, and myth. As such it can serve as the basis for the propagation of a cult and for the maintenance of tribal solidarity, for it is only the record that the old-timers of the tribe remember or wish to have remembered. They can use the "official" history to influence the current actions of the tribe, remembering only such parts of it as will serve their own immediate ends. By means of this selective history the tribal leaders can control the tribe, swaying it in this or that direction, against this or that enemy, behind this or that leader. In the absence of the full historical record, the only history that remains is official history—that is, the history that is remembered by those who participated in it and is passed on by them in the form of memoirs.

In more sophisticated societies the pressure to write this type of official history is felt especially by those who are employed as government historians. They enjoy a monopoly of historical sources and can therefore determine what and how much shall be made available to scholars, to the public, and to the formulators of public policy. If the historian employed by government arranges the data of history to suit the prejudices of his employers and does not show the past as it really was, he degenerates into a bureaucratic time-server. He may be competent, industrious, and intelligent, but he always remains thoroughly disciplined and never critical of his superiors. He thus becomes a member of the claque and acquires a vested interest in perpetuating a forced and biased interpretation of history. He is the "rememberer" who stands behind the man of action to provide historical sanction for his decisions, whether wise or unwise. He shows or at least pretends to show a kind of "protective stupidity," in Orwell's phrase, which will guarantee him both personal security in his job and security for the bureaucratic party of which he is a member. He does not deviate in either opinion or action from official orders, and even when orders are not issued he divines them by a kind of extrasensory perception and obeys them. He agrees that all policy decisions that have been made in the past by his superiors have been perfect decisions and that his bureaucratic masters have a record of complete infallibility. All he must do is dig up the evidence that will sustain their infallibility and suppress that which does not sustain it. As he thus resolves every queston in favor of withholding information, he ceases to be a historian and reduces his role to that of a public censor.

As a censor he follows the maxim: *éraser l'infâme*. When he finds something in history that offends him or his official heroes, he obliterates it. He presents the past in the light of his own purposes or the preoccupations of his own age. If he conspires to perpetuate only the facts that are officially acknowledged, he and his historical craft can be made to serve the same purposes as the official rememberers in primitive societies. He will use history as a means not of seeking and publishing the truth about the past but of establishing and maintaining authority. In any contest between moral integrity and power, he will support the latter and will allow his historical skills to be used as an instrument of power politics.

In the words of Professor Gaetano Salvemini, who resisted the perversion of history under the fascism of Mussoiini, such a historian-propagandist "selects according to his own bias the facts which he is to expound and those which he is to conceal. And when he cannot conceal a version different from his own, he distorts the arguments which militate in its favor, and thus attempts to persuade his public to believe something they would not believe if they were given all the facts and arguments for or against his version."[7] "Propaganda agents," he continues, "always introduce themselves as open-minded and impartial historians or social scientists; they are wolves in sheep's clothing." Salvemini, speaking of this kind of history, so-called, has gone so far as to say that "The collections of diplomatic documents which Foreign Offices from time to time issue to justify their activities are as a rule more or less skillful forgeries. . . . The 'yellow book' which in the summer of 1914 the French Foreign Office published on the events leading to the outbreak of the World War is a classical example of this kind of mystification."[8] The Red, White, and Blue books issued by the Creel Committee during World War I to stimulate the war spirit of the American people against Germany, Austria, and Italy were thoroughly exposed immediately after the war to be only "skillful forgeries." Another example is the so-called China White Paper, prepared under the supervision of the chief of the historical division of the state department in Washington and published in August 1949. Its egregious omissions, its inaccurate paraphrases, and its tendentious editorializing expose it, when compared with the full documentation on relations of the United States with China, not yet published, to be nothing but a propaganda document fobbed off as history.

History, particularly official history, may therefore be used to condition the people to the supposed requirements of

---

[7] Gaetano Salvemini, *Historian and Scientist* (Cambridge, 1939), pp. 83–84.

[8] *Ibid.*, pp. 40–41.

a political situation, not to enlighten them. It aims at converting them to an official point of view. The historian's synthesis of the past envisages predicatorily what ought to be in terms of what he says has been. He uses his science to shape the future by selective editing of the past or by perversion and destruction of historical records. He thus reduces history to a single lifetime—his own—and foreshortens the whole vast term of man's experience on this earth. The best that can be said for him is that he has fallen into the rut of a "presentist subjectivism," the worst that he betrays his calling for hire and willfully fails to illustrate the present by showing up its problems in accurate and full perspective. His history then becomes only an apology for state policy. By reason of the suppression and perversion of historical information, the realities of our world vanish in part. As we lose the rationale of our present, we lose also a part of our past, to our own misfortune.

Our scientific age has been made possible by the discovery of the method of the working hypothesis as a substitute for dogma. By this method, scientists formulate conclusions on the basis of all available evidence, and as new evidence appears they scrap their old conclusions in favor of new ones. If the physical scientists had never questioned the Ptolemaic theory of the universe, their science would undoubtedly have disappeared and the atomic age would still perhaps be four hundred years in the future. This method of "dogma eat dogma" has opened up to modern man expanding and seemingly illimitable visions of new truth.

This is a method which history, as one of the sciences—a word which in the literal sense, *sciencia*, means simply knowledge—shares with all the other sciences. Historians cannot afford to be any more satisfied with truths discovered in the past than can the natural scientists. They should not be content simply to repeat traditional ideas but must push beyond the old frontiers into new areas of research and interpretation. For "the truths of history," as Goldwin Albert Smith has written, "are usually wild and leaping things. They do not lie asleep and still when we peer behind the curtain of the night. They are always joined to other truths, many of which we do not understand."[9] A historian who makes an unconditional commitment to a certain set of historical formulas forgets that absolute truth is not found in any one historical work, or in any one historical school, or indeed in all of them put together. The reality of life can never be captured or imprisoned in a system.

Historians reject this principle when they base their history not upon the facts but upon their preconceptions. Repudiating their science, they fall back upon the will to believe. They make history an act of faith. Their science then becomes only intuitive and emotional. It moves into the realm of the romantic and becomes doctrinaire, oracular, and intellectually irresponsible. It concerns itself no longer with the meanings of things or even with things themselves but is content to parrot the accepted jargon about things. The genuine historian is distinguished from the historical charlatan by the tentativeness of the conclusions which he holds, for history cannot be dogma. Embalmed truth, in history as in every other science, is falsehood.

History therefore must be a science in perpetual evolution. It must take account of all the hard resilient facts of human experience. It must adapt old experience to new situations and necessarily must be at the same time both destructive

---

[9] *The Heritage of Man: A History of the World* (New York, 1960).

and constructive—destructive of outmoded historical concepts and constructive of new patterns of action for the future based upon experience.

The bridge over which history—and indeed all science— moves from the orthodoxy of yesterday to the orthodoxy of tomorrow is known as revisionism. We all acknowledge in our saner moments that no advancement in insight and wisdom is possible unless we continue to call in question and reconsider what we have previously taken for granted. Professor Samuel Eliot Morison, in paying tribute to Edward Channing, observed that "Channing's most striking characteristic as an historian was his ability to wipe his mind clear of preconceived interpretations and theories, even if he had been teaching them all his life; to study every question and period anew, from the sources, and to reach fresh conclusions."[10]

The function of the historian is to be constantly correcting and completing the image of the past. He is concerned not only with what is true in the past, but also with what is false. Indeed he does not think in terms of true and false, because he is concerned with everything that has happened in the past, with analyzing and explaining it, and with showing its relatedness to the present. He must be ready to penetrate beneath conventional expressions and disguises. For him no subject is taboo and hence closed to further discussion. To represent history as more dignified than human nature is to tamper with the truth. "The historian," J. R. Pole of University College, London, has written, "has a responsibility to

---

[10] Samuel Eliot Morison, "Edward Channing: A Memoir," in *By Land and by Sea* (New York, 1953), p. 323.

the past, but it is not that of deciding within what limits he can recommend it to the approbation of his readers."[11]

The first obligation of the historian is to write down exactly what happened. Like all the sciences, history must be fact-bound. The function of the historian, Polybius wrote in the second century B.C., is "to record with fidelity what was actually said or done, no matter how commonplace it may be."[12] The historian must, in Salvador de Madariaga's vivid phrase, "set down the black and white of everyone of us in due relation to the black and white of the others."[13] The starting point of all historical science must be: What was? It must tell the whole truth with complete frankness, must undeviatingly adhere to the rules of evidence, and must draw only justifiable conclusions from the facts. The historian must be diligent in ferreting out all the facts of an episode—not just those that confirm either his own preconceptions or the prevailing interpretation of it. He must perform his work neither as a zealot nor as an apologist. He must study all the actors in the historical play. He must show neither friendship nor enmity. He is neither a prosecutor nor a counsel for the defendant. He must conserve and present all the facts, and if he fails in this task, if he suppresses or falsifies a single piece of evidence, he neglects his supreme duty as a historian. Both his loyalty to truth and his public service responsibilities enjoin him, therefore, to pursue end-

---

[11] "Historians and the Problem of Early American Democracy," *American Historical Review,* LXVII (1962), 632.

[12] Quoted by James Harvey Robinson in *The New History* (New York, 1912), p. 29.

[13] Salvador de Madariaga, *The Rise of the Spanish American Empire* (New York, 1947), p. xviii.

lessly his search for new historical facts and to examine critically all such facts as he may find.

The sciences differ from religion in that, if they are honest, they do not rest upon revelation. They advance only by accepting contradictions and criticisms. If history is, as Pieter Geyl says, "an argument without end," it will be useful and can justify itself only so long as it allows *pro* and *con*.[14] If it becomes all *pro*—*pro* this or that political figure, *pro* this or that political party—it loses both its savor and its utility. For though history deals with politics it can have no politics. Treating of religion, it nevertheless cannot be sectarian. It embraces all politics, all religions, all peoples. The historian, wrote Carl Becker, "must espouse, with the enthusiasm, the cause of not espousing any cause."[15]

History must reflect the diversity that is man, and though it may acquire sense and meaning from the analysis bestowed upon it by a certain historian, it must be allowed to acquire a different sense and a different meaning from the analysis bestowed upon it by a different historian. The historian who after evaluating the evidence arrives at conclusions which he considers soundly based and then rules out all the *cons* is stultifying his labor, both in the search for new facts, which might vitiate his conclusions, and in the development of his imagination in historical interpretation. "We may compare this attitude," declares Cassirer, "to the frame of mind of those adversaries of Galileo who consistently refused to look through the telescope and convince themselves of the truth of Galileo's astronomical discoveries

---

[14] *Use and Abuse of History* (New Haven, 1955).

[15] "Detachment and the Writing of History," *Atlantic Monthly,* CVI (October 1910), 524–36.

because they did not wish to be disturbed in their implicit faith in the Aristotelian system."[16] When a historian thus closes his mind, he makes it his only object to erect a structure that can be admired even though it may not represent reality. It becomes all white, and his critics become all black. He presumes to have imprisoned reality for all times. But in fact he has become the captive of his own myths.

Myth has its uses, and as long as it is believed it may be a powerful instrumentality for governing men. It represents a crystallization of primitive truth and serves as the justification for ritual and cult. But, as soon as it ceases to be believed, the priestcraft who perpetuate it lose their authority, the hero-cult upon which it is based loses its sanctity, and the world of the myth is seen to be only an artificial world, a mere make-believe. One of the functions of the true historian is to strip away the falsities of myth and to reveal it as mere myth. He should never conspire to manufacture a myth or to perpetuate it as the truth.

One of the characteristics of our time is the antihistoricism of the historians. The absence of a truly inquisitive, scientific history may explain the alarming development in our own time of the power of myth.[17] New interpretations of history, like new discoveries in science, can expect to encounter opposition from the deposit of prejudices which attach themselves to each scholar, to the accretion of dogmas which for each scholar come to assume the role of revealed religion. It is reprehensible enough in a scholar to close his mind to new interpretations, but it is professionally criminal for him to suppress the evidence which supports a

---

[16] *An Essay on Man,* p. 240.

[17] See Ernst Cassirer, *The Myth of the State* (New Haven, 1946), p. 3.

new interpretation and to commit professional murder upon those who suggest it. An entire school of historical writers since the mid-1930s, nevertheless, has violated a simple but cardinal principle of history, namely, examination of the original evidence instead of the many interested versions. We have therefore been led into an obscurantist maze, gloomy and prefigured, that fixes not only our pattern of action but also many of our modes of thought about our modern world.

These historians have developed their own conformities and dogmatisms, and, like Procrustes of old, they lop off every oversize idea to make it fit their bed. They not only reject the idea of the wholesomeness of contradiction, but they smear their critics. Their dogma requires the suppression of contradictory facts and opposing hypotheses. But, as Salvemini has warned, such "scholars," when "no longer stimulated by free competition, lose their capacity to renew their vitality, become mummified by the very monopoly they enjoy, and lapse into lazy repetition of official propaganda. If they do not demand free competition not only for themselves but for their rivals as well, the historian and the social scientist, more than any other scholars, accept both moral and intellectual degradation."[18] A science that adapts itself too closely to its environment, that takes on the protective coloration of its age, is already moribund. It seems ironical that in this enlightened twentieth century those who argue against revelation as an explanation of what has happened in history should be thrown on the defensive and that those who argue for the scientific method in history should be castigated, even by some of their professional colleagues.

---

[18] Salvemini, *op. cit.*, p. 113.

The eighteenth century used history to bring about societal changes, which helped to generate the great upheaval of the French Revolution. History became a branch of polemics. Clio, rechristened the goddess of Illusion, was made to enter the lists, her clothing tattered and shredded, and to give the sanction of destiny to what was being done. But she had her ultimate revenge. The leaders of the New France, who began their historical epoch with the Year One and a new calendar, found that their era was actually thousands of years old. They soon repeated the very historical cycle that they condemned.

As they thus turned their backs upon their fabricated history, spun out of their dreams of a new heaven and a new earth, they laid the basis for that scientific history which was one of the glories of the nineteenth century. History, conceived as a study of the process of growth and development, became a counter-revolutionary force. When it sloughed off both its revolutionary and its counter-revolutionary preachments and ceased to be used for ends considered good by the historian, it became a profound interpreter of the thoughts, sentiments, and mode of behavior of human beings through the ages. It held up the mirror to nature but did not seek to change nature. It thus opened up undreamed-of possibilities of understanding the contemporary world.

History in our time, as contrasted with the scientific history of the nineteenth century, must be characterized as simplistic. We have succumbed to the conviction that history, instead of resulting from decisions taken by men and carried out by men, results only from intentions that are implicit in objects, and that those intentions must be blindly and inexorably fulfilled by men. Men therefore are only the victims or tools of materialistic forces—and this theory lies at the heart of the Marxian dialectic. One of the main defects of Marxism is its naive oversimplification of the actual historical forces in human society, as for example by its overemphasis on the class struggle as a single formula explaining society. As Professor J. H. Hexter has shown, many modern historians, whether knowingly or unknowingly, write their history from the Marxist point of view, particularly his theory of the class struggle in history and the consequences flowing from it. Hexter writes: "Historians were rightly impressed by Marx's insight into the conflict of classes. It gave them a whole new set of exciting insights into the way things happened. But when they picked up the notion of class conflict, they quite unconsciously picked up with it Marx's theory of social change. They bought themselves a package deal."[19] Professor Hexter's claim of innocence for his fellow craftsmen in this respect may be questioned, but his charge of the all-pervasiveness of the Marxist viewpoint in modern historiography cannot be disputed. And in addition to the class-struggle theme which permeates much of modern historiography, the theme of the inevitability of the historical process—another Marxist teaching—dominates our historical schools. As a result, history is once more being predominantly used to justify rather than to explain, to glorify rather than to criticize, to prove that everything that was done was rightly done. As it is paralyzed by *raison d'état,* it becomes only illusion and deception, a thing of unreality and myth, deprived of its critical faculty, and prostituted to serve ambition and hero-worship. As history thus surrenders its claim to untrammeled investigation and criticism, it loses its role as a free and independent force in our world. When

[19] J. H. Hexter, *Reappraisals in History* (New York, 1961), p. 15.

historians become accomplices to bureaucrats, history becomes a means not of enlightening the people but of keeping
them in ignorance.

"The historian who pretends to an independent authority
to certify the documents or verify the claims of a government
department must be as jealous and importunate as the cad of
a detective who has to find the murderer amongst a party of
his friends," writes Professor Herbert Butterfield of Cambridge University. And, he continues, "if an historian
were to say: 'This particular group of documents ought not
to be published because it would expose the officials concerned to serious misunderstandings,' then we must answer
that he has already thrown in his lot with officialdom—
already he is thinking of their own interests rather than
ours." Furthermore, he adds, "supposing there are gaps anywhere in the documentation . . . then there should be no
limit to the detective work put into the matter and no limit
to the precision in the account that is given to historical
students."

What is even more serious, Butterfield declares, is the
effort of official historians "to lull us to sleep" by telling us
that the materials which are withheld "do not matter for
purposes of historical reconstruction. Here is a point," he
concludes, "that goes to the very basis of historical science."[20] It also goes to the very basis of the principle of the
right of the people to know the full truth and to have the
information necessary to exert an effective and intelligent
control over the officials to whom they have temporarily
entrusted the powers of government. After all, public offi-

[20] Herbert Butterfield, *History and Human Relations* (London: 1951),
pp. 194–206.

cials are only custodians of the official records. They are not the owners. What will become of our system of government if the facts on which the people must base their decisions are suppressed or distorted and then only a partial record is promulgated by "historians" as the full truth?

It is here, in this spadework of the profession, that the historian working in the official bureaucracy has an immense responsibility. By his selection of the documents revealing the experience of the nation in both its domestic politics and its foreign relations, he can color the historical interpretation of his epoch for generations to come. His responsibility for the coloration that historical writing will take is enormous. At this first fact-collecting stage, the historian must primarily let the facts speak for themselves. He should therefore exercise a more than Olympian objectivity and be influenced neither by political predilections nor by official friendships. If he remains steadfast in his calling, he will not allow himself to become either a politician or a bureaucrat. Upon him is laid the duty of pursuing all leads, examining all documents, and sweeping all relevant pieces of information into his work. To do less is to fail to let history serve the role of usefulness which it ought to serve in this modern world. History, said Lord Acton, "to be above evasion or dispute, must stand on documents, not on opinion."

The independent scholar, no less than the official historian, must scrupulously guard against subservience to the partisanships and personalities of the moment. History was too narrowly defined by Edward A. Freeman in the nineteenth century as "past politics," but it is now sometimes conceived even more narrowly as only "present politics." As history in modern times has beome thus politicized, the historians, like the politicians, uncritically accept the prevalent assumptions of the current age and make their craft an instrument of political force. "The twentieth century historian is training potential civil servants, whereas the nineteenth century historian trained statesmen," suggestively observes Professor A.J.P. Taylor.[21]

The conformitarian pressures of our times and the increasing role that governments play in all human situations impose upon the modern historian, both official and private, the obligation to be more than usually inquisitive and skeptical. He must do this not only for the selfish aim of defending his chosen profession against the onslaughts of its enemies, but also for the enlightened purpose of making history serve the large role in public affairs which he must believe is indispensable to a sane and peaceful world. History conceived only as a dogma will destroy itself. When any branch of learning becomes a closed system and reaches a stage of speculative completeness, it loses its interrogative function. It then ceases to have a dynamic quality. It succumbs to a self-hypnosis of finality. A history that denigrates itself either to dogma or to myth is on the way out. As it resists reason, it becomes irrational. By stifling criticism, it yields itself to the fallacy that it can become authoritarian and still survive.

The handmaiden role of history, it is explained, has been made necessary by the modern emphasis upon centralization of authority in government, which historians themselves have quite generally encouraged. Centralism is now widely accepted as the very marrow of history. For the pervasive idea that virtue resides mainly in large slabs of power, modern historians must bear considerable responsibility. They have been carried away by their urge for system, logic,

---

[21] *The Origins of the Second World War*, p. 9.

order, and unity. They have succumbed to the view that history, in Américo Castro's phrase, is only "universalizable culture" and has no local or national tone.[22] History is proceeding, and proceeding rightly, according to them, toward centralized control, greater collectivities, and stronger government. The innumerable sacrifices which human individualism has made in resisting authority have been submerged in the centralizing tradition which history has consecrated. The recipe for secure individual living and harmonious international relations is found, say the historians, in ever-enlarging agglomerations of power. History has therefore become preoccupied with the search for absolute law and a universal order. In this search, it has created an ideal structure of abstractions which, according to its own preconceptions, reduces to a minimum the role of freedom in history. Progress has come to be embodied in certain authoritarian persons and institutions.

Affirming the preachment of modern historians that centralism represents an inevitable projection of a long historical process, Liu Shao-chi, the official spokesman of the Chinese Communist Party, declared, in early 1956, that this "is the road that all humanity must inevitably take, in accordance with the laws of the development of history." The inexorably centralist character of Soviet communism was starkly disclosed during World War II. It then appeared to be only a latter-day version of Czarist autocracy. But this type of government seemed to respond to the postwar demand for governments of the positive or welfare-state variety. It appealed to many who were now convinced of the

---

[22] Américo Castro, *The Structure of Spanish History* (Princeton, 1954), p. 39.

need for more effective action at local and national levels. The climate of the postwar era favors centralization of power and deprecates the local and community values which seemed important in the prewar period and which at that time gave Soviet communism its aura of respectability and utopianism.

The change of historical fashion in this respect is well illustrated by contrasting the current interpretation of Soviet communism with that of the 1920s and 1930s. At that time, the seeming rejection of the stereotype of centralism by Soviet communism was one of the reasons for its appeal to young intellectuals in the Western world. Soviet Russia was represented as a system in which initiative welled up from the local communities and was successfully reflected in action at higher and higher levels of government. This was one of its attributes which seemed most alluring to the British scholars Sidney and Beatrice Webb, who, it must be remembered, won their academic laurels through their monumental studies of English local government before they turned to their influential study of *Soviet Communism.*[23] Nor did the American scholar Walter Russell Batsell, in his *Soviet Rule in Russia,* emphasize the suppression of individualism that was taking place in Russia under the Politburo and the OGPU; rather, the Soviet government machine seemed to be only an efficient mechanism for implementing the work of the virtuous citizen in his home and community living.[24] So represented, it exerted a mighty appeal to those who believed in the freest possible community action and the largest possible individual fulfillment, and who at the

---

[23] *Soviet Communism: A New Civilisation* (New York, 1938).
[24] Walter Russell Batsell, *Soviet Rule in Russia* (New York, 1929).

same time distrusted centralized authoritarianism as a means of achieving these ends.

Traditional history was primarily concerned with individual action. It was as Pieter Geyl says, "the guardian of the particular."[25] It emphasized originality, experimentation, and difference. If it propounded theses, it also recognized antitheses. But, when it became concerned only with the totality and lost its interest in the particular and the unique, it was converted into a weapon for structuring the future.

Today a belief in centralism or gigantism enthralls our intellects and stimulates our imaginations. It colors our interpretation of the past and has produced—and in part been produced by—a new school of centralist historians, each of whom is an "organization man." As history is thus rewritten to justify the centralizing tendencies in our society and to give the authority of secular inevitability to present tendencies, it becomes the proselyting determiner of things to come. The idea of progress, which when it first appeared represented a reaction against a medieval statics imposed by Providence, has now, by its own apotheosis of centralization, created a new statics, a new anthropo-centrism, which is represented as an inexorable creature of "the laws of the development of history." Emphasis is placed upon the principle of centralized authority as being essential to order at the sacrifice of the principle of freedom, which is equated with disorder. The force of freedom, writes the Peruvian philosopher Alejandro O. Deústua, "could not be regarded as a danger, as a threat to the happiness which had been conquered. . . . The new could be imposed by only the command

---

[25] *Use and Abuse of History* (New Haven, 1955), p. 66.

of authority, representative of prescient wisdom and of irresistible power."[26]

This neo-Hegelian or, more accurately, neo-Marxist historiography needs to be critically examined. The present emphasis upon the centralizing forces in history means the neglect of the forces of decentralization, regionalism, particularism, localism, and individualism. The ultimate centralization is totalitarianism. How many civilizations that succumbed to conquerors in the long record of the past were themselves highly centralized? May it not have been the centralization that Athens established in its Delian League, for example, rather than its persistence in particularism that brought about its downfall in the Peloponnesian War? The art work of that Etruscan civilization, which has been so reprobated for its political disunity, surpassed the art of the conquering centralized Romans in many respects. Was not the founder of Christianity himself executed by the most powerful central authority of his day?

Has not the long history of political thought and action been more concerned with the restraint than with the exercise of centralized power? The greater part of history, quantitatively measured, is the record of men's activity at local levels, in their own communities. A centralized government has usually been tolerated by a people only when it appeared to be the only alternative to national extinction. Have the effects, whether intended or unintended, of weak rulers upon the process of individual development and popular self-government been fairly interpreted for us? *Rois*

---

[26] Quoted in Aníbal Sánchez Reulet, ed., *Contemporary Latin-American Philosophy* (Albuquerque, 1954).

fainéants have also made historical contributions. A great many things have happened without the intervention or instigation of great men. The dangers of centralism and its effects upon the integrity of citizens were warningly stressed with impeccable historicity by Edward Gibbon in his *Decline and Fall of the Roman Empire,* written in an age of hastening centralization. May not the struggle for individual freedom, individual expression, and local self-government have been at least as important in the historical process as the struggle for authoritarianism? Has the latter been so unfailingly and universally triumphant as to deserve so much historical accolade? And should we not reconsider the idea, implicit in much modern historiography, that because mankind has been moving from isolation to union he has therefore been advancing from war to peace? Centralized government has often established itself only by victory in battle. Has sufficient thought been given to the fact that praise of centralism is praise of force as the final arbiter in human affairs?

The idea that periods of centralization are the only or even the main examples of progress in history overlooks the oscillations that have occurred in the historical process, such as the rise and fall of political systems, the seesaw of action and reaction, the relativity of historical evolution. The mature historian sees that the historical process is eternal pulsation. It is, as Gerald Heard has written, "the systole and diastole of Time itself." As some societies have been moving toward centralization, others have been retreating from it. At least as much of human history has been devoted to rebellion against the tyranny of centralization as has been directed toward its establishment. The recurring triumphs of centralism, therefore, should be treated not as achievement and consummation—not as new plateaus which man has fought for and won—but as episodes in a continuing struggle between centralism and particularism, between authoritarianism and individualism, between tyranny and freedom.

Without challenging the idea of progress, which is seemingly built inextricably into modern history, it may be suggested that the characteristic phenomenon of human development over the long run is not progress toward centralization but rather oscillation or cyclical change in accordance with the German concept of *zeitgeist* or spirit of the time. Historical interpretations which overemphasize the theme of centralization, when looked at from the viewpoint of eternity, appear as actual errors of fact. History, if it is to be accurate, must give a prominent place to the continuous attempts at the reconciliation of individualism on the one hand and authority on the other. In history, as in the physical world, the centripetal forces are balanced by the centrifugal. If it were not so, human life would be snuffed out by the pressures of an eccentric universe. We need a history in the round that will give due importance to all the currents and forces in man's evolution. "History," Américo Castro has observed, "exists in a vital dialectic of things present and things absent, of positive and negative values."[27]

History has a disconcerting way of confronting us when we are least ready to meet her. In the shadows behind every statesman addressing an international conference or affixing his signature to a treaty stands this enigmatic muse. She belongs to no party except the party of truth, and she stands watch serenely while heroes wax and wane.

The past is all we can know, for the future is concealed

---

[27] Américo Castro, *op. cit.,* p. 548.

from us and the knife-edge of the present is too brief to be fully comprehended. The present is in any case unintelligible without the past. But, as the present is determined by the past, it can also be used to determine the past. As we seek to build a whole in the present, we sometimes undertake to work the past into that whole and use it to justify the whole, even though we must distort the past in order to accomplish this result. The only durably satisfactory present that we can fashion, however, must be constructed upon a frank appreciation of the realities of the past. This is to argue not for a canonization of the past but for such an understanding of the past as will illuminate and provide guidance in the present. If the present is made to rest upon only an officially approved past or an ideally conceived past, its foundations are shifting sand. And a future built upon such a present becomes increasingly shaky. An accurate reading of the past, therefore, is an essential precondition to every satisfying present and every successful future.

Essay Ten

Official History

Herbert Butterfield

Herbert Butterfield has been professor of modern history at Cambridge University since 1944. He has served as president of the Historical Association (1955 to 1958) and as editor of the Cambridge Historical Journal *(1938 to 1952). He is the author of* The Historical Novel *(1924),* The Peace Tactics of Napoleon, 1806–08 *(1929),* The Whig Interpretation of History *(1931),* Napoleon *(1939),* The Statecraft of Machiavelli *(1940),* The Englishman and His History *(1944),* The Study of Modern History *(1944),* George III, Lord North and the People *(1949),* The Origins of Modern Science *(1949),* Christianity and History *(1949),* History and Human Relations *(1951),* Christianity in European History *(1951),* Christianity, Diplomacy and War *(1953),* Man on His Past *(1955),* George III and the Historians *(1957),* International Conflict in the Twentieth Century *(1960), and* The Universities and Education Today *(1962).*

I

Much has been said about contemporary history from the point of view of the expert, but the issues that are raised belong to a court of wider jurisdiction. A word on this subject will perhaps be allowed, therefore, to the student of historiography who tries to see the experts themselves in their due relationship with everything else. The experts have a great advantage in the nature of things, and when they have the peculiar position of being "official" historians (or even "officially favored" historians) so that they can say "We have seen the evidence and you have not; besides, our ways are hidden ways"—in such conditions they might well feel themselves out of reach of criticism. I, for my part, can only cross-examine the experts and analyze the situation itself from the point of view of a general historian who exercises the prerogatives of a critic in respect of a field or a period not his own. I do indeed have one qualification for speaking on contemporary history which, without betraying any secrets, I can say that all people do not possess. I am not an official historian employed by the British or any other Foreign Office; I am not limited by special obligations under the Official Secrets Act in the communication of what

I do happen to know; and if I feel that I have anything to write or say, I do not belong to that new class of so-called independent historians, who have first to submit their scripts to the check or censorship of a Foreign Office official.

Of all the principles which touch the life of states and peoples it seems to me that the most important in the secular sphere is the one which insists upon freedom of thought, by which I mean of course freedom in the expression of thought—freedom (supposing I am in a minority of one) to attempt the task of converting the majority. Under the shelter of this general principle, there will exist (when the body politic is healthy) an independent science of history, not hostile to the government but standing over against it— a science which will seek to present the cause of historical truth as distinct from the things which might be promulgated from motives of *raison d'état* or for the sake of a public advantage or in order to cover the imprudences of politicians and government servants. Our predecessors recognized perhaps better than we do, however, that such an independent science of history would always tend to find the dice loaded against it for the time being; for it is difficult for men to place truth above public advantage when public advantage might mean the winning of a war, the circumvention of a diplomatic crisis, the covering of a reputation, or even an improvement in general welfare. Against those who demanded that the historian should more directly serve his time and age, the German historian Meinecke, even in 1916, asserted in a moving manner the long-term advantages of academic history; but it must be remembered that in more pressing times it is easy to feel that the historian should serve the government—easy to overlook the long-term benefits of an historiography which insists on keeping a higher altitude. In a case where a change in the relationship of the state to historical study is in question, causes may be lost by the selling of very little passes—even by unconscious compliances and complicities. Eighteenth-century Whiggism was correct in stressing the point that when men have inherited freedom, and have not had to fight for it themselves, they easily allow it to slide away, not realizing that concessions apparently innocuous, when made to people whom we happen to like and trust, become at the next remove the ground from which a new generation of men can make a more serious encroachment on liberty. Some of our nineteenth-century historians wrote as though they remembered much more clearly than we do that freedom is always a fight, always a striving, always a matter of vigilance and alertness. The relations of a government with historical study are on a different footing from those which exist in the case of any of the other sciences. It is necessary for the outside student, therefore, always to be on his guard.

The relationship of technical historians to "official history" in our days is no doubt good for official history which can only benefit from the connection. It is even calculated to bring out some revelations earlier than might otherwise have been the case, though we must never forget that it enables other things to be kept concealed with the greater impunity. The good which is produced for the time being turns to serious evil, however, if the new situation has the effect of blurring old distinctions; and one of the disturbing symptoms of the present time is the fact that attempts have indeed been made to blur the distinctions, as will appear from some examples given below. It is necessary not to allow the new state of affairs to conceal the fact that what we have to deal with is still official history. If that point were to be overlooked in a universal absence of mind or suspension of criticism, too good a bargain would have been made for the state, and an important cause would have been put in jeopardy. In any case, there is need for a very precise code of guarantees to assure one that the interests of independent historical science have been guarded in a watertight manner, considering the pitfalls that exist. Official historians are serving the public, it is true; their labors are sometimes of colossal magnitude; but they get the reward that is certainly due to them. If they are true to the ideal of academic history they will agree that all forms of official history should be regarded with the greatest caution, the greatest critical alertness; and they will see that their own hands are strengthened by the very clamor of criticism, the very importunity of their enemies. It may be necessary that official history should be produced. It is equally necessary that it should be subjected to unremitting scrutiny.

II

If I may be allowed to give what at least is not an unconsidered opinion, I must say that I do not personally believe that there is a government in Europe which wants the public to know all the truth. If there is one which does have the desire, it has an easy way of proving its good intentions, for it has only to open its archives to the free play of scholarship—to friends, enemies, neutrals, devil's advocates and independent observers, so that everything may be put into the crucible and we may know the worst that the eagle eye of hostile critic may pounce upon, the clash of controversy ultimately producing a more highly tested form of truth. There are two maxims for historians which so harmonize with what I know of history that I would like to claim them as my own, though they really belong to nineteenth-century historiography: first, that governments try to press upon the historian the key to all the drawers but one, and are very anxious to spread the belief that this single one contains no secret of importance; secondly, that if the historian can only find out the thing which government does not want him to know, he will lay his hand upon something that is likely to be significant.

My own teacher and predecessor, Professor Temperley, stood at what I should call an intermediate stage in the development of modern "official history"; for, along with Dr. Gooch, he held what now seems to me a peculiarly independent position as editor of the *British Documents on the Origins of the War of 1914*—negotiating with the Foreign Office not from the inside, so to speak, but from a more arbitral position outside. And we know that serious tension existed at times in the course of that publication, for after some volumes had appeared the editors found it necessary to announce their threat that they would resign if their decisions were not followed; though I believe it is true to say that the tension was due to the difficulties raised by other powers, and not to any anxiety that our Foreign Office then had on its own account. Since it seems to me that the editors of the *British Documents* knew as much about the relations between historians and governments as any Englishman of their generation, there are three of Professor Temperley's utterances on this subject which have a peculiar significance and which invite us to serious reflection. First of all, in his inaugural lecture in Cambridge in 1930 he expressed grave misgivings concerning the harm that might come to history from both the patronage of government and the growing popular interest in the subject. Secondly, in almost the last article—if not the very last—that he wrote (an article published in 1938 in the *Cambridge Historical Journal*) he depicted the decline of frankness—the growing significance of secret diplomacy—in the policy of English Foreign Secretaries during the hundred years that ended with Sir Edward Grey. He closed that article with words which throw a curious light on the inferences that he was inclined to make upon the whole of his experience, for he said: "It is indeed evident that no statesman in our own generation will approach the standards of candor in diplomacy upheld by Palmerston or by Canning." Thirdly, in a manuscript which appeared in the *Cambridge Historical Journal* in December 1948, he set down some views concerning the origin of the war of 1914—views somewhat different from those commonly accepted as a kind of semiofficial orthodoxy today; but even in the unusually independent position that he occupied as an editor of the *British Documents* I am interested to note that he felt himself under some constriction; for, though he wrote down these views in 1927, he particularly specified that his name should not be attached to any publication of them until the last of these volumes of documents had appeared—which in fact proved to be a decade later.

After the First World War, a special situation was created by the existence of revolutionary governments not unwilling to discredit the dynasties or the regimes which they had displaced, and therefore not unready to make a generous publication of diplomatic documents which should throw light not merely on the immediate origins of the war itself but also on the events of the preceding years. These revelations had the effect of springing the secrets of other Foreign Offices, too, of course; and the result was bound to be unsatisfactory to these latter, for the simple reason that one's diplomatic secrets do not appear at their best when revealed in the papers of another government. Other governments were encouraged, therefore, to publish their own diplomatic documents in turn; and within a single decade after the conclusion of peace in 1919 an extraordinary development had taken place in the whole historiography of the origins of the war of 1914. This was particularly remarkable in the minute researches, the intricate collation of documents, and the detailed detective work which are evident in certain major writings of the late 1920s. The original simple "melodrama" of 1914 was transformed into a story of higher organization altogether—a story possessing that texture which a piece of history seems to acquire when, instead of burying the recalcitrant fact and the inconvenient discrepancy, it allows itself to be driven by these very things to a higher synthesis altogether.

The rise of Hitler and the consequent political strain or fever seem to have had a serious effect on that whole type of scientific enquiry in England. Not only was the great task discontinued, but there occurred one of those remarkable throwbacks which occasionally take place in the history of historical science—we had a general return into currency of the primitive, garbled, wartime versions of the origins of the war of 1914. The view that what happened was in reality a retrogression can be supported by tests of an external kind, tests which might be put forward as affording general criteria for a judgment of quality on works of contemporary history. Firstly, in the return to the older version of the origins of the war of 1914, it is difficult to see a fraction of that scholarship which had been so impressive in the late 1920s and to which I have never come across any authentic or scholarly answer. Secondly, there does not appear to be the same texture in the narrative—a texture which results when history is written with a due respect for the complexity of events. Thirdly, the spirit of scientific enquiry—the desire to learn the truth whatever the consequences—is a recognizable thing; and we can discern it in a particular manner in that work of the 1920s to which reference has been made. It is the subsequent writers who so often make it clear that they are writing the history with their eye on a certain policy that they desire for the present; So that constantly somebody is trying to bluff us into forgetting the distinction between historical enquiry and political propaganda, though the distinction is a palpable one, and the modes of procedure are widely divergent. Finally, if an hysterical cry goes up when a person questions the popular or prevailing views on the origins of the war of 1914—if a Nazi-like howl is raised when anybody recalls the views of some of the writers in the late 1920s, and historical problems are settled by nicknaming the offender as a "pro-German"—this itself is a sign and proof that the times are not fitted for sober enquiry or judicious decision. Indeed, one must have grave misgivings concerning any contemporary history that is produced in such an atmosphere.

III

A second world war, on the top of what I have described, has produced in the field of contemporary history a situation not without its disquieting features. Even before the end of the war a mere outsider could hardly escape the impression that governments were preparing to race one another in the endeavor to state their case, whether by official histories or by the publication of selected documents. This we must regard as an object legitimate in itself, and academic students would be overarrogant if they were to think that governments exist only in order that historians should be able to write about them afterward. But we must never lose sight of the separate interests of officialdom on the one hand and academic history on the other, never allow the distinction to be blurred or the tension and conflict between the two to be quietened. A book was published during the Second World War and it happened that some time later I mentioned in print a curious howler that it contained. It was not very long before I was told that I ought not to be severe on the author on the ground that the book had been written for the Ministry of Information, in the Ministry's office, and in time spent as the servant of the Ministry. An outsider could not have realized this fact, but I am clear that work produced in this way should always bear distinct signs of its origin, and never be published in a form that would make the ordinary reader think it a normal example of disinterested and independent scholarship. In various other forms there is appearing a sort of history not avowedly official—pseudo-official perhaps, or semi-official, or sub-official—and I can well believe that in a certain sense of the words it would deny that it had any official character. Similarly there are "independent" academic historians, yet half-entangled in officialdom, controlled by the Official Secrets Act, even amenable to instructions, and not authorized to tell all the truth they know. It is not always quite clear that our leaders made the best possible bargain for the cause of independent history, a cause for which (in any case of default) it may happen that brother will have to fight brother.

We are now following the practice of the Germans in their days of victory and securing that we—not they—shall control that most subtle of all historical tasks, the selection of such of the diplomatic documents of the defeated power as we shall allow to be published to the world. The Americans have produced on their own account a volume of these German documents relating to Nazi-Soviet relations in 1939, and the book in two prefaces which are worded with extreme care and delicacy makes its bid to appear as the work of "independent" historians, a point concerning which there is a tendency sometimes to protest too much. The elements of policy in the commanding of this special series of documents at the time at which it was produced make it necessary to suggest (as one of those delicate matters which seem small but are really pivotal) that the term "independent historian" is in danger of undergoing a subtle change of meaning in our time. It is just by gradations of this sort that one would fear to see the situation deteriorate. It is just such hints of an inclination to compliance which justify our asking whether the official historians are fighting as unremittingly as we should wish and fighting always on our side.

We easily recognize fallacy and foolishness in the foreigner, and a useful way in which we can test either our own integrity or the wisdom of a technical measure is to remember what our reactions are when the parallel thing is done in a foreign country, especially a country that we happen to be observing with a certain jealousy. One of the gravest signs of what seems to me to be a decline from the principles explicitly instilled into me when I was young is an inability to step out of one's own shoes—and even a deprecation of any attempt to step into the shoes of others—and this is a sin which involves the overthrow of the essential discipline of history. In communications concerning our presumptuous view that we can "reeducate" the Germans in history, I have seen humor so far lost that, while German historiography has been regarded as national, whether it was Nazi or not, there has been a sublime and awful assumption that our own current version of the course of ages was the uncolored "scientific" history—a thing appropriate to be imposed by direct transmission upon a defeated power. When I was an undergraduate we were taught to mock the simplicity of German historiography in the Bismarckian era, which went so far as to produce "contemporary history" under Bismarck's wing, using the documents the great man himself chose to have revealed, and even allowing him to influence and interpret the historical accounts of his own activity. The future historian will certainly find it useful if all the Bismarcks are allowed to say as much as possible for themselves; but I seem to have noticed a tendency to believe that what was naïveté when it was done by the contemporaries of Bismarck is virtue now, and one is made to feel as though one were hitting below the belt if one suggests (what is certainly true) that there are many booby-traps for the historian in such a policy.

A Foreign Secretary once complained that, while he, for his part, was only trying to be helpful, Professor Temperley (as one of the editors of the *British Documents*) persisted in treating him as though he were a hostile power. Certainly it is possible for the historian to be unnecessarily militant, and even a little ungracious in his militancy; but what a satisfaction it is to the student if he can be sure that his interests have been guarded with unremitting jealousy! And if we employ a watchdog (which is the function the independent historian would be expected to perform on our behalf), what an assurance it is to be able to feel that we are served by one whom we know to be vigilant and unsleeping! The ideal, in this respect, would certainly not be represented by the picture of a Professor Temperley and a Foreign Secretary as thick as thieves, each merely thinking the other a jolly good fellow; for the historian who is collecting evidence—and particularly the historian who pretends as an independent authority to certify the documents or verify the claims of a government department—must be as jealous and importunate as the cad of a detective who has to find the murderer amongst a party of his friends. One of the widest of the general causes of historical error has been the disposition of a Macaulay to recognize in the case of Tory witnesses a need for historical criticism which it did not occur to him to have in the same way for the witnesses on his own side. Nothing in the whole of historiography is more subtly dangerous than the natural disposition to withhold criticism because John Smith belongs to one's own circle or because he is a nice man, so that it seems ungracious to try to press him on a point too far, or because it does not occur to one that something more could be extracted from him by importunate endeavor. In this sense all is not loss if our historian-detective even makes himself locally unpopular; for (to take an imaginary case) if he communicates to us his judgment that the Foreign Office does not burn important papers, the point is not without its interest; but we could only attach weight to the judgment if he had gone into the matter with all the alertness of an hostile enquirer and with a keenly critical view concerning the kind of evidence which could possibly authorize a detective to come to such a conclusion. And if an historian were to say: "This particular group of documents ought not to be published, because it would expose the officials concerned to serious misunderstandings," then we must answer that he has already thrown in his lot with officialdom—already he is thinking of their interests rather than ours; for since these documents, by definition, carry us outside the framework of story that somebody wants to impose on us, they are the very ones that the independent historian must most desire. To be sure, no documents can be published without laying many people to grievous misunderstanding. In this connection an uncommon significance must attach therefore to the choice of the people who are to be spared. The only way to reduce misunderstanding is to keep up the clamor for more and more of the strategic kinds of evidence.

In keeping with this view, no matter whether the papers in question are those of one's own government or those of an enemy power, it would be essential, when documents are to be published, that editors should insist on seeing the whole range of original papers, known or inferred or suspected—seeing the originals themselves and not more photostats provided for them: never saying that they have seen documents if they have only seen photostats, and never resting content if, say in the case of a German collection of photostats, they have seen only copies, possibly reduced in number, after rephotographing in some allied government department. It is essential that editors, if they suspect the existence of further documents, should pursue them unrelentingly, and, if they fail to find them, should give an account of this, making it their object to serve the historical student rather than to vindicate officialdom. And supposing there are gaps anywhere in the documentation—particularly in those sinister cases where a gap may exist at what for the government concerned happens to be a strategic point in the story—then there should be no limit to the detective work put into the matter and no limit to the precision in the account that is given to historical students. For at some time or other the world will take notice of this.

It is a mistake to imagine that the influence of government would ordinarily operate today in the kind of cases we are considering (any more than in the case of the press) by the older, cruder modes of direct censorship; and both official historians and the general public are anachronistic when they formulate the issue, as they sometimes seem to do, in these simple terms. Where the publication of select documents is concerned there is one matter which the outsider cannot very well know about (but must wish to know), and that is the question of the machinery or the series of processes through which documents pass at their various stages of selection and elimination, particularly if there are places or cases where people other than historians (representatives of government departments for example) have any participation at all in the work or the discussions. It would even be useful if all the rules governing the work of official historians could be published; since it is conceivable, for example, that regulations restricting certain powers or privileges to a chief editor would raise an issue of some significance. But outside such realms as these there are ways of keeping official history "safe," just as there are ways (one is permitted to gather) in which a modern newspaper can be induced to exercise its own self-discipline in the interests of government. It is essential for everybody to be aware that the whole problem of "censorship" today has been transformed into the phenomenon of "auto-censorship"—a matter to be borne in mind even when the people involved are only indirectly the servants of government, or are attached by no further tie than the enjoyment of privileges that might be taken away. It is even true that where all are "pals" there is no need for censorship, no point where it is necessary to imagine that one man is being overruled by another. And in any case it is possible to conceive of a state in which members of different organizations could control or prevent a revelation with nothing more than a hint or a wink as they casually passed one another amidst the crowd at some tea party. I do not think that I am merely day-dreaming when I feel that in certain circles near to government a kind of contagious unanimity seems to exist at a certain level, even amongst men who, if we took them at a more superficial level, would say that they were only conscious of being in perpetual controversy with one another. It is like the case of Emerson, who, fighting perpetually against the New England Puritans, never suspected that he would be remembered in history only as another New England Puritan. Such being the situation, I think it was true even long ago that nothing could be more subtle than the influence upon historians of admission to the charmed circle; and in many fields besides the history of historiography we are able to confirm the fact that certain contacts (even if they are between churchmen and the state) produce unconscious complicities and acquiescences—a well-run state needs no heavy-handed censorship, for it binds the historian with soft charms and with subtle, comfortable chains.

Essay Eleven

The Monstrosity of Government

John A. Lukacs

John A. Lukacs was born in Hungary in 1923, arrived in the United States in 1946, and became a naturalized U.S. citizen in 1953. He is professor of history at Chestnut Hill College, where he joined the faculty in 1947, and has been a lecturer at La Salle College since 1949. He has also been a visiting professor at Columbia University. He is the author of The Great Powers and Eastern Europe, A History of the Cold War, and The Decline and Rise of Europe.

Toward the end of an age more and more people lose their faith in their institutions: and finally they abandon their belief that these institutions might still be reformed from within.

At the beginning of the twentieth century among the civilized peoples of the world faith in political reform was still strong. Their political vocabularies—"Right," "Left," "conservative," "liberal," "radical," "nationalist," "socialist"—still made much sense. Only a few groups of extremists professed a cynical indifference to the potential benefits of constitutional government.

Except for two republics (France and Switzerland), as late as 1910 every European state was still a monarchy, but the actual political power of the monarchs was dwindling everywhere. Using the terms in their classical sense, it could be said that the peoples of the Western world before 1914 were governed by a mixed system of democracy and aristocracy. On the one hand the rise of democracy was being accepted almost everywhere, and universal suffrage existed in more and more countries. On the other hand governmental influence was still largely exercised by a relatively small class of people, a kind of functioning bourgeois aristocracy which was no longer a nobility whose distinctions had been based on birth. The distinction of this amorphous class rested largely, though not exclusively, on wealth or, rather, on the large and nearly limitless influences that wealth could procure around that time.

In retrospect we can see that the influence of this kind of transitional aristocracy was bound to disappear rather fast. Developments such as the passing of the House of Lords Bill in Britain or Theodore Roosevelt's measures in curbing the powers of plutocracies in America showed this even before the cataclysm of 1914.* All of this meant a gradual increase in governmental intervention in the lives of citizens. In certain states in Central and Eastern Europe a considerable portion of the population was employed by the state, in one way or another. Still, as A. J. P. Taylor put it: "Until August 1914 a sensible, law-abiding Englishman could pass through life and hardly notice the existence of the state, beyond the post office and the policeman."

> He could live where he liked and as he liked. He had no official number or identity card. He could travel abroad or leave his country forever without a passport or any sort of official permission. He could exchange his money for any other currency without restriction or limit. He could buy goods from any country in the world on the same terms as he bought goods at home. For that matter, a foreigner could spend his life in this country without permit and without informing the police. . . . The Englishman

---

* The shortsightedness of the Marxians was apparent even then. They were still agitated about the powers of a capitalist aristocracy whose authority was diluted each year. A few intelligent thinkers around 1900 saw further: they were aware that thoroughgoing reforms of society were to be stultified by an entirely new factor, by the emergence of managerial bureaucrats, including those within socialist parties and trade unions.

paid taxes on a modest scale . . . rather less than eight percent of the national income. The state intervened to prevent the citizen from eating adulterated food or contracting certain infectious diseases. It imposed safety rules in factories, and prevented women, and adult males in some industries, from working excessive hours. The state saw to it that the children received education up to the age of thirteen. Since January 1, 1909 it provided a meager pension for the needy over the age of seventy. Since 1911, it helped to insure certain classes of workers against sickness and unemployment. This tendency toward more state action was increasing. Expenditure on the social services had roughly doubled since the Liberals took office in 1905. Still, broadly speaking, the state acted only to help those who could not help themselves.*

"All this was changed by the impact of the Great War." The Great War, as wars usually are, was a power motive force in the further development of democracy. It united peoples more than anything before it (or perhaps even after). The influence of the upper classes continued to wane. As usual, governments were slow in catching on. They were, generally, incapable or unwilling to realize the new necessities of the welfare state. Parliaments and parties began to look old and weak. This made certain people, mostly intellectuals, talk about radical political solutions. Some of them considered anew the virtues of Marxism, no matter how bankrupt these had proven in practice. The constitutional dishonesty of most of these intellectuals was such that they refused to see what was rather obvious: that the communists won in Russia because Russia was still much of a barbarian country, the government of which became even more barbarian after the revolution than it had been before.

Between the two world wars the failure of democratic

---

* *English History 1914–45* (Oxford, 1965), p. i.

governments was not that they governed too much but that they governed too little. This is why most of them were no match for the new kind of government that arose in Central and Southern Europe, where the democratic evolution of the masses was, on occasion, exploited by national and centralized dictatorships. In the classic Aristotelian terminology, therefore, the new mixture was that of democracy with monarchy—or, in modern terms, it was dictatorship with mass consent. It provided potent and sometimes efficient governments of a kind that other people envied, not altogether without reason. In the United States the democratic reforms toward a long overdue governmental administration of welfare were presided over by Franklin Roosevelt, for all practical purposes an elective monarch. In Europe the rise of Germany under Hitler was so spectacular that she could have dominated much of the Continent by the reputation of her governmental efficiency alone. For some reason, however, Hitler was not sufficiently confident of this; he wanted to make this kind of German domination unquestionable. The result was the Second World War, at the end of which his monstrous government was destroyed. In most of Western Europe, freed mainly by American and British armies, a partial restoration of liberal democracy took place after the war. In most of Eastern Europe another monster, Russia, imposed her form of government, with or without the consent of the Atlantic democracies. The United States had become, not only economically but militarily, the greatest power of the world, with the result that the originally, and constitutionally, limited powers of the executive arm of the American government grew to enormous proportions.

At the time of this writing the United States and the Soviet Union are still the two supergovernments of the world. The governmental bureaucracies of the smaller Western nations have been growing, too, though generally at a lesser rate. Unlike before the last war, however, fewer and fewer people feel that their governments are not powerful enough: rather the contrary. During the last few decades not only the different forms of governments but the different words designating political ideas have become empty of meaning. A "conservative" in Russia designates a Stalinist. In the United States "conservatives" distinguish themselves by their espousal not of the Constitution but of the FBI. "Liberals" in the United States and earlier in Britain long ago turned advocates of the socialist state. In many European countries the socialists have turned middle-class par excellence. Elsewhere, the communists have become anti-revolutionaries. During the last war "nationalists" in many countries distinguished themselves by advocating that their country surrender to Germany. Like the ancient designations "Right" and "Left," less and less of this makes sense any longer.

Today disillusionment with politics and with government is widespread to an extent which was not foreseeable even a decade ago. It is not only found among people who are ruled by dictatorships or authoritarian governments, such as exist in Eastern or Southern Europe or in South America, or among people whose politics have been palpably corrupt or inefficient, like those of the French in the 1930s. It has begun to spread among the peoples of the oldest and most stable democracies of the world. It is no longer only the attitude of an oversensitive and largely irresponsible intellectual class: it has begun to penetrate the minds and the hearts of large numbers of people.

To some extent this development was predictable. When were peoples ever satisfied with their government? Not very often: certainly not in modern times, when it seemed as if they appreciated the relative virtues of their governments only in retrospect (*"comme la République était belle sous l'Empire,"* said the French). But here is the difference: in the past, disillusionment with politics was one thing, the dislike of government another. When politics were rotten, people looked forward to a new kind of government; when government was tyrannical, people looked forward to a new political system. Now, however, disillusionment with politics and with government go hand in hand.

In the Western democracies the respect for politics depreciated before the respect for government. This is registered by our languages. The word *politic* three or four hundred years ago meant something akin to "wise," "temperate," "civic-minded," in England. In France the *politiques,* at the end of the sixteenth century, were the moderate Catholic party, a party of reason, of Henry IV and of Montaigne: the noun had a largely approbatory meaning, since it contrasted them with the *fanatiques,* the Holy League men during the religious civil wars that racked and grieved the French. But by the twentieth century "he is a politician"; "politicking"; "playing politics"; "politiquant"; "espéce de député" are, all, condemnatory. Significantly, the older the democratic practice of politics, the more condemnatory they are.

At the end of the Middle Ages, having literally become sick and tired of the violent and unpredictable rule of aristocracies, people had welcomed the strong rule of the first national monarchs. The middle classes, nearly everywhere, profited from the rise of the centralized state. Four hundred years later the modern state and its centralized form of government have become so enormous that large numbers of people fear, distrust, dislike and disrespect it.

To point out the evils of centralization does not belong here: most of the conservatives and a few thoughtful radicals of the nineteenth century wrote about these things well enough. But I must say that the argument for decentralization which has recently become somewhat fashionable, will not go very far in our times, when people have begun to question not only the distribution of power, but its very exercise, not only the structure of government, but its very nature.

Of course it is very often true that officials of a central government, sitting in their capital, gravely and injudiciously interfere with the lives and properties of citizens in distant provinces or towns, without having consulted them at all, and without either considering or understanding their particular problems. But there is no longer any guarantee (if there ever was) that people elected or appointed locally will be more capable or even more considerate. In the United States, for example, federal authorities have often acted more considerately than have local authorities in matters involving the civil rights of certain groups. Of course there have been many instances when the reverse has been true. But the newfangled advocates of decentralization have not asked themselves this question: Why is the election of supervisors of townships, or mayors of small towns, an even less inspiring exercise of one's civic duties than the election of a governor or a president? Is it because people feel that in these times of centralized government these locally elected men have little power? Not necessarily: the budgets that local governments and school boards handle nowadays are enormous, their powers of regulating properties are very large indeed. The answer, I submit, is to be found elsewhere. People have become distrustful of the kind of men and women who are interested in holding this kind of power at all.

In the long run the rule of aristocracy has been succeeded not by the rule of democracy but by the rule of bureaucracy. Let us examine this pallid aphorism a little more closely. If one does not like aristocracy one is, most probably, a democrat by preference; or the other way around. But one's exasperation with bureaucracy is a different matter: it is at the same time more superficial and more profound than our dislike of either form of government. The democratic exercise of periodic elections does not compensate people sufficiently against their deep-seated knowledge that they are being ruled by hundreds of thousands of bureaucrats, in every level of government, in every institution, on every level of life.

These bureaucrats are not the trainees of a rigid state apparatus, or of capitalist institutions, as their caricatures during the nineteenth century showed them. They are the interchangeable, suburban men and women of the forever present, willing employees of the monster Progress. They, without exception, are employed in the external administration of life, at a time when people are becoming aware of the frightening condition that the internal freedom of their lives is shrinking. Hence the monstrosity of government even in the most democratic of nations.

During the second quarter of the twentieth century it seemed that a very new kind of monstrous government had arisen in the form of the totalitarian state, exemplified by those of Hitler, Stalin, and of their numerous imitators and satellites. Monstrous as they surely were, the word "totali-

tarian" (a stammering sort of word, at that) does not really
fit them. Total government is an impossibility, even under
Hitler, even under Stalin. In retrospect, it is surprising how
many fields of everyday life were—sometimes deliberately—
actually touched by these cruel regimes. (This does not
mean that fanatical ideologues would not rather see the
entirety of the lives of peoples governed by regimes that
incarnate their own ideology: but there is little that is new
in that.)

Relatively new, however, were three or four features of
these modern dictatorships. First, they were democratic, at
least in the sense that they ruled with the consent, sometimes
active, sometimes passive, of the large majority of their people. (This was especially true of Hitler's Germany.) Second,
they were capable of vast misdeeds because of the instruments of modern science. (No gas chambers: no Ausch-
witz. The SS may have killed one million Jews at random,
but not four million.) Third, the execution of such crimes,
together with all of the huge operations of the regime, was
made possible not so much because of the existence of a
minority of radical fanatics and perhaps not even because of
the existence of large insensitive majorities as because of
the existence of a considerable number of sufficiently efficient and sufficiently indifferent bureaucrats (indifferent,
that is, not to their own lives and careers but to moral
standards and considerations that lay outside their authority). Fourth, for more or less sensitive people the most hor-
rible trait of these regimes was not so much their practice
of injustice as their propagation of untruth.

Now, the monstrous matter with modern government is
this: every one of these features exists within our mass
democracies, too. The consent, sometimes active, sometimes passive, of the majority for governmental misdeeds in

the name of efficiency; the criminal application of modern technology; the eagerness of professional specialists to be employed by the government; the prevalence of untruth (practiced, to be sure, not by hardheaded government censors but by eager or stupid journalists). Thus it sometimes seems that the differences between a modern dictatorship and a modern democracy are merely differences of degree, not differences of kind.

Let us not underestimate differences of degree! They are very important, except for those who believe in the possibility of something like perfect government on earth— utopian idealists who are often potential fanatics, whether they know this or not. The actual extent of these differences of degree is manifested by the movement of the people who flee, whenever they can, from Communist Eastern Europe to democratic Western Europe, or from Castro's Cuba to Nixon's United States; there were very great differences of degree, too, distinguishing, say, a dictatorship of the Franco kind from Hitler's. Nevertheless, at the end of an age, the elements of governmental evil are probably alike, no matter how tempered they are by separate traditions and, what is more important, by different national characteristics. As Bernanos wrote after the Second World War: "The democracies have been decomposing, too, but some decompose more quickly than others. They have been decomposing into bureaucracies, suffering from it as a diabetic does from sugar, at the expense of his own substance. In the most advanced states, this bureaucracy itself decomposes into its most degraded form, police bureaucracy. At the end of this evolution, all that is left of the state is the police. . . ."

More than one hundred and thirty years ago Tocqueville, in a famous passage, attempted to describe the "sort of despotism democratic nations have to fear." It would not be like the tyranny of the Roman Caesars. Modern democratic despotism "would be more extensive and more mild; it would degrade men without tormenting them. . . . [The] same principle of equality which facilitates despotism tempers its rigors." But this was scant consolation; he went on. "I seek in vain for an expression that will accurately convey the idea . . . the old words *despotism* and *tyranny* are inappropriate: the thing itself is new, and since I cannot name, I must attempt to [describe] it."

> I seek to trace the novel features under which despotism may appear in the world. The first thing that strikes the observation is an innumerable multitude of men, all equal and alike, incessantly endeavoring to procure the petty and paltry pleasures with which they glut their lives.
> Above this race of men stands an immense and tutelary power, which takes upon itself alone to secure their gratifications and to watch over their fate. That power is absolute, minute, regular, provident, and mild. . . . It covers the surface of society with a network of small complicated rules, minute and uniform, through which the most original minds and most energetic characters cannot penetrate, to rise above the crowd. The will of man is not shattered, but softened, bent, and guided; men are seldom forced by it to act, but they are constantly restrained from acting. . . .
> I have always thought that servitude of regular, quiet, and gentle kinds which I have just described might be combined more easily than is commonly believed with some of the outward forms of freedom, and that it might establish itself under the wing of the sovereignty of the people.

In 1945, when a new edition of Tocqueville's *Democracy in America* was published, American critics declared that Tocqueville had been unduly pessimistic, that he put too much emphasis on the tyranny of the majority. Twenty-five years later this kind of reaction is nowhere to be found. Not only disgruntled conservatives or conventicles of intellectuals but millions of people now experience a sense of impersonality and of powerlessness: impersonality, because of the hugeness of democratic organizations and the myriads of interchangeable human beings who make up most of their personnel; powerlessness, because of the knowledge that votes, appeals, petitions amount to so very little at a time when people have become accustomed to accept the decisions of planners, experts and powerful governmental agencies. The result is the sickening inward feeling that the essence of self-government is becoming more and more meaningless, even though the outward and legal forms of democracy remain. In spite of recent advances of civil rights, in spite of recent juridical extensions of constitutional freedoms (sometimes permitting the propagation of all kinds of licentiousness), people sense that they are facing a growing erosion of privacy, of property and, yes, even of liberty.*

Yet at the very time when this soulless kind of democratic despotism has arisen, fulfilling to the jot and tittle the prophecies of Tocqueville, symptoms have begun to appear of a development that he could not foresee. As I wrote earlier, the growing disinterest in politics has developed into

---

* Another element in the growing disillusionment with democracy (the very word itself has become bland and meaningless, and not only because practically every government in the world now claims to be "democratic," very much including the communist "people's democracies") is the growing realization of its abstract character. For who are "the people"? Rule by "the people" is not only difficult, it is abstract. While it is possible to find out (and later relatively easy to reconstruct) what a certain ruler or even a certain ruling group wanted, who can say what "the people" want? When do "the people" really speak? A statement by Napoleon is a statement by Napoleon: a statement by the people is, almost always, a statement made *in the name* of the people—a profound difference.

disillusionment with government in general. The recent rebelliousness of young radicals whose ideas otherwise are rather unoriginal (since they are seldom anything but extreme projections of radical and anarchistic ideas that had been articulated many decades earlier) would be unimportant and ineffectual in the long run, were it not for another, emerging factor: at the very time when modern governments have accumulated enormous powers and fantastic weapons, their very powerlessness is beginning to appear. The monstrous growth of modern democratic government seems to carry within itself the fast-sprouting corpuscles of decay.

Tocqueville saw that in the age of democracy great revolutions would become rare (let us not forget that Hitler or Mussolini assumed power through largely nonrevolutionary means). His foresight proved extraordinarily accurate for one hundred and fifty years, which may be the undisputable world record for political thinkers. What he could not foresee was that for many people existence in a technological and standardized society might become so meaningless as to be intolerable—either because of their appetite for individual freedom, including many of its excrescences, or because little in their education had prepared them to live on their inner resources in the midst of a standardized and depersonalized external world.

There are only three basic forms of government, Aristotle said: monarchy, aristocracy, democracy. Others, as for example Montesquieu, added that in essence every government is a mixture of these forms in one way or another. For a long time it seemed that liberal democracy would eventually degenerate into a new kind of elective monarchy, that increasing centralization and the degeneration of elections to the levels of vast popularity contests would lead to this. This danger is by no means past. But another possibility has now arisen: a new compound of democracy and aristocracy—the latter, however, not a spiritual or hereditary or financial or intellectual aristocracy, but a novel kind of aristocracy of brute power.

I find it not at all impossible that the disintegration of regular civic authority might eventually lead to the establishment of a new kind of relative safety and order desired by people in neighborhoods and small towns—which, however, would no longer be imposed by the traditional and lawful authorities alone. It would depend upon the cooperation of criminal gangs who had grasped and maintained portions of power and authority in their neighborhood during the time when traditional authority was disintegrating. The gangs that already control certain very clearly delimited portions of streets and blocks that their members call "turfs"; the successful criminal who is a hero among the young people of a neighborhood or perhaps of an entire social or racial group; the tightly knit group of adult criminals who, indirectly or directly, secure contracts from this or that arm of the government and consequently guarantee safety and profit for those who do not object to cooperating with them—all of this, including the actual cooperation of certain elements of the police with certain groups of criminals, reminds one of the beginnings of feudalism in the Dark Ages, of the end of one thing and the beginning of something else from which a new kind of law and a new kind of order would eventually grow. At least in the United States we have suddenly traveled very far from Tocqueville's centralized democratic government whose power is "absolute, minute, regular, provident, and mild."

The idealist (or, more properly, the sentimentalist) radicals among our young people are therefore quite mistaken in thinking that because of the bankruptcy of the established political and institutional ideas they, and their ilk, are bound to inherit authority and power, whereafter the building of a new Jerusalem may begin. To the contrary, power will be quickly grasped by those who want it for themselves, who would sneer or laugh at the notion that after the old order comes down, the first item of business would be the discussion of the new philosophical ideas that should govern new institutions. Something like this happened in the autumn and winter of 1917 in Russia, or during the ridiculous play at revolution by the students in Paris in May 1968, toward the end of which juvenile criminals from outlying districts began to appear in the university buildings, terrorizing and blackmailing students and their girls who already after two weeks were exhausted from debating and playing at revolution. Their compatriot Proudhon, a much deeper seer than Marx, was, after all, entirely right in saying that people react less to ideas about social contracts than to the realities of power.

Does the history of government alternate between periods in which authority prevails, degenerating eventually into tyranny, and other (usually much shorter) periods in which liberty prevails, degenerating eventually into anarchy? It seems so: and the best times in the history of modern civilization were those decades when there existed a tolerable compound of authority and liberty. In these matters, however, the compounds are marked not by the proportions of their quantities but by their qualities. In our times, then, when the principle of popular democracy is supreme, when elections are popularity contests at the same time when the common citizen before government is powerless; when he is the potential victim of atomic accidents, of atmospheric booms, of exploding gases or chemicals, at the same time when he is at liberty among pictures, advertisements, books, theater and moving-picture scenes representing the mutual degradations of naked men, women and children, to talk of a balance of authority and liberty is nearly nonsense: it is tyranny and anarchy that are beginning to hold each other in sway.

Essay Twelve

The Guaranteed Economy
and Its Future

Jonathan R. T. Hughes

Jonathan R. T. Hughes is professor of economics at Northwestern University. He is the author of The Vital Few, Industrialization and Economic History, Social Control in the Colonial Economy, *and* The Governmental Habit.

This essay is reprinted from chapter six from The Governmental Habit: Economic Controls from Colonial Times to the Present, *by Jonathan R. T. Hughes. Copyright © 1977 by Basic Books, Inc., Publishers, New York. Reprinted by permission. All rights reserved.*

Whereas, in order to stabilize the economy, reduce inflation, and minimize unemployment, it is necessary to stabilize prices, rents, wages, and salaries . . . Now therefore, by virtue of the authority vested in me by the Constitution and Statutes of the United States, including the Economic Stabilization Act of 1970 . . . it is hereby ordered as follows. . . .

Richard Nixon, 1971

Triumphant Controlled Capitalism in Doubt

On August 15, 1971, Richard Nixon added his mite to the history of government control over American capitalism. His actions, imposing an assortment of direct controls, came under blanket delegation of such power by Congress in 1970. There was virtually no resistance to Nixon, and it appeared capitalism's "vested interests" of yore had vanished. Cynics suggested that had he frozen profits and prices on the New York Stock Exchange the ghost of free-enterprise capitalism might have appeared to raise objection. But by 1971 the idea of government intervention had become the norm, and it was people like the redoubtable Milton Friedman, of the University of Chicago, raising their voices in defense of the price mechanism as a form of social control, who were considered to be the radicals. That turning of the ideological worm resulted from the wars and crises which had produced a steady expansion of nonmarket controls from 1941 on.

The economic impact of World War II was, like its 1917–18 predecessor, both an acceleration of recent historical trends and a glimpse of the future. Anyone familiar with our institutions of nonmarket control will recognize that most of the New Deal innovations remained, some of them, like the Commodity Credit Corporation and the Agriculture Department's bureaucracy, still stuck in the ruts of the 1930s. The laws of the 1930s could be dangerous in the 1970s, but institutional inertia is powerful. Thus, in 1973, as the first food shortage since colonial times gathered momentum, the federal government was still paying farmers to restrict acreage and was still subsidizing exports (the Haugen-McNary nostrum). It thus subsidized the Soviet government into the largest wheat purchase in history, stripping the grain elevators.

Other traditions remained. Nixon's comprehensively inept control system came with such ease because of the institutional changes of World War II, the Korean War, and the Cold-War aftermath. By 1971 there were few pockets of resistance left to federal direct controls. Public Law 91-379, the Economic Stabilization Act of 1970, passed by Congress as a challenge to Nixon on responsibility for inflation, said: "The President is authorized to issue such orders and regulations as he may deem appropriate to stabilize prices, rents, wages, and salaries. . . ." That, he proceeded to do. But, as the reader of this book will readily comprehend, far more than Vietnam and previous wartime experiences had combined to produce this sad denouement of American capitalism. From butter to steel, available supply was the product of one or another government policy, agency, or bureau. Transportation, by water, land, or air, communications, by satellite, post, telephone, television, or radio, the price of money, the utilization of land—there was little left of the pure form of "free enterprise" that was not now subject to federal nonmarket controls. Ten percent of the goods and services output was controlled by federal regulatory agencies; an estimated eighty percent of all economic activity in the private sector was subject to antitrust control. But government expenditure had removed some thirty-five percent of economic activity from private uses; in 1973 twenty percent of the GNP was utilized directly by the federal government, and fifteen percent by state and local governments through processes which involved little free-market allocation. Those figures in 1929 had been about twelve percent in total, with budgeted expenditures of the federal sector (*smaller* than those of state and local sectors) just over $3 billion, which was only 2.9 percent of the GNP. By 1973 the GNP was ten times the 1929 figure (current prices), but the federal sector had grown *by a factor of eighty-six*. All these developments reduced capitalism in its pure form, the private ownership and *control* of productive resources, to a mere shadow of its former self. One way or another, government had become the silent partner of most enterprises.

It has been a comfortable partnership, however. In 1940, GNP was $100.5 billion, or $770 per capita. In 1971, GNP was $1,140 billion, or $5,420 per capita. In constant dollars (1958 prices) from 1941 to 1972 real GNP grew just over 208 percent ($263.7 billion to $812.4 billion) while the population increased only about sixty-one percent. Also, of course, per capita income is higher in the United States than in most other advanced countries, save Norway, Sweden, and Switzerland, and, apart from the industrial countries and Arab oil sheikdoms, incomparably higher than that enjoyed by two-thirds of mankind. If it is argued (and it is, by distinguished economists) that the steady imposition of nonmarket controls over economic life made the American economy less efficient than it otherwise would be, it can hardly be argued in these sorts of crude aggregate terms that many other major economies supply their citizens with more goods and services. Perhaps such considerations also entered into the profound lack of serious objection in August 1971 to Nixon's speech and the ensuing controls. The system worked, whatever you wanted to call it.

But there is something else. In 1942, the great economist Joseph Schumpeter published a brilliant, provocative, and much underrated book about capitalism and its future.[1] *Capitalism, Socialism, and Democracy* is generally a gloomy book, because Schumpeter was an admirer of classical capitalism for its economic achievements and the resulting lifestyle, especially the individual freedom associated with capitalism. He believed, however, that capitalism would fade away, not for Marxian reasons, but for the opposite reasons—its inexorable successes as a system of production.

The system would reach its greatest productiveness, he wrote, under the leadership of giant firms exploiting scale economies, mainly utilizing the late nineteenth-century organizational innovation, the generalized corporate form. These giant firms would reduce to impotence the private entrepreneur, the small-scale capitalist. In so doing, the corporation would undermine the social and political raison d'être of the middle class, that group whose values created the commercial milieu of industrial capitalism. The giant firm would rob the bourgeoisie of its leadership and vanguard function in the capitalist economy. Hence: "The true

---

[1] Joseph Schumpeter, *Capitalism, Socialism, and Democracy* (London: Allen and Unwin, 1943).

pacemakers of socialism were not the intellectuals who preached it but the Vanderbilts, Carnegies and Rockefellers."[2] The separation of ownership from control via the sale of stocks fatally weakened the capitalist enterprise as a social organism:

> The capitalist process, by substituting a mere parcel of shares for the walls of and the machines in a factory, takes the life out of the idea of property. It loosens the grip that once was so strong. . . . Dematerialized, defunctionalized and absentee ownership does not impress and call forth moral allegiance as the vital form of property did. Eventually there will be *nobody* left who really cares to stand for it—nobody within and nobody without the precincts of the big concerns.[3]

Moreover, the intellectual defenses of capitalism were doomed, again by success. A far larger proportion of the population would achieve higher education and thus a sharpened critical understanding of capitalism's shortcomings and inequities. With no practical experience of any other system to temper their remarks, the intellectuals' withering criticism would pick away at the moral supports of capitalism: ". . . capitalism inevitably and by virtue of the very logic of its civilization creates, educates and subsidizes a vested interest in social unrest."[4]

By the late 1960s corporate concentration in the American economy was astonishing. By 1967, of the 200,000 active corporations in the manufacturing sector, a mere 200, or 0.1 percent, shipped forty-two percent of all manufacturing production, delivered forty percent of the manufacturing

---

[2] *Ibid.,* p. 134.
[3] *Ibid.,* p. 142.
[4] *Ibid.,* p. 146.

payroll, and employed over a third of all employees. Other sectors were even more concentrated. There were, by 1971, 13,687 commercial banks. The fifty largest, a mere 0.36 percent of the total, held roughly forty-eight percent of total bank assets in the nation. There were 1,805 life insurance companies, and the ten largest owned fifty-seven percent of the industry's assets; the top fifty, only 2.8 percent of the total, held eighty-two percent of the whole industry's assets.[5] As we recall, fear of the rising corporations motivated the late nineteenth-century reforms, which had introduced and multiplied federal controls.

As for the intellectual props of capitalism—the "work ethic" of Richard Nixon, or, as usually expressed, the "free enterprise" and "rugged individualism" of the Elks club and chamber of commerce luncheons, the stock-in-trade of hopeful conservative politicians—they had been rocked seriously by the events of 1929–33. But the assumption of federal responsibility for aggregate output and employment, together with constant surveillance under the regulatory commissions and the Antitrust Division, had cast a further pall over private capitalism. Faith in *caveat emptor* was a fading belief—a fadeout accelerated by inferior, dangerous, defective products made by the nation's largest and most profitable firms, and their sensational exposure by Mr. Ralph Nader and other consumer militants. The scholarly purist might think of the ancient doctrine of *assumpsit* and weep. Moreover, the long Cold War years had intertwined the interests of the Pentagon with those of: (1) politicians needing

---

[5] *Statistical Abstract of the United States* (Washington, D.C.: Government Printing Office).

the votes that came from defense spending in their districts, (2) universities needing research funds, and (3) industrial enterprises whose profits depended upon the federal defense largesse—all these had, in fact, undermined motives for independence from government. In the military-industrial complex, a wide-open stomping ground was produced for advocates of a realignment of the nation's priorities, such as Professors J. K. Galbraith and Seymour Melman.[6] Their work exposed the way defense expenditures, channeled through the upper reaches of the industrial and intellectual system, had seduced thousands of firms and millions of workers into dependence upon government for their daily bread.

The Vietnam War added to all these troubles. The American business community had routinely "supported the President," as it always had in the nation's wars. But this time patriotism compromised it severely, and what might be called "Schumpeter's army"—the millions of young people in colleges and universities who opposed the Vietnam adventure—linked their righteous indignation over the war with the alleged war-profiteering of a hawkish business community. The system's total involvement in an aggressive Asian war was made the more insupportable because the war drained off vital government financial resources from the civil rights movement. As Martin Luther King said of it: "The bombs we drop in Vietnam will explode in America's cities." There followed a unique alienation of millions from

---

[6] J. K. Galbraith, *The Affluent Society* (Boston: Houghton Mifflin, 1958); *The New Industrial State* (Boston: Houghton Mifflin, 1967); Seymour Melman, *Pentagon Capitalism* (New York: McGraw-Hill, 1970).

both the American political system and American capitalism that staggered the nation, drove a president from office, and may well have left American capitalism with the weakest popular commitment it had since the depths of 1932.

With a government ruthlessly pursuing a foreign military adventure, paid for largely by mounting deficits, inflation continued: the Nixon government, unwilling to pay the price of the war by increased taxation, fell back upon direct controls, the third such policy commitment by the federal government since 1941. The results in 1972–73 were farcical, and such was no surprise since so much of the Nixon program was economic nonsense, or else, like the price freeze of the summer of 1973, a simple blueprint for disaster. What saddened the student of American economic history was the supine acceptance of the Nixon programs by American business leaders. Here the dark accuracy of Schumpeter's vision was demonstrated. There seemed to be no one left who cared. In his speech of August 15, 1971, the President spoke of "a new prosperity without war," of "greatness in a great people," of the plan to "break the back of inflation . . . without the mandatory price and wage controls that crush economic and personal freedom." He went on to speak of that "inner drive called the competitive spirit," the need to be "number one." But who he imagined was his audience for such effusions is a mystery. By 1971, wars and crises for three decades had pushed nonmarket controls far beyond the legacy of Roosevelt and the New Deal. Not people but government made things happen, caused inflations, stopped them. People went to work and paid taxes. Businessmen watched the government regulations that affected them and they worked with their partner, the IRS, sharing in the revenues.

Flood Tide of Nonmarket Controls

Federal government controls were greatly expanded in World War II, and since then. Mobilization for war began long before the Japanese attack on Pearl Harbor. Utilizing powers existing from World War I legislation, Roosevelt set up the National Defense Advisory Commission in May 1940. In so doing he avoided confrontation with a Congress already hostile because of the Selective Service Act. The NDAC was an umbrella organization, and it was from this that the main apparatus of the economic war effort was developed. The Commission was placed within the Executive Office in the Office of Emergency Management, safely away from congressional scrutiny. Similarly, utilizing Civil War legislation, the National Defense Research Council was set up in June 1940 at the urging of Dr. Vannevar Bush to mobilize scientists.

This organization inherited defense research done under the leadership of the Bureau of Standards, and then, from the day before Pearl Harbor, another subsidiary, the Office of Scientific Research and Development, took over the research which led to the development of the atomic bomb project.

From the NDAC came, ultimately: The Office of War Mobilization (1943), the War Production Board (1942), and the Office of Price Administration (1942). The Controlled Materials Plan began in 1942, and in that year the War Powers Act authorized the President to allocate vital materials by priorities. This was done primarily by the WPB. In the Stabilization Act of 1942 price control powers were provided and the OPA administered these. With the rationing of some consumers goods (for example, gasoline), price controls, priorities established for vital materials, and exemptions from Selective Service to move personnel to essential employments, the vast enterprise of economic mobilization was carried through. The World War I experience had supplied the New Deal with men and ideas. Now the New Deal provided essential managerial and organizational talents for a new war effort. Prominent New Dealers held the crucial posts at the top: Donald Nelson heading the WPB, Leon Henderson in charge of OPA, James Byrnes at the Office of War Mobilization.

The reformed banking system was utilized to help absorb the deficits. The Federal Reserve System piloted into the banking system a vast increase in the national debt as the federal deficits mounted. The figure for gross federal debt, about $49 billion in 1941, stood at nearly $259 billion in 1945. The private banking system absorbed about $70 billion of this increase, the Federal Reserve Banks increased their own holdings by $22 billion, the various fund-holding government departments and agencies invested in another $40 billion or so, and bond sales, payroll savings, and other smaller investments accounted for the rest. The long-run consequences of this effort hung over the financial sector for years. Management of these vast sums led the nominally independent Federal Reserve System into an unhappy collaboration with the Treasury which ended only in the early 1950s. During the inflation of the late 1940s there was little scope for offsetting monetary policies by the Federal Reserve. The Federal Reserve authorities agreed to support government bond prices while the private sector liquidated its federal debt to acquire funds for rebuilding private securities portfolios.

Part of the war expenditures was covered by increased taxes. Total government receipts, $7.1 billion in 1941, rose to $44.5 billion in 1945, but with expenditures of $98.4 billion that year and a deficit of nearly $54 billion, the role which debt finance had to play is fairly obvious. The individual income tax yielded $1.4 billion in 1941 and $19 billion in 1945. These taxes were increased by raising the rates, imposing surtaxes, and lowering exemptions; then, in 1943, the Current Tax Payment Act created the pay-as-you-earn system. Here was a crucial turning point. This wartime measure, which became permanent, was a profound change. For the first time in American history, the federal government had an automatic and easily collectable cut of the income of every working person. Most of American income was earned by the millions of wage earners. Now these sources could be readily tapped by the federal government. Not surprisingly, American history did not repeat itself. Unlike the periods following the Civil War and World War I, the aftermath of World War II did not include a major decrease in government taxation.

There followed a shift in incidence of taxation away from business firms and onto individual wage and salary earners. Corporate income taxes, including the excess profits tax, rose from about $2.6 billion in 1941 to $16 billion in 1945. For the future of the federal government's command over resources, the pay-as-you-earn tax was now crucial. By 1950 corporate income taxes were down to $10.8 billion, but individual income taxes were $17 billion. By then the Cold War was intensifying, with the outbreak of hostilities in Korea. In 1953 corporate taxes were $21.6 billion and individual income taxes were $31.6 billion. Increasingly, the burden of higher government expenditures fell upon the individual income-tax payer. By 1960 those taxes were $40.7 billion, while corporation income taxes were only $21.5 billion.

At that point the Social Security taxes came into play as a device to finance those government expenditures that could classify as social reform. Those taxes, $11.2 billion in 1960, grew to $46.4 billion in 1972. The Social Security tax is one of the most regressive in our system. Individual income taxes were $86.5 billion in 1972, but in that year corporation income taxes were merely $30.1 billion, even though corporate profits were the highest in history, and the stock market, not surprisingly, reached unprecedented heights. Thus a social reform measure of the 1930s became an invaluable source of increased tax revenues to meet the country's social needs while the defense budgets mounted. This episode, hardly one of the more celebrated progressive breakthroughs of the era, might be labeled "soak the poor." Social Security taxes, combined with the pay-as-you-earn income tax, became the basis of a fiscal transformation. In 1960 individual income taxes were forty-four percent of total federal tax receipts, corporation income taxes twenty-three percent, and Social Security taxes sixteen percent. In 1974 individual income taxes yielded forty-five percent of the total, corporate income taxes a mere sixteen percent, and Social Security taxes had increased to twenty-six percent.[7] As the writer Mary Gray Hughes described the system, "Socialism for the rich, capitalism for the poor."

For the most part, the World War II system established lasting precedents, despite the postwar efforts of both the President and the Congress to dismantle different parts of

---

[7] *Statistical Abstract of the United States.*

it. But just as the New Deal revived and gave extended life to institutional innovations of World War I, so the Korean War emergency, only five years after V-E Day, produced reincarnations of World War II control practices.

The exigencies of continuous cold-war pressures enfolded many of these wartime practices into the regular federal control structure. Also, the legitimacy of federal controls became an accepted part of economic life. What was once considered an extraordinary imposition of federal power, say, automatic payroll deduction of the income tax, became normal. Even the extraordinary tax rates of wartime came to be accepted as reasonable in perpetuity.

The Korean War produced another emergency, but mobilization was only partial, and the emergency was over by 1954, fiscally by 1953. The experience after World War I, however, was repeated after the Korean War, as it had been after World War II. Once expanded by the fiscal force of war expenditures, the size of government, measured by spending outlays, did not then contract back to prewar levels. Another zero was added to the federal numbers. This phenomenon occurred after each of our major wars from the Civil War onward. The calculations are simple enough, and show in the more expensive wars a permanent change in order of magnitude of government expenditures.

In the five peacetime years from 1856 to 1860, means federal budget expenditures were $69 million per year; in the five postwar years from 1866 to 1870, mean expenditures were $378 million per year. Federal expenditures *never* fell back to prewar levels again. In the five years from 1912 to 1916, mean annual expenditures were $712.8 million; 1919 marked the high point of World War I expenditure, $18.4 billion. Starting peacetime calculations in 1920, the mean annual rate of expenditure from 1920 to 1924 was $4.2 billion. Again, prewar levels of expenditures, below a billion dollars a year, were never seen again. In the five New Deal years from 1937 to 1941, mean budgeted federal expenditures (excluding social insurance payouts from 1936 throughout these calculations) were $9.2 billion. From 1947 to 1950 (we exclude 1946 as a year of "war"—$60.4 billion, in a fiscal sense), mean expenditures were $37.8 billion. The New Deal levels, now considered small, were never seen again. Mean expenditures in the Eisenhower years after the Korean War were $71 billion, nearly double the previous peacetime levels from 1947 to 1950.[8]

Each war inflated the economy and gave the federal spending mechanism a scope it did not previously have. The historical expansion of the federal sector has been mainly achieved by a few short bursts of wartime spending, not by a steady rise related to the country's population growth, or the GNP it produced. After each war there were expanded interest payments, new veterans benefits, as well as the actual growth of government costs. Once a new plateau of expenditures was achieved the gains were held. For this reason alone, those who proposed some abatement of federal expenditures in the post-Vietnam War period had little reason to hope. The tax system ensured self-financing of government expansion.

The enlarged government share occurs automatically when the government begins to inflate the economy by deficit finance. These expenditures inflate personal incomes, automatically enlarging the federal cut of GNP because the

---

[8] *Historical Statistics of the United States* (Washington, D.C.: Government Printing Office, 1957), and *Statistical Abstract of the United States.*

fixed progressive income tax rates shave off increasingly more as income rises. Automatic deductions from wage and salary earners thus support the present federal establishment on a scale unimaginable to the New Dealers. Inflation makes federal deficit spending self-financing via progressive income tax schedules. Government does not fear inflation; in fact, inflation tends to ease the problems of government finance.[9]

It is thus no wonder that the federal government expenditures have increased eight times as fast as has the GNP since 1940, and it is no wonder that among the federal programs proposed each year the one no one seriously advocates is the big reduction of the federal sector. What the big revenues encourage is bold new spending. What has been lacking has been any politically viable major alternative to military procurement to sop up the flood of tax money that automatically pours into the Treasury each year. Continued budgetary expansions are necessary to avoid surpluses and deflation. The military-industrial complex may thus be seen as partially the consequence of the pay-as-you-earn income tax of 1943 made permanent. The economy has responded to these changes, now thirty-five years in existence, with the sad result in the 1970s that whole sectors of American life— industries, cities, settled populations—have no way to live except as steady recipients of federal expenditures.

There was never anything like this in our history before. This is the real "welfare problem" in the American economy, and it has nothing to do with the poor, with black welfare mothers, or with unemployment-compensation "chis-

---

[9] Sir John Hicks, *A Theory of Economic History* (London: Oxford University Press, 1969), pp. 97–99.

elers." With automatic taxation paid in upon the very processes of creative economic life and an unrestrained ability to create debt and then to monetize it through the financial system, with guaranteed fiscal fulfillment from the ensuing inflationary consequences, the federal government's own outlays have become the greatest growth sector, by far, in the American economy. Those who can share in this ever-growing treasure trove gain accordingly. A fifth of GNP is now directly absorbed by the federal government on a nonmarket basis: taxation and spending programs are politically determined. One consequence is a nightmare: our economy supports the largest arms-producing machine in history. Much of the product cannot be absorbed by our own forces and is openly for sale to an unstable world, making it the more unstable. It is naturally considered unpatriotic to criticize this development even though the American democracy has been changed out of all recognition by it.

This is our version of Sir John Hicks's "administrative revolution":[10] Government expenditure is no longer based upon established need; instead, the size of GNP establishes the need for government expenditure to funnel the river of taxes back into the private economy via the continuous government spending stream. Like so many of the control devices established since 1887, the taxing mechanism continues without question, and obviously is not going to magically disappear, or reduce itself, of its own accord. Like the regulatory agencies, the federal tax system has become established with a life of its own, kept going by automatic inclusion of all, with taxpayers "voluntarily" assisting in the preparation of the necessary paperwork, Form 1040.

---

[10] *Ibid.*, pp. 99, 162, 166.

The Korean War occasioned the re-creation of a skeletal version of the World War II control system. The crucial elements of the Korean War institutions of physical control were then absorbed into the permanent federal establishment. The basic legislation, the Defense Production Act of September 8, 1950, was still law, as amended in 1974. Congress then began the motions to abolish the DPA after it was discovered that the act had been used to shelter the oil companies from antitrust laws.[11] This legislation empowered the President to shield businesses from the antitrust laws in the interests of national defense. The explicit power to control wages and prices granted in the act ended in 1953, but similar powers were granted again by Congress in 1970. And since this power is one of the oldest government powers, there is no real question of its legitimacy.

The Office of Defense Mobilization, established in 1950, was merged in 1959 with the Federal Civil Defense Administration to form a new Office of Civil Defense and Mobilization. In 1961 the Kennedy administration changed the OCDM to the Office of Emergency Planning, lodged in the Executive Office of the President, where it remained until 1973.[12] When the oil crisis struck, the OEP turned in a laughable performance, its head having left office with no plans and with no certainty as to the disposition even of its records.

A controlled materials plan, like that of World War II, was established in 1950, and the Department of the Interior established a Defense Materials Administration in the same

---

[11] *New York Times,* October 13, 1974.

[12] H. H. Liebhafsky, *American Government and Business* (New York: Wiley, 1971), p. 559.

year. The system had among its chores not only defense materials acquisition, but also materials for the Atomic Energy Commission. A National Production Authority was established in the same year in the Commerce Department to create a system of defense priorities. When the NPA was abolished in 1953 its functions were transferred to the Commerce Department's Business and Defense Services Administration, which then had the power to determine priorities and allocate vital materials.[13]

In an age of recurring crises and priority needs, a modern nation clearly must secure its vital material supplies, and the necessary control can hardly depend upon the price mechanism to assure supplies for extraordinary or emergency government needs. Nonmarket controls are required, and ours partly represent hard-won experience from our war emergencies. For example, the Atomic Energy Commission was set up under civilian control in 1946 as an independent agency following the wartime development of nuclear capability under military control, once the scientific progeny of Vannevar Bush's council began the road to Hiroshima. The AEC's business extends into the military and into the civilian economy as well. It requires extraordinary powers for acquisition and allocation to meet critical needs, and these powers are now securely lodged in various parts of the government. Defense materials have been stockpiled by the General Services Administration. In 1968 the Business and Defense Services Administration's priorities, together with the Defense Materials System, acquired materials for the Atomic Energy program, for the National Aeronautics and Space Administration, and for the Defense Department.

---

[13] *Ibid.,* p. 558.

Acquisitions for such purposes, including food stockpiling, cannot depend upon the price mechanism alone, yet actual physical availability must be achieved when it is needed.[14] Since the price mechanism is not to be utilized alone, something else—offices, agencies, departments—must be set up in its stead.

Such are the arguments justifying the federal establishment. Yet in the many-sided crises of 1973–74, centering on food, fuel, and materials, the federal bureaucracy was woefully inadequate. Inflation, not the bureaucracy, rationed the goods. The poor simply went without. Despite all the nonmarket controls, the price mechanism solved the problems for the most part with the highest peacetime inflation in American history, distorting the flow of expenditures and income distribution, and contributing in 1974–76 to the worst recession since the 1930s.

Bureaucratic Parthenogenesis—Possibilities

There is a further dimension to the growth of intragovernmental controls, and that is a legislative one. The idea of governmental legislation *without Congress* is an oddity, given our Constitution. Yet it is common enough; rule-making by regulatory agencies and special offices in the executive branch is precisely that. But there are still constraints. The day has not yet come when mere presidential edict is considered sufficient legislative activity to be considered law. For example, in *Youngstown Sheet and Tube Company* v. *Sawyer,* when the Supreme Court overruled

---

[14] *Ibid.,* p. 559.

President Truman's order authorizing the federal government to take over the steel mills during a crippling strike, Justice Black wrote: "The Constitution does not subject . . . lawmaking power of Congress to Presidential or military supervision or control."[15] Yet agency rule making is an everyday occurrence, as it must be, in a governmental apparatus of such proportions as ours. The citizen still has access to the courts, as, for example, when he runs afoul of the mercurial rules of the IRS, or when a firm contests a ruling of a regulatory agency such as the FTC. Also, most of the control agencies have internal appeals procedures. However, the rules and procedures of so many different control agencies are a mass of confusion, and the amount of nonmarket control is now so extensive that some coordination of rule making would doubtless be of advantage. But coordinated rule making by the control agencies would be potentially far more powerful than the noncongressional legislative activity that we have seen thus far in our history. In fact such is now under way. In the General Services Administration's list of independent offices and establishments of the federal government, along with such august organizations as the ICC, the VA, the FRS, the FCC, or relatively new ones, such as the National Foundation on the Arts and Humanities, the Atomic Energy Commission, and the National Aeronautics and Space Administration, a little-known title appears: the Administrative Conference of the U.S. What is this? The Administrative Conference of the U.S. is an assembly which attempts to coordinate the rule-making activities of the regulatory bodies, and as such, could be the beginning of our version of France's *conseil*

---

[15] 343 U.S. 579 (1951) 588.

d'état. The agencies of nonmarket control each represent *a specific solution to a specific problem*. As such, they hardly represent a coherent system of planning and control, but rather a congeries. They now face the possibility of becoming a real system under Public Law 88-499 of 1964, the Administrative Conference Act. This organization's growth is worth watching.

The structure of our independent agency establishment would be, for the reader of this book, a shorthand history of perceived or imagined failures of the price mechanism as a social control system since the *Wabash* case in 1886. The ICC, the FTC, and the Federal Reserve System represent the beginnings. The Federal Maritime Commission is the legatee of the Shipping Act of 1916; the Federal Power Commission and the Veterans Administration (1930) come from the relatively quiet twenties. The New Deal flurry is represented by such control bodies as the TVA, FCC, NLRB, SEC, CAB, and FDIC. The Atomic Energy Commission, the Environmental Protection Agency, the National Aeronautics and Space Administration, and the National Foundation on the Arts and the Humanities reflect more modern experiences. These are but a selection from many with a similar historical provenance.

These organizations are indeed little historical monuments. But they still function, and the questions must be, how well, and what continuing functions do they serve, if any. It should be borne in mind that there is an economic cost involved. Configurations of productive activity achieve results which differ from those the price mechanism alone would produce. If this were not true, then there would be no justification whatever for the controls. But since the price mechanism would produce a different balance of consumers' and producers' preferences—in terms of economics alone—the costs and benefits of the nonmarket controls deserve to be constantly scrutinized. For example, clearly the Environmental Protection Agency has an ongoing function. The environmental movement is of recent origin, and the job of restructuring what is left of the natural ecology and managing the country's lifestyle to preserve and protect the land, air, and water is one which now commands the support and enthusiasm of millions. But is the Environmental Protection Agency to last forever? And if not, why not? At this moment in time the answer might well seem to be yes. We would be wise, though, to keep some options open, and this has not really been done. We still have all of the original major independent agencies, or their direct successors, as if the problems they were introduced to solve had never changed or been solved. In October 1973 it was proposed by the natural gas producers that the FPC control of pipeline transmission should be suspended. The initial reaction was that a return to the allocation of the price mechanism was unthinkable. It should have been thinkable, or else the slow accretion of nonmarket control in this country would eliminate the elements of efficiency in the price system even more than is now the case. By 1974 the FPC's control over gas prices and transmission was seriously questioned and in 1976 it seemed about to be lifted. A good argument could clearly be made that the lives of the control agencies should be made renewable, or not, on a regular basis. How many, given our present railroad system, would now renew the ICC if some other options were regularly available? The economy would gain if nonmarket control bureaucracies were constrained in order periodically to prove their superiority to the price mechanism.

In the Executive Office of the President, the options for renewal and change exist more readily. We saw how Roosevelt reorganized this part of our government by executive order in 1940, and then proceeded to utilize it during World War II without the necessity of normal congressional scrutiny. President Truman continued the technique. For example, when the Senate refused to cooperate in the establishment of the International Trade Organization, following the Havana Conference in 1947–48, the President fell back upon General Agreement on Tariffs and Trade, which he had endorsed by Executive Agreement and which the Office of the Special Representative for Trade Negotiations in the Executive Office was established to implement.[16] We got international cooperation on trade and tariffs despite Congress. The Executive Office is used to provide freedom and flexibility for the President that would be difficult to achieve with the older apparatus of government represented by the classic government departments.

Like the list of independent agencies we just considered, the fifteen offices and councils of the Executive Office of the President listed by the General Services Administration embody bureaucratic artifacts of modern American history. The Office of Management and Budget represents not only the Roosevelt era, but, as we recall, efforts to reform the federal budgetary process back to President Taft and be· yond. Only in 1974 did Congress make a serious effort to provide its own equivalent to the OMB, in response to the budgetary crisis.[17] The Council of Economic Advisers is the

---

[16] Raymond F. Mikesell, "Trade Agreements," *International Encyclopedia of the Social Sciences* (New York: Macmillan, 1968), 8:129–36.

[17] *The New Congressional Budget Process and the Economy* (New York: Committee for Economic Development, December 1975).

artifact of the depression and wartime experiences that resulted in the Employment Act of 1946. The National Security Council is the product of the Cold War, and as we have seen, so was the Office of Emergency Preparedness—with historical trailers going back as far as World War I. The domestic activist moods of the Kennedy-Johnson era are represented by such offices as the Office of Economic Opportunity, the Office of Consumer Affairs, and the Council on Environmental Policy. The advances in technology of our age and the government's needs to keep abreast of them have produced the National Aeronautics and Space Council, the Office of Telecommunications Policy, and the Office of Science and Technology (which fell, at least temporarily, because of President Nixon's dislike of intellectuals). These control devices can come and go mainly by executive initiative, and the associated apparatus has not the permanence of the established agencies, foundations, boards, commissions, corporations, and services, whose line of descent in modern times begins with the ICC. Officials of the Executive Office, like the foreign-affairs specialists W. W. Rostow and Henry Kissinger, or domestic specialists like those of Watergate fame, do not hold office with the same long-term tenure as do those in the independent regulatory establishments. The failure to establish President Nixon's putative doctrine of executive privilege as an umbrella of prerogative over the Executive Office in 1973 further assured that these parts of the nonmarket control system would remain more sensitive to changing public needs than is the case with the independent agencies.

In both of these parts of the federal control apparatus our history has bequeathed us the physical reality of government outside the tripartite divisions of the federal Constitution.

The regulatory government is as real as is the regular government of the congressional, judiciary, and executive departments. The small beginnings of the Populist era have yielded a fulsome harvest of bureaucracy blessed by the older traditions of colonial America and its mercantilist and Britannic parent.

Stagflation as a Lifestyle

When Lyndon Johnson went to war in 1965, federal budget expenditures were at an annual rate of $118 billion. In 1973 the annual federal expenditure rate was $260 billion, an increase since 1965 *greater than all the previous increases of federal expenditures in our entire history.* By 1976 the federal government was struggling to hold expenditures at the level of $400 billion. Such considerations bring us back to the Employment Act of 1946, its consequences, and its problems. Let it be said that such expenditures did not, and do not, produce full employment, but have produced the highest rate of peacetime inflation in our history. What these expenditures did to "promote free enterprise and the general welfare," as the act puts it, is probably not best dealt with in a study such as this.

The administrative device of the 1946 Employment Act was the Council of Economic Advisers, economists appointed by the President and supported by an appropriate research apparatus. For the most part the members and chairmen of the CEA have been academic and financial establishment figures. Since the tools available to the Council and government in our circumstances are insufficient to achieve almost any policy aims, it is pointless, even unkind, to criticize the Council for anything, except possibly mis-steps like the sophomoric blunders of the 1973 price freeze, which could not help but produce automatic shortages. The Council only makes recommendations, one source of in-formation input into a governmental taxing and spending machine that receives an infinity of other inputs regarding how much money should be spent, by whom, paid to whom, and where. For whom the Council's statements are prepared is something of a mystery, since it is clear that the Execu-tive rarely follows their advice, and the public merely has its intelligence insulted by such predictions as those in the 1972 *Economic Report* of the President, prepared by the Coun-cil, which, among other things, confidently predicted that inflation was about over.[18] The real novelty of the Council is not what Professor Galbraith called the "feckless incom-petence" of the 1973 Council, but the implications of its very existence. By 1976 a new Council was still predicting the end of the inflation, and also a recovery from the re-cession. Someday it is bound to be correct, if only by chance.

In terms of ideological history the federal government's direct assumption of responsibility for employment and wel-fare was as nearly a total reversal as one could imagine. The reversal had two parts. The first part, the legal turnabout with acceptance of such responsibility in Washington, we discussed earlier. The second part assumes that the federal government can in fact work such control over economic life as to guarantee the future level of full, or nearly full, employment. By 1976 doubt had deepened about this as-

---

[18] Carl F. Christ, "The 1972 Report of the President's Council of Eco-nomic Advisers," *American Economic Review* 63, no. 4 (1973).

sumption. Against the wisdom and possibility of such control was our understanding of the country's past economic development and of what could possibly be achieved by free enterprise if it were to continue to exist. In the first instance one had the idea of capitalist development, expressed best by Professor Schumpeter. Depressions, deflations, and unemployment were necessary aspects of capitalist development. These were the periods of forced realignment of productive factors necessary to achieve the efficient combinations which would enable the next period of expansion to succeed. In the second instance was the sheer physical problem of control over such a vast thing as a consumer-oriented capitalism with its billions of annual decisions independently and simultaneously made. This view held that the prospect of really effective control was about as likely to succeed as King Canute's orders to the ocean waves. This popular wisdom was expressed in 1931 by Senator Gore of Oklahoma when he said that passing laws would no more improve the economy ". . . than you can pass a resolution to prevent disease. This is an economic disease. You might just as well try to prevent the human race from having a disease as to prevent economic grief of this sort."[19]

The abandonment of such pessimism was partly the result of the World War II mobilization, during which full employment, with massive armed forces, was finally achieved, and partly the result of the policy implications of Keynes' *General Theory*. With cyclically balanced budgets and the right fiscal and monetary policies, a guaranteed full employment

---

[19] Arthur M. Schlesinger, Jr., *The Age of Roosevelt,* v. I, *The Crisis of the Old Order 1919–1933* (Boston: Houghton Mifflin, 1957), p. 226.

economy seemed a real possibility. But there was one facet which came to be forgotten by the CEA's practitioners of the "dismal science," and that was *price stability,* a part of the original promise of the managed economy. In the first flush of post-World War II enthusiasm for the managed economy, the "strategic principles" of fiscal and monetary management were thought generally to be the following: "Government tax revenues should be higher relative to government expenditure in periods of high employment than in periods of substantial unemployment," and "Money and credit should be relatively tight in periods of high employment and relatively easy in periods of substantial unemployment."[20]

That was 1950, and the eminent economists who penned that statement were diverse spirits—Emile Despres, Milton Friedman, Albert Hart, Paul Samuelson, and Donald Wallace. Behind their statement lay a set of axiomatic beliefs about both economic theory and historical reality relating to the American experience with the peacetime business cycle. A federal budget balanced only over the course of the whole business cycle, if at all, together with adroit monetary management which stimulated expenditures in slumps and constrained them in booms would do the trick. Prices might fluctuate relative to each other, but a faithful execution of policy relative to agreed-upon theory and facts would avoid any "marked trend" in prices.

In any event, those forces which made price stability in the American economy unattainable proved to be the rock upon which the original fiscal policy ideals were broken. The dream could not be realized, given the facts.

---

[20] "The Problem of Economic Instability," *Readings in Fiscal Policy* (Homewood, Ill.: Richard Irwin, 1955), p. 419.

Whether full employment with price stability could actually have been achieved in a peacetime economy remained unknown, because in 1950 began an era of ceaseless increases in government expenditures, the "great Keynesian updraft," related to continuous large-scale military and quasi-military expenditures, which have never ended and whose long-run consequences have produced secular inflation. Real shortages in 1973–74, combined with Federal Reserve efforts to offset the mounting federal deficit with a resolute tight-money policy, produced *both* the highest peacetime interest rates and highest price increases we have ever known.

In 1951, when Korean War expenditures were mounting, Professor Arthur Smithies foresaw not only the war's destabilizing consequences regarding policy-making, but glimpsed things to come in the structural sense:

> It is likely that the long period of military preparation on which we are now embarking will bring permanent changes in the relation of government to business, and control measures that are inconsistent with private enterprise today may be permanent and compatible features of the economy tomorrow.[21]

Since reality cannot be deduced from general principles, Smithies could not foresee precisely how the new perpetual military establishment would exist in a private economy like ours. But less than a decade later, President Eisenhower had a more vivid premonition of the future, recognizing the changes that had taken place during his administration:

> We annually spend on military security more than the net income of all United States corporations.

---

[21] Arthur Smithies, "The American Economic Association Report on Economic Instability," *ibid.,* p. 442.

This conjunction of an immense military establishment and a large arms industry is new in the American experience. The total influence—economic, political, even spiritual—is felt in every city, every statehouse, every office of the federal government. We recognize the imperative need for this development. Yet we must not fail to comprehend its grave implications. Our toil, resources, and livelihood are all involved; so is the very structure of our society.

In the councils of government we must guard against the acquisition of unwarranted influence whether sought or unsought, by the military-industrial complex. The potential for the disastrous rise of misplaced power exists and will persist.[22]

By now there are scarcely words of sufficient drama to describe the consequences: a trillion dollars spent on military demand since 1950; an international situation in which such a condition has come to be considered normal, perhaps even desirable; a constant need for new, more sophisticated weaponry (and more expensive on each round). It came to pass that military waste no longer counted. Politicians competed with each other in denouncing welfare chiselers, education, and school lunches, but the billions lost on the ABM site in North Dakota, or further billions wasted on the cost overruns of the C5A cargo plane, brought scarcely a comment from the presidential candidates of 1976.

A decade after Eisenhower's speech Professor Seymour Melman ended his definitive study of the consequences, *Pentagon Capitalism,* with another such warning, beyond the eleventh hour:

Rarely does a single social force have a controlling influence in changing, swiftly, the character of life in a large and complex society. The expansion of the Pentagon and its state-management is such a force. Failing decisive action to reverse the economic

---

[22] Reprinted in Melman, *Pentagon Capitalism,* app. B.

and other growth of these institutions, then the parent state, if it is saved from nuclear war, will surely become the guardian of a garrison-like society dominated by the Pentagon and its state-management.[23]

This study is not the place to pursue this subject further. From our viewpoint the Pentagon's power is another vast imposition of nonmarket control upon American capitalism, a direct removal from the GNP of a large portion, perhaps ten percent (counting all the quasi, or hidden, military expenditures in the federal budget), for straight military needs on what appears to be a permanent basis. Congress has shown little enough willingness to constrain seriously the gross military demand, and as Alain Enthoven and K. Wayne Smith pointed out out in their book, *How Much Is Enough?* the Pentagon's ability to apply standard criteria of efficiency to military procurement proved largely fruitless during Enthoven's regime at the Systems Analysis office.[24]

The military expenditure is triply inflationary: first, because the financing of its aggregate size usually requires deficit spending; second, because military expenditures generate income in the civilian economy in the form of money demand, but *return no product* to the civilian economy to help soak up that demand; third, because military expenditures notoriously allow leeway for seller-induced price increases, for example, under "cost plus" contracts. Cost overruns have been the inexorable consequences of such procedures and have become common; some have been quite unbelievable—for example, the ill-fated F-111.

---

[23] *Ibid.*, p. 227.

[24] Alain Enthoven and K. Wayne Smith, *How Much Is Enough?* (New York: Harper & Row, 1971).

What can be said of military expenditure can be said also, perhaps to a lesser degree, of most other federal outlays, and one is reminded of Adam Smith's commentary in 1776 on such matters:

> Great nations are never impoverished by private, though they sometimes are by public prodigality and misconduct. The whole, or almost the whole public revenue, is in most countries employed in maintaining unproductive hands. Such are the people who compose a numerous and splendid court, a great ecclesiastical establishment, great fleets and armies, who in time of peace produce nothing, and in time of war acquire nothing which can compensate the expense of maintaining them, even while the war lasts. Such people, as they themselves produce nothing, are all maintained by the produce of other men's labor . . . Those unproductive hands, who should be maintained by a part only of the spare revenue of the people, may consume so great a share of their whole revenue, and therefore oblige so great a number to encroach upon their capitals, upon the funds destined for the maintenance of productive labor, that all the frugality and good conduct of individuals may not be able to compensate the waste and degradation of produce occasioned by this violent and forced encroachment.[25]

We need not go all the way with Adam Smith to get the point: resources used by the government are not available to the private sector.

The remorseless increase of federal spending is partly achieved by visible taxation, and partly by a defter method —inflation. In either case the consequence, the removal of goods and services from private use, is the same; in the first instance because money demand is directly expropriated and transferred in the form of taxes; in the second instance

---

[25] Adam Smith, *The Wealth of Nations* (New York: Modern Library, 1937), pp. 325–26.

because government buys whatever it wants at whatever is the necessary price, and consumers pay for it by nonconsumption, finding their own money incomes insufficient to compete with government purchasing. In the first case, the expropriation is achieved by democratic means: Congress authorizes the expenditures openly. In the second case the method of expropriation is less obvious: Congress raises the debt limit (an action the average citizen cannot comprehend), deficit spending occurs, and the price mechanism, together with timely actions of the Federal Reserve System, is used to remove goods and services from the nongovernment economy. The result is an increase in the national debt and, in due course, in the money supply. Because of income multiplier effects, prices, the money supply, GNP, and the federal government's progressively structured tax haul increase proportionately more than does the initial increase in the national debt. The euphemism for this form of expropriation in the jargon of economics is an "income-adjusting economy," and the people are told they are better off thereby. The hoax is transparent, but is infinitely more acceptable politically than would be direct expropriation of goods and services to foot the federal bills.

Table 1
Federal Finance and the National Economy

Year	Gross Debt ($ Billions)	Consumer Prices (1967 = 100)	Money Supply*	GNP	Federal Revenues	Industrial Production (1967 = 100)	Percent Unemployed
			($ Billions)				
1965	320.9	94.5	315	684.9	116.8	89.2	4.0
1973	457.1	150.0	540	1,235.5	240.0	120.0	5.0
Percent Increase	42.4	58.7	71.4	80.4	105.5	34.5	25.0

SOURCE: *Statistical Abstract of the United States.*
* Currency outside the banking system plus demand and time deposits.

Table 1 illustrates the workings of the system of secular inflation between the massive expansion of the Vietnam War outlays in 1965 and the last full year of the Nixon regime, 1973. The smallest increase, in terms of percentages, was the federal debt, with increased consumer prices next. The money supply increase represented a directly related variable, deposit creation and currency increases. GNP, its normal expansion swollen by increased money demand (and prices), rose even faster, and federal revenues, geared for this by the progressivity of the tax tables, rose the most rapidly of all these inflationary indicators. Hence the government's inflationary action actually enhanced its own revenue position. But, of course, only a continuing deficit and expanding GNP could produce these results. In the 1974–76 downturn the thing went haywire. "Fine tuning" was forgotten.

In real terms the figures yield a much different result. Industrial production rose only some thirty-five percent in 1965–73, a mean annual rate of just over four percent. As for the promise of full employment, there are problems. What is the definition of full employment? There is none. The 1965 rate, four percent, is not awfully high, but it was lower in 1953 and in 1969, and it was higher in aggregate by more than twenty-five percent in 1973. So, however it might be defined, unless the definition of full employment is entirely political, it was not achieved. In 1974–76, with stagnating output and even higher prices, unemployment exceeded eight percent of the labor force. Unemployment among minorities was double the national average in any case, and rates differed widely across the United States. Low real growth and high unemployment during periods of rising nominal GNP is stagflation, the modern world of aggregate economics. Instead of price stability with full employment, we speak now of wage-push, or cost-push, inflation with an assumed trade-off between inflation and unemployment. In 1976 one hoped, at least, for a return to Nixon-style stagflation from the pain of the 1974–76 recession.

Stagflation, the logical consequence of an economy suppressed by nonmarket controls of all sorts, topped by a total government absorption of more than a third of everything produced and a government structure which, at all levels, *employs every sixth person in the labor force*—these are major components of the economic world we have produced and must live with. A world of full employment and price *stability,* envisaged by the economists of 1950, now seems utterly utopian.

Essay Thirteen

Violence as a Product
of Imposed Order

Butler D. Shaffer

Butler D. Shaffer graduated from the University of Chicago Law School in 1961. For several years he practiced law in Omaha, Nebraska, specializing in business and real estate development, corporate law, and labor law. Currently he is an associate professor in the College of Business Administration at the University of Nebraska at Omaha.

Professor Shaffer has published articles in the Creighton Law Review, Labor Law Journal, *and* Rampart Journal. *He is writing a book on the origins of governmental regulation of business.*

This essay resulted from a research fellowship awarded under the Law and Liberty Project of the Institute for Humane Studies. It is a slightly revised version of an article that appeared in the University of Miami Law Review, *v. 29, no. 4 (Summer 1975), and is reprinted by permission. Copyright © 1975 by the* University of Miami Law Review. *All rights reserved.*

Recent years have witnessed a marked increase in explorations into the causes of violence in America. The convergence of increases in crime rates, violent public demonstrations, urban riots (accompanied by the seemingly indiscriminate killing of people and the looting, burning, and other destruction of property), police brutality, street-corner gang warfare, and other similar forms of interpersonal aggression has led researchers to attempt to identify causal factors related to the origins of violence, with a hopeful view to eliminating such causes. Many hypotheses have been presented for consideration, ranging anywhere from economic causes (i.e., discriminatory hiring practices, unemployment, inability to fulfill economic expectations, etc.) to a general breakdown in moral and ethical values. Proposals to eliminate the causes of violence have included a revamping of social welfare programs and elimination of discriminatory employment practices on the one hand, to "cracking down" on lawlessness by upgrading local law enforcement agencies and imposing stiffer criminal penalties on the other. There are doubtless as many views as to the causes and cures for violence as there are

observers, each view tinged with the value system, prejudices, philosophies, and epistemological attitudes of each
such observer. It is the purpose of this article to focus
attention on one possible source of violence—not necessarily "the" source, but one that might very well be found
deserving of a share of the burden for having contributed
to the conditions that have led to increased violence. This
chapter will explore the possibility that the effort to impose
social order may in fact lead to a breakdown of order, and
that any formal legal structure may contain within it dysfunctional elements, which lead to such a result. Employing
the basic frustration-aggression hypothesis, it is the principal contention of this chapter that the incidence of violence
in our society may be, in part, a product of the frustration
that people perceive in connection with their expectations of
benefits to be derived from a formal system of law; that, in
other words, people have sanctioned the political system out
of a belief that the institution of law will produce a reasonably predictable level of social order, the failure of which
to be realized results in frustration, which in turn serves to
encourage aggression. That there are numerous additional
explanations for the causes of violence and societal disorder
is not to be denied; nor is it to be suggested that imposed
order will always lead to aggression or violence. It is only
being suggested that any system of imposed order, to the
degree people perceive its activities as frustrating their own
expectations, will serve to increase the tendency toward aggression and violence.

It is well, at this point, to define the terms used in this
chapter. "State" shall mean a formal organization that enjoys a monopoly of the use of coercion within a specific geographical area, and that is sanctioned by a sizable enough

portion of the population of that area to permit it effectively to exercise universal decision-making functions therein. "Law" shall be defined in positivist terms as formal rules enacted and enforced by the state in furtherance of any policy as defined by the state. While the article will refer to the writings of such "natural law" advocates as John Locke, an attempt shall be made not to confuse the definitions. The chapter will, instead, refer to "law" solely in political terms as those formal rules that a political state can enact and enforce within a given area. The effort to regulate human conduct within such an area by the use of such rules of law shall thus constitute efforts to "impose order," the content of said "order" being determined by those persons exercising effective decision-making through the state. Such definitions shall therefore be considered in a totally "value-free" setting, and no effort shall be made herein to evaluate any rules of law in terms of consistency with any socio-political philosophy or other premise. The effort shall be a *descriptive* one, with the only *subjective* factor being a consideration of the reaction that people may have to rules of law that are promulgated by the state, but without regard to whether, in the eyes of the writer, such reactions are "good" or "bad," or "right" or "wrong."

This article shall, therefore, limit its scope to an examination of *formal* systems of political and legal order, and shall not consider the systems of "order" that prevail throughout any society, and that are the product *not* of political law-making, but of informal "rule making" found within social institutions (such as the family, economic, religious, and social organizations), or spring from the mores, customs, manners, and habits of people. It is fairly well recognized, in fact, that without such informal sources of order, no meaningful social structure could long endure. Contrasted with the political efforts to *impose* order by coercion or the threat of coercion, then, are those informally, voluntarily developed rules of behavior that shall be referred to as "natural order."

I. A Theory of Government Regulation

A. The "Hygienic" Function

Any effort to characterize the expectations of such an amorphous abstraction as "society" or "people" must constitute the height of presumption. While human beings are continually being collectivized into various groupings in order to assist in the generalization of human behavior, it is well not to confuse the abstraction with reality, but to remember that "society" consists of many separate individuals with unique tastes, values, motivations, experiences, and goals. With this caveat in mind, an attempt shall nonetheless be made to identify what appears to be at least the minimum functions that most people would expect a formal system of law to serve. That different persons might have various *additional* expectations from "law" is not to be denied; it is only being proposed that one can identify a fairly universal attitude as to the minimum functions that "law" ought to serve, and that such minimum functions constitute the basis upon which most people grant their sanction to the "law" and the "state." These minimum functions have been identified by such philosophers as Thomas Hobbes and John Locke.

Hobbes observed that, in a state of nature, the basic equality of men's abilities would lead to conflict in the realization of essentially equal goals among men, adding that "if any two men desire the same thing, which nevertheless they cannot both enjoy, they become enemies."[1] As long as such a condition exists "without a common power to keep them all in awe," said Hobbes, men will find themselves in a state of "war of every man against every man." The result of such a state was eloquently described by Hobbes:

> Whatsoever therefore is consequent to a time of war, where every man is enemy to every man, the same is consequent to the time wherein men live without other security than what their own strength, and their own invention, shall furnish them withal. In such condition, there is no place for industry, because the fruit thereof is uncertain; and consequently no culture of the earth; no navigation, nor use of the commodities that may be imported by sea; no commodious building; no instruments of moving, and removing, such things as require much force; no knowledge of the face of the earth; no account of time; no arts; no letters; no society and, which is the worst of all, continual fear, and danger of violent death; and the life of man, solitary, poor, nasty, brutish, and short.[2]

To avoid such adverse consequences, Hobbes concluded that men introduce "restraints upon themselves" by the creation of a "commonwealth," through which they will get "themselves out from that miserable condition of war" with a view "to live peaceably amongst themselves, and be protected against other men." Thus, even though Hobbes articulated a justification for the authoritarian state, he acknowledged that the fundamental role of the state is to

---

[1] Hobbes, "Leviathan," in *Great Political Thinkers* 366, 367 (W. Ebenstein 3d ed. 1965).

[2] *Ibid.* at 368.

provide order and security for the lives and property of its citizens.

John Locke was even more explicit as to what he considered to be the basic function of the state. He noted that, in a state of nature, every man has a right to restrain those who would seek to interfere with his right to his life and property, declaring that such interference creates a "state of war" between the transgressor and his victim: "[H]e who attempts to get another man into his absolute power does thereby put himself into a state of war with him: it being . . . understood as a declaration of a design upon his life."[3] Locke further stated:

> To avoid this state of war . . . is one great reason of men's putting themselves into society, and quitting the state of nature. For where there is an authority, a power on earth from which relief can be had by appeal, there the continuance of the state of war is excluded, and the controversy is decided by that power.[4]

To Locke, then, government serves in the capacity of an "agent" for members of society, empowered to do those acts—and only those acts—that such members of society could have rightfully done for themselves in a state of nature. Since individuals have the right, in nature, to protect their lives and property from acts of interference by other men, these same individuals have the right to authorize government to perform, in their behalf, this same function. As Locke reasoned:

> A man, as has been proved, cannot subject himself to the arbitrary power of another; and having, in the state of nature,

---

[3] Locke, "Two Treatises of Government," in *Great Political Thinkers* 393, 397 (W. Ebenstein 3d ed. 1965).

[4] *Ibid*. at 399.

no arbitrary power over the life, liberty, or possession of another, but only so much as the law of nature gave him for the
preservation of himself and the rest of mankind, this is all he
doth, or can give up to the commonwealth, and by it to the
legislative power, so that the legislative can have no more than
this.[5]

Contrary to Hobbes, then, Locke argued that the right of
each man to his life and to his property circumscribes the
proper limits of governmental action, and that any act of
government that goes beyond the function of *protecting*
such rights and begins to *interfere* with them exceeds the
claims of legitimacy:

The supreme power cannot take from any man any part of his
property without his own consent. For the preservation of property being the end of government and that for which men
enter into society, it necessarily supposes and requires that the
people should have property, without which they must be supposed to lose that by entering into society which was the end
for which they entered into it; too gross an absurdity for any
man to own. Men therefore in society having property, they
have such a right to the goods, which by the law of the community are theirs, that nobody hath a right to their substance,
or any part of it, from them without their own consent; without
this they have no property at all. For I have truly no property
in that which another can by right take from me when he pleases
against my consent. Hence it is a mistake to think that the
supreme or legislative power of any commonwealth can do
what it will, and dispose of the estates of the subject arbitrarily,
to take any part of them at pleasure.[6]

It is not the purpose of this chapter to debate the "proper"
limitations of government action, but only to point out that
both Hobbes (who laid an intellectual foundation for an

---

[5] *Ibid*. at 406.
[6] *Ibid*. at 408.

omnipotent state) and Locke (who narrowly restricted the functions of the state) agreed that the *primary* purpose for which men create institutions of government and law is the protection of their lives and property from interferences by other men. At the risk of oversimplification, it would appear that this view, which seems to find fairly general support among people as a definition of the basic purpose of government and law, could be summarized as follows: Men, in order to engage in productive enterprises and to have the opportunity for maximizing pleasure and seeking personal fulfillment, must be free from the actions of other men that, whether intentional or unintentional, violate by force or by threat of force their persons or property. Men have a need, in other words, to be free from acts of victimization; to be free from having their will violated with respect to their persons or property. For this reason (at least theoretically) men have sanctioned the political state, whose function it is to provide protection from such acts. This shall be referred to herein as the "hygienic" function of law, consisting of those actions of government that are designed to eliminate (or, at least, to reduce) those negative influences by which some people physically violate (or threaten to physically violate) the person or property of others, and thus restrict or otherwise interfere with the right of people to make decisions concerning their own lives.

Acts of victimization may be either "intentional" or "unintentional." The legal system may respond to intentional wrongdoings (e.g., murder, rape, burglary, arson, assault) through the institution of criminal proceedings or civil actions by the victim, while the unintentional acts (e.g., breach of contract, tortious conduct leading to personal injury or property damage) are almost always left to the victim to seek redress through civil proceedings. In either event, it would seem safe to conclude that the sanction which most people have for a formal legal system has, as its fundamental consideration, the expectation that the system will effectively *minimize* such negative social influences in order to protect them from victimization, to provide them the opportunity to maximize their life, psychic growth, and economic potentials, and to facilitate the free flow and expression of their choices.

B. The "Structuring" Function

As indicated earlier, the element that distinguishes the political state from other institutions is its enjoyment of a monopoly on the use of coercion within a specific geographical area. The rationale for the existence of such a monopoly, whether justified or not, has always been that the state, in order effectively to restrict acts of violence and other disorder, must have the ultimate reservoir of power. Or, as one writer observed: "The function of the police power of the state is to maintain a threshold of force to deter and/or contain the ever-present margin of anti-social acts by individuals and groups."[7] Assuming, *arguendo,* that such a contention is correct, a fundamental question immediately arises: Can an institution that has been imbued with a monopoly on mechanisms of coercion for the purpose of protecting the lives and property of its citizens from acts of victimization be prevented from becoming an instrument used by some people for the purpose of imposing their will upon others, in effect realizing Locke's fear that the state would become the *source* rather than the *remedy* for victimization?

---

[7] Nieburg, "Violence, Law, and the Social Process," 11 *Am. Behavioral Scientist,* March-April 1968, at 17.

If the political philosophers are correct in concluding that the nature of men is such that they will, given the opportunity, seek to take advantage of other men and to impose their will upon them, it is then not unreasonable to assume that these same men would seek to gain control of a monopolistic instrument of coercion such as the political state in order to effectuate such a design. Nor is it so incredible that such men would, in order to make the social environment more conducive to their own purposes and objectives, seek to redefine the terms and conditions of the "order" that the state is mandated to preserve. Given these human tendencies, it can be seen that there exists the possibility that men and women of differing political, economic, and social persuasions will begin to modify the concept of "order" so as to embrace an ever-widening range of subject matter. The result of this process would be that "order" is no longer solely perceived in terms of the "hygienic" function of eliminating acts or threatened acts of aggression and violence, but instead is perceived as including the organization and structuring of human relationships in order to permit some men, through the use of state coercion, to make the behavior of other men more predictable for their objectives, and more conducive to their control. That such, in fact, has been the history of man's efforts with political processes cannot be denied by any realist. "Order," at least on the American scene, has come to mean more than simply eliminating crime in the streets: To the businessman it means a system of laws to restrict the competitive practices of one's competitors,[8] to the educationalist it means the adoption of

---

[8] See, e.g., G. Domhoff, *The Higher Circles: The Governing Class in America* (1970); G. Kolko, *The Triumph of Conservatism* (1963); J. Weinstein, *The Corporate Ideal in the Liberal State, 1900–1918* (1968).

state-enforced standards of instruction applicable to all; to
the "moral reformer" it means the banning of drugs, alcohol,
and pornographic books; to the labor union it means the
elimination of lower-priced sources of labor through minimum wage laws; to the manufacturer it means the restriction
of competitive foreign imports through tariffs and import
quotas; to the environmentalist it means restriction of the
development of natural resources; to the railroad or telephone company executive it means the assurance of restricted entry of would-be competitors and the comfort of
knowing that existing competitors may not engage in effective price competition through reduced rates;[9] to the farmer
it means governmental maintenance of artificially high
prices for farm products; to the doctor, lawyer, barber, den-
tist, funeral director, electrician, and car dealer it means
control over the trade practices of one's competitors through
systems of licensing; and to the real estate developer it
means the regulation through zoning laws of the use that
other men may make of their property. In short, while the
political state continues to be presented to the public as a
system of order designed to *protect* them from acts of victimization, in truth it functions as a mechanism for the
ordering, regulation, and restriction of human conduct to
the end of maintaining a "status quo" for the benefit of those
who would stand most to lose whatever advantage they
presently enjoy were men permitted a greater degree of
flexibility and opportunity for change in their economic and
social relationships. Such "order," enforced by the political
state, is reminiscent of the "order" existing within a cartel,
in which, in the words of one observer, "the goal is to restrain disturbing influences, to stabilize prices, and to assure

---

[9] See, e.g., G. Kolko, *Railroads and Regulations: 1877–1916* (1965).

those in the business the comfortable feeling that their position is secure."[10]

The "hygienic" function of the state in attempting to restrict acts of victimization can be contrasted, then, with this latter function of seeking to structure personal and institutional behavior so as to interfere with the normal processes of change that would accompany human interrelationships not subject to such restrictions. This shall be referred to as the "structuring" function of the state, having both the purpose and effect of imposing restraints on the noncoercive activities and decision making of individuals in order to prevent such individuals from acting contrary to the interests of those persons or groups that have been successful in obtaining the imposition of such restraints.

The "hygienic" function, being designed only to protect people against acts of victimization, *theoretically* precludes the condition in which the power of the state is used by some people to victimize others. The "structuring" function, on the other hand, is *designed* to allow some men to interfere with the peaceful activities of others. Its purpose is to permit the monopolistic power of the state to be used to control the activities and the environment of other men to the end that those successful in achieving such control may effectively limit the choices and decisions of other people.

C. Conflict in the Relationship Between the "Hygienic" and "Structuring" Functions

Once the role of the state expands to include the "structuring" function, a conflict of purpose arises, and to the degree such a conflict is perceived by members of society,

[10] H. Fleming, *Ten Thousand Commandments* 42 (1951).

the seeds of potential discontent are sown. For if the state theoretically exists in order to protect people from acts of victimization and to provide a threshold of safety and security from interference for persons and their property such as will allow them to seek to maximize their well-being and happiness, it becomes difficult to justify the state becoming the *source* of negative restraints upon personal behavior, functioning as the very *limitation* upon individual free choice and action that it was designed to eliminate. The perception of such a dichotomy can lead to a feeling of frustration, a feeling that becomes heightened if the viewer is made aware not only that the "structuring" function interferes with the "hygienic" function, but also that the state is failing adequately to carry out the "hygienic" function—a realization brought home to people through continually rising crime rates, public disorders, and riots. The continuation of such a sense of frustration can lead not only to acts of aggression, as shall be seen, but also to a weakening of the sanction that individuals are willing to grant to the state and upon which the ultimate power of the state must depend. If people sanction the state in order to realize protection from acts of victimization, and not only fail to receive such protection, but also find themselves subject to restrictions placed upon them by the state, it would be naïve to suppose that the continuation of such a situation would not have adverse personal and social consequences.

The expectation of the public that the state will protect their lives and property is quite obviously that which motivates the proponents of most legislation seeking to restrict and structure some phase of human behavior to present such legislation in terms consistent with the public's expectation. A group of dairy producers, desirous of eliminating price competition from their industry, would never consider going before the public or the legislature and arguing that they cannot match the efficiency of their lower-priced competitors and, therefore, that the consuming public should be forced to pay a higher price for milk through the institution of minimum milk prices. Such an appeal would constitute a blatant admission that the law was being used simply to victimize consumers and efficient producers. Instead the appeal is presented in terms of "protecting" the consumer and the milk supply for small children since a higher price for milk will assure the continued existence of the less efficient dairies. To the degree people perceive that such legislation is for their benefit and protection, it is unlikely that any crisis of confidence in the state will be engendered. Perceived in those terms, people will simply conclude that such action is in proper fulfillment of the "hygienic" function of the state. Examples of efforts at "structuring," which have successfully been "sold" to the public in terms of satisfying the "hygienic" function, are many. They include licensing procedures promoted as a means of protecting the public from incompetent practitioners of a trade or profession, when the real purpose is to restrict entry and to control the practices of competitors; antitrust legislation that has been offered as a means of protecting consumers from monopolistic practices, when the true purpose has been to restrict competition; and tariffs that have been presented to the public as a device for protecting domestic employment.

The factors that stimulate the desire of some men to impose a system of "order" upon other men and institutions by restricting the opportunities for change and by controlling human conduct for the benefit of those seeking to impose such order are varied and would constitute a worthwhile subject for deeper study. The critical factor, however, would appear to stem from a basic need that men have to make the world about them *predictable* and subject to influence by their purposeful action.[11] Man, being a reasoning animal, cannot rely on instinct to guide his behavior, but must perceive reality and consciously devise action that will effectuate a desired result. The more man's *perception* of reality conforms to reality, and the more competent he is at identifying cause and effect relationships, the greater degree of success he will have in realizing his intended goals. Quite obviously, then, the more predictable a man's environment is in terms of his being able to discern recurring patterns of behavior, the better able he should be to engage in efficacious activity. In order to maximize his well-being, a man must be able to predict with reasonable certainty the consequences of his actions, and this necessarily implies his being able to influence his environment. As one observer has noted:

> Man is motivated to achieve outcomes which are consistent with his evaluative beliefs about himself, his evaluative beliefs about others, and the degree to which he believes that there is one set of values (whatever they may be) to guide behavior in this world.[12]

Or, in short: "Regularity is . . . a condition of personal security and the ability to plan our lives in fruitful ways."[13]

---

[11] As one writer has added, however, it is not every kind of predictability that men find desirable and conducive to social order: "To be regularly subject to the violence of others is not to be secure—quite the opposite," Berger, " 'Law and Order' and Civil Disobedience," 13 *Inquiry* 254, 258 (1970).

[12] Korman, "Organizational Achievement, Aggression and Creativity: Some Suggestions Toward an Integrated Theory," 6 *Organizational Behavior & Human Performance* 593, 595 (1971).

[13] Berger, *supra* note 11, at 258.

But perhaps the most significant part of man's environment is *other* men; most of man's activities are conducted in relation to other men. There thus exists the same need to have the actions of such other men be predictable as there is with respect to the predictability of man's physical environment. The need men have to be free of negative influences that restrict their ability to engage in predictable, efficacious action in order to maximize their well-being encompasses a need to have the behavior of others brought within parameters that do not interfere with the realization of such objectives. Such is the motivation underlying the "hygienic" function of the law; namely, to make the social environment as free as possible from victimizing behavior that would reduce the opportunities for productive and pleasurable activity. Men do have a need for predictable certainty that their relationships with other men will be free from acts of trespass, theft, assault, murder, and other forms of violence, and that they can go about their day-to-day functions free from such disorder. The maintenance of "orderly" social relationships is, then, an adjunct of man's basic metaphysical need for an environment providing a "consistent outcome" for his actions.

If the ordering functions of the state were limited to the "hygienic" function, few objections would probably be raised (assuming the state was capable of performing that function). As has been seen, however, the state becomes the object of a power struggle among competing groups seeking to employ the force of the state against other groups in order to restrict the scope of the other groups' activity. This "structuring" effort is likewise motivated by a desire to make the socio-economic environment predictable and more subject to the influences of the groups that prevail in such a power struggle. The consequence of this method of imposing order is the creation of a conflict with the basic assumption underlying the existence of the political state; namely, the elimination of victimization. It is at this point that a "crisis of confidence" arises that will (to the degree men perceive a discrepancy between the enunciated objectives of the state and the realized results, and especially if the action of the state interferes with some important activity of such men) lead to a feeling of frustration that, consistent with the "frustration-aggression" hypothesis, may result in some manifestation of aggression, including possibly violence.

II. A Theory of Frustration and Violence

A. The "Frustration-Aggression" Hypothesis

The "frustration-aggression" hypothesis received its modern impetus from a classic study by Dollard, Doob, Miller, Mowrer, and Sears[14] and has been reinforced by a significant amount of research by others. The essence of the hypothesis is that interference with the goal-directed activity of an individual (i.e., frustration) "can produce an instigation to aggression,"[15] or, as Neal Miller stated, "Frustration produces instigations to a number of different types of response, one which is an instigation to some form of aggression."[16]

Daniels and Gilula elaborated on this hypothesis:

> The frustration view states that aggressive behavior occurs after an interference with ongoing purposeful activity. (This theory

---

[14] J. Dollard, L. Doob, N. Miller, O. Mowrer & R. Sears, *Frustration and Aggression* (1939).

[15] L. Berkowitz, *Aggression* 28 (1962).

[16] Miller, "The Frustration-Aggression Hypothesis," in *Roots of Aggression* 29, 30 (L. Berkowitz ed., 1969).

often equates aggression with destructive or damaging violent behavior.) The primary effect of frustration is to raise the motivational state of the individual, with the destructive response itself being a learned behavior. A person feels frustrated when a violation of his hopes or expectations occurs, and he may then try to solve the problem by attacking the presumed source of frustration.[17]

Spiegel defined "aggression" in these terms:

Aggression is behavior involving the use of force or its symbolic equivalent to effect an outcome in line with the intentions, or goals, of the aggressor acting against the intentions or goals of an adversary. It usually, but not always, occurs in an agonistic situation characterized by a conflict of interests.[18]

The relationship of frustration to social disorder has been stated as follows:

According to the basic frustration-aggression hypothesis, instability results from unrelieved social frustration. One form of systematic frustration occurs when there are wide gaps between the needs, expectations or demands of the population and their achievement.[19]

It is important to note at this point that in assessing the frustration experienced by a given individual, one must compare the levels of "expectation" and "achievement" *not* by

---

[17] Daniels & Gilula, "Violence and the Struggle for Existence," in *Violence and the Struggle for Existence* 405, 410 (D. Daniels, M. Gilula & F. Ochberg eds. 1970).

[18] Spiegel, "Toward a Theory of Collective Violence," in *Dynamics of Violence* 19, 21 (J. Fawcett ed. 1972).

[19] Feierabend & Feierabend, "Conflict, Crisis and Collision: A Study of International Stability," 1 *Psychology Today,* May 1968, at 28. *See also* Ilfield, "Environmental Theories of Violence," in *Violence and the Struggle for Existence* 79, 86 (D. Daniels, M. Gilula & F. Ochberg eds. 1970).

"absolute" or "objective" criteria, but rather in terms of the disparity felt by the individual himself. As Crawford and Naditch have stated, we must look to "the level of achievement or deprivation *relative* to some standard employed by the individual as a basis of comparison or self-evaluation."[20] Or as Jerome D. Frank summarized: "The amount of frustration depends less on the amount of deprivation than on the size of the gap between what a person has and what he expects or believes he is entitled to have."[21]

That frustration caused by differences between a person's expectations and achievements can lead to violent social behavior is well-documented in the literature. Gurr has observed, for example, that

> the necessary precondition for violent civil conflict is relative deprivation, defined as actors' perception of discrepancy between their *value expectations* and their environment's apparent *value capabilities.* Value expectations are the goods and conditions of life to which people believe they are justifiably entitled. The referents of value capabilities are to be found largely in the social and physical environment: they are the conditions that determine people's perceived chances of getting or keeping the values they legitimately expect to attain.[22]

Violence resulting from other sources of frustration is also noted in the literature. For example, as Frank has ob-

---

[20] Crawford & Naditch, "Relative Deprivation, Powerlessness, and Militancy: The Psychology of Social Protest," 33 *Psychiatry* 208, 208 (1970).

[21] Frank, "Psychological Aspects of International Violence," in *Dynamics of Violence* 33, 39 (J. Fawcett ed. 1972).

[22] Gurr, "Psychological Factors in Civil Violence," in *Anger, Violence and Politics: Theories and Research* 33, 37–38 (I. Feierabend, R. Feierabend & T. Gurr eds. 1972).

served, the failure of the state to perform its "hygienic" function can lead to violence:

> Group conflict arises when each group perceives its goal as achievable only at another's expense. Domestically, this type of conflict becomes violent when groups feel intolerably frustrated or threatened, and have lost faith in the institutions of society to satisfy their claims or to protect them.[23]

Fred R. Berger is even more explicit. Where

> certain segments or groups within the population are systematically exposed to these weaknesses in the ability of the legal system to provide or protect security, those subjected to such treatment come to feel "left out" of the social process, come to regard themselves as the "victims" of the social and political scheme, rather than full participants in it. In such circumstances, respect for law and the lives and property of those who *do* enjoy the benefits of the order the legal system provides may be considerably weakened. Such conditions tend to foster counter-violence and retaliatory disorder, either out of revenge, frustration, a desire to take one's "share" of the goods of society, or merely the need to assert one's "manliness" and no longer to "take it lying down." And that the legal system may very well foster and permit such conditions which lead to such widespread, relative disorder in a community can no longer be reasonably denied.[24]

B. Violence Resulting from "Powerlessness"

But the failure of the state to perform its "hygienic" function is not the only way in which the actions of the state may lead to violence. The "structuring" function, by limiting,

---

[23] Frank, *supra* note 21, at 34.
[24] Berger, *supra* note 11, at 262–63. See also L. Coser, *Continuities in the Study of Social Conflict* 97 (1967).

regulating, or prohibiting various types of human conduct, creates in the mind of the person so affected a sense of "powerlessness," an inability to control or influence his immediate environment in order to make decisions meaningful to his basic life goals. This is perhaps the ultimate sense of frustration: the inability to achieve a sense of efficacy over one's own life, due, in large part, to the imposition of barriers and restrictions by the very institution that one was told would *eliminate* such negative influences. The relationship between powerlessness and violence has been pointed out by Rollo May: "Violence comes from powerlessness; . . . it is the explosion of impotence."[25] "As we make people powerless, we promote their violence rather than its control."[26] (May, of course, speaks of "power" in terms of the ability to make decisions, not in the sense of the use of force or coercion.)

The full impact of this condition of powerlessness was eloquently expressed by Grinker:

> I believe that we are witnessing at all levels of our social network a conflict based on dualistic thinking, the polarities of which are personal or individual freedom as against social structures maintaining the functions of regulation and control. Each has moved speedily and quantitatively to become antagonistic and reactionary to the other. The greater the demand for freedom, the more repressive measures are set into action. The more restrictive controls to dampen freedoms, the more protest and violence as the final common pathway of many causes.[27]

---

[25] R. May, *Power and Innocence* 53 (1972).

[26] *Ibid.* at 23. See also Ransford, "Isolation, Powerlessness, and Violence: A Study of Attitudes and Participation in the Watts Riot," 73 *Am. J. Sociology* 581, 583 (1968).

[27] Grinker, "What is the Cause of Violence." in *Dynamics of Violence* 64, 64 (J. Fawcett ed. 1972).

Rollo May added this thought:

> To admit our own individual feelings of powerlessness—that we cannot influence many people; that we count for little; that the values to which our parents devoted their lives are to us insubstantial and worthless; that we feel ourselves to be "faceless others," as W. H. Auden puts it, insignificant to other people and, therefore, not worth much to ourselves—this is, indeed, difficult to admit. I cannot recall a time during the last few decades when there was so *much* talk about the individual's capacities and potentialities and so *little* actual confidence on the part of the individual about his power to make a difference psychologically or politically. The talk is at least partially a compensatory symptom for our disquieting awareness of our very loss of power.[28]

In short, as Anthony Storr has summarized: "When our drive to master the environment, or take from it what we need, is obstructed, we become angry. . . ."[29]

C. The "Displacement" Theory

A factor that appears to influence how an individual responds to a given frustrating experience is the degree of sanction he accords the frustrating agency. Reviewing the studies done in this area, Burnstein and Worchel concluded that "frustrations which are perceived to be reasonable or nonarbitrary are accepted with much less overt aggression than those which are perceived to be arbitrary or unreasonable."[30] Gurr also noted that the learning and socialization

---

[28] R. May, *supra* note 25, at 21.

[29] A. Storr, *Human Aggression* 92 (1968). See also Ilfield, "Overview of the Causes and Prevention of Violence." 20 *Archives of General Psychiatry* 675, 685 (1969).

[30] Burnstein & Worchel, "Arbitrariness of Frustration and Its Consequences for Aggression in a Social Situation," in *Roots of Aggression* 75, 75 (L. Berkowitz ed. 1969). See also Gurr, *supra* note 22, at 42.

processes can modify the tendencies both as to the perception of and response to frustrations.[31] To the degree one sanctions, or at least reveres, the agency responsible for an interference with an expectation that results in frustration, there may develop a tendency for that individual to shift his aggressive response from the causal agency to a substitute target. This practice, known as "displacement," has been described as the "shifting of an effect and its behavioral correlates from the original object to a substitute object, presumably one that is similar to the original object on certain perceptual or cognitive dimensions."[32]

The displacement theory has been used to explain the higher incidence of lynching during times of economic recession.[33] One can only wonder how much of the recent violence—some part of it directed by blacks against their own deteriorated neighborhoods, other parts of it directed against banks and businesses with large defense contracts—may be the product of displaced aggression against an amorphous but highly structured "social order" that is created, maintained, and enforced by the political state for the purpose of restricting human activity and interfering with the processes of change, thereby frustrating the expectations of millions of people seeking greater fulfillment in their lives. It may well be that much of the violence experienced in recent years has grown out of frustrations developed through the imposition of "order" by a highly regulative political system, but that, in Kaufmann's words, the frustrated individual

---

[31] Gurr, *supra* note 22, at 35.

[32] H. Kaufmann, *Aggression and Altruism* 32 (1970).

[33] See, e.g., H. Cantril, *The Psychology of Social Movement* 78–122 (1941).

realizes that the original object would have been too dangerous an object of attack. Therefore, he now selects a new target which, even though a little less dangerous, is in some way "similar" to the original tormentor, and thereby still provides sufficient balm for the aggressor's self-esteem, so that he can persuade himself that he is not an utter coward, and that he has behaved in a manly fashion.[34]

III. Frustration as a Product of Government Regulation

A. Examples of Government Regulation That Produce Frustration

1. *Social reform measures.* Many programs have been offered to the public with the promise that they will eliminate various causes of discontent and promote a greater degree of self-control and direction for all people. Yet the promised results are often not the real reason for the program. For example, minimum wage laws are suggested as a means of increasing the earning capacity of marginal workers, but the immediate effect of such laws is to increase the number of unemployed marginal workers because such laws increase the labor cost of employers.[35] Such legislation has been promoted *not* out of humanitarian impulses, but out of the desire of labor unions to eliminate lower-priced sources of labor and the desire of employers who are already

---

[34] H. Kaufmann, *supra* note 32, at 32.

[35] See, e.g., Benewitz & Weintraub, "Employment Effects of a Local Minimum Wage," 17 *Ind. & Lab. Rel. Rev.* 276 (1964); Douty, "Some Effects of the $1.00 Minimum Wage in the United States," 27 *Economica* (*New Series*) 137 (1960); Peterson, "Employment Effects of State Minimum Wages for Women: Three Historical Cases Re-Examined," 12 *Ind. & Lab. Rel. Rev.* 406 (1959); Peterson, "Employment Effects of Minimum Wages, 1938–50," 65 *J. Pol. Econ.* 412 (1957).

paying higher wages to impose higher costs upon their competitors. Whether or not the supposed beneficiaries of such legislation recognize the causal relationship between these laws and increased unemployment, the overall effect is nevertheless detrimental to their interests by depriving them of an expected benefit. Likewise, urban renewal legislation has been fostered (at least in theory) as a means of eradicating slums and providing higher-quality housing for lower-income people. Yet the history of this program has been that blacks and other residents of slum areas have been forced out of their existing homes—thus disrupting their personal lives and removing them from familiar surroundings—while their residences were torn down to make way for new apartments, *not* for them, but for middle-income tenants. Whether or not slum residents are aware that such programs have been undertaken in order to benefit real estate investors and insurance companies,[36] or whether they even recognize the causal relationship between urban renewal programs and the failure to solve the problem of low-income housing, a sense of frustration must be expected from those who *expected* results that were not delivered.

Along the same lines, rent control laws have been enacted with an express purpose of providing low-income tenants with reduced rents. The effect of such laws has been to make it unprofitable for landlords to make needed improvements on such property, thus leading to the deterioration of such property, a consequence that can be expected to increase the frustration of tenants who anticipated improved living conditions. What, too, of the effects of the building codes,

---

[36] M. Anderson, *The Federal Bulldozer* (1964). For the related topic of the effects of legal intervention into land use, see B. Siegan, *Land Use Without Zoning* (1972).

enacted at the behest of contractors and labor unions seeking to protect their positions, which prevent the reduction of construction costs by restricting the usage of modern modular building techniques, and which thus interfere with efforts to supply lower-cost housing?

One can further imagine the frustration felt by young men and their families who have been subjected to the military draft, their lives disrupted and threatened with death or serious injury, especially since the stated purpose of the military establishment has been to *protect* its citizens, not send them off to foreign lands to be killed, and has been to promote peace rather than to find itself embroiled in the sort of continuous pointless wars envisioned by Orwell in *1984,* wars that serve to promote the interests of the state, rather than of its citizens.[37]

Then, too, people are told that their being subjected to the restrictions of economic planning has been to provide for greater economic stability, increased productivity, and higher standards of living. What feelings of frustration must follow from the fact that such programs have not only failed to *prevent,* but may well have *caused* such phenomena as recession, inflation, higher unemployment, scarcity of some goods and services and surpluses of others, balance of payments deficits, and devaluation of the dollar, with proposed "cures" consisting of even tighter economic controls that further restrict and limit the choices people may make, thus interfering with their opportunity to control their own lives and maximize their own well-being.[38] One writer has

---

[37] R. Bourne, *War and the Intellectuals, 1915–1919* (1964).

[38] M. Rothbard, *America's Great Depression* (1963).

suggested that this process not only *leads* to violence, but *is* violence:

> The books are full of laws passed, not by the pressure of the voters, but by the pressure of wealthy businessmen, powerful labor unions, and influential politicians. This often results in social injustice, and such injustice is clearly a form of violence.[39]

Freud recognized this same point in his declaration:

> It is a general principle, then, that conflicts of interest between men are settled by the use of violence. . . . The justice of the community then becomes an expression of the unequal degrees of power obtaining within it; the laws are made by and for the ruling members and find little room for the rights of those in subjection.[40]

Minority group members, for years the victims of discrimination in employment practices, are told that "fair employment practices" leigslation will open up all sorts of job opportunities. Yet—some ten years later—the results have not measured up to the promises, and more and more persons are finding themselves being pigeonholed into a highly structured "quota" system for hiring, under which people who had asked only for the opportunity to be considered for employment on their merit are once again finding themselves considered for employment on the basis of their racial, religious, sexual, or ethnic profile. Is it surprising to find such people experiencing a profound sense of frustration under the circumstances?

---

[39] R. N. Johnson, *Aggression in Man and Animals* 225 (1972).

[40] Letter from Sigmund Freud to Albert Einstein, September 1932, in *The Dynamics of Aggression* 13 (E. Megargee & J. Hokanson eds. 1970).

In each of the areas just discussed, it is important to point out that the experienced frustration does not necessarily derive from people actually perceiving the relationship between the regulated activity and the failure of the program to achieve the desired result. It is enough that people have an expectation of a desired result, and that such result does not materialize. A slum tenant may not be aware that urban renewal programs or rent control laws have interfered with his acquiring better housing, but he does know that the promises made to him have not been fulfilled, and he will likely experience frustration as a consequence.

2. *Police activities.* A practice that must rank near the top in terms of the frustration of the expectations of people involves the failure of the police, in the exercise of the "hygienic" function, to realize what, as has been seen, is regarded by most people as the basic purpose of a formal political-legal structure: the protection of the person and the person's property from acts of victimization by others. This purpose theoretically casts the police in the role of *protectors* of personal rights and safety, and yet in practice such has not always been the case. Not only has this system failed to halt rapidly advancing crime rates—a consequence that, by itself, could be expected to generate frustration within those who had endorsed and sanctioned such a system out of an expectation that crime would thus be minimized—but it also has become the source of additional frustration to persons, especially minority group members and other low-income people, who have found themselves the objects of fairly routine acts of victimization by the police themselves. While there may be a tendency by some persons to over-react and regard *any* action by a police officer as "police brutality," a far more unrealistic reaction is naïvely to as-

sume that the metropolitan police forces of this country are characteristically staffed by officers who view themselves as simply "public servants," desirous only of promoting the "general welfare" of the community, while being ever-mindful of the basic rights of all men. The informed reader needs no recitation of the fairly systematic abuse of minorities by the police on the streets, or of suspects within the confines of the precinct station, or of sleeping families whose homes have been broken into by police officers during the course of an illegal search. Add to this the documented acts of violence initiated by the police during the course of demonstrations, the tendency of many police officers to be "gun-" or "nightstick-happy," the Supreme Court's recent decision extending the power of search incidental to traffic arrests,[41] and the like, and one gets the picture of a system that, far from *protecting* those who come into contact with it, provides a *threat* to their safety. One can only wonder how much violence has been generated by the police themselves as a result of their ofttimes arbitrary treatment of criminal suspects. To what extent, in other words, does submission to arbitrariness constitute an attack upon one's own self-esteem, or pride, and thus encourage violence as a response? As one individual observed:

> The right to resist unlawful arrest memorializes one of the principal elements in the heritage of the English revolution: the belief that the will to resist arbitrary authority in a reasonable way is valuable and ought not to be suppressed by the criminal law. In the face of obvious injustice, one ought not to be forced to submit and swallow one's sense of justice.[42]

---

[41] Gustafson v. Florida, 414 U.S. 260 (1973).

[42] Chevigny, "The Right to Resist an Unlawful Arrest," 78 *Yale L. J.* 1128, 1137–38 (1969).

One of the most pressing needs people have today is for protection *from* the police and, more importantly, from the structuring of the police system into a self-serving system that no longer makes a pretense of existing to serve and protect the interests of the community.[43] It may be argued that a strawman has been set up, and that such criticism of the police is overly abusive. But nothing here suggests that all police officers or all police departments are ill-motivated. What is being suggested, however, is that the police function in America has become a highly structured system acting in pursuit of its own objectives, a system that not only has failed to *eliminate* the negative influences of victimization, but has become the *source* of such behavior, the net consequence of which has been to frustrate the expectations of persons subject to it.

3. *Economic controls.* It should not be assumed that racial minorities or low-income persons are the only ones subject to the experience of frustration as a result of the actions of government. While such persons may be the ones most in need of the benefits of change with which legal restrictions interfere, middle-income people are also subject to imposed restraints that interfere with economic processes of change (thus frustrating opportunities), and are further subject to the burden of an enormous income and property taxation system, which deprives such persons of a sizable portion of their earnings, channeling it into uses that they do not perceive as serving their objectives. That violence is essentially a product of lower-income areas is a myth which is being eroded by the realization of increased violence in white middle-income suburban America, and by the recog-

---

[43] S. Putney, *The Conquest of Society* 30 (1972).

nition that attitudes of frustration, "powerlessness," and despair transcend all social, economic, and geographical lines. That such consequences may be the product of the frustrations flowing from systems of imposed order that do not serve the expectations of people is a possibility worthy of deeper examination.[44]

B. *"Autosystems"*

As has been indicated, frustration may result when people perceive that the imposition of "structured" forms of order by a political-legal system is in conflict with the system's role of preventing acts of victimization.[45] This perceived sense of frustration is accentuated by a factor that is associated with the operation of virtually all hierarchical structures; namely, a tendency to treat the inputs of persons subject to the organization as secondary to the interests of the organization itself. Whether an organization is political, religious, economic, or social in nature, it develops an atti-

---

[44] Such a question might, for example, explore the role that "displacement" has in accounting for different forms of aggressive behavior among middle-income and lower-income persons. It may be that middle-income people, on the whole, tend to revere the political-legal system more than do lower-income people (i.e., they may identify their interest more clearly with it) and, thus, displace their aggression onto other objects, while lower-income people may have a greater tendency to attack the political-legal system more directly (e.g., attacks upon police officers).

[45] We get confirmation of the proposition that political institutions are not meeting the expectations of people from studies, such as the one conducted at the University of Michigan's Center for Political Studies. This study documents a steady decline from 1958 to 1972 (for whites) and from 1964 to 1972 (for blacks) in public trust and confidence in government. A. Miller, T. Brown, and A. Raine, *Social Conflict and Political Estrangement, 1958–1972* (available through the Center for Political Studies, University of Michigan, Ann Arbor, Michigan). The question that needs to be faced is the one presented herein: What are the hidden personal and social costs

tude early in its life that the perpetuation of the organization is to be regarded as the paramount operational consideration. The organization becomes its own *raison d'être,* and the persons for whose benefit the organization was initially formed suddenly become a means to the organization's ends. In the words of sociologist Snell Putney: "[T]he basic problem is that large systems over a period of time take on objectives of their own, distinct from the objectives of the men who created the systems in the first place."[46] Putney defines such a system as an "autosystem": "a social system which comes to pursue its own objectives by its own means and ceases to be under the effective control of men."[47] These autosystems, in order to guarantee their own continuation, "persuade their participants that there is no possible conflict of interest between man and system."[48]

The process through which this attitude develops involves the same elements that cause men to want to make their environment subject to their influence in order to achieve a high degree of predictability favorable to their objectives. There is a sense of security and certainty in learning a particular pattern of behavior and in having that pattern remain constant. This is the great attraction of bureaucratic procedures: Those within the system can simply respond to any decision-making situation with a reference to a known set of rules and an attempt to fit the *situation* to the *rules.* The

---

associated with the practice of imposing political direction and control over the lives and property of individuals? Is it realistic to expect such institutions to continue frustrating personal expectations without a consequent increase in aggression?

[46] S. Putney, *supra* note 43, at 10.

[47] *Ibid.*

[48] *Ibid.* at 11.

eventual consequence, however, of this process is to insulate the system from the feedback of those persons subject to the system. Korman has reached the following conclusion regarding the tendency of men to desire "structured" organizations:

> First, the high reliance by authority figures on programming and rule specification implies that the world is stable and unchanging enough to permit the utilization and reliance on general rules and programming. Second, the reliance on relatively permanent specialization of activities, as opposed to variation, encourages a belief system that general rules and routine are the order of things while variations, difference, and lack of rules as guides are not.[49]

It might be appropriate at this point to consider the role played by one's metaphysical outlook toward other men as a factor in the incidence of "structuring" as a means of providing "order" within society. To what extent, in other words, is "structuring" a reflection of the view that men are, by nature, untrustworthy and must therefore be subjected to force—or the threat of force—as a means of maintaining any semblance of social harmony? There seems to be a slow deterioration of this attitude in a number of areas, most notably in education and industrial management.[50] With a weakening of the doctrine of "original sin," so to speak, men may someday generally recognize that there is no basic conflict between individual selfishness and social order, and that a world of self-directed, self-centered individuals does not

---

[49] Korman, *supra* note 12, at 601.

[50] See, e.g., McGregor, "Theory X: The Traditional View of Direction and Control," in *People and Productivity* 190 (R. Sutermeister ed. 1963); McGregor, "Theory Y: The Integration of Individual and Organizational Goals," in *People and Productivity* 198 (R. Sutermeister ed. 1963).

necessarily imply either chaos or the collapse of social institutions.

Healthy organizations—such as those normally found in the marketplace—must not only *respond* to feedback, but, in order to enlarge upon their support, actively seek out such feedback in an effort better to plan their operations. (Product market surveys are an example of this effort.) The greater responsiveness of market organizations to feedback is not due to any greater sense of maturity on their part, but is dictated by the competitive nature of the market in which consumers are neither compelled to pay for the product of any given organization (as they are with tax-supported government organizations) nor prohibited from transferring their business from one organization to another. The fact that the business community has been responsible for fostering the antitrust laws in order to *restrict* such competitive conditions[51] is evidence of the desire of virtually all organizations to so structure their environments in order to interfere with the processes of change, thereby helping to maintain a status quo situation consistent with those patterns of behavior that the organization has found to be most conducive to the realization of its goals.

An organization that is responsive to feedback, then, will develop a flexibility designed to adapt its procedures to meet the new inputs of those subject to the organization. While the "structural" system (or, as Putney calls it, the "autosystem") seeks to make the situation conform to its operational procedures, the healthy organization will devise procedures to meet the situation. The forces favoring structuring, however, tend to gain prominence within any orga-

---

[51] See, e.g., books cited in note 8 *supra.*

nization, and the healthy, responsive system soon becomes a structured one. As Putney declared:

> Systems decay and become stupid through *ossification;* the process by which the decision-making centers of a system come to derive their decisions independently of the information inputs and feedback. The decisions become increasingly unrelated to what is happening within and without the system.[52]

And Putney further observed: "There seems to be no way of preventing ossification. It is a natural process in social systems."[53]

If this process of structuring is inherent in all organizations, even those subject to competitive influences, it must be wondered what degree of structuring exists within political systems that do not depend for their existence upon satisfying people who are free either to accept or reject such systems. Since they enjoy a position that is founded upon a monopolistic use of force, and in which financial support is guaranteed through the taxation process while compliance with system objectives is assured by the absolute power to command, political systems not surprisingly become indifferent to the needs and desires of their subjects, and impose a bureaucratic structure that serves the *system,* but not necessarily the people under it. In short, as Putney noted: "[B]ureaucracies also tend to become autosystems. As such, they lose sight of the individual and attempt to force all cases into their standardized categories."[54]

Under such conditions, is it surprising to find people experiencing a sense of frustration because of their inability

---

[52] S. Putney, *supra* note 43, at 37.

[53] *Ibid.* at 41.

[54] *Ibid.* at 113.

to communicate their needs to the political system and to have that system respond to their expectations?[55] The failure of the public school system to accommodate the desires of a parent regarding the education of his child, the refusal of a local planning commission to permit a property owner to convert his real estate to a more profitable use, the inability of the police system to provide the individual with adequate protection of his person or his property, and the inflexibility of political administrators and bureaucrats in responding to a particular person whose needs do not happen to fit within the procedural norms of a governmental agency—all serve to demonstrate the frustration of one's objectives that is experienced at the hands of government. When men are told that such systems exist to serve and protect them, only to find that these systems have come to regard their *own* welfare as paramount, even when that means sacrificing the interests of the systems' theoretical beneficiaries, should feelings of frustration be so unexpected?

C. Nonsatisfaction of Needs

The degree to which the state fails to respond to the needs of the people is demonstrated by its tendency to react to

---

[55] Ilfield states, for example: "Among the multitude of frustrations in America today, several seem to stand above the rest in current importance: those of the failure of many minority group individuals to achieve dignity and self-pride, and of poor communities to communicate effectively their grievances and attain control of their own destinies. Expectations have been increased but not fulfilled. For many of our people the conditions of poverty, discrimination, unemployment, and lack of skills, when combined with unfulfilled expectations for improvement, foster disillusionment and disappointment and tear away at self-esteem and dignity." Ilfield, *supra* note 19, at 89.

expressions of social discontent in much the same way most employers have attempted to deal with employee dissatisfaction: disburse more money. The faith that most organizations have in money as a cure-all for frustration shows how far out of touch such organizations are with the people they theoretically serve. More often than not, discontent within an organization stems from a failure of that organization to satisfy wants totally unrelated to monetary considerations.

The late Abraham H. Maslow, in a pioneering work in the area of human motivation,[56] discerned a hierarchical ordering of human needs and concluded that the lowest level of needs will serve to motivate men until such needs have been satisfied, and that men will not proceed up the hierarchy to the higher order of needs until the lower needs have, in fact, been satisfied. He observed, further, that a need once satisfied no longer serves to motivate behavior (unless, of course, that need arises again at a later time). Maslow's hierarchy of needs, from the lowest to the highest level, is as follows:

1. *Physiological needs.* These are the basic biological needs associated with the maintenance of bodily functions and include, among others, the need for nourishment, oxygen, water, and constant body temperature. It should be fairly evident that an individual who has not satisfied these needs is unlikely to be concerned with any higher order of needs until they have been satisfied. Maslow also pointed out, however, that if all the higher-order needs of a particular person are unsatisfied, he is likely to become dominated by these physiological needs (such as compulsive eating).

---

[56] Maslow, "A Theory of Human Motivation," in *People and Productivity* 71 (R. Sutermeister ed. 1963).

Normally, though, the satisfaction of these basic biological needs will cause a new (and "higher") level of needs to emerge.

2. *Safety needs.* One who has resolved the need for his biological maintenance will find himself concerned with a need to make his environment as "safe" and "secure" as possible, and hopefully to eliminate any threats to his well-being. It is this need that undoubtedly leads individuals to seek the "predictability" discussed earlier in this article, and that accounts for efforts to structure the social environment by the imposition of legal restrictions upon the activities of other individuals. Maslow noted this need as arising in childhood, concluding that one "generally prefers a safe, orderly, predictable, organized world, which he can count on, and in which unexpected, unmanageable or other dangerous things do not happen. . . ."[57]

As has been seen, the need for a predictably "safe and secure" environment is not, among most persons, confined to the elimination of threats and violence, trespass, or other injury to their person or property ("hygienic" function), but is extended to the "structuring" of the behavior of other persons and institutions in order to make their entire world as predictable as possible, even at the cost of restraining the freedom of action of others. This latter behavior is not unlike Maslow's description of the "compulsive-obsessive-neurotic" who will

> try frantically to order and stabilize the world so that no unmanageable, unexpected or unfamiliar dangers will ever appear. They hedge themselves about with all sorts of ceremonials, rules and formulas so that every possible contingency may be provided for

---

[57] *Ibid.* at 77.

and so that no new contingencies may appear. They are much like the brain injured cases, . . . who manage to maintain their equilibrium by avoiding everything unfamiliar and strange and by ordering their restricted world in such a neat, disciplined, orderly fashion that everything in the world can be counted upon.[58]

It is then, perhaps, the efforts of men to satisfy their needs for safety, security, and predictability that cause some to want to place restraints upon the activities of others. The problem, of course, which arises from this is that such restraints interfere with the efforts of other men to seek the satisfaction of *their* needs, and such restraints impose negative influences that deprive other men of *their* need to make *their* environment predictable and conducive to *their* control and influence.

3. *Love needs*. The general satisfaction of the physiological and safety needs will result in the development of a need for love, or what Maslow has referred to as the "love and affection and belongingness needs." Such needs are fairly self-evident as to their content and include the seeking of affectionate relationships through group acceptance as well as individual sources of affection.

4. *Esteem needs*. It is a well-accepted conclusion nowadays that people have a fundamental need to have a good view of themselves, a need for "self-esteem." This need, Maslow noted, is next in the hierarchical structure, and its satisfaction is dependent not upon false praise, but "upon real capacity, achievement and respect from others."[59] Satisfaction of these self-esteem needs leads to a feeling of effi-

---

[58] *Ibid.* at 78–79.
[59] *Ibid.* at 79.

cacy, an ability to deal effectively with reality both through accurate sensory perception and the identification of causal relationships that permit one to take predictable action. As Maslow stated, such satisfaction "leads to feelings of self-confidence, worth, strength, capability and adequacy of being useful and necessary in the world. But thwarting of these needs produces feelings of inferiority, of weakness and of helplessness."[60]

It may well be that self-esteem needs contribute, indirectly, to the need some people have to impose order upon others. If it is correct to conclude that men have a need to make their world certain and predictable, that men's self-esteem needs are satisfied and reinforced by being able to function effectively in that world, and that the element of "predictability" enhances the opportunities for efficacious behavior, is it then not likely that men will have a strong motivation to so structure institutions and social relationships as to facilitate such predictability? After all, if other men are unrestricted in their decision making and can act and modify their actions freely in response to the wishes of others or to the conditions in the marketplace; if, in other words, other men can function as completely self-directed individuals in pursuit of their own objectives, the ability accurately to predict the behavior of such other persons is lessened. Greater predictability can be realized by employing the lawmaking function to limit the autonomy of other persons.

5. *Self-actualization needs.* The highest order of needs, according to Maslow, is that for "self-actualization," which he defined as

---

[60] *Ibid.* at 80.

the desire for self-fulfillment, namely, to the tendency for him to become actualized in what he is potentially. This tendency might be phrased as the desire to become more and more what one is, to become everything that one is capable of becoming.[61]

This need, then, encompasses man's need for intellectual awareness, growth, and creativity, and can involve virtually any area of human conduct, including, for example, literary or artistic creativity, business or professional competency, and, in Maslow's terms, "the desire to be an ideal mother."[62] That relatively little is known about self-actualizing people (because there are so few of them) or the self-actualization process is readily acknowledged. Suffice it to say, however, that it involves the process of personal growth, of an individual seeking to maximize his potential, or, as Maslow stated: "What a man *can* be, he *must* be."[63]

While it should be pointed out that Maslow regarded most behavior as consisting of an effort to satisfy more than one level of needs (e.g., sexual activity could satisfy physiological, love, and esteem needs), the escalation from lower- to higher-order needs is dependent upon the basic satisfaction of such lower needs, such that, for example, a man facing the threat of starvation is not likely to be motivated by a need for self-actualization while his hunger needs go unsatisfied. As Maslow declared:

[T]he most prepotent goal will monopolize consciousness and will tend of itself to organize the recruitment of the various capacities of the organism. The less prepotent needs are minimized, even forgotten or denied. But when a need is fairly well satisfied,

---

[61] *Ibid.*
[62] *Ibid.*
[63] *Ibid.*

the next prepotent ("higher") need emerges, in turn to dominate the conscious life and to serve as the center of organization of behavior, since gratified needs are not active motivators.[64]

How do Maslow's conclusions relate to the effects on individuals of interference with goal-directed activity? They would appear to be completely consistent with the frustration-aggression hypothesis:

> Any thwarting or possibility of thwarting of these basic human goals, or danger to the defenses which protect them, or to the conditions upon which they rest, is considered to be a psychological threat. . . . It is such basic threats which bring about the general emergency reactions.[65]

Superimposing the frustration-aggression hypothesis over Maslow's hierarchical structure of needs, one would appear warranted to conclude that men have a highly developed and ever-changing scale of needs, ranging from those that are purely physical to those that are purely intellectual, encompassing every conceivable area of human activity from romance to commercial enterprise, from artistic expression to the joining of social organizations, from athletic competition to gardening. These needs differ from one person to another and, within a given person, from one moment to the next. To the degree that individuals are free to engage in goal-directed activity in response to these needs, there is a greater likelihood of need satisfaction, leading to a greater sense of self-fulfillment and the opportunity to develop higher-order needs. But to the degree such activity is interfered with, such as by the imposition of formal restrictions limiting the choices and the actions of the individual, the

---

[64] *Ibid.* at 89.

[65] *Ibid.* at 90.

individual so affected will experience a frustration of his expectations, with the consequence being an increased likelihood of aggression or violence. While, as has been seen, men do have a need to make their world predictable, they also have a need to act in response to a wide range of ever-changing goals, a need to grow and to develop higher-order goals, a need that presupposes a condition of change and the opportunity to act in response to such change. Implicit in the concept of "self-actualization" is the need for flexibility and self-directed activity. It is thus fairly obvious that if a given individual is interfered with and restrained, whether by acts of victimization from other individuals or by impositions of controls by formal systems of "order," he will experience frustration of his efforts to satisfy his needs.

Reconsidering Maslow's observation that "gratified needs are not active motivators," an additional point of significance to the subject matter of this article arises. Just as many employers have learned that they cannot hope to motivate a man who is seeking to satisfy the third, fourth, or even fifth level of needs by offering an incentive (such as money) that is designed to satisfy the first or second level of need, so too must those seeking a solution to social problems—including violence—learn to dig through the veneer of stereotyped "solutions" to find out precisely what needs people do have, and how they are being hindered from satisfying those needs by a stifling form of imposed order. The common response of many is to assume that an increase in welfare payments to low-income people will relieve their sense of frustration by providing them with an increase in their means for value satisfaction.[66] This line of reasoning

---

[66] Gurr, *supra* note 22, at 45.

is reminiscent of the response of automobile manufacturers to employee demands during contract negotiations: offer them more money. There is a sizable body of opinion which holds that the strong demands—enforced by periodic strikes—of the auto workers are not so much a product of wage dissatisfaction (auto workers are quite highly paid) as a response to the employees' felt sense of frustration at being locked into a highly structured work environment, characterized by the orderly, impersonal, and predictable assembly line. While these employees, like anyone else, are always interested in more money, the real needs that they are seeking to satisfy are those relating to attaining a sense of identity, having greater control and influence over their work environment, and realizing a greater sense of fulfillment from their work. Unable to realize these needs, they revert, as Maslow points out, to the expression of the lower-order needs as a substitute.

If highly paid auto workers are seeking to break free of the frustrations of a highly structured assembly line, can we not also assume that lower-income people are also desirous of freeing themselves from the dehumanizing, overregulative and overbureaucratized legal structure, which they perceive as interfering with their opportunities for self-fulfillment? If the classic response to such dissatisfaction—namely, increasing transfer payments to welfare recipients—does provide the solution, then why do we continue to find the greatest amount of violence and social dissatisfaction originating in areas where the inhabitants are the prime recipients of such payments? Might it not be that men are seeking something more than just an increased supply of money? Is it not possible that they are seeking to free themselves from restrictions that limit their opportunities to make the changes necessary to improve their well-being? Is it not within the realm of possibility that such persons experience a deep sense of frustration not only at having their expectations thwarted by the system, but also at having the system so completely misread their needs as to assume that they can be "bribed" into more submissive conduct with a few dollars? In the words of one psychiatrist: "In correcting social conditions which produce intolerable frustration it should be recognized that 'give-aways' and paternalism do little to enhance the recipient's dignity and self-esteem."[67]

The conclusion that interference with efforts to realize one's potential (i.e., the "self-actualization" process) leads to violence has been noted in the literature:

> The self-actualization hypothesis suggests that some men effectively are prevented from using legitimate channels of self-expression. When this occurs, as it does frequently in the ghetto, violence may offer an alternative road to achievement.[68]

Melges and Harris made the following observation on the subject:

> If a person feels that he no longer has any control over what will happen to him—if he feels his own actions will have little effect—he may then feel at the mercy of others. . . . Since the person essentially feels unable to direct himself toward his own goals, he feels unduly influenced by the demands of the immediate environment, particularly the demands of other people. This feeling of being influenced may culminate in a persecutory delusion. But even with lesser degrees of distortion the feeling that one has little control over his own destiny may lead to at-

---

[67] Ilfield, *supra* note 29, at 686.

[68] Bittker, "The Choice of Collective Violence in Intergroup Conflict," in *Violence and the Struggle for Existence* 181, 181 (D. Daniels, M. Gilula & F. Ochberg eds. 1970).

tempts to restore oneself as an active agent. This may involve attacking those who appear to be influencing and controlling the individual.[69]

An essential prerequisite to the process of seeking to maximize one's potential, or even the effort to make a less significant improvement in one's well-being, is, as has been seen, a condition of change—change resulting from free-functioning individuals modifying their behavior or acting in response to opportunities to gain desired benefits. The substance of both personal and societal development is change, and change necessarily implies the absence of restrictions or of efforts to maintain a status quo. Those who seek to preserve existing relationships by erecting a system of rules and other restrictions do more than simply protect their position; they interfere with the efforts of other men to improve their own relationships. The consequence of the erection of these barriers is not only to frustrate the dreams, hopes, and expectations of those seeking the fulfillment of their own lives, thereby increasing the likelihood of aggression and violence, but also to break down the Anglo-American concept of "equal protection of the laws." Those who are successful in having the kind of order imposed that is satisfactory to themselves are thus able to realize the sort of world *they* want, not only for themselves, but for others; while those whose expectations have been thus interfered with do not realize the kind of environment they want even for themselves. The "structuring" process, then, by its very nature, results in a situation in which some men have, by law, put themselves and their objectives in a position supe-

---

[69] Melges & Harris, "Anger and Attack," in *Violence and the Struggle for Existence* 97, 120 (D. Daniels, M. Gilula & F. Ochberg eds. 1970).

rior to that of persons whose freedom of choice and action has thus been denied. Under such a system, to paraphrase Orwell, "all men are equal, but some men are more equal than others."

IV. Conclusion

A factor that seems to have hindered an objective examination of the relationship between a system of politically imposed order and the phenomenon of violence has been a broadly based consensus among Americans that political structuring and "social engineering" are necessary to the functioning of a complex society. One may safely criticize any given political program or challenge the competency of a given political leader effectively to carry out desired programs, but faith in the process of political intervention, direction, and planning goes unchallenged in the minds of most people. The political ordering of society has become a basic tenet of American life, to the end envisioned by Herbert Spencer that "no form of cooperation, small or great, can be carried on without regulation, and an implied submission to the regulating agencies."[70] While there is a recognition that certain "excessive" political practices (e.g., police brutality and corruption of political leaders) may have dysfunctional effects upon the social structure, there is an unwillingness to consider that the very institution of imposing order upon people and, in the process, interfering with their personal objectives and the direction of their own lives may have the same consequences. As with any institu-

---

[70] Spencer, "Laissez Faire," in *Great Political Thinkers* 635, 652 (W. Ebenstein ed., 3d ed. 1965).

tion cloaked with reverence and awe, there is a reluctance to consider uncomfortable questions regarding its basic foundations. Those of intellectually honest persuasion might well choose to examine in greater depth the degree to which "order," imposed by the state, may have created a general milieu in which people perceive a frustration of their personal, economic, and social expectations, a frustration that may lead to acts of violence and other forms of disorder. Such an examination must consider the nature of the political process, not from the viewpoint of a *polemicist,* but of a *realist.* One must be willing to hold in abeyance such doctrines as "social contract" and the "general will" long enough to see if man does, in fact, experience a felt sense of frustration and victimization as a result of the political ordering of his life even though, according to some philosophic precept, he is only being "forced to be free."

It has been the purpose of this chapter to draw a distinction between the "hygienic" and "structuring" functions of political-legal systems, and to raise the question of the relationship between the activities of these systems (both as to the efforts to impose social order through the "structuring" process and the failure to fulfill the "hygienic" function) and the increased incidence of violence and other forms of disorder. The conventional examinations of causes of violence have tended to focus on such social factors as income disparity, living conditions, and opportunities for employment and upward mobility. This chapter has not attempted to deny or affirm any of these possible explanations, but has offered for consideration—and, one hopes, further inquiry —the hypothesis that there may be something inherent in any form of imposed order, which leads to a sense of frustration among persons whose expectations come into conflict with the expectations of the system and which, when such disparity is perceived by such persons and when the alternatives to relieving the disparity fail, may lead these persons to take up violence in an attempt to eliminate that disparity. A formal system of legal and political order may, then, be a dysfunctional institution serving to contribute to the very phenomenon of violence that it is theoretically designed to control and eliminate.

It would not seem an exaggeration to say that "law" has become almost synonymous with "political power," and that, transposing Thrasymachus, law "means nothing but what is to the interest of the stronger party." With the elaborate growth of "law" into every conceivable sector of human activity, there is little pretense expressed anymore that law is designed only to serve the "hygienic" function, or that the parameters of its dictates are governed by anything more than the basic consideration that influences any power structure: "How much interference will be sanctioned by the victims thereof?"

This chapter has, one hopes, served to focus attention on a possible explanation for a source of violent behavior that has been all but ignored. Time has not permitted exploring a tangential question here, one raised by Robert Ardrey and Konrad Lorenz;[71] namely, the relationship between the violation of territorial boundaries and the occurrence of aggression. The extent to which legal interference by the state—with the use, enjoyment, and decision making over one's property—has contributed to personal frustration is a question that, alone, justifies a separate examination. If, after all, people experience frustration from having their personal activities subjected to restraints that interfere with their

---

[71] R. Ardrey, *The Territorial Imperative* (1966); K. Lorenz, *On Aggression* (1966).

goals, it could hardly be doubted that this same sense of frustration would extend to interference with the use of their own property.

Neither has this chapter inquired into alternatives to systems of imposed order, but such would merit further exploration. It would appear justifiable to conclude that men have a need to strengthen and encourage the natural and informal system of order as found in the operations of such voluntary systems as the marketplace and various social institutions. Attention should ultimately be focused, perhaps, on the relationship between the value systems and psychological maturity of individuals and the degree of order experienced as a consequence of such factors. Insight into the foundations for true social order might well be found in the works of such men as Abraham Maslow and in the realization that the conditions for the process of "self-actualization" require flexible social institutions that are responsive to the individual needs of their members. As a consequence, the conclusion might be drawn that the basis for any true system of social "order" comes from *within* individuals—and is not imposed from without—and that such order is promoted by an environment in which people are encouraged to be responsible for their choices and actions. That such conditions are inconsistent with the maintenance of regulative and oppressive practices by political-legal systems that seek to *restrict* rather than *encourage* the process of growth and change implicit in "self-actualization" is evident upon examination.

The reader may, perhaps, have a tendency to assume a polarization here between the alternatives of "imposed order" and "disorder," and to assume that the choice is between living in a society characterized by chaos, violence, and insecurity, and living under a "structured" system, which, while perhaps not perfect, constitutes a more desirable alternative. If such were the only available choices, the system of "imposed order" might well be preferred. But like many questions, this too is not susceptible of such limitations of choice, and such a polarization may only be a reflection of the reader's assumptions regarding the nature of man. For purposes of this discussion, it is not necessary again to polarize the issues in terms of whether men are, by their nature, "inherently good" or "inherently bad." It is sufficient to observe only that men are, by nature, disposed to act in pursuit of goals that they have set for themselves, that they will voluntarily organize themselves in order to realize those goals, and that all men disapprove of their own victimization and thus seek means of preventing it. The problem, then, is not one of choosing either "imposed order" or "disorder," but of recognizing that a system of "imposed order" *fosters* "disorder," and of seeking methods of social organization that can, in fact, *promote* the degree of social order that most people desire in order to facilitate the goal-directed activity of each person. In the words of Rollo May:

> In its best sense and by itself, order ought to mean the forms and conventions by which we live and work together; order ideally is freedom from disturbing interruptions of peace, physical safety which in turn gives the psychological security for the pursuit of intellectual, emotional, and spiritual aims. But when coupled with law, it implies a rigid clinging to old forms of acting, a prevention of the very changes made necessary by our transitional age.[72]

---

[72] R. May, *supra* note 25, at 59.

Essay Fourteen

Kinds of Order
in Society

F. A. Hayek

Friedrich A. von Hayek, corecipient of the 1974 Nobel Memorial Prize in Economic Science, received doctoral degrees both in law and economics from the University of Vienna. For half a century, this distinguished scholar has lectured throughout the world and engaged in an active career of teaching and research in Austria, England, Germany, Japan, and the United States. He is a Fellow of the British Academy, Honorary President of the Mont Pelerin Society, and Professor Emeritus of three universities—Chicago, Freiburg, and Salzburg.

This essay was published in the New Individualist Review, *v. 3, no. 2, 1964, and is reprinted by permission. The author used this essay as the basis for the second chapter of his book* Law, Legislation and Liberty *(Chicago: University of Chicago Press, 1973).*

W e call a multitude of men a society when their activities are mutually adjusted to one another. Men in society can successfully pursue their ends because they know what to expect from their fellows. Their relations, in other words, show a certain order. How such an order of the multifarious activities of millions of men is produced or can be achieved is the central problem of social theory and social policy.[1]

Sometimes the very existence of such an order is denied when it is asserted that society—or, more particularly, its economic activities—is "chaotic." A complete absence of an order, however, cannot be seriously maintained. What presumably is meant by that complaint is that society is not

---

[1] The concept of order has recently achieved a central position in the social sciences largely through the work of Walter Eucken and his friends and pupils, known as the Ordo-circle, from the yearbook *Ordo,* issued by them. For other instances of its use, see J. J. Spengler, "The Problem of Order in Economic Affairs," *Southern Economic Journal* (July 1948), reprinted in J. J. Spengler and W. R. Allen, eds., *Essays on Economic Thought* (Chicago: Rand McNally, 1960); H. Barth, *Die Idee der Ordnung* (Zurich: E. Rentsch, 1958); R. Meimberg, *Alternativen der Ordnung* (Berlin: Duncker & Humblot, 1956); and, more remotely relevant as a treatment of some of the philosophical problems involved, W. D. Oliver, *Theory of Order* (Yellow Springs, Ohio: Antioch Press, 1951).

as orderly as it ought to be. The orderliness of existing society may indeed be capable of great improvement; but the criticism is due mainly to the circumstance that both the order which exists and the manner in which it is formed are not readily perceived. The plain man will be aware of an order of social affairs only to the extent that such an order has been deliberately arranged; and he is inclined to blame the apparent absence of an order in much of what he sees on the fact that nobody has deliberately ordered those activities. Order, to the ordinary person, is the result of the ordering activity of an ordering mind. Much of the order of society of which we speak is, however, not of this kind; and the recognition that such an order exists requires a certain amount of reflection.

The chief difficulty is that the order of social events can generally not be perceived by our senses but can only be traced by our intellect. It is, as we shall see, an abstract and not a concrete order. It is also a very complex order. And it is an order that, though it is the result of human action, has not been created by men deliberately arranging the elements in a preconceived pattern. These peculiarities of the social order are closely connected, and it will be the task of this essay to make their interrelation clear. We shall see that, although there is no absolute necessity that a complex order always be spontaneous and abstract, the more complex the order at which we aim, the more we shall have to rely on spontaneous forces to bring it about, and the more our power of control will be confined in consequence to the abstract features and not extend to the concrete manifestations of that order.[2]

---

[2] For a more extensive treatment of the problem of the scientific treatment of complex phenomena, see my essay, "The Theory of Complex Phenom-

The terms "concrete" and "abstract," which we shall have to use frequently, are often used in a variety of meanings. It may be useful, therefore, to state here in which sense they will be used. As "concrete," we shall describe particular real objects given to observation by our senses, and we shall regard as the distinguishing characteristic of such concrete objects that there are always still more properties of them to be discovered than we already know or have perceived. In comparison with any such determinant object, and the intuitive knowledge we can acquire of it, all images and concepts of it are abstract and possess a limited number of attributes. *All* thought is in this sense necessarily abstract, although there are degrees of abstractness.[3] Strictly speaking, however, the contrast between the concrete and the abstract, as we shall use it, is the same as that between a fact of which we always know only abstract attributes but can always discover still more such attributes, and all those images, conceptions, and concepts which we retain when we no longer contemplate the particular object.[4]

An abstract order of a certain kind may comprise many different manifestations of that order. The distinction becomes particularly important in the case of complex orders based on a hierarchy of ordering relations, where several

---

ena," in Mario A. Bunge, ed., *The Critical Approach: Essays in Honor of Karl Popper* (New York: Free Press of Glencoe, 1963).

[3] It is customary to describe the relatively less abstract in contrast to the more abstract as (relatively) concrete. And the distinction between an abstract and a (relatively) concrete order is, of course, the same as that between a concept with a small connotation (intention) and a consequently wide denotation on the one hand, and a concept with a rich connotation and a correspondingly narrow denotation on the other.

[4] For a helpful survey of the abstract/concrete relation and especially its significance in jurisprudence, see K. Englisch, *Die Idee der Konkretisierung in Rechtswissenschaft unserer Zeit* (Heidelberg: *Abhandlungen der Heidelberger Akademie der Wissenschaften,* Phil.-Hist. Klasse, I, 1953).

such orders may agree with respect to their more general ordering principles but differ in others. What is significant in the present context is that it may be important that an order possesses certain abstract features irrespective of its concrete manifestations, and that we may have it in our power to bring it about that an order which spontaneously forms itself will have those desirable characteristics, but not to determine the concrete manifestations or the position of the individual elements.

The simple conception of an order of the kind that results when somebody puts the parts of an intended whole in their appropriate places applies in many parts of society. In the social field, the kind of order achieved by *arranging* the relations between the parts according to a preconceived plan is called an *organization*. The extent to which the power of many men can be increased by such deliberate coordination of their efforts is well known, and many of the achievements of man rest on the use of this technique. It is an order we all understand because we know how it is made. But it is not the only nor even the chief kind of order on which the working of society rests; nor can the whole of the order of society be produced in this manner.

The *discovery* that there exist in society orders of another kind, which have not been designed by men but have resulted from the action of individuals without their intending to create such an order, is the achievement of social theory. Or, rather, it was this discovery which has shown that there was an object for social theory. It shook the deeply ingrained belief of men that where there was an order there must also have been a personal orderer. It had consequences far beyond the field of social theory since it provided the conceptions that made possible a theoretical explanation of the structures of biological phenomena.[5] And in the social field it provided the foundation for a systematic argument for individual liberty.

This kind of order, which characterizes more than biological organisms (to which the originally much wider meaning of the term *organism* is now usually confined), is an order that is not made by anybody but that forms itself. It is for this reason usually called a "spontaneous" or sometimes (for reasons to be explained) a "polycentric" order. If we understand the forces that determine such an order, we can use them by creating the conditions under which such an order will form itself.

This indirect method of bringing about an order has the advantage that it can be used to produce orders that are far more complex than any order we can produce by putting the individual pieces in their appropriate places. But it has the drawback that it enables us to determine only the general character of the resulting order and not its detail. Its use in one sense thus extends our powers: It places us in a position to produce very complex orders, which we could never produce by putting the individual elements in their places. Our power over the particular arrangement of the elements in such an order is, however, much more limited than it is over an order that we produce by individually arranging the parts. All we can control are certain abstract features of such an order, but not its concrete detail.

All this is familiar in the physical and biological fields. We could never produce a crystal by directly placing the indi-

---

[5] All three independent discoverers of biological evolution, Darwin, Wallace, and Spencer, admittedly derived their ideas from the current concepts of social evolution.

vidual molecules from which it is built up. But we can create the conditions under which such a crystal will form itself. If for that purpose we make use of known forces, we are nevertheless unable to determine the position an individual molecule will occupy within a crystal or even the size or position of the several crystals. Similarly, we can create the conditions under which a biological organism will grow and develop. But all we can do is create conditions favorable to that growth, and we are able to determine the resulting shape and structure only within narrow limits. The same applies to spontaneous social orders.

In the case of certain social phenomena, such as language, the fact that they possess an order which nobody has deliberately designed and which we have to discover, is now generally recognized. In these fields we have at last outgrown the naive belief that every orderly arrangement of parts which assists man in the pursuit of his ends must be due to a personal maker. There was a time when it was believed that all those useful institutions which serve the intercourse of men, such as language, morals, law, writing, or money, must be due to an individual inventor or legislator or to an explicit agreement of wise men who consented to certain useful practices.[6] We understand now the process by which such institutions have gradually taken shape through men learning to act according to certain rules—rules that they long knew how to follow before there was any need to state them in words.

But if in those simpler instances we have overcome the

---

[6] Cf., e.g., the examples given by Denys Hay, *Polydore Vergil* (Oxford: Clarendon Press, 1952), ch. 3.

belief that, wherever we find an order or a regular structure which serves a human purpose, there must also have been a mind which deliberately created it, the reluctance to recognize the existence of such spontaneous orders is still with us in many other fields. We still cling to a division, deeply embedded in Western thought since classical antiquity, between things that owe their order to "nature" and those that owe it to "convention."[7] It still seems strange and unbelievable to many people that an order may arise neither wholly independently of human action nor as the intended result of such action, but as the unforeseen effect of conduct that men have adopted with no such end in mind. Yet much of what we call culture is just such a spontaneously grown order, which arose neither altogether independently of human action nor by design, but by a process that stands somewhere between these two possibilities, which were long considered as exclusive alternatives.

Such spontaneous orders we find not only in the working of institutions like language and law (or, more conspicuously, the biological organisms), which show a recognizable permanent structure that is the result of slow evolution, but also in the relations of the market, which must continuously form and reform themselves and where only the conditions conducive to their constant reconstitution have been shaped by evolution. The genetic and the functional aspects can never be fully separated.[8]

---

[7] Cf., F. Heinimann, *Nomos und Physis* (Basel: F. Reinhardt, 1945).

[8] On the inseparability of the genetic and the functional aspects of these phenomena as well as the general relation between organisms and organizations, see Carl Menger, *Untersuchungen uber die Methode der Sozialwissenschaften und der politischen Oekonomie insbesondere* (Leipzig: Duncker & Humblot, 1883), which is still the classical treatment of these topics.

That division of labor on which our economic system rests is the best example of such a daily renewed order. In the order created by the market, the participants are constantly induced to respond to events of which they do not directly know, in a way that secures a continuous flow of production and a coordination of the quantities of different things, so that the even flow is not interrupted and everything is produced at least as cheaply as anybody can still provide the last quantities for which others are prepared to pay the costs. That it is an order which consists of the adaptation to the multitudinous circumstances which no single person can know completely, is one reason why its existence is not perceived by simple inspection. It is embodied in such relations as those between prices and costs of commodities and the corresponding distribution of resources; and we can confirm that such an order in fact exists only after we have reconstructed its principles in our minds.

The "ordering forces" that we can use in such instances are the rules governing the behavior of the elements which form the orders. They determine that each element will respond to the particular circumstances which act on it in a manner that will result in an overall pattern. Each of the iron filings, for instance, which are magnetized by a magnet under the sheet of paper on which we have poured them, will so act on and react to all the others that they will arrange themselves in a characteristic figure of which we can predict the general shape but not the detail. In this simple instance the elements are all of the same kind. The known uniform rules that determine their behavior would enable us to predict the behavior of each in great detail if we only knew all the facts and were able to deal with them in all their complexity.

Some order of a determinant general character may form itself also from various kinds of different elements, i.e., of elements whose response to given circumstances will be alike only in some, but not in all, respects. The formation of the molecules of highly complex organic compounds provides an example from the physical sciences. But the fact is especially significant for many of the spontaneous orders that form themselves in the biological and social spheres. They are composed of many different elements that will respond to the same circumstances, alike in some respects but not in others. But they will form orderly wholes because each element responds to its particular environment in accordance with definite rules. Thus, the order results from the separate responses of the different elements to the particular circumstances that act on them, and for this reason we describe it as a "polycentric order."[9]

The physical examples of spontaneous orders we have considered are instructive because they show that the rules which the elements follow need of course not be "known" to them. The same is true, more often than not, where living beings and particularly men are the elements of such an order. Man does not know most of the rules on which he acts;[10] and even what we call his intelligence is largely a system of rules which operates on him but which he does not

---

[9] Cf., Michael Polanyi, *The Logic of Liberty* (London: Routledge and Kegan Paul, 1951), p. 159.

[10] On the whole issue of the relation of unconscious rules to human action, on which I can touch here only briefly, see my essay, "Rules, Perceptions, and Intelligibility," *Proceedings of the British Academy*, v. 48 (1962-63).

know. In animal societies and, in great measure, in primitive human society, the structure of social life is determined by rules of action, which manifest themselves only in their being obeyed. It is only when individual intellects begin to differ sufficiently (or individual minds become more complex) that it becomes necessary to express the rules in communicable form so that they can be taught by example, deviant behavior can be corrected, and differences of view expressed about what is to be decided.[11] Though man never existed without laws that he obeyed, he did exist for millennia without laws that he knew in the sense that he was able to articulate them.

Where the elements of the social order are individual men, the particular circumstances to which each of them reacts are those that are known to him. It is only when the responses of the individuals show a certain similarity, or obey some common rules, that an overall order will result. Even a limited similarity of their responses—common rules that determine only some aspects of their behavior—suffice, however, for the formation of an order of a general kind. The important fact is that this order will be an adaptation to a multitude of circumstances that are known only to the individual members but not as a totality to any one of them; and that such an order will result only because, and in so far as, the different individuals follow similar rules in these responses to the particular circumstances known to them.

---

[11] There thus seems to be some truth in the alleged original state of goodness in which everybody spontaneously did right and could not do otherwise, and to the idea that only with increased knowledge came wrongdoing. It is only with the knowledge of other possibilities that the individual becomes able to deviate from the established rules; without such knowledge, no sin.

This does not mean, nor is it necessary for the production of an order, that in similar circumstances different persons will do precisely the same thing. All that is meant and required is that in some respect they follow the same rule, that their responses are similar in some degree, or that they are limited to a certain range of actions which all have some attributes in common. This is true even of the iron filings in our former illustration, which may not all move with the same speed because they will be different in shape, smoothness, or weight. Such differences will determine the particular manifestation of the resulting pattern which, in consequence of our ignorance of these particulars, will be unpredictable; but the general character of the pattern will be unaffected by them and will therefore be predictable.

Similarly, the responses of human individuals to events in their environment need be similar only in certain abstract aspects in order that a definite overall pattern should result. There must be some regularity—but not complete regularity —in their actions: they must follow some common rules, but these common rules need not be sufficient to determine their action fully; and what action a particular individual takes will depend on further characteristics peculiar to him.

The question of central importance both for social theory and social policy is what rules individuals must follow for an order to result. Some such common rules individuals will follow merely because of the similarity of their environment or, rather, because of the similar manner in which this environment reflects itself in their minds. Others they will all follow spontaneously because they are part of the common cultural tradition of their society. But there are still others which it is necessary that they be made to obey, since it would be in the interest of each individual to disregard them, though the overall order will be formed only if the rule is generally obeyed.

The chief regularity in the conduct of individuals in a society based on division of labor and exchange follows from their common situation: they all work to earn an income. This means they will normally prefer a larger income for a given effort—and possibly increase their effort if its productivity increases. This is a rule that is sufficiently generally followed, in fact, for those who follow it to impress upon society an order of a certain kind. But the fact that most people follow this rule in their actions leaves the character of the resulting order yet very indeterminate, and it certainly does not by itself insure that this order will be of a beneficent character. For this, it is necessary that people also obey certain conventional rules, i.e., rules which do not follow simply from the nature of their knowledge and aims but which have become habitual in their society. The common rules of morals and of law are the chief instances of this.

It is not our task here to analyze the relation between the different kinds of rules that people in fact follow and the order that results from this. We are interested only in one particular class of rules that contribute to the nature of the order and that, because we can deliberately shape them, are the chief tools through which we can influence the general character of the order that will form itself: the rules of law.

These rules differ from the others that individuals follow chiefly by the circumstance that people are made to obey them by their fellows. They are necessary because only if the individuals know what means are at their respective disposals, and are made to bear the consequences of their use of these means, will the resulting order possess certain desirable attributes. The appropriate delimitation of these individual spheres is the main function of the rules of law, and their desirable content one of the chief problems of social policy. This is not altered by the fact that their desirable form has been found largely by the accumulated experience of ages and that their further improvement is also to be expected more from slow, experimental, piecemeal evolution than from redesign of the whole.

Though the conduct of the individuals which produces the social order is guided in part by deliberately enforced rules, the order is still a spontaneous order, corresponding to an organism rather than to an organization. It does not rest on the activities being fitted together according to a preconceived plan, but on their being adjusted to one another through the confinement of the action of each by certain general rules. The enforcement of these general rules insures only the general character of the order and not its concrete realization. It also provides only general facilities, which unknown individuals may use for their own ends, but does not insure the achievement of any particular results.

In order to enforce the rules required for the formation of this spontaneous order, an order of the other kind, an organization, is also required. Even if the rules themselves were given once and for all, their enforcement would demand the coordinated effort of many men. The task of changing and improving the rules may also, though it need not, be the object of organized effort. And insofar as the state, in addition to upholding the law, renders other services to the citizens, this also requires an organized apparatus.

The organization of the apparatus of government is also effected in some measure by means of rules. But these rules, which serve the creation and direction of an organization, are of a different character from those that make possible the formation of a spontaneous order. They are rules that apply only to particular people selected by government; and they have to be followed by them in most instances (i.e., except in the case of judges) in the pursuit of particular ends also determined by government.

Even where the type of order chosen is that of an organization and not a spontaneous order, the organizer must largely rely on rules rather than specific commands to the members of the organization. This is due to the fundamental problem that all complex order encounters: the organizer wants the individuals who are to cooperate to make use of knowledge that he himself does not possess. In none but the most simple kinds of social order is it conceivable that all activities are governed by a single mind. And certainly nobody has yet succeeded in deliberately arranging all the activities of a complex society; there is no such thing as a fully planned society of any degree of complexity. If anyone did succeed in organizing such a society, it would not make use of many minds but would, instead, be altogether dependent on one mind; it would certainly not be complex, but very primitive—and so would soon be the mind whose knowledge and will determined everything. The facts that enter into the design of such an order could be only those that could be perceived and digested by this mind; and as only he could decide on action and thus gain experience, there could not be that interplay of many minds in which a lone mind can grow.

The kind of rules which govern an organization are rules for the performance of assigned tasks. They presuppose that the place of each individual in a fixed skeleton order is decided by deliberate appointment and that the rules which apply to him depend on the place he has been given in that order. The rules thus regulate only the detail of the action of appointed functionaries or agencies of government—or the functioning of an organization created by arrangement.

Rules that are to enable individuals to find their own places in a spontaneous order of the whole society must be general; they must not assign to particular individuals a status, but rather leave the individual to create his own position. The rules that assist in the running of an organization, on the other hand, operate only within a framework of specific commands that designate the particular ends which the organization aims at and the particular functions which the several members are to perform. Though applicable only to particular, individually designated people, these rules of an organization look very much like the general rules underlying a spontaneous order, but they must not be confused with the latter. They enable those who have to carry out commands to fill in details according to circumstances that they, but not the author of the command, know.

In the terms we have used, this means that the general rules of law aim at an abstract order whose concrete or particular manifestation is unpredictable; while both the commands and the rules, which enable those who obey commands to fill in the details left open by the command, serve a concrete order or an organization. The more complex the order aimed at, the greater will be the part of the circumstances determining its concrete manifestation which cannot be known to those whose concern it is to secure the formation of the order, and the more they will be able to control it only through rules and not through commands. In the most complex type of organizations, little more than the assignment of particular functions to particular people will be determined by specific decisions, while the performance of these functions will be regulated only by rules. It is when we pass from the biggest organization, serving particular tasks, to the order of the whole of society which comprises the relations between those organizations as well as the relations between them and the individuals and among the individuals, that this overall order relies entirely on rules, i.e., is entirely of a spontaneous character, with not even its skeleton determined by commands. The situation is, of course, that, because it was not dependent on organization but grew as a spontaneous order, the structure of modern society has attained a degree of complexity which far exceeds that which it is possible to achieve by deliberate organization. Even the rules that made the growth of this complex order possible were not designed in anticipation of that result; but those peoples who happened to adopt suitable rules developed a complex civilization which prevailed over others. It is thus a paradox, based on a complete misunderstanding of these connections, when it is sometimes contended that we must deliberately plan modern society because it has grown so complex. The fact is rather that we can preserve an order of such complexity only if we control it not by the method of "planning," i.e., by direct orders, but, on the contrary, aim at the formation of a spontaneous order based on general rules.

We shall presently have to consider how in such a complex system the different principles of order must be combined. At this stage it is necessary, however, at once to forestall a misunderstanding and to stress that there is one way in which it can never be sensible to mix the two principles. While in an organization it makes sense, and indeed will be the rule, to determine the skeleton by specific command and regulate the detail of the action of the different members only by rules, the reverse could never serve a rational purpose. If the overall character of an order is of the spontaneous kind, we cannot improve upon it by issuing to the elements of that order direct commands, for only these individuals and no central authority will know the circumstances that make them do what they do.

Every society of any degree of complexity must make use of both ordering principles that we have discussed. But while they must be combined by being applied to different tasks and to the sectors of society corresponding to them, they cannot successfully be mixed in any manner we like. Lack of understanding of the difference between the two principles constantly leads to such confusion. It is the manner in which the two principles are combined which determines the character of the different social and economic systems. (The fact that these different "systems"—which result from different combinations of the two ordering principles—are sometimes also referred to as different "orders," has added to the terminological confusion.)

We shall consider further only a free system that relies on spontaneous ordering forces not merely (as every system must) to fill in the interstices left by the commands determining its aim and structure, but also for its overall order. Such systems not only have many organizations (in particular, firms) as their elements, but also require an organization to enforce obedience to (and modify and develop) the body of abstract rules which are required to secure the formation of the spontaneous overall order. The fact that government is itself an organization and employs rules as an instrument of its organization, and that beyond its task of enforcing the law this organization renders a multitude of other services, has led to a complete confusion between the nature of the different kinds of rules and the orders that they serve.

The abstract and general rules of law in the narrow sense (in which "the law" comprises the rules of civil and criminal law) aim not at the creation of an order by arrangement but at creating the conditions in which an order will form itself. But the conception of law as a means of order-creation (a term which, as a translation of the equally ambiguous German *Ordnungsgestaltung,* is now invading Anglo-American jurisprudence)[12] in the hands of public lawyers and civil servants who are primarily concerned with tasks of organization rather than with the conditions of the formation of a spontaneous order, is increasingly interpreted as meaning an instrument of arrangement. This conception of law, which is the conception prevailing in totalitarian states, has characteristically been given its clearest expression by the legal theorist who became Hitler's chief legal apologist, as "concrete order formation" (*konkretes Ordnungsdenken*).[13] This kind of law aims at creating a concrete preconceived order by putting each individual on a task assigned by authority. Although this technique of creating an order is indispensable for organizing the institutions of government and all the enterprises and households that form the elements of the order of society as a whole, it is wholly inadequate for bringing about the infinitely more complex overall order.

We have it in our power to assure that such an overall

---

[12] Cf., e.g., E. Bodenheimer, *Jurisprudence, the Philosophy and Method of Law* (Cambridge: Harvard University Press, 1962), p. 211.

[13] See Carl Schmitt, *Die drei Arten des rechtswissenschaftlichen Denkens* (Hamburg: Schriften fur Akademie fur deutsches Recht, 1934).

order will form itself and will possess certain desirable general characteristics, but only if we do not attempt to control the detail of that order. But we jettison that power and deprive ourselves of the possibility of achieving that abstract order of the whole if we insist on placing particular pieces into the places we wish them to occupy. It is the condition of the formation of this abstract order that we leave the concrete and particular details to the separate individuals and bind them only by general and abstract rules. If we do not provide this condition but restrict the capacity of the individuals to adjust themselves to the particular circumstances known only to them, we destroy the forces making for a spontaneous overall order and are forced to replace them by deliberate arrangement which, though it gives us greater control over detail, restricts the range over which we can hope to achieve a coherent order.

It is not irrelevant to our chief purpose if, in conclusion, we consider briefly the role that abstract rules play in the coordination not only of the actions of many different persons, but also in the mutual adjustment of the successive decisions of a single individual or organization. Here, too, it is often not possible to make detailed plans for action in the more distant future (although what we should do now depends on what we shall want to do in the future) simply because we do not yet know the particular facts that we shall face. The method through which we nevertheless succeed in giving some coherence to our actions is that we adopt a framework of rules for guidance which makes the general pattern, though not the detail, of our lives predictable. It is these rules of which we are often not consciously aware—in many instances rules of a very abstract character—which make the course of our lives orderly. Many of these rules will be "customs" of the social group in which we have grown up, and only some will be individual "habits" that we have accidentally or deliberately acquired. But they all serve to abbreviate the list of circumstances that we need to take into account in the particular instances, singling out certain classes of facts as alone determining the general kind of action that we should take. At the same time, this means that we systematically disregard certain facts which we know and which would be relevant to our decisions if we knew all such facts, but which it is rational to neglect because they are accidental partial information which does not alter the probability that, if we could know and digest all the facts, the balance of advantage would be in favor of following the rule.

It is, in other words, our restricted horizon of knowledge of the concrete facts which makes it necessary to coordinate our actions by submitting to abstract rules rather than to attempt to decide each particular case solely in view of the limited set of relevant particular facts that we happen to know. It may sound paradoxical that rationality should thus require that we deliberately disregard knowledge which we possess; but this is part of the necessity of coming to terms with our unalterable ignorance of much that would be relevant if we knew it. Where we know that the probability is that the unfavorable effects of a kind of action will overbalance the favorable ones, the decision should not be affected by the circumstance that in the particular case a few consequences which we happen to be able to foresee should all be favorable. The fact is that, in an apparent striving after rationality in the sense of more fully taking into account all the foreseeable consequences, we may achieve greater irrationality, less effective taking into account of remote effects, and an altogether less coherent result. It is the great lesson which science has taught us that we must resort to the abstract where we cannot master the concrete. The preference for the concrete is to renounce the power that thought gives us. It is therefore not really surprising that the consequence of modern democratic legislation, which disdains submitting to general rules and attempts to solve each problem as it comes on its specific merits, is probably the most irrational and disorderly arrangement of affairs ever produced by the deliberate decisions of men.

Index

This book was linotype set in the Times Roman series of type. The face was designed to be used in the news columns of the *London Times*. The *Times* was seeking a type face that would be condensed enough to accommodate a substantial number of words per column without sacrificing readability and still have an attractive contemporary appearance. This design was an immediate success. It is used in many periodicals throughout the world and is one of the most popular text faces presently in use for book work.

Book design by Design Center, Inc., Indianapolis
Typography by Weimer Typesetting Co., Inc., Indianapolis
Printed by North Central Publishing Co., Saint Paul